616 738 0968

Here @ cottage

340 Big Bay Drive

WOODROW WILSON

AND

THE GREAT BETRAYAL

Professor Thomas A. Bailey was born in San Jose, California, and studied at Stanford University. He is the author of *America Faces Russia, A Diplomatic History of the American People,* and *The American Pageant.* He is at present Professor of American History at Stanford University.

Woodrow Wilson
and the
Great
Betrayal

by THOMAS A. BAILEY

Q

QUADRANGLE PAPERBACKS

Quadrangle Books / Chicago

THIS IS an account of one of the supreme tragedies of human history—the Great Betrayal which occurred when the United States turned its back on Wilson's pledges and failed to ratify the Treaty of Versailles and join the League of Nations.

The narrative presented herewith is a sequel to *Woodrow Wilson and the Lost Peace,* although each of the two volumes is an entity in itself and is designed to stand on its own feet. The first deals with peacemaking; the second deals with peacebreaking, with special emphasis on the role of the United States. My original plan was to tell the whole story in one book, but the exigencies of time and space, to say nothing of other considerations, suggested the desirability of two separate volumes.

My purposes are essentially those set forth in the preface of the preceding account. History never repeats itself, but statesmen and their people repeat the same mistakes. I am presenting this narrative, from the American point of view and *with emphasis on what went wrong,* in the hope that we may better recognize certain disastrous pitfalls, and not stumble into them again.

If the American people are handicapped by ignorance of what happened in connection with the making of the peace, they are no less handicapped by wrong notions as to what happened in connection with the breaking of the peace. The tendency is to resort to the absurd oversimplification of saying that Senator Henry Cabot Lodge alone kept us out of the League of Nations. People are lazy, and they like mental short cuts; people are sentimental, and they like real villains in their dramas—villains with long whiskers. Hence Senator Lodge occupies a conspicuous place in American demonology.

My object is neither to kick the corpse of Lodge nor to whiten the tomb of Wilson. Neither the whitewash brush nor the tar brush is going to help us much if we seek a real appreciation of the many forces that entered into this vast tragedy, some of which forces exist today in latent or active form. I fear for the future if the American people are still so simple-minded as to think that one wicked man was to blame for everything that happened.

I must again confess that I am in complete sympathy with Wilson's broad program and with his vision for the future. He spoke with unchallengeable realism when he said that isolationism had been repealed by the forces of history; he spoke with prophetic vision when he said that if we did not set up an agency to prevent war, another and more terrible holocaust would engulf the next generation.

I agree with Wilson that it would have been desirable for the United States to ratify the Treaty of Versailles without any reservations whatever. But, since that proved impracticable, I feel that an agreement on reservations should have been worked out, *in keeping with the American way of resolving deadlock by compromise.* The United States had a world to gain and virtually nothing to lose by joining the League of Nations.

As this narrative unfolds, it will become increasingly clear that Wilson's tactlessness and stubbornness had much to do with our colossal failure. I realize that it is ungracious to criticize an eminent man with a noble vision who did unreasonable things—especially a sick and crippled man. But the historian is not a Hollywood script writer; and he serves neither the cause of an exacting truth nor the cause of a fumbling humanity if he glosses over pertinent but unpalatable facts.

Wilson presumably had the highest motives for what he did, and he doubtless had valid reasons in his own mind for the unyielding course he took. His experiences with compromising had not been altogether happy, and he distrusted some of the men with whom he had to compromise. Although it is possible to argue that he was right in demanding all or nothing, the present account is written with the conviction that in complicated matters of this nature mankind, if it moves forward at all, must proceed "leg over leg" and demand not what is ideally desirable but what is practically attainable.

Every generation has to make its own blunders, and no doubt ours will. An old English proverb says, "Wise men learn by other men's mistakes, fools by their own." On the one hand, there is grave danger in ignorance of the past; on the other, there is grave danger in misapplied knowledge of the past. We must not attempt to scrap the entire machine—as certain earnest souls urge—simply because some parts of it failed to work. What we did right, we should do again; what we did wrong, we should avoid doing again.

These two books on Wilson may serve, I hope, as a rough guidepost to the future. The labor of preparing them will not have been altogether in vain if they do something to show the public that peacemaking is immensely difficult and complicated, that peoples should be tolerant of a failure to achieve the impossible, that to wait for perfection is to wait forever. Peace ratifying and peace execution require a high degree of intelligence, patience, persistence, and vigilance, as well as a courageous assumption of responsibility, and a clearheaded pursuit of long-range rather than short-range interests.

A number of individuals have graciously provided information, among them the Honorable Bainbridge Colby, the late Senator William E. Borah, and Mr. Robert V. Shirley, Clerk of the Senate Committee on Foreign Relations. Dr. Thomas S. Barclay, professor of political science at Stanford, helpfully criticized several chapters relating to political developments. The distinguished Finnish diplomat, Dr. Rudolf Holsti, now a member of the faculty at Stanford, was kind enough to check my observations on the Lodge reservations against his extraordinary background of thirteen years of official participation in the work of the League. Dr. Victor E. Hall, professor of physiology at Stanford, read the manuscript with particular attention to medical problems, and saved me from several embarrassing errors. My present chief, fifteen-year colleague, and former teacher, Dr. Edgar E. Robinson, Margaret Byrne professor of history at Stanford, read the manuscript with meticulous care and prepared a masterly critique, most of the suggestions in which I was able and happy to accept. He also placed at my disposal certain personal data, including copies of letters from James M. Cox, Josephus Daniels, Homer S. Cummings, and others. I am also indebted to Dr. Robinson for his maps on the elections of 1916 and 1920, which appear in his *The Presidential Vote, 1896-1932* (Stanford University, 1934), and which are herewith produced in slightly modified form with the blessing of Mr. Will A. Friend, manager of the Stanford University Press.

I am indebted, as before, to the staffs of the Stanford University Library, especially to Miss Ruth Scibird; of the Hoover Library on War, Revolution, and Peace (Stanford University); of the Widener Library at Harvard University; of the Boston Public Library; and of the Periodicals Division, Library of Congress. Miss Ruth S. Watson, of the Nebraska State Historical Society, cooperated by providing me with an important Hitchcock manuscript. President Charles Seymour and Mr. Russell G. Pruden graciously extended courtesies in connection with the Yale House Collection. For assistance in examining manuscript materials in the Library of Congress, my thanks are due to Dr. St. George L. Sioussat, Chief of the Division of Manuscripts, and to Miss Katharine E. Brand, Special Custodian, Woodrow Wilson Collection. I am particularly grateful to Mrs. Woodrow Wilson for permission to use this valuable collection.

My wife, Sylvia Dean Bailey, typed notes, helped edit the manuscript, read and constructively criticized both galley and page proofs, assisted in the preparation of the index, and tolerated my irascibility. *Nihil est superius benigna conjuge.*

THOMAS A. BAILEY

STANFORD UNIVERSITY, CALIF.

TABLE OF CONTENTS

ix

LIST OF MAPS

WOODROW WILSON

AND

THE GREAT BETRAYAL

CHAPTER ONE

THE RETURN OF THE MESSIAH

"Dare we reject it [the League] and break the heart of the world?" WOODROW WILSON, *July 10, 1919.*

1

ON JUNE 29, 1919, the presidential liner, *George Washington,* steamed out of Brest harbor, France, filled with singing boys in baggy khaki. But their eminent fellow passenger, Woodrow Wilson, was not singing. To him home meant not quiet and repose but the beginning of yet another battle to secure ratification of the Treaty of Versailles, a copy of which he was bringing back with him.

Wilson was not altogether happy over the pact which he had helped frame, even though it did contain the League of Nations. He had done his very best in the face of superhuman obstacles, but no one in far-away America could possibly appreciate the web of difficulties in which he had become entangled. He was painfully aware that he had been forced to mortgage some of his ideals in order to salvage others. But he confidently hoped that the inevitable contradictions and injustices of the treaty would eventually be smoothed away by a powerful League of Nations, of which the United States would be both a charter member and a guiding force.

The ten-day trip through smooth July seas was relatively uneventful, despite rumors of loose mines in the path of the ship. The *George Washington* was met outside New York harbor on the morning of July 8 by a flotilla of superdreadnoughts, headed by the *Pennsylvania,* carrying members of the Cabinet and of Congress. The presidential liner was escorted to the pier at Hoboken, New Jersey, by battleships, destroyers, subchasers, airplanes, and dirigibles. Even smoky

Hoboken looked beautiful to Wilson, for it was home; and he was glad to be there, although bitter struggles lay ahead.

The much-traveled President was taken by automobile from the Twenty-third Street ferry to Carnegie Hall, where he was to make his first public speech. Along the way full-throated cheers rose from the jostling mass of humanity, demonstrations which brought him to his feet, hat in hand. School children waved, and white-haired women leaned from windows to throw him a tearful "God bless you!"

The climax came at Carnegie Hall, where four thousand throats were supplemented by shrilling police whistles. When the din died down, Wilson spoke briefly and "from the heart" —a "homesick" heart. He described the peace as a just one which, if it could be preserved, would "save the world from unnecessary bloodshed." But he made no specific reference to the much-debated League of Nations.

The speech was a disappointment to those who had expected a concrete explanation of what Wilson had done "over there," and why he had done it. Instead, he spoke in characteristically exalted tones of "unselfishness," "distant horizons," and "new tasks."

Leaving Carnegie Hall, Wilson entrained for Washington, and late that same night reached the Union Station in the nation's capital. Some ten thousand people, defying the late hour, were there to give a warm welcome to their most distinguished fellow townsman. A few hundred of the curious were also waiting at the White House grounds. Among them was Mrs. Alice Roosevelt Longworth, who nourished all the bitterness of her Rough Riding father for the professor-president. As the presidential party passed, she made the sign of the evil eye, and muttered, "A murrain on him, a murrain on him, a murrain on him!"

The weary warrior was now home to stay, after an unprecedented six months abroad. There was much point to the current quip that Wilson was visiting rather than returning to the United States. "Just think," exclaimed the Macon *Telegraph*, "we will have a President all by ourselves from now on!"

2

Wilson's next important step in peacemaking was to submit his official copy of the treaty to the Senate, even though that body had secured an unofficial copy about a month earlier. Thereby hangs a curious tale.

When preliminary terms were presented to Germany in May, 1919, Wilson and his colleagues had agreed to keep the exact provisions secret until they were final. This was to prevent the inevitable outcry that would go up in Allied countries if the original draft was softened in response to German complaints.

Yet the Germans were not bound by the non-publication agreement, and within a short time copies of the treaty were being sold all over Europe for a trifle. When this became evident, Wilson could well have asked to be released from his promise so that he might do the Senate the honor of submitting an unofficial draft to it.

But the President was a proud and stubborn Southern gentleman. He had given his word; and besides it seemed ridiculous to communicate a draft treaty to the Senate, and then a month or two later present another draft with the request that the Senate forget all about the first one. Wilson often found it difficult to perceive that a man may be technically right but politically wrong.

The premature publication of the treaty further rasped senatorial sensibilities. Wilson had told the senators before he left for Europe that they would know all that he was doing. Yet they had been kept pretty much in the dark. They were a coordinate part of the treaty-making power. Yet others had received a copy of the pact before they had. The senators had approved the very first of Wilson's Fourteen Points: "Open covenants of peace, openly arrived at . . ." Yet Wilson could now be represented—though unfairly—as a champion of secret covenants.

Various unofficial versions of the treaty speedily reached the United States. The Chicago *Tribune,* a violently anti-League newspaper, secured and published a copy. Senator Henry Cabot Lodge was shown one which had been procured through Thomas W. Lamont, one of the American financial experts at Paris and a member of the House of Morgan. This revelation aroused a great uproar in senatorial circles about the sinister hand of Wall Street. Things had come to a pretty pass indeed when the Senate could not have a copy of the treaty, whereas Wall Street could. The unthinking masses found in this incident strong confirmation of their suspicion that Wall Street was really running the government.

Senator William E. Borah of Idaho, a bitter opponent of the treaty, secured a newspaper copy and on June 9 had it read into the *Congressional Record.* This was highly unconventional, for the Senate is supposed to consider only treaties formally laid before it by the President, not garbled documents in the draft stage. But Borah was highly unconventional, unalterably determined to undo the pact, and completely impervious to caustic remarks about "sagebrush diplomacy."

This whole pother over publication irregularities, trivial though it may now seem, was most unfortunate. It rubbed salt in old sores, confused an issue that was already confused enough, and diverted attention from the main business at hand. It further ensured that the official treaty, when presented, would have a chilling reception.

3

On the afternoon of July 10, 1919, President Wilson, immaculately dressed, arrived at the Senate chamber carrying a bulky copy of the treaty under his arm. A burst of applause greeted him, principally from the galleries and from the Democratic side of the aisle. The Republican senators for the most part sat in stern silence.

The presentation speech was not one of Wilson's best, either in content or in delivery. Perhaps he sensed that a large part of his audience was unsympathetic, for now and then he stumbled over a word. At times it seemed as though he were speaking to the people in the gallery and beyond the gallery, rather than to the senators themselves.

Wilson dealt throughout, as was his wont, in generalities. He explained that time did not permit a detailed account of what had happened at Paris. But he issued a significant invitation when he made it clear that he was at the disposal of the Senate and of the all-important Senate Committee on Foreign Relations, "either informally or in session, as you may prefer . . ." The League Covenant, he said, not only was the most important part of the treaty but was inseparable from the treaty. "Shall we or any other free people hesitate to accept this great duty? Dare we reject it and break the heart of the world?"

At the very end Wilson laid aside his manuscript, and in a superbly eloquent passage pleaded with his audience to "follow the vision" of leadership which we had "dreamed at our birth." His moving words were greeted by an ovation from the galleries and from the Democratic senators, with an occasional "rebel yell" rising above the hand clapping. Yet, ominously, only a scattering of the Republican members were seen to applaud.

Comments on the speech among senators ran the whole gamut of partisanship. The Democrats regarded it as clear, effective, informative, convincing. Senator Williams of Mississippi described it as "the greatest thing ever uttered by any President of the United States since Lincoln died."

The Republicans, as usual, found Wilson's apocalyptic prose too vague, too idealistic, too full of "glittering generalities." Senator Medill McCormick of Illinois declared that

it was "soothing, mellifluous, and uninformative"; Senator
Brandegee dismissed it as "soap bubbles of oratory and soufflé
of phrases"; while Senator Harding (Wilson's successor) criticized this appeal of the "internationalists" as "utterly lacking
in ringing Americanism."

Clearly Wilson, in his first appearance before Congress in

It Doesn't Happen to Be a Parrot
(Courtesy of Chicago *Tribune*; cartoonist Orr)

seven months, had not made the most of an unusual opportunity. Foes of the treaty were spreading broadcast the seeds
of doubt and misinformation; and the presentation of the
pact provided an enviable chance for the President to meet
his enemies head on and regain much ground that had been
lost during his absence. This was what Secretary of Agriculture Houston urged him to do; but Wilson, for reasons that
no doubt seemed valid, ignored such advice. Instead, he appeared aloof, noncontroversial, and confident, refusing to take

the people into his confidence by telling them what had happened, and thus giving further support to the charge that he was arrogant and uncompromising.

4

The irregular publication of the pact and Wilson's rather inept manner of presenting it were not the only incidents that confused the picture in July, 1919. There was also the French Security Treaty, and thereby hangs another curious tale.

At Paris, Wilson had finally persuaded the French to give up their claims to the German Rhineland in return (among other things) for a treaty of guarantee. This unprecedented pact pledged both the United States and Great Britain to spring to the aid of France should she again be wantonly attacked by Germany.

Surprisingly enough, considerable approval was expressed in the United States for the French treaty. It was only a temporary arrangement, pending the effective establishment of the League of Nations. It merely put on paper what most Americans felt: that having gone across to save France (and their own skins) in 1917, they would do so again (as they did). The memory of our debt to the land of Lafayette was still fresh.

But many Americans voiced serious objections to the French Security Treaty. It was an alliance; and George Washington had solemnly warned against alliances. It seemed to take the war-declaring power out of the hands of Congress. Finally, it complemented the League of Nations; and the League of Nations was a red flag to many ardent nationalists and isolationists both in and out of the Senate.

Yet it is a significant fact that many of those who were unfriendly to the Treaty of Versailles, such as Senator Henry Cabot Lodge and the journalist, George B. M. Harvey, were not unfriendly to the idea of a French pact of guarantee, *pro-*

vided it could be divorced from the League and specifically limited to five or so years.

But the Security Treaty had been signed, and according to the explicit terms of the fourth article, it was to be submitted to the Senate simultaneously with the Treaty of Versailles. This Wilson signally failed to do. In a statement for the newspapermen he said that he had not had time to prepare a message, and he wanted to take up the issue separately because it was "complicated."

The senatorial foes of Wilson roundly condemned him for not carrying out the plain dictates of the Security Treaty. They made much of the fact that he (and not Germany) was the first to violate the terms of the Paris settlement. The clamor finally became so loud that Wilson on July 29, 1919, *nineteen days late,* submitted the pact with an appropriate message.

Having insisted on speed in submission, the Senate displayed lethargy in taking action. The Security Treaty, to which France pinned extravagant hopes, was not even reported out of the Foreign Relations Committee. It lay for many months silently yellowing in a senatorial pigeonhole. There was obviously no point in taking action on this pact until it was clear that we were going to ratify the Treaty of Versailles. When we failed to do so, the Security Treaty was forgotten in America, but not in France, where Wilson and the United States were bitterly charged with betrayal.

Wilson clearly should have submitted the French pact on the day stipulated; and in neglecting to do so he laid himself open to legitimate criticism at home and abroad. But the people in America who condemned him had already been condemning him on other grounds, and it is difficult to prove that his action (or inaction) had any appreciable bearing on the final tragic failure of the Treaty of Versailles.

5

If the Senate was irked by Wilson's handling of both the French Security Treaty and the Treaty of Versailles, Wilson was no less irked by what had been going on in the Senate. On the same day that he presented the main pact, he gave a most revealing interview to the newspapermen. Obviously annoyed by the efforts of the Senate Republicans to sever the League Covenant from the treaty, and disturbed by their preparations to load the pact down with vexatious qualifications, he struck sharply at the proposed reservations.

One of the correspondents spoke up and asked whether the treaty could be ratified if the Senate were to adopt reservations. Wilson replied bluntly: "I do not think hypothetical questions are concerned. *The Senate is going to ratify the treaty.*"

Such statements as these, taken in connection with Wilson's general aloofness, reveal a spirit of confidence, not untinged with arrogance, which subsequent events were to prove but poorly grounded. What is the explanation?

Wilson's faith in the sound judgment of the masses, once the facts were laid before them, was still unshaken. He shared Thomas Jefferson's conviction that in the long run, if not in the short run, the people could be counted upon to decide correctly on a great moral issue, such as the League of Nations. The truth was mighty and would prevail.

This perhaps is sound doctrine, where the issues are clearly drawn, and where truth and righteousness stand openly arrayed in shining armor against ignorance and deceit. But what will happen when the issues are blurred or falsified by master confusionists like Senators Lodge and Borah and Johnson?

Wilson also had unbounded confidence in his power to appeal to the people and lead them into the paths of right thinking. He had suffered a severe setback in November, 1918, when he had pleaded for a Democratic Congress and had got a Republican majority. But that was a different matter. Even though Congress was Republican, he certainly could marshal enough nonpartisan support to carry the day. Surely, if the enthusiastic outpourings in New York and Washington meant anything, the great mass of the voters was behind him on this issue.

Wilson had not yet learned—perhaps he never learned—that not all those who come to stare and mayhap to cheer will follow the object of their acclaim through fire and water. H. H. Kohlsaat, the well-known Chicago newspaperman, was of the opinion that the people were behind Wilson—but some little distance behind him.

The supreme self-confidence of the President was fortified by a consciousness of his powerful strategic position. Every kind of agency for revealing public opinion—polls, resolutions of legislative bodies and mass meetings, speeches, editorials, letters to the press—showed that the masses were demanding some kind of League to prevent a repetition of the horrors which were still fresh in mind. Even Senator Lodge admitted that all "the vocal classes" were friendly to the League.

While at Paris, Wilson had remarked in the presence of Colonel Stephen Bonsal that the "Senators do not know what the people are thinking. They are as far from the people, the great mass of our people, as I am from Mars." This almost certainly was not true; but, even if true, it bespoke a dangerous attitude of mind.

6

Wilson had other sound reasons, aside from the support of public opinion, for his feeling of confidence.

The Senate had never before rejected a peace treaty, though the one with Spain in 1899 had squeezed through by the narrow margin of two votes.

The Senate could not separate the Covenant of the League of Nations from the treaty, and kill the one while approving the other. Wilson had foreseen the possibility of such a move, and had cleverly forestalled it. He had interwoven the Covenant with the treaty and with the other peace settlements so intimately that the League could not be cut out without unraveling the whole arrangement. Wilson not only had planned it this way, but had unfortunately boasted of his strategy in public. Some of the senators were angered because the President had deliberately confronted them with a horrible dilemma. Apparently they had to kill all or accept all; and they wanted to do neither.

The Senate could not even seek the hollow solace of delay. The people were clamoring to get the war officially over and to bring the rest of the boys home. Bankers and merchants and manufacturers and shippers were demanding that peace be concluded at once so that the Allies would not get a head start in the race for enemy markets.

And what valid reason could be offered for delay? The Republican senators, in their resounding Round Robin of March, 1919, had announced that they could not vote for the League in "the form now proposed." But it was no longer in "the form now proposed." Reluctantly, and at the behest of senatorial and other critics, Wilson had gone back to Paris in March, 1919, and had secured safeguarding amendments. He had not done it gracefully, but he had done it. "I am yielding to the judgment of men," he groaned, "who have little knowledge or appreciation of the world situation, but who, alas! control votes."

Finally and unanswerably, the Senate could not escape its moral obligation. The League could not be torn from the treaty; so the only choice was to approve the treaty, or to reject the treaty and make such terms as we could with Germany.

A separate peace-during the war had been regarded as treasonable; it still seemed treasonable. We could not honorably forsake our recent comrades in arms and leave them still bleeding on the common field of battle. We could not turn back when the task was only half done, for we should break faith with the dead, and the mothers of the dead, whom Wilson had promised to make this a "war to end wars." We could not refuse to honor the commitments which Wilson as President had made in the name of the American people. We could not betray the high hopes of the lesser nations of Europe who were counting on us to finish the job. We could not cravenly reject the world leadership which the logic of events had forced upon us.

In a speech several months earlier Wilson had spoken of the poor people of Europe who had trustingly thrust flowers upon him. "It is inconceivable that we should disappoint them," he declared, "and *we shall not*."

7

With all the high cards seemingly in his hand, Wilson may perhaps be pardoned for having developed considerable complacency in his attitude toward the Senate. The Democrats could be counted on to support him. If they did not, he would flourish the patronage bludgeon, and appeal to their constituents not to reelect them. The Republicans could in the end be counted on to support him. If they did not, he would brandish the bludgeon of public opinion. He could not lose.

At Paris the situation had been different, and Wilson had been different. He had been considerate, acquiescent, open to compromise. He had stooped to conquer. He had walked into the French Foreign Office to visit Foreign Minister Pichon, instead of waiting, as custom dictated, for Pichon to visit him.

Wilson might approach the diplomats of Europe on a friendly and conciliatory basis, because he knew them not. But the Senate he had had "on his hands" for six long years. With his characteristic intolerance of inattentive students and sluggish brains, he entertained little respect for the senatorial representatives of the sovereign people. "Bungalow minds" and "pygmy minds" were favorite expressions of his when referring to certain members of Congress. There were in fact many important senators, especially among the Republicans, with whom he had already had some kind of brush. Finally, he had never before faced a Republican majority in either house of Congress; *now hostile majorities controlled both the Senate and the House of Representatives.*

Colonel House had urged Wilson in Paris to treat the senators with more deference, and even to extend the olive branch to Hoke Smith, Democratic senator from Georgia, with whom the President had been "feuding" for many years. Smith and Wilson had both hung out their law shingles in Atlanta in the same month of the same year. Smith was a "hustler," and he had prospered; Wilson was a gentleman, very much on his dignity, and he had failed. "That man is an ambulance-chaser," exclaimed Wilson to House with blazing eyes. "I scorn to have any relations with him whatsoever."

House remonstrated that even if the man had chased ambulances thirty years ago, his vote was now necessary to save civilization. But Wilson was imperturbably confident. He did not think Smith's vote important; certainly not decisive. He would "receive him, of course, as the senator from Georgia, if he calls, but, House, no nosegays, no olive branches in that direction."

Wilson's attitude toward the Senate had, understandably enough, gradually taken on a degree of belligerence. He had with good reason been angered by the Republican Round Robin during the previous March, and had flashed back defiance in his speech of March 4, 1919, at the Metropolitan Opera House. Senator Martin of Virginia, then the Democratic Senate leader, had expressed doubts as to whether a two-thirds vote for the treaty could be mustered. "Martin!" snapped Wilson. "Anyone who opposes me in that, I'll crush!"

In the late spring of 1919 Wilson had been further aroused by the attempts of the Republican senators to amputate the League Covenant from the treaty, and particularly by efforts to propose reservations to the all-important Article X, which undertook to guarantee peace by pledging all members of the

League to protect one another against external aggression (see page 385 for text). On May 24, the President cabled Secretary Lansing that the Senate would have to accept this vital Article X or reject the entire treaty and abide the consequences. He hoped that the friends of the treaty in America would take a most militant and aggressive course, *such as he meant to take the minute he got back.*

Herbert Hoover, then in France, undertook to criticize certain aspects of the treaty, and Wilson, regarding this as a personal affront, flashed back angrily and thenceforth excluded Hoover from his private councils. Colonel House's parting words at Paris, the last he ever spoke to his chief, were an admonition to deal with the Senate in a conciliatory manner. But Wilson sternly rejected such timid advice.

8

It is clear that Wilson returned home in a mood that did not augur well for an amicable adjustment of differences with the Senate. He held the highest office; he held the highest trumps. It was unthinkable that the Senate would dare reject the treaty; we simply could not go back to our fallen foe and beg for new terms. Then why should he accept compromise of any kind, especially reservations and amendments, when he was sure to have his way anyhow? He had the Senate in a bad corner, and he would press his advantage mercilessly.

Dr. Nicholas Murray Butler records in his reminiscences that, in June, 1919, he worked out certain tentative reservations to the treaty which proved satisfactory to an important group of Republican senators. Jules Jusserand, French Ambassador in Washington, cabled the draft to Paris and subsequently was informed that it was acceptable to both the French and the British foreign office. Jusserand then went directly to the White House and said that if Wilson would consent to these reservations the treaty would certainly be ratified. To

Jusserand's horror, the President replied in a stern voice: "Mr. Ambassador, I shall consent to nothing. *The Senate must take its medicine.*"

As we see it now, Wilson would have been well advised not to press the Senate so remorselessly. A stitch in time saves nine; a minor compromise or two in July probably would have saved a half-dozen major ones in October. In July, when the tide was running strongly for the League, the Republicans probably would have accepted trivial concessions which would have enabled them to save face. In October, the advantage was more definitely with them, and it was they who pressed their advantage relentlessly.

It is easy to criticize Wilson for not having seen what is now plainly evident. Most statesmen cannot see their errors as they make them. In fairness to Wilson we must note that almost everyone in July took it for granted that the treaty would be approved substantially as it was signed at Versailles, with perhaps a few face-saving reservations. Even the bitterest foes of the League in the Senate were nursing no more than a forlorn hope. The ill concealed despair of this little group of "irreconcilables" is convincing proof that Wilson was not altogether unjustified in his confidence and optimism.

CHAPTER TWO

THE PARADE OF PREJUDICE

"We of all peoples in the world . . . ought to be able to under-
derstand the questions of this treaty . . . for we are made up
out of all the peoples in the world." WOODROW WILSON, *at Colum-*
bus, Ohio, September 4, 1919.

1

THE UNWARY observer is apt to conclude that during the summer and autumn of 1919 the one consuming interest of the American people was the treaty with its League of Nations. This is not true. If it had been, the story might well have been different.

Only a sprinkling of Americans had more than the foggiest notions as to what the treaty was all about. The pact itself, of which the League was the very first section, filled a bulky book of 268 large quarto pages. If a copy had been placed in the hands of each voter, it still would not have been read. It was too long, and the language was so technical as to be largely incomprehensible to the lay mind. "This is a strange world," lamented the Peoria *Transcript*. "Nobody is competent to discuss the Versailles Treaty until he has read it, and nobody who would take the time to read it would be competent to discuss it."

The League of Nations Covenant was of course much less technical. It was written in simple language and could be read in about twenty minutes. Hundreds of thousands of copies were scattered broadcast by newspapers and interested pressure groups, but we have no way of knowing how many people read them. One observer took an informal poll of the voters of a middle western city and found that only one in twenty-five had done so. This seems like a high percentage, certainly if we stipulate a comprehending reading.

The disconcerting conclusion is that what little the "average American" knew about the treaty came to him second-, third-, or fourth-hand. Others read the pact and interpreted it for him. Or others read the interpretations of others and then did some additional interpreting of their own. The small-town newspaper editor, the lurid magazine writer, the ill informed local forum, or the loud-mouthed tub-thumper were primary sources of information or misinformation. It must ever be thus when immeasurably complex issues are thrown into the turmoil of public debate.

The American people certainly wanted no more of wars, and they hoped that their leaders would work out some kind of inexpensive and self-operating organization to prevent future conflicts. But the man in the street was too inert or too unintelligent or too preoccupied to give these delicate issues sustained thought. Overpowering problems on his very doorstep clamored for immediate attention. While Wilson was still in Paris, twenty-six Democratic members of the Massachusetts legislature actually cabled that the American people wanted him to come home and reduce the high cost of living, "which we consider *far more important than the League of Nations.*"

The world will never stånd still while men debate the issues of peace and war. As the statesmen in their frock coats moved the pawns back and forth on the diplomatic chessboard, the men in blue denim worked and sweated and played and married, as they ever will. Foreign affairs cannot be conducted, much less discussed, in a vacuum. In all our history there have been few times when outside dangers seemed more fearful than domestic dangers; and the post-Armistice period appears not to have been one of them. The power of autocratic, Prussianized Germany had been broken, apparently forever. With the setting of each sun the recent war seemed less real, and the prospects of a future war so remote as to cause little concern.

Delay was the great enemy of the peacemakers in America.

For delay was the culture bed for all the prolific forces of prejudice, partisanship, confusion, and doubt.

2

A mere catalogue of some of the distractions and worries of
the American people during these hectic months will shed a
flood of light on the problem of the peace-ratifiers.

Seldom have times been more out of joint for great masses
of Americans. A restless army of some four million men had
to be demobilized, and each discharged soldier had to find a
peaceful niche in civilian life. Some were maimed, some were
shell-shocked, and most of them were in need of more or less
emotional and mental reconditioning. And the one gnawing
question above all others in their minds was: "Will the old
job be there, or a new one in its place?"

Industrial demobilization was a colossal undertaking. To
the capitalist, financial losses were inevitable; to the laborer,
transitional unemployment was inevitable. To the businessman who faced general insecurity and possible bankruptcy,
the League of Nations did not seem an unmixed blessing.
Would it be, as alleged, a superstate which would beat down
our tariff barriers, flood the nation with the sweated handiwork of foreign labor, and force the American producer to
the wall?

Labor was restive. The cost of living had shot up like a
whale spout; wages, as usual, had lagged behind. Profiteering
and the high cost of living were burning issues well into the
1920's. The labor market was in danger of being glutted by
destitute hordes from Europe.

It had been unpatriotic to lay down one's tools during the
war; now the lid was off. Serious strikes broke out among the
steel workers of Gary, Indiana, and among the begrimed host
of John L. Lewis' coal miners. The very foundations of government trembled when in September of 1919 the police of
Boston struck and left the city at the mercy of hoodlums, who

smashed windows and defiantly rolled dice on the Boston Common—near the "cradle of American liberty."

Some of the labor disorders shaded off toward radicalism. The Socialists were unusually active; the I.W.W.'s were on the loose. The fear was widespread that Russian Bolshevism would sweep the United States. In the spring of 1919 a total of more than thirty bombs, addressed to prominent personages, was found in the mails. Several bombs were thrown, including one which, on June 2, 1919, wrecked the home of Attorney General A. Mitchell Palmer. Palmer, with understandable zeal, redoubled his efforts to herd "reds" behind bars or harry them out of the land. Conservatives were turning witch-hunters, and talking of rope and lampposts and "100 per cent Americanism."

3

The railroads were in a muddle. Taken over as a war measure for war purposes, they had been administered by Wilson's son-in-law, Secretary of the Treasury William G. McAdoo. They had been "McAdoodled," said conservative critics like George Harvey, who did not want government in business except when it helped business.

The Negro problem had been made more explosive. Colored men had gone North, or to France, and they had enjoyed undreamed-of privileges. When they came home it was more difficult to "keep them in their place." Terrifying race riots broke out in Washington, Chicago, Omaha, and elsewhere. Scarcely more than a week after Wilson returned from championing the rights of suppressed minorities, a frightening outburst occurred between blacks and whites almost under the White House windows.

Vexatious legislative issues were still unsettled. The fight for a woman suffrage amendment to the Constitution was going into its final rounds. The Eighteenth Amendment was riveted to the Constitution, but the "wets" and the "drys" were still doing battle over enforcement legislation. The boys in khaki were muttering that while they had been abroad fighting for human liberty, the "bluenoses" had taken advantage of their absence to "put over" this infringement on their personal liberty.

Even when Americans looked up from the harrowing domestic scene, their eyes did not necessarily seek Europe. American boys were still fighting Wilson's undeclared war against the Bolsheviks in the vastnesses of Siberia, and there was a growing demand that they be brought home. Relations with Mexico were normal—that is, teetering on the precipice of war.

The current crop of headline diversions was more than ordinarily thrilling. The air was dark with transatlantic airplanes or dirigibles, guided by men seeking either a watery grave or immortality. The British dirigible *R-34* made the crossing while Wilson was en route, thus crowding him from the front page.

New sports idols were springing into prominence. On July 4, while the President was in mid-ocean, Jack Dempsey battered the huge Jess Willard into a bleeding pulp, and thus became one of the most potent and unpopular of heavyweight champions. The baseball season was now on, with "Babe" Ruth thumping the ball over right-field walls with unprecedented frequency, and with the Chicago White Sox (soon to become the "Black Sox") about to treat the public to the most reverberating scandal in the history of the game.

One South Carolina newspaper half jokingly concluded that the people were getting more interested in the National League than in the League of Nations, and another journal discovered that some Americans actually thought that the new League of Nations was a baseball league.

4

Ignorance, apathy, inertia, and preoccupation were only negative obstacles in the path of the treaty. More dangerous in many ways were the active ingredients of the opposition, for they were able to bend large bodies of public opinion to their way of thinking.

Noisy rather than numerous, yet withal exceedingly influential, were the liberals. In view of later condemnations of the Treaty of Versailles it is highly significant that they alone of the purely American groups thought it too severe; most Americans thought that it erred, if at all, on the side of leniency.

The liberals had pinned their faith to Wilson and his Fourteen Points. Yet he had sat down in secret conclave with international "brigands," he had seemingly bartered away his ideals, and he had brought back a "hell's brew" that would merely beget World War II. The American liberals, joined by many of their brethren abroad, pronounced a solemn curse on Wilson and his handiwork.

The most important liberal journals to turn their guns against the treaty were the *New Republic* and the *Nation*. The *New Republic,* which was widely regarded as a mouthpiece for Wilson on progressive issues, broke with him and fought ratification, lock, stock, and barrel. This decision cost the magazine much of its circulation and presumably some of its prestige.

The *New Republic* published serially a part of John Maynard Keynes' devastating indictment of the treaty. Keynes was one of the British experts who had resigned in protest; his book, *The Economic Consequences of the Peace,* became a non-fiction best seller, and undoubtedly had a powerful effect in stirring up opposition both within and without the halls of Congress.

The venerable New York *Nation* was then under the militant editorship of Oswald Garrison Villard (grandson of the fanatical abolitionist William Lloyd Garrison), a professional pacifist with a high degree of sympathy for the German point of view. He fought the entire treaty with all the slashing weapons at his command. He was somewhat embarrassed to find himself·in the company of such bitter reactionaries as

"Boss" Boies Penrose and Henry Cabot Lodge, but politics makes strange bedfellows.

Not all liberal sheets, notably the Springfield *Republican,* broke with Wilson. But in general, as is usually true of liberals, they tended to seek perfectionism. Only dimly aware of the practical problems that had confronted Wilson at Paris, and of the necessity for give and take, they insisted on the whole loaf or none. When they saw that the loaf was not whole, they fought for none—and got it.

Former Progressives—those who in 1912 had fought to purge the Republican party and many of whom had sung "Onward, Christian Soldiers"—may be roughly classed with the liberals. Prominent among them were Senators Johnson of California, Borah of Idaho, Norris of Nebraska, La Follette of Wisconsin (who represented a constituency where many Germans lived), and ex-Senator Beveridge of Indiana.

Strangely enough, progressives in domestic affairs became reactionaries in foreign affairs. Those who had been crusaders for internal reform became crusaders against international reform. Possibly some of them felt that adventures abroad would interfere with housecleaning at home. But hatred of Wilson, pro-Germanism, and pure partisanship were curiously commingled with the most exalted liberal ideals.

5

Even louder and more bitter than the liberals were the immigrant groups in America, commonly referred to as "hyphenates"—German-Americans, Irish-Americans, Italian-Americans, and the others—all of whom were tied to the mother country by an umbilical hyphen three thousand miles long. Millions had been born in the "Old Country"; other millions —wives, husbands, children—fell under the same influence.

Ironically enough, Wilson expected that the United States would be the most eager of all powers to accept the League of Nations, for we were a league of nations in miniature. Millions of people from all races and climes had been dumped into the giant melting pot, and they had fabricated the New America. The United States seemed to be living proof of the workability of the League of Nations.

But the comparison proved to be misleading. People can live side by side in peace, but nations find it more difficult to live side by side in peace. The ties of nationalism are long and enduring, tenaciously resistant to the heat of any melting pot. This was why the British ambassador could sneer, after the outbreak of war in 1914, that we were "no nation, just a collection of people who neutralize one another."

The Irish-Americans were probably the most important politically of the hyphenate groups arrayed against the League; but they fall into a special category and will be treated later.

The German-Americans were a force of tremendous power, especially in the Middle West. Those of German birth and those with at least one German-born parent numbered about 7,000,000, or approximately 7 per cent of the population. A great body of them had patriotically supported the recent war effort; others had been bulldozed into silence and browbeaten into buying Liberty Bonds. It was now safe for them to come out of their holes, give vent to their pent-up emotions, and work for the Fatherland.

These people hated Wilson for having asked Congress to declare war, and for having prosecuted the war. They hated him for having visited a punitive peace on Germany, with its reparations, territorial excisions, and various humiliations— all seemingly in violation of the Fourteen Points. They were completely impervious to the argument that if it had not been for Wilson the peace would undoubtedly have been more severe than it actually was.

The German-Americans held rousing mass meetings, and undertook to organize their several million voters for the anti-League presidential candidate in 1920. At the forefront of these propagandists was George Sylvester Viereck, who castigated the Covenant as the "League of Damnations," and who was later, during World War II, to serve a prison term as an alien agent.

The Republican foes of the League assiduously wooed the German-Americans, though this group needed little wooing. To preserve America it seemed necessary to appeal to the prejudices of non-American groups in our midst.

Nor did the anti-League agitators overlook the hundreds of thousands of Italian-American voters, who were especially numerous in New York and Massachusetts, and who bitterly resented Wilson's persistent efforts to force the Yugoslav port of Fiume from the grasp of Italy. On Columbus Day, 1919, one Dr. Joseph Santosuosso, speaking to a crowd of Italian-Americans in Boston, vigorously attacked Wilson's Fiume policy, and evoked hisses for the name of Mrs. Wilson when he condemned her for having accompanied her husband to Europe. Fiorello H. La Guardia, then president of the New York City Board of Aldermen and future mayor of the metropolis, was active in organizing Italian-American strength against Wilson.

Other hyphenate groups blamed Wilson because their national aspirations had been denied, or grudgingly granted. Among them were the Poles, the Czechs, the Jews, the Chinese, and the Japanese. Some of these carried no real political weight, but they all added up to a loud, snarling, embittered opposition which controlled millions of votes. There was much point in the remark of a Boston journal that "the United States is a country of quiet majorities and vociferous minorities."

6

A final hyphenate group of great importance was the Irish-Americans. These colorful people had been closely associated during the war with German-Americans and pro-Germanism, not because they particularly loved Germany but because they violently hated Britain.

The mercurial sons of the shamrock were more important politically than the Germans, though outnumbered by them nearly two to one. First of all, the German-Americans were normally Republicans anyhow, and could be counted on to oppose the Democratic Wilson. Secondly, the Irish were generally Democratic and were vital elements in the great urban machines which controlled pivotal states like New York and Massachusetts. Every Irishman whom the Republicans could turn against Wilson represented a gain of more than one vote: one taken away from the Democrats and one added to the Republicans.

The Irish in America, it has often been said, are more Irish than the Irish of Ireland. Certainly those who came to the United States kept their memory of England's sins, real and fancied, as verdant as the landscape of their Emerald Isle. American politicians had long since learned that it was politically profitable to twist the British lion's tail periodically, and receive the acclaim, often in a rich brogue, of hate-ridden Irish voters. It is significant that Senator David I. Walsh of Massachusetts, himself of Irish lineage, was one of the few Democratic senators who refused to support Wilson foursquare on the League. He could not overlook the Boston Irish or the Massachusetts Italians, nor for that matter could his senior colleague, Henry Cabot Lodge.

In the late spring of 1919, the British ambassador in Washington told Henry White that he had been approached by two "prominent Republicans" (possibly senators), who confessed that their party would have to attack England on the Irish question but they wanted it known privately that they felt no real animosity toward the Mother Country.

The Irish problem in America would have been less troublesome if during 1919 and 1920 conditions in the ever vexed and ever turbulent isle had not verged on civil war. Rioting, burning, and murdering were daily occurrences. Irish prisoners of the British went on "hunger strikes," notable among them Terence MacSwiney, Lord Mayor of Cork, who died on October 25, 1920, after a voluntary fast lasting seventy-four days.

"President" Eamon de Valera, of the so-called Irish "Republic," toured the United States in the spring and summer of 1919, stirring up fresh hate. The champions of Irish independence held overflow mass meetings, at which the League of Nations was viciously assailed, and the name of Wilson was repeatedly booed and hissed.

"No European Entanglements"

(From New York *Tribune*; courtesy of *Herald-Tribune*; cartoonist Darling)

German-Americans and Irish-Americans made it a point to attend public meetings en masse, and by their vocal and manual approval of attacks on the treaty they gave the false impression that public sentiment was overwhelmingly opposed to the League. The Brooklyn *Eagle* was not far from the mark when it complained, "Too many people in this country are enjoying the right of free screech."

7

One of the chief grievances of the Irish-Americans against Wilson was that he had failed to secure self-determination for Ireland. At Paris he had courteously but informally talked with an Irish delegation from the United States, though privately confessing that his first impulse was to tell them "to go to hell." Yet he refused to accede to their wishes and press for Irish self-determination, primarily because the problem of Ireland was not relevant to the task in hand.

The United States had fought Germany, not Britain (though some Irish-Americans would have preferred to fight Englishmen); and self-determination was generally applied only to former enemy territory. Wilson had enough insoluble and vexatious problems worrying him at Paris without taking up the questions of self-determination for India, Afghanistan, Egypt, and Ireland. Yet the Irish-Americans never forgave him for not doing the impolitic and the impossible.

The Irish were also infuriated by Article X of the League Covenant, which obligated each member of the League to assist its fellow members against "external aggression." In the voluble mouths of pro-Irish agitators this meant that American boys of Irish ancestry might be sent abroad to help England crush out an Irish revolt. How then could Ireland ever win her independence?

This of course was malicious misrepresentation. By no stretch of either imagination or phraseology could an internal revolt in Ireland be interpreted as "external aggression" against the British Empire.

No less damaging in the mouth of the demagogue was the article of the Covenant which gave the British Empire six votes in the Assembly of the League, while assigning only one to the United States. Wilson, it was hotly charged, had been taken into camp by the wily British diplomats. Henceforth Great Britain would dominate the world, and the Land of the

Free would play second fiddle to King George V of England. This, too, was malicious misrepresentation or inexcusable ignorance. We shall later consider the problem in some detail, but for the moment we may note that while the British Dominions had six votes in the Assembly, they had only one, like the United States, in the all-important Council. *And our one vote could block any decision on any question except where we were parties to a dispute.*

After viewing the intemperate Irish outbursts, and considering our proposed mandate over Armenia, the Philadelphia *Press* concluded that the League should not ask "Uncle Sam to be mandatory for nations abroad until after he has successfully mandated a few things right here at home."

8

Closely allied with the professional Irishmen were the professional British-haters. They were the men who had not outgrown the influence of their fife-and-drum textbooks, and who were still shooting Redcoats at Bunker Hill and New Orleans. They hated the British, and, like the Irish, feared that something was being "put over" on the United States. Specifically, they pointed to the undeniable fact that the League in its preliminary stages had been largely drafted by such eminent Britons as Smuts, Cecil, and Phillimore. England under George III had failed to enslave America in 1776 by force of arms; now she was seeking to do it under George V by trickery —the trickery of Article X and six votes to one. The United States would have none of a Smuts-sired League.

The high priest of the Anglophobes in the Senate was James A. Reed of Missouri. Neither pro-German nor pro-Irish as such, he castigated the British-controlled League, and satirically nominated for its presidency "that great British statesman" "Sir Herbert Hoover," whom he scorned for having lived many years under the British flag.

Most influential of all the British-haters was William

Randolph Hearst, who marshaled his newspaper empire, with its 3,000,000 or so henchmen, against Britain and the "British-spawned League." His syndicated blasts of hostility were unrelenting, and he directed his fire indiscriminately against both the white peril of British imperialism and the yellow peril of Japanese expansionism.

George Bernard Shaw is reported to have said that the two great English-speaking peoples are separated—not united—by a common language. The British could read what we said about them, and we could read what they said about us. Expressions of sympathy in America for Ireland, whether passed by Congress or by other bodies, were resented in England—and we resented their resentment. Soon influential British writers like Horatio Bottomley in *John Bull* were muddying the waters by crying that America came into the war "not to save her honor but to save her skin," and that Uncle Sam "filled his pockets years before he filled his cartridge belt."

Ere long this transatlantic bickering broadened into an utterly senseless debate as to who had won the war. Before the Armistice there had been some dispute among the American forces as to whether the marines or the infantry deserved the real credit. Now responsible British commanders like Field-Marshal Sir Douglas Haig were saying to English audiences (for home consumption) that Britain had won the war. This seemed like an intolerable insult to the American dead.

During the war America had accelerated her gigantic naval construction program in the face of the German threat. Now the war had stopped, but the riveters had not. Against whom could we be building, unless England? At the rate we were going we should soon be able to wrest Neptune's trident from her grasp.

This general atmosphere of acrimony drove the two nations farther apart at a critical time in world history. Working together, the two great Anglo-Saxon powers could preserve the peace; pulling in opposite directions, they would surely bring about the downfall of the League.

9

Fundamentally more important than any other group was the great mass of isolationists in the United States—those who wanted to keep out of the broils of Europe, and who thought they could do so by merely trying to mind their own business.

The myth still persists that a few wicked men, like Senators Lodge and Borah and Johnson, converted the American people to an isolationist course, and thus engineered the ruin of the League.

This is paying far too high a tribute to the persuasive powers of these master obstructionists. The truth is that the American people had always been basically isolationist in their aspirations, that they had been forced into the war by German U-boat attacks, and that they had temporarily lost sight of their ancient policy under the enthusiasm of war and the lofty exhortations of Wilson.

When the shooting stopped, and the menace to our security was (temporarily) enchained, the natural tendency of the American people was to slip back into the old groove. The New York *Sun* confidently and accurately predicted that "a lot of people will pick up their 1913-14 thoughts right where they laid them down." The foes of the League recognized that this would happen, and their great fear was that action might be pressed on the treaty before the nation had cooled off. Time must be purchased at any price.

France had fought in 1914 because she was attacked; Britain had fought because her age-old policy had been to keep any strong power from occupying the Lowlands and pointing a pistol at her heart; America had fought because she was attacked by Germany. When the war was over, France went back to her ancient policy—older than Louis XIV—of seeking to dominate the continent. Britain went back to her ancient policy—older than Queen Elizabeth—of trying to prevent any one power from becoming too dominant on the continent.

America went back to her ancient policy—older than George Washington—of attempting to keep out of the political broils and wars of the mother continent.

"Nationalism" would be a better description than "isolationism" for the postwar mood of the United States. Wilson had been belatedly converted to a policy of internationalism, and hence his quarrel was with nationalism wherever he found it. He fondly believed that he represented a world constituency rather than an American constituency. He opposed Italian nationalism, and was frustrated by Orlando and others; he opposed French nationalism, and was thwarted by Clemenceau and others; he opposed British nationalism, and was blocked by Lloyd George and others.

When Wilson came home his struggle was still with nationalism. Instead of Orlando and Clemenceau and Lloyd George, he encountered Borah and Lodge and Johnson. And the subsequent battles were more bitter, and the results even less successful, than the battles had been in Europe. Borah was a more obdurate "irreconcilable" than Clemenceau, because he wielded power without commensurate responsibility. The Senate foes of the League, who at first glance may have seemed like less redoubtable antagonists than the European diplomats, were even more formidable because they could be sure of a definite term in office, and be reasonably sure of reelection.

10

Wilson could do battle with live men, and he did. But he could not do battle with dead men. Some of his most formidable antagonists were in the spirit world: George Washington, Thomas Jefferson, James Monroe, and even Theodore Roosevelt. Skeleton hands as well as muscular hands pulled the United States back from the threshold of the League of Nations.

The sacred policy of George Washington—of keeping out

of the broils of Europe—was sanctified not only by time but, said the isolationists, by common sense. Washington would stir uneasily in his tomb at Mount Vernon if he should learn that we were going to underwrite a League of Nations and keep an army of American boys ready to fight strange peoples in strange lands—all at the behest of some superbody. Senator Philander C. Knox of Pennsylvania cried out in the Senate that accept-

Not Room for Both
(Courtesy of San Francisco *Chronicle*; cartoonist Bronstrup)

ance of the League would mean "centuries of blood-letting."

Why surrender our sovereignty to some foreign superstate? In isolationist eyes the League was a species of self-emasculation, a fundamental change in our government, a subversion of our great Constitution. Ex-Senator Beveridge insisted that America was being inveigled into a partnership "where Europe furnishes the liabilities and the United States supplies the assets." It was a sinister conspiracy that would, in the judgment of the New York *Sun,* mark the "sunset of our independence." A League for the Preservation of American Independence was actually organized.

Critics of the League beat the tomtoms of nationalism, and cried out against denationalization. "If I were an Englishman, a Frenchman, or an Italian," cried George Harvey, "I should want this League. But I am an American." His vitriolic *Harvey's Weekly* condemned the "Denationalists," the "League of Denationalization," and the "Covenant of Denationalization." It published "The International Hymn," a part of which ran:

> Our foreign countries, thee,
> Lands of the chimpanzee,
> Thy names we love . . .

As a political issue denationalization had tremendous possibilities, especially in the hands of the unscrupulous rabble rouser. Senator Reed of Missouri made the most of the potent new issue—of a hybrid flag flapping above the glorious Stars and Stripes. "I decline," he shouted, "to set up any government greater than the government of the United States of America!"

Inconsistency was a bugbear that did not trouble the isolationists and nationalists. We must keep free from the broils of the Old World; yet we must rush into the broils of Ireland. The League was such a powerful "superstate" that it would submerge our independence; yet the League was such a weak "sewing circle" that it would be a waste of time to join it. The League was a vicious entanglement; yet the League was "as entangling as any other rainbow."

But the enemies of the League had no scruples about being all things to all men. Such a horrible calamity awaited America that the end would justify the means. And the great mass of the people would not note these inconsistencies. There would be a doubt for everyone, and the gullible could seize upon the doubt which most alarmed them. "Senator Borah," said the Des Moines *Register,* "is not an unthinking man. But he voices the sentiments of the unthinking."

A great many of the isolationists were no doubt as sincere as they were shortsighted. It made sense to them that we should follow the time-honored precepts of Washington, steer clear of foreign broils, and keep our necks out of the noose of internationalism. Aloof from the century-old quarrels of Europe, disinterested, detached, and powerful, the United States as a free agent could best throw its weight on the side of peace. We could dole out loaves to the hungry, proffer do-good advice to the quarrelsome, and preen ourselves on our righteousness. Or, as one journal put it, we could serve most usefully by being a sister to the world rather than by marrying it.

11

Hardly less important than isolationism in the tragedy which befell Wilson and the world was what is known as "the slump in idealism."

Until the Armistice, Wilson had been able to sustain the idealism of the people at a high pitch, high enough in fact to bring the self-denial of prohibition. Even if he had been able to do at Paris all that was expected of him, the slump doubtless would have come sooner or later, as in fact it did in Europe. Human nature is able to sustain an emotional orgy for only a relatively short time.

The barometer of idealism was visibly falling even before Wilson brought the treaty back from Paris. In the heat of combat one does not usually feel so keenly the pain of wounds. But we now had time to take stock of the situation: to scan our incoming casualty lists, and our outpouring disbursements to the Allies. There was the chill that comes with the doctor's bill. We were weary of well-doing. We were tired of war and wartime restrictions and wartime taxes; we recoiled from the very thought of troublesome and expensive international police.work.

Many unselfish souls in America had been shocked by the scrambling for spoils at the peace table, and they were disillusioned because their ideals had gone sour. Others felt that they had been victimized by Allied propaganda. Men like Senator Johnson of California had entered the war with the highest motives; they had listened respectfully to the eloquent preachments of Allied spokesmen—spokesmen whose pockets all the while bulged with secret treaties. When the veil was ripped aside at Paris, these senators branded the whole lot as a gang of double-crossing crooks, and vowed to wash their hands of the whole business.

If the Allies had proved faithless, our newly found friends of the succession states were little better. Nations like Poland had received much, but they were greedily reaching out for more. The Balkans were still a caldron of hate and warfare. Peace had not come to earth. "The trouble with the new nations," remarked the Greenville (S.C.) *Piedmont*, "is that they have the old quarrels." Everywhere men were sneering, "Where is Wilson's millennium?"

The President had gone to Paris, seeking nothing for the United States but peace. We not only had lost the friendship of Italy, China, and Japan, but had gained nothing from the whole mess except a questionable League of Nations, while the imperialistic powers had apparently made off with valuable oil reserves and other properties. Observers like the Socialist Victor L. Berger could say with more than a grain of truth that all America got out of the war was the flu and prohibition. Others would add high prices, heavy taxes, and bad debts.

This general picture of course was not fair to the Allies, but it was the picture that a large number of Americans retained.

12

Nor was this all. The "ingrate" nations of Europe, while cursing us for our sins of commission and omission, were stretching bony arms across the Atlantic and begging for more food, more money. Would the appalling cost of this thing ever stop? The Brooklyn *Eagle* struck a popular note when it said, "We don't mind feeding the small nations, but we should like them to stop fighting between meals."

Every returning passenger ship dumped into American ports a fresh cargo of homesick and disillusioned soldiers. They had gone abroad to save the world, believing from their storybooks that war was something romantic and glamorous. They had received a deflating dose of trenches, poison gas, mud, hardtack, and lice. Mark Sullivan tells of the returning Negro soldier who gazed rapturously at the Statue of Liberty from a transport, and solemnly vowed, "Lady, once I gets behind you, I promise I never will look at yo' face again."

All had not been harmonious on the other side. Our boys had engaged in fisticuffs with their British cousins. They had been overcharged by French shopkeepers. The baseless rumor had spread that our government had actually had to pay rent for the trenches our doughboys occupied. The starry-eyed lads in khaki had reached France believing that Frenchmen wore wings and Germans horns. Now that many of our warriors had seen the clean German cities and the clean German people, they were not so sure as they had once been that they had fought on the right side. Anyhow, they were home, and home to stay, and they were not going to be summoned from their plows by any superstate blowing a blast on the trumpet of Article X.

Saddened and disgusted though they were, the "Yanks" at least had the satisfaction of knowing they had won the war. Yet now Field-Marshal Haig was openly proclaiming that the British had turned the trick!

The titanic conflict which had been fought to "make the world safe for democracy" and to "end wars" had turned to dust and ashes. A score or so of minor wars now grew where only one had grown before. Our military leaders were talking openly of peacetime conscription; the War Department was asking Congress for a standing army about five times the normal complement. There was a growing feeling that, as one journal put it, "until the League proves itself, we had better beat our swords into convertible plowshares."

Wilson had won the war by arousing the American people to the fervor of a great moral crusade. He could win an acceptance of the peace, and above all a carrying out of our responsibilities under the peace, only by arousing them to a new idealistic crusade. But would he be able to do so in the face of the obstacles confronting him? A sober review of the forces in opposition reveals little to justify his optimism.

CHAPTER THREE

THE PALL OF
PARTISANSHIP

*"No party has a right to appropriate this issue [the treaty] and
no party will in the long run dare oppose it."* WOODROW WILSON,
March 4, 1919.

1

BLIND PARTISANSHIP, as much as any other single factor,
ruined the League of Nations in the United States. This is not
to condemn any one individual or group of individuals; it is
merely to state a fact which, in the circumstances, was as inescapable as the law of gravitation.

The treaty was too much bound up with Wilson, and especially with Wilson's League of Nations, to leave any room for
hope that the issue could escape the reefs of partisanship. One
competent writer has estimated that four-fifths of the opposition to the League was nothing more than unreasoning hatred
of Wilson. This is probably an exaggeration, but there can be
no doubt that the Republican leaders, and many of the Republican rank and file, hated the President with a consuming
bitterness, and were prepared to stop at nothing to bring about
his downfall and at the same time (so they claimed) save the
Republic.

The Republicans could not forgive Wilson for having
beaten them in 1912, especially since his victory was their
own fault. They could not accustom themselves to the role of
a minority party: this was contrary to the natural order of
things since 1861. They could not forgive Wilson for having
won again in 1916, by the narrowest of margins and with the
slogan, "He kept us out of war." It was in fact the first time
an incumbent Democrat had been elected since the redoubtable Andrew Jackson, in 1832.

The Republicans distrusted Wilson because he was a Southerner, with Southerners in his Cabinet, and with long-lived Southern Democrats in control of the Congressional committees. He was believed to be conspiring to impoverish the North to the advantage of the South through the income tax and other devices. The New York *Tribune* charged that Wilson's internationalism was developed as a screen to cover his Southernism. William E. Dodd alleges that certain "eminent" Republicans announced in his presence that it would have been better if the South had won the Civil War, for "then we should have escaped Wilson."

Wilson believed that a President should lead, and he had stood over Congress with a dictatorial rod. Worse than that, he had liberal ideas about the tariff and trusts and income taxes, all of which notions were anathema to Republican big business. Republican journals referred angrily to the "crimes of Wilson"; and the oil magnate, Edward L. Doheny, later to be besmeared with the Teapot Dome scandal, growled that the President was a "college professor gone Bolshevik."

Bitterly though the Republicans reacted against Wilson's peacetime leadership, their resentment increased when war came and Wilson ("Kaiser" Wilson) assumed the dictatorial powers that were lawfully his under the Constitution. The Republicans could not reconcile themselves to the fact, nor forgive themselves for it, that a Democrat was running the biggest of our wars up to that time. They cried out against huge expenditures of money, as if penny-pinching were in order when the fate of America was at stake; and their bitterness mounted to fury when, search though they did, they could find no real taint of scandal.

2

Wilson not only had run the war, but had kept prominent Republicans from winning glory and making political capital out of it. General Leonard Wood, a potential Republican President and a close friend of ex-President Theodore Roosevelt, was suddenly ordered away from the embarkation port and condemned to stay at home while the troops which he had trained went overseas. Colonel Theodore Roosevelt, who was regarded as the logical Republican nominee in 1920, almost got down on his knees before the hated Wilson, pleading for a chance to take a division of volunteers to France and inspirit the flagging Allied cause. Wilson austerely rebuffed him, thus visiting upon the graying Rough Rider the greatest disappointment of his life.

Wilson of course had good or at least plausible reasons for snubbing both Wood and Roosevelt; but the important point is that the Republicans neither forgot nor forgave. Roosevelt had once shown some friendliness to the idea of a league of nations, notably in his address accepting the Nobel Peace Prize. But when Wilson espoused the League, Roosevelt attacked it with all his unbridled vehemence. He literally plotted on his deathbed to defeat the yet unborn League of Nations.

The venom engendered by the Roosevelt-Wilson feud persisted, and gave strength to the foes of the League during those dark hours when it seemed as though theirs was a losing cause. Looking back through the mists of thirteen years, Mrs. Alice Roosevelt Longworth, the doughty Rough Rider's doughty daughter, could write, "How we did cherish and nourish our hatreds in those days!"

During the war, politics had been nominally "adjourned." Both partisanship and pro-Germanism took cover, but they were still very much alive. Now that the shooting had stopped, partisanship could flare forth with all the greater explosiveness for having been repressed.

Wilson, it must be conceded, played directly into the hands of the Republican partisans. Before going to Paris, he bluntly called upon the country for a Democratic Congress to uphold his policies; then, when the voters returned Republicans, he snubbed the Senate by refusing to consult with its leaders and by taking abroad a peace commission of five which contained no senators and only one Republican, a minor figure at that. Wilson was going to make a Wilsonian peace, a Democratic peace, with the glory unipartisan but with the responsibility bipartisan. All right, said the Republicans, that was a game that two could play.

Partisanship in some degree could not have been kept out of

The Stars and Stripes First

(From New York *World*; cartoonist Kirby; reprinted by permission)

the death struggle over the treaty. Yet if Wilson had been more deferential to the Republicans, if he had honored them with prominent places in his councils, if he had accepted more of their ideas, he would no doubt have removed some of the sting. Certainly he would have given the Republicans less excuse for going before the country in a blaze of indignation crying that the President was playing politics with the treaty.

In short, the Republicans were forced to oppose the League, at least in unamended form, if for no other reason than that it was a Wilson League. As the Greenville (S.C.) *Piedmont* baldly put it, "The Senate's chief objection to the League idea is that Wilson is a Democrat." A few prominent Republicans, notably ex-President William Howard Taft, could rise above their dislike of Wilson and support the League with unflagging devotion. But such men were the exception. The Columbus *Ohio State Journal* whimsically remarked, "The attitude of most of us thoughtful Republicans seems to be that we're unalterably opposed to Article X, whether we know what's in it or not."

3

The high officials of both parties naturally considered their position on the League issue in the light of their political fortunes. The chairman of the Republican National Committee, Will H. Hays, was in constant touch with the party leaders, senatorial and otherwise, as to what attitude the Republicans should take. Should they accept the Wilson League? Should they strive to amend it slightly, or fundamentally? Or should they scrap the whole thing, as Senators Borah and Brandegee and Johnson were demanding? Would not the ringing cry of "Americanism versus internationalism" win the most votes in the end? The Republicans, in brief, were striving to find the winning issue; the Democrats, to maintain one.

Neither party ever lost sight of the relation of the League to the presidential election of 1920. The Republicans were confident that on domestic issues alone they could defeat any possible Democratic candidate: they had merely to capitalize on war-weariness and a desire to get back to "normalcy." But if Wilson should shove his grandiose scheme through the Senate, his increased prestige would be dangerous. So overshadowing a world figure might he become that he would perhaps dictate

a Democratic successor—possibly his son-in-law, William G.
McAdoo.

Even more disquieting was another possibility. Once the
League was approved, would it not be logical that Wilson
should stay in office at least another term to see that it got off
to a proper start? The two-term tradition was still strong, but
world reorganization was a grave responsibility. Wilson might
consent to run by persuading himself that he was the "indispensable man." Worse than that, he might be able to persuade
the voters that he was the "indispensable man." The night-
mare of four more years of Wilsonism caused cold chills to run
down Republican spines.

The hated professor might even aspire to head the League
of Nations and become president of the world. Possibly this
was his desire. Irwin H. ("Ike") Hoover, the White House
usher, referring to the period shortly after Wilson's return
from Europe, recalls that the President once turned to him
and asked if he would like to go back to Geneva.

4

One of Wilson's gravest mistakes, it now seems, was his
failure to announce early in the fight that under no circumstances would he attempt to shatter the two-term tradition.
Partisanship would have remained; but a great deal of the
personal spleen would have been removed, and the battle
would have been fought out at ordinary partisan levels. As it
turned out, a vast amount of Republican effort was devoted
to thwarting and humiliating Wilson, largely because he was a
potential candidate for a third term. He was in fact freely
mentioned as such, down to the very week in 1920 when the
Democrats nominated James M. Cox.

Wilson, as his private papers now reveal, was fully aware of
this situation. On May 17, 1919, an editorial in the influential
Springfield *Republican* called upon him to announce that

he was not a candidate for a third term, and thus eliminate his personality from the debate. This editorial reached Wilson in Paris, and on June 2 he cabled his private secretary in Washington, Joseph P. Tumulty, asking for a consensus of opinion among his advisers as to what he should do.

Tumulty did not make it clear in his reply of the next day whether he had consulted anyone or not. But he vigorously advised against accepting a third nomination, even though the great majority of the Democratic leaders favored one. Another four years would not add to Wilson's dignity and honor. But in any case, Tumulty concluded, the time was not ripe for an announcement, because the Democrats were sorely depressed by their 1920 prospects.

Wilson did not reply to this urgent cablegram, but it is significant that he refrained to the very end from making a public pronouncement. We do not know whether he was impressed by Tumulty's advice, or whether he was moved by other reasons. Several possibilities offer themselves.

Before the two-term tradition was shattered in 1940, the President's power waned as his second term neared its end. Everyone knew that the king was dying. Perhaps Wilson wished to cultivate the third-term threat so as to hold his Democratic followers, many of whom were grumbling, securely in line. Perhaps he was actually keeping his mind open on the question of a third term, waiting to see whether it was necessary to arrange to have himself "drafted." Possibly he felt that a formal act of abdication would be not only unnecessary but slightly ridiculous: the two-term tradition had already become a part of the unwritten Constitution. And Wilson habitually recoiled from the unnecessary or the slightly ridiculous.

In politics one must often stoop to conquer. Wilson never fully learned that one must do irrelevant, repetitious, or even somewhat foolish things to attain the larger end. At least, he never learned to do these things willingly or gracefully.

5

The presidential election of 1920 was not the only one that cast a dark pall over the League issue.

In the campaign of 1912 the Republicans had broken into two snarling factions, and had defeated themselves. The penalty was Wilson and his works. At all costs the Republicans must not split again in 1920. Whatever position they took, it must be one which all of them, or the great majority of them, could support. If that position squared with world order and the cause of humanity, so much the better; but, if it did not, the nobler cause would have to go out the window. There must be unity at any price, for disunity might mean another 1912, with a triumphant Wilson or his heir apparent enthroned for four more years.

Much that is not otherwise understandable becomes transparently clear when we remember that the preliminary stages of the election of 1920 were fought on the floor of the Senate in 1919, with the League as the chief whipping boy. When the Republican leaders wavered under pressure of public opinion, and seriously considered accepting some kind of amended Wilson League, there were always bolters like Borah and Johnson to threaten that they would organize a third party in 1920 and repeat the horrors of 1912.

Our presidential form of government has many virtues, but in the field of foreign affairs it has serious drawbacks. Elections must come not by the crisis, as in England, but by the calendar; and the calendar is no respecter of events. The momentous debate of 1919–1920 was conducted with one eye on the political arena.

Both parties, it must be emphasized, were looking at the calendar. Democrats accused the Republicans of partisanship; Republicans accused the Democrats of partisanship. It was the age-old story of the pot calling the kettle partisan; purely political motives were absent on neither side. This is a fact

that has often been overlooked by overzealous friends of the
League, who have upbraided the political maneuvers of the Republicans while completely ignoring those of the Democrats.
The innermost feelings of the Democrats were betrayed by one
South Carolina newspaper which remarked, "The world has
been made about as safe for democracy as this country for
the Democratic party."

Democratic partisanship was quieter, less conspicuous, more
subtle. The Republicans appeared to be flagrantly partisan,
for they were attempting to pull down or at least reshape the
Wilsonian League. They seemed to be attacking world peace.
The Democrats on the other hand, while supporting Wilson's
scheme for what were in some cases largely partisan motives,
appeared to be fighting for peace on earth and good will among
nations. They could make political capital out of Wilson's
glowing successes, while professing to support the League for
only the noblest motives. They sought partisan credit; the
Republicans could not permit them to get unalloyed partisan
credit.

The various newspaper polls show beyond a doubt that
where the Democratic party was strong, sentiment for the
League was strong. The Solid South was solidly behind the
League. Where the Republicans were strong, opposition to an
unamended Wilson League was strong. In the Senate, the
Democrats lined up almost unanimously for an unamended
League. If on the one hand there was blind Republican partisanship, on the other hand there was blind Democratic party
loyalty. Both are partisanship.

6

Viewed in the large, the League of Nations was a national
issue—a world issue—which should have been completely
divorced from politics. There was nothing inherent in the
League that should have enlisted the support of the cotton-

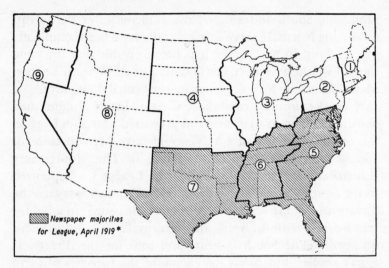

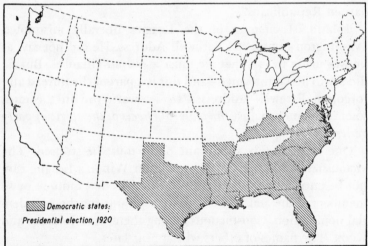

Newspaper majorities for League, April 1919*

Democratic states: Presidential election, 1920

* Based on *Literary Digest* poll (April 5, 1919, p. 15) of 1,377 daily U. S. newspapers on League of Nations. Responses by section: (1) 40 yes, 14 no, 41 conditional; (2) 122 yes, 37 no, 104 con.; (3) 166 yes, 48 no, 132 con.; (4) 85 yes, 29 no, 70 con.; (5) 75 yes, 13 no, 24 con.; (6) 45 yes, 4 no, 7 con.; (7) 88 yes, 8 no, 21 con.; (8) 33 yes, 8 no, 30 con.; (9) 64 yes, 20 no, 49 con. Total: 718 yes, 181 no, 478 con.

producing South and aroused the antagonism of the wheat-producing North. If party barriers could have been completely beaten down in the Senate, it is inconceivable that the same line-up would have been for and against the Wilson League. Men did not vote their consciences; they voted their party.

If the Republican candidate, Charles Evans Hughes, had defeated Wilson in 1916, and had presented a Hughes League, the Solid South almost surely would have been in favor of adding reservations to it or rejecting it. The Montgomery *Advertiser* was frank to admit that the League was supported in the South "largely because Southern Democrats regard the Treaty and its ratification as a Democratic issue." In a lighter but no less truthful vein, the Greenville (S.C.) *Piedmont* quipped: "The South is heart and soul for the Treaty. It hasn't read it, but it has read some of the speeches of them darned Republicans."

Isolationist enemies of the League liberally misquoted Washington's immortal Farewell Address. He did not say, as he was made to say, that we must avoid *all* alliances. But he did say to his countrymen—and this is a part of the unread and forgotten Farewell Address: "I . . . warn you in the most solemn manner against *the baneful effects of the spirit of party generally.*"

One other highly significant point must be stressed. The viciousness of the senatorial attacks on Wilson's League cannot be entirely disassociated from the fact that a dozen or so members of the Senate were active aspirants for the presidential nomination. Conspicuous among them were Johnson and Knox. The names of others will appear later.

The attacks which some of these men launched against the League, notably Johnson, were not currently popular, but, given time, the tide might turn against internationalism and in favor of rousing nationalism. It is always easier to implant doubts than to dig them up. Unquestionably much of the oratory and parliamentary jockeying in the Senate was related to the great national conventions of 1920. "Patience, Europe," counseled one Southern newspaper. "We can't bother with these little world-problems until we decide who is to get the office."

In political warfare as in military warfare the first casualty is the truth. The imminence of the battle of 1920 was all the more reason why Wilson, as noted elsewhere,* should have striven to keep a detailed League Covenant out of the treaty, so that it might be considered later in a less impassioned and less partisan atmosphere.

7

Partisanship and prejudice merged imperceptibly with pride of prerogative in the Senate fight over the League.

The Senate is the more important half of one of the three coordinate branches of the United States government. In normal times it is a coordinate body; in wartime it tends to become a subordinate body, because the Constitution confers upon the President dictatorial powers. When the war is over, the Senate naturally seeks to reestablish its former importance. This it did when the Civil War came to a close in 1865; this it did when the World War came to a nominal close in 1918. Lincoln died before the battle was fully joined, leaving Johnson to do unsuccessful battle; Wilson lived on, gave unsuccessful battle, and was crushed.

Wilson's position was in some respects even less favorable than Lincoln's would have been had he lived to face the music. From the very beginning of his administration in 1913, Wilson had "crowded" Congressmen in his attempts to drive through a sweeping program of reform. By 1919 there was a growing list of members who were not loath to pay off old scores.

The senators, by being left off the Peace Commission, had been ostentatiously denied an opportunity to help write the treaty in Paris; now was their opportunity to do a little re-

* See T. A. Bailey, *Woodrow Wilson and the Lost Peace*, pp. 190–192, 352–353.

writing on their own in the form of reservations. They owed it to their wounded pride to put some kind of senatorial stamp, major or minor, on Wilson's handiwork. They were in fact the first representative body in our democracy to have a chance at it. Wilson's group of experts ("The Inquiry") had been solely appointive; his Peace Commission of five had been solely

"Looks Black to Me"

(From New York *Evening World*; cartoonist Cassel; reprinted by permission)

appointive, and largely rubber stamps. If democracy had any validity, the people's elected representatives were entitled to a microscopic look at a treaty which had been negotiated behind guarded doors.

8

Wilson, it now appears, took an unduly narrow view of the constitutional powers of the Senate regarding treaties. To him advice and consent meant that the Senate would give its advice and consent *after* the completed pact had been laid before it, not while the pact was in the process of negotiation.

Such was the procedure that had ordinarily been followed in dealing with routine treaties, though previous Presidents had occasionally sought advice in advance of senatorial action. Wilson was legally justified in pursuing a policy of aloofness; but it was politically unwise. Ordinary methods would not suffice. This was more than an ordinary treaty: it was a charter for a new world order. The Senate would doubtless have been flattered, and probably to some extent mollified, if it had been invited to have some kind of share in the treaty's making.

The two-thirds rule interposed a formidable hurdle, but there it was, and Wilson had to play the game within the rules unless he was prepared to engineer a successful *coup d'état*. The Founding Fathers, with their distrust of George III, had piled up obstacles in the path of executive action, and had set the stage for deadlock. A prudent Wilson would have left no stone unturned in his efforts to avert the deadlock.

Wilson felt strong, because, as we have noted, public opinion was generally behind him. He knew that he was wiser than the Senate in that he could see the world aspects of the problem, whereas the mental ceiling of the senators from the sheep-and-corn country was relatively low. He believed that when the Senate was presented with an accomplished fact in peace-making it might grumble but could do no other than surrender.

This, as we shall see, was a woeful misjudgment of the temper of the prerogative-proud Senate. Public opinion might favor the League, but public opinion could be changed or confused. Besides, election day for individual senators was approximately two, four, or six years away; and the voters have an incredibly short memory. One wit has well said, "The President proposes, the Senate disposes, while the country dozes."

Two-thirds of the Senators would be in office after Wilson's two terms came to an end. The Senate in 1919 was composed of iron-willed, independent-minded men: the Brandegees, the

Reeds, the Borahs, the Johnsons, and the Shermans. They would not jump when the President cracked the whip; they would give more advice than consent. If Wilson made them angry enough, they would willingly commit political suicide provided, in so doing, they could but drag this vile League into the grave with them.

A certain amount of partisanship would of course have been present even if Wilson had treated the Senate with the deference of a Lord Chesterfield. But he would have lost nothing if at the very beginning he had tried to make partners of the senators rather than vicious partisans. By July, 1919, he had affronted them so seriously that it was difficult if not impossible to recover lost ground.

Wilson was now dimly aware of this situation, and under the proddings of his advisers undertook to make some conciliatory gestures in the direction of the Senate. But it was evident to all that he would extend no "nosegays" to the "pygmy-minded" members of that body.

CHAPTER FOUR

THE CAVE OF THE WINDS

"God made the world in seven days, but he didn't have a senate
to deal with." Greenville (S.C.) PIEDMONT, *September, 1919.*

1

THE FOCAL point of the fight over the treaty was the Senate of the United States—what the presiding officer, Vice President Thomas R. Marshall, remembering his classical mythology, whimsically called "the cave of the winds." The opinions of the senators ran the whole gamut from enthusiastic approval of the treaty as it stood, to flat rejection of all it contained. An analysis of these various groups is indispensable if one is to understand precisely how the treaty met its doom.

The Democrats may be considered first. When the treaty was submitted to the Senate there were 47 Democrats and 49 Republicans. The Democrats not only lacked a simple majority but fell far short of the necessary two-thirds. Not only that, but four of the Democratic senators were outright opponents of an unreserved "Wilson treaty": the unbridled Gore of Oklahoma, the independently minded Shields of Tennessee, the Irish-sired Walsh of Massachusetts, and the leather-larynxed Reed of Missouri. By far the most important of these four Democratic "irreconcilables" or near "irreconcilables" was the silver-thatched Reed, an accomplished rabble-rouser with a withering tongue and a buzz-saw voice. He seems to have turned against the treaty primarily because of his isolationist and anti-British prejudices.

The Democrats not only lacked numbers but lacked forensic power. They had no one who could stand up against the oratorical blasts of Borah and Johnson, or match the sarcastic sallies of Brandegee and Moses. Reed could, but he deserted to the other side.

The Democrats also lacked parliamentary skill. Not even their ablest member could cross swords on equal terms with Lodge, one of the cleverest and most resourceful parliamentarians in the history of the Senate.

Altogether, the Democrats were conspicuously short of intellectual resources and general ability. In brilliance of mind, Senator Walsh of Montana, a bloodhound for facts who later made his mark in the Teapot Dome prosecutions, could, after careful preparation, stand up against Knox or Lodge, but he was lacking in personal force and adaptability. His older colleagues were in general average if not mediocre figures.

Most of the Democratic senators were from the Solid South, where party loyalty was a fetish closely associated with racial supremacy and the "Lost Cause" of 1861–1865. They were generally the products of a one-party system, and some of them had been elected and reelected for decades with little or no opposition. It was said with more than a grain of truth that if a Southern Democrat maintained his party allegiance, voted the straight ticket, and kept out of jail, he could be reasonably sure of being returned to Congress. This situation did not make for the ablest type of legislator.

2

The Democrats also lacked effective leadership. Their minority leader, the seventy-two-year-old Senator Martin of Virginia, had been seriously ill for more than six months, and was confined to his home. He died during the debate over the treaty. The acting minority leader was Gilbert M. Hitchcock of Nebraska, a newspaper editor with an honorable record and moderate ability, who was called upon to defend the breach against Lodge, the master parliamentarian. When we consider Hitchcock's mediocrity, his relatively little experience with the tricks of parliamentary jockeying, and his demoralizingly uncertain status as acting leader, it is surprising that he did as well as he did.

Hitchcock was further handicapped by not enjoying the complete confidence of Wilson, at least not at the outset. Having received two years of his education in Germany, the senator had developed a higher degree of sympathy for the German point of view than was common, and in a strongly worded letter to the President he had protested against going into the war. When he declared himself foursquare for the League, Wilson felt more kindly disposed toward him, but still there was lacking that close cordiality which was essential for effective cooperation.

After Wilson's physical collapse, an additional barrier was erected between the two men. Yet it must be confessed that before this time Wilson had not made the most of his opportunities. On the day he submitted the treaty to the Senate he incorrectly told his press conference that reservations could be added only by a two-thirds vote. This was extremely embarrassing to Hitchcock and other Democrats, for they had just been arguing on Capitol Hill that a simple majority would suffice.

The Democrats, for all their weaknesses, had three powerful advantages. One was party loyalty. Whatever their personal convictions, only four members of the entire group deserted the ranks, until it was clear that the battered ship was sinking. The great body of Democrats was blindly loyal to the ablest leader they had raised up since the days of Andrew Jackson. The dying Senator Martin wrote Wilson from Virginia, on July 27, 1919, that when the time came to vote he would get into the drawing room of a train, come to Washington, vote for the treaty, and return home.

The second Democratic advantage was a good cause—what at the outset seemed to be the superior moral cause. But in the mouths of skilled sophists the better position may be made to appear the worse, and the Republicans had a superfluity of skilled sophists.

The third great advantage of the Democrats was Wilson's leadership. He was President of the United States, with all the prestige and power of that exalted office. He was a gifted leader who could sway opinion and turn the tide of events. But he was the only real leader the Democrats had. This was all the more reason why he should have worked closely with his following in the Senate, while carefully husbanding his energy and safeguarding his health.

3

Complicated though the situation was in the Democratic camp, it was simplicity itself when compared with that on the Republican side.

No single Republican group unqualifiedly favored the treaty as it stood. For the sake of the party, the Republicans could not permit a Wilson pact to go through without some kind of alteration—without "Americanizing" it or, to put it crudely, "Republicanizing" it. If they did this, they could save face, and in some measure share the glory, claiming that it was now a Republican as well as a Democratic treaty.

Many of the Republicans (as well as some Democrats) had honest doubts about the treaty. They were afraid that our sovereignty might be jeopardized, that we could not control our own tariff barriers or our immigration flood dikes. They wanted reservations added to the treaty, of greater or less force, to safeguard the interests of the United States, to clarify our obligations, and to glorify the Republican party.

The reservationists among the Republicans divided into two groups: those who favored mild reservations, and those who favored strong reservations or amendments.

The "strong reservationists," cleverly led by Henry Cabot Lodge, not only wanted to amend outright certain objectionable parts of the treaty, but insisted that the signatory powers formally accept these changes. The "strong reservationists" numbered about twenty, and included such dependable party hacks as Harding of Ohio (later President) and Curtis of Kansas (later Vice President). It is probable that some of these men did not want the treaty in any form, but lacked the courage to attack it frontally.

Our Senatorial Hamlet
[To ratify or not to ratify]
(Courtesy of Spokane *Spokesman-Review*;
cartoonist Morris)

The "mild reservationists" (also called "middle grounders" or "moderates") included about twelve of the ablest and most liberal-minded senators, such as Kellogg (later Secretary of State) and McNary (Republican Vice Presidential nominee in 1940). They favored certain rather innocuous reservations which would protect our interests without undermining the basic structure of the treaty or requiring further action by the signatory powers.

The dozen or so "mild reservationists" played a crucial role in the unfolding of this great drama, and one that has not been properly appreciated. They were evidently sincere in wanting the treaty approved, and their reservations were relatively unobjectionable, differing hardly at all except in phraseology from the reservations which the Democrats themselves were belatedly willing to accept. If the 43 dependable Democrats had joined with the dozen "mild reservationist" Republicans, the Democrats would still have been short of a two-thirds majority, but *they would have had comfortably more than a simple majority.*

This is a fact of immense importance. The much-maligned Lodge reservations were all added by a simple majority vote. If the Democrats had opened their arms to the "mild reservationists," the resulting coalition *could have voted down every Lodge reservation;* more than that, *it could have voted through its own relatively innocuous reservations.* Even then the two-thirds vote might not have been obtainable; but the remaining Republicans would have been confronted with the painful alternative of defeating the treaty outright or getting onto the bandwagon. It is possible that under pressure of this kind enough "strong reservationists" would have swung over to insure victory.

One of Wilson's gravest strategical errors was his failure to hold out the olive branch to the "mild reservationists" in the summer of 1919, when they were in a mood to be bargained with. But Wilson, for understandable reasons, was cold to the whole idea of reservations. When he stingingly rebuffed the "mild reservationists," they had to respond to the tuggings of party loyalty and the growing popular demand for reservations. So they fell in behind Lodge; but they went unwillingly, with Kellogg freely damning Wilson and wishing "the treaty was in Hell."

4

As far as the public was concerned, the small phalanx of Republican "irreconcilables" overshadowed all other Senate groups. Numbering about fourteen, and irreconcilably opposed to the treaty in any form, they were also known as the "bitter-enders" and the "Battalion of Death."

The "irreconcilables" held the balance, or more than the balance, in oratorical ability and obstructive power. They dominated the Senate Foreign Relations Committee, and thus were able to pursue their strategy of delay. They had the loudest voices, the voices of Borah and Johnson, and they could shout down and silence their opponents. They could monopolize the Senate debate, and at times did, all the while dragging out the discussion, and further confusing the public mind with irrelevant or baseless arguments, against which their opponents were forced to dig up answers.

Nor were the "irreconcilables" merely noise. They had brains on their side as well, the brains of Knox and Brandegee. In parliamentary as well as in military warfare the advantage is usually with the side which is able to seize and hold the initiative. This advantage lay with the "Battalion of Death." Attacking the treaty with satire, ridicule, and invective, they could throw its proponents on the defensive. The League lent itself to ridicule; the "irreconcilables" did not lend themselves so well to ridicule, for they were proposing nothing. Their role was to tear down, and they did.

The compact little group of "irreconcilables" also held the balance of power in the voting. They joined with their Republican colleagues in saddling the treaty with as strong reservations as possible, and then joined with their Democratic opponents to vote the whole thing down.

This seemed like hypocrisy, and the "bitter-enders" were roundly condemned for it. But, to give the devil his due, they were playing the game within the rules. They believed—no

doubt, some of them sincerely—that the Republic was faced
with the most awful peril in all its history, and they were determined to forestall, by fair means or foul, this "unholy thing
with a holy name." To them the end justified the means. If
the rules permitted them to defeat the treaty by loading it
down, they would be foolish not to take advantage of the rules.
The Democrats, had they been in the shoes of the "irreconcilables," almost certainly would have done the same thing.

5

The "irreconcilables" had one other potent weapon: the
threat to bolt. They constantly brandished it over the head of
Lodge, loudly threatening to go over to the Democrats and
vote down the Republican reservations, unless a substantial
part of their wishes was granted.

Worse than that, these "bitter-enders" repeatedly declared
that they would desert the party in 1920 if the Republicans
surrendered to White House dictation. The bolters of 1912
had brought in Wilson; whatever the cost, there must be no
bolters in 1920.

The stock in trade of the "irreconcilables" was obstruction,
not construction. They were heatedly accused of not proposing
anything constructive; of not coming forward with any practicable alternative. As the Syracuse *Post-Standard* remarked,
"The League of Nations Covenant has flaws in plenty, but we
should like to see the document that Senators Lodge, Borah,
Johnson, Reed and Sherman could agree on." Yes, one would.
But the "bitter-enders" felt no call to propose anything. They
were quite content that the United States should stay out of
any or all Leagues, and they made it their aim to bring this
about.

The "irreconcilables" presented an almost perfect example
of minority rule; theirs was the philosophy of the filibuster.
They, and only they, saw the true light; theirs was the ultimate
wisdom. They would prevent this treaty calamity even though

some 80 per cent of their colleagues and an overwhelming majority of the American people favored the League in some form.

Almost fanatical in their desire to save the Republic, the "bitter-enders" did not scruple to use any weapon that came to hand. Senator Sherman openly appealed to religious prejudice when he asserted that Catholic peoples would predominate in the League, and that the new order would be ruled by the Pope. Senator Reed openly appealed to racial prejudice when he declared that colored peoples would outnumber whites in the new League of Nations.

It is impossible to determine with certainty the motives of each of the "irreconcilables." At best, emotions and motives tend to merge. Some of the senators, traditionalists and isolationists like Borah, appear to have really believed that the Republic had to be rescued from imminent peril. Others, like Johnson, probably saw the possibilities of using the senatorial sounding board for the advancement of their presidential candidacies—though it must be conceded that at the outset the fiery Californian took the unpopular side. Others were no doubt aware of the political profit to be derived from appealing to the Irish and German vote.

A detailed analysis of the motives or probable motives of the "irreconcilables" would doubtless reveal that their state of mind was compounded of varying amounts of traditionalism, ignorance, bigotry, fear of the untried, prejudice, personal pique, partisanship, political ambition, and a natural bent for destructiveness. But, whatever the motives, the result was the same. This group was one of the vitally important elements in keeping the United States out of the League of Nations.

6

The "irreconcilables" were such a colorful crew, and their names will appear so often in this narrative, that it would be well to make the acquaintance of some of them.

There was Medill McCormick of Illinois, relative of the inventor of the McCormick reaper, former publisher of the violently isolationist Chicago *Tribune,* husband of the daughter of Mark Hanna, and a senator who through his polish and connections was expected to go far.

There was George H. Moses, small-town newspaper editor from New Hampshire, filled with Yankee shrewdness and political craft, and noted for his gabbiness, flippancy of tongue, and cheap wit.

There was Albert B. Fall of New Mexico, with drooping mustaches, wide-brimmed western hat, and a wide-brimmed conscience, who, after having "saved" his country from European thieves, was to deliver his country's oil reserves to 100 per cent American thieves.

There was Philander C. Knox of Pennsylvania, "the brain" of the "bitter-enders." A distinguished lawyer whose mind had been whetted on the grindstone of corporation law, he had served as Secretary of State under President Taft. Short of stature, bald of head, rotund of paunch, he was dubbed by Theodore Roosevelt that "sawed-off cherub." Impeccably dressed, with striped trousers and wing collar, he looked like a statesman, and was still considered, despite his sixty-six years, presidential timber. He provided much of the legal acumen, the shysterlike shifts and dodges, which the "Battalion of Death" needed in waging what seemed at the outset to be a losing battle.

There was Frank B. Brandegee of Connecticut, the "tongue" of the "irreconcilables"—that is, the rapier tongue. A Connecticut Yankee, bitter to the point of vindictiveness, and so intense as later to commit suicide, he dressed like a fop and spoke in a peculiarly high, whining, nasal voice. Mrs. Alice Roosevelt Longworth, who was a constant visitor to the Senate galleries, especially enjoyed hearing him speak. He was usually brief, and though in deadly earnest he threw off sparks of sardonic humor. When Mrs. Longworth complimented him he replied, "Well, I get going and I can't stop, like a cat with a ball of catnip." He was one of the original "bitter-enders," and one of the few who never lost confidence that the League would be killed.

There was Hiram W. Johnson of California, the "noise" of the "irreconcilables." Thickset, ruddy-faced, silver-thatched, he was probably the most accomplished rabble-rouser of them all. If Brandegee wielded a rapier, Johnson wielded a meat-ax. Having made his reputation as a smasher of the corrupt Southern Pacific political machine in California, and having become governor and senator largely on the strength of that achievement, he continued to smash things. His noise-making ability came to be a standing joke: he did not attack, he "flayed." Yet no one could deny that the man had bulldog tenacity, a ripsaw voice, and the ability to move great crowds.

Friends of the League decried Johnson's cave-man mentality and his completely closed mind. They said if he was sincere then God deliver us from the sincere bigot. Probably he was sincere; but he was also sincere in desiring the presidency. He was also consistent. The fires of his presidential ambitions reduced to ashes, his stentorian voice reduced to a whisper, he was still holding the same antiquated castle twenty-five years later.

7

William E. Borah was the "soul" of the "irreconcilables." Tall of frame, massive of face and head, bushy of hair, and almost eccentric in appearance, the "Idaho lion" was generally regarded as the most eloquent and inspiring speaker of the Senate, if not of his generation. Admirers compared him with the "godlike" Daniel Webster. The murmured announcement that Borah had the floor was enough, during a critical debate, to depopulate the House floor and galleries. This was a compliment paid to few if any other orators of his generation.

Borah's eloquence was sincere, simple, lofty, moving. One did not have to agree with his isolationist convictions in order to admire his oratory. At one time during the Senate struggle, the bored presiding officer, Vice President Marshall, scribbled a note for Borah: "May a mummy say that you almost galvanized him to life?"

By instinct and training Borah was a conscientious objector. His daily horseback ride in Rock Creek Park was as unfailing as the Washington Monument; and one of the stock jokes of the capital was to express amazement that the senator would consent to go in the same direction as the horse. His mind naturally sought reasons why something should not be done, rather than why it should be done.

Borah's official biographer claims that he was "the original irreconcilable." As early as 1916 the senator was voicing vehement opposition to Wilson's proposed forsaking of the paths of isolationism. Early in 1919, when American public opinion overwhelmingly favored the League, and when the Republicans were timidly thinking that the best they could do would be to "Americanize" or "Republicanize" the Covenant, Borah demanded that the whole wicked contraption be hurled back across the Atlantic into the teeth of its authors.

After Borah's great speech of February 21, 1919, Lodge came to him with a word of congratulation, but added with a deprecatory wave of his hands: "What are you going to do? It's hopeless. All the newspapers in my state are for the League." Other admirers of Borah chimed in: "That was great; that was fine; we agree with you; but we have got to have some sort of League; everybody is for it." The faint-hearted Senator Harding told Borah: "Bill, I'd like to get in the fight against this League of Nations, but the people of my state are all for it I'm afraid." (In 1937 Borah told the present writer that Harding was the "biggest moral coward" he ever knew in public life.)

It was Borah, probably more than any other man, who stirred up and crystallized public opposition to the League, at least in the early stages. He demonstrated that with the passage of time, and with the proper strategy, an anti-League program might prove to be politically profitable.

The leonine Idahoan was completely uncompromising. He declared that if he had his way the League would be "Twenty Thousand Leagues under the Sea." He wanted "this treacherous and treasonable scheme" "buried in hell," and he insisted that he would not change his course if Jesus Christ himself should come to earth and plead for the Covenant.

Newspapers might call Borah, as the Philadelphia *Public Ledger* did, a "political antiquarian and a pottering troglodyte"; but few doubted his sincerity. Borah had the rare ability to smash everybody's pet scheme and yet retain the friendship if not the admiration of those whose plans he had reduced to rubble. Completely free of a mean and petty spirit, he alone of the "bitter-enders" retained the respect of President Wilson.

To the very end the "irreconcilables" seem to have thought that they had done a noble thing: they had saved the Republic from dangers to which all others were blind. Borah's official biographer, writing with the Idahoan's sanction, says, "The Senator is proud of his part in keeping the United States out of the League . . ."

8

Closely associated with the "irreconcilables," at least in the public mind, was the leader of the "strong reservationists," Henry Cabot Lodge. He was so important in the treaty fight that one might almost say he was a group in himself.

Lodge was slender, narrow-shouldered, and aristocratically bewhiskered. Sprung from the stony soil of Massachusetts, and nurtured by the New England aristocracy, he fell heir to all the advantages of wealth, education, culture, travel, and social position. Educated at Harvard University, where he took the degree of Ph.D. in history, Dr. Lodge early undertook a literary career. From his pen poured a succession of books, chiefly on historical subjects, some of which had their brief day, but none of which has lived or has deserved to live. He also re-

vealed a flair for politics, and by faithful party service he secured a strangle hold on his seat in the Senate, and became
chairman of the Senate Committee on Foreign Relations.
Cold, cautious, aloof, aristocratic as he was, one wonders at the
secret of his appeal to the masses.

Three Little Elephants
(Courtesy of Brooklyn *Eagle*; cartoonist Harding)

For many years Dr. Lodge enjoyed the distinction of being
"the scholar in politics." Then came Professor Wilson, whose
political and scholarly attainments eclipsed those of Lodge,
and the senator's flattering sobriquet dropped into disuse.
This was no doubt displeasing to the learned solon.

All of Lodge's forbears had reached America before the
Revolutionary War; all of Wilson's had come well after the

establishment of the Republic. Lodge took naturally to nationalism; Wilson more naturally to internationalism—possibly as a result, in part, of his heredity.

Yet Lodge, before the arrival of Wilson on the scene, had shown signs of broadening horizons, as had other leaders of the traditionally expansionist and imperialistic Republican party. He had warmly supported his bosom friend, "dear Theodore" Roosevelt, in the various international adventures upon which the brandisher of the Big Stick embarked. He had made speeches in favor of some kind of international organization for peace, and in 1915 had even come out for *a* league of nations. But shortly thereafter Wilson began to advocate *the* League, and Lodge found himself in the other camp. The senator in his apologia strongly denies that this was anything but mental growth. Chronology and circumstance suggest that it was not disassociated from the feud with Wilson.

Contrary to a general misconception, Lodge was not an isolationist of the Borah or Johnson stripe. On the eve of the Peace Conference he was willing to go even further than Wilson in making the United States a part-guarantor of the European settlement. He said repeatedly that, League or no League, the world could count on us again to spring to the defense of Western civilization against ruthless aggression.

9

The whole bent of Lodge's thinking had naturally predisposed him to entertain kindly thoughts toward the Covenant that Wilson brought back from Paris. But it was a Democratic League, from which the Democrats could make political capital, and all the partisan instincts of the senator rose to the surface.

Above all things Lodge was a partisan, a narrow and bitter partisan, who believed that the Republican party was the embodiment of all the virtues. In 1914 he had made an elo-

quent speech about politics stopping "at the water's edge";
but this was pure rhetoric. He probably would have denied
that he would basely subordinate the interests of his country
to those of his party, but so ingrained was his Republicanism
that he did not find it difficult to convince himself that the
interests of both were identical. With him party regularity
was a religion.

Lodge realized as clearly as anyone that it would be politically unwise for the Republicans to permit Wilson and his
Democratic following to garner all the glory from the League.
The Republicans must be allowed to add something to it, just
enough to pose as co-authors of the pact.

With disarming candor, Lodge outlines in his posthumous
book the strategy which he employed. He would load the
treaty down with Republican reservations, and in this way
"Americanize" or "Republicanize" the document, thus safeguarding both the country and the party. If Wilson accepted
the Lodge reservations, then the Republicans would be sharers
of the glory; if he did not, then the onus for rejecting the entire
pact would be on the President's shoulders, not on those of
the Republicans. Either way the Republican party could make
political capital.

When the corpse of the treaty was finally dragged from the
senatorial arena, the friends of international cooperation
pointed the finger of accusation at Lodge, and since then have
kept it unwaveringly there.

This is a gross oversimplification. The struggle was exceedingly complex; there were all shades of opinion; there were
varying and conflicting motives; there were currents and cross-
currents. To say that one senator alone killed Cock Robin is
to betray obtuseness or mental inertia.

So poisonous were the hatreds stirred up by Lodge that his
position has seldom been viewed in proper perspective. He
was chairman of the Foreign Relations Committee. He was
majority leader, not because of personal charm, but because
men respected his skill as a party manager and parliamentarian.

His speeches were able, dignified, and usually on a high plane. His two-hour condemnation of the League, on August 12, 1919, was delivered at a time when the galleries were crowded with marines who had returned from Château-Thierry. The unprecedented roar that greeted his peroration lasted for three minutes, and sounded like the ovation accorded the home-town hero who knocks the ball into the right-field bleachers.

Lodge's responsibilities were heavy and conflicting. He was a foremost defender of senatorial prerogative. He was leader of the party in the Senate and the official spokesman for the various factions within the party. His immediate task was two-fold: first, to propose and carry through a specific program of reservations; second, to keep the party ranks intact, and pre-vent any such schism as had developed in 1912. His primary duty, as he conceived it, was not to unite the world but to unite the party.

The Massachusetts senator was in the plight of one attempt-ing to ride three horses trying to go in three different direc-tions. The body of the Republican senators—the "strong reser-vationists"—were not too difficult to manage; they were going down the middle of the track. But on one side the dozen "mild reservationists" were momentarily threatening to coalesce with the Democrats. On the other side the "bitter-enders" were threatening to bolt the party completely, or go over to the Democrats and vote through reservations objectionable to Lodge. At one time the Massachusetts senator complained that the "irreconcilables" were addressing him in language which "no man of my age should be obliged to hear."

While Lodge was trying to curb the three horses, he had to keep closely in touch with the party managers outside the Senate so that the strategy of the campaign of 1920 could be carefully mapped. Above all, he had to restrain his personal dislike of Wilson for fear that he would appear to be a "sore-head." It has been well said that Lodge had "a hard enough time keeping his temper without stopping to consult his con-science."

10

The bitterness of feeling between Lodge and Wilson was intense and was perhaps the most formidable single barrier in the way of compromise.

The two men simply rubbed each other the wrong way. Lodge insists that his distrust of Wilson was wholly on public grounds, and began with the administration's alleged misconduct of relations with Mexico. The feud broke out into the open in 1916, when Lodge accused Wilson of suppressing certain vital information regarding the *Lusitania* negotiations. Wilson, in a not altogether candid reply, delicately branded the senator a liar, and from then on the breach widened.

Colonel Bonsal talked with Lodge about the League Covenant in November, 1919. "As an English production it does not rank high," said Lodge, perhaps half jokingly. "It might get by at Princeton but certainly not at Harvard." Colonel House observed at Paris that President Wilson "bristled" whenever Lodge's name was mentioned. On the few occasions when the President and the senator had to meet, the interchanges were severely formal, and the atmosphere could seemingly be cut with a knife.

Both the senator and the President were bitter partisans, lasting haters. In life, Lodge outwardly restrained his innermost feelings, at least in public. But he forgot about the Old Testament patriarch who expressed the desire that his "adversary had written a book." The senator prepared an elaborate, posthumously published apology, in which his embittered spirit rose from the grave to reveal what he had previously been at pains to conceal.

"I never had the slightest personal hostility to Mr. Wilson," writes Lodge. He goes on to say that Wilson was not a true scholar at all, and as proof stresses the fact that, unlike Lodge, the Princeton professor did not stud his speeches with classical allusions—which any sterile wit may crib from compilations of quotations.

The senator finally convicts Wilson of not having been a scholar, and perhaps not even an educated man, when he gleefully reveals that on the one occasion when he found the Princetonian using a classical reference, it was used incorrectly. Wilson committed the terrible error of having Hercules, rather than Antaeus, renew his strength as he touched Mother Earth.

This does not prove that Wilson was unscholarly. All it proves is that Lodge had a jealous and petty spirit.

CHAPTER FIVE

THE STRATEGY OF
STRANGULATION

"The mere fact that President Wilson wants something is not an argument against it." Philadelphia PUBLIC LEDGER, *quoted in the* LITERARY DIGEST, *December 6, 1919.*

1

ONCE THE Treaty of Versailles was formally before the Senate, it was referred as a matter of course to the powerful Foreign Relations Committee, a traditional graveyard of presidential hopes. The signs did not point to a hospitable reception.

When Congress had convened nearly two months earlier, the Republicans controlled the Senate by a narrow margin, and thus it was that Lodge became head of the Foreign Relations Committee. The "scholar in politics" went to great pains to see to it that the newly appointed members of his committee were not too kindly disposed toward the League.

Four new places were to be filled by Republicans. Kellogg of Minnesota was a logical choice for one of them, but the firmness of his opposition to the League was suspect. Lodge made it clear to him that he might have a place if he would promise in advance to support the chairman's decisions and carry out his policies. But Kellogg's self-respect would not permit him to be a Lodge rubber stamp, and he said as much. The vacancy was then filled by Moses of New Hampshire, a relative newcomer but an unflinching "irreconcilable."

The four new Republican members (Harding of Ohio, New of Indiana, Johnson of California, and Moses of New Hampshire) were all at least "strong reservationists." Two of them, Johnson and Moses, were among the most active "bitter-enders." Of the two new Democratic members (with whose

72

appointment Lodge had nothing to do) one, Shields of Tennessee, was so independently minded on the League question as to be an "irreconcilable."

Altogether, there were ten Republicans and seven Democrats on the committee. Only one of the Republicans, McCumber of North Dakota, favored the treaty without alteration. Six of the ablest and most bellicose Republican "irreconcilables" (out of a total of fourteen) now had places on the committee. In addition to Moses and Johnson, there were Borah of Idaho, Brandegee of Connecticut, Knox of Pennsylvania, and Fall of New Mexico. *Thus the "bitter-enders," though constituting about one-seventh of the Senate, were able to outvote the Republican majority representatives on the Foreign Relations Committee.*

Why did Lodge, who professed to want the treaty with adequate reservations, pack the committee with "irreconcilables" whose avowed purpose was to bring about the complete ruin of the treaty? The scholarly senator vouchsafes no answer in his apologia except to say, "It will be seen at once that this was a strong committee and such as the existing conditions demanded." Verily, it was.

Fair-minded persons naturally condemned this flagrant packing of the committee. Ex-President Taft openly voiced his dissatisfaction in public speeches. Even some of the Senate Republicans were quietly unhappy, while their Democratic colleagues protested stridently. When Senator Thomas of Colorado (Democrat) accused the Republicans of stacking the cards against Wilson by packing the committee, Senator McCormick of Illinois (Republican "irreconcilable") replied that Wilson had "stacked the Peace Conference with Democrats." This, unfortunately, was uncomfortably close to the truth.

2

We remember that when Wilson submitted the treaty to the Senate he announced that he was ready to confer with the members and give them such information as he had. Nearly a week went by, and there was no response to the invitation. Wilson then decided to take matters into his own hands by summoning individual senators to the White House for conferences. About twenty Republicans were invited and put in an appearance.

This, on the face of it, seemed like a conciliatory gesture; and in some ways it was. If it had been made before Wilson went to Paris, it might have had far-reaching results; but it now came much too late. The President, as a matter of fact, undertook these conferences with great reluctance. Senator Hitchcock later recalled that it was difficult to persuade him to employ such tactics: he was temperamentally unable to flatter and coax.

Hitchcock assisted in making up the list of Republican senators who were to be invited. Some of the proposed names, Wilson rejected out of hand. Finally, the list was complete, and invitations were sent out by letter in three batches. The Democrats were not included in these individual conferences, although Wilson talked with eleven of them at one time late in July. They could be counted upon to support the administration anyhow.

The great body of Republican invitees was drawn from the "mild reservationists" and from those of the "strong reservationists" who seemed open to reason. The bitterest of the "bitter-enders" were completely passed by; invitations were sent to only two of the "irreconcilables," Fernald of Maine, who came; and Norris of Nebraska, who in a courteous letter declined to come. He gave as his reasons, first, that he would be honor bound not to discuss afterward any of the matters considered, some of which were public property anyhow; and second, that it would take too much of Wilson's valuable time to confer with each senator. It would be better, he said, for the President to send over to the Senate, in the usual way, such information as he wished to submit.

Wilson's omission of most of the "bitter-enders" seems to

have been fully justified. It would have been a complete waste of time to try sweet reasonableness with rigidly closed minds. Yet, because the Foreign Relations Committee was packed with "irreconcilables," only three of its ten Republican members were invited, and Lodge was not one of them.

3

The time-consuming private conferences with the Republican senators ran about an hour each. On one day Wilson was closeted individually for three hours with three; on another day he talked four hours with four during successive appointments. Most of the senators spoke freely to the reporters about their experience, and from these accounts we may piece together what went on behind White House doors.

The conferees were virtually unanimous in agreeing that Wilson did not try to browbeat them into accepting his views. He evidently conceived of his role as explicatory rather than hortatory. He explained what had happened at Paris; the reasons for certain decisions; and the nature of some of the secret data. He emphasized the necessity for haste, and especially the desirability of avoiding reservations. These, he said, would necessitate a reopening of the conference, cause further delay, and encourage Germany to make additional demands.

The senators were likewise unanimous in agreeing that Wilson's remarks had not altered their fundamental position, although Senators Capper and McNary admitted that he had somewhat softened their opposition to the so-called "surrender" of the Chinese province of Shantung to Japan. Many if not most of the senators made it clear to the President that the treaty simply could not be ratified without reservations of some kind.

Senator Watson of Indiana was the only one of the invitees who published his recollections of the event. He found Wilson very cordial, and asking, "Where am I in the Senate on this fight?" "Mr. President," replied Watson, "you are licked."

Wilson expressed amazement when Watson said that the administration could count on only twenty-four votes for the proposed mandate over Armenia. As the conference ended, Watson said to the President that there was only one way to take America into the League, and that was, "Accept it with the Lodge reservations."

"Accept the Treaty with the *Lodge* reservations?" Wilson replied scornfully. "Never! Never! I'll never consent to adopt any policy with which that impossible name is so prominently identified." Watson almost certainly did not remember Wilson's exact words, and possibly he misread their spirit; but the general import of his version squares with the President's known views.

It is doubtful whether these individual conferences helped the cause of the League in any appreciable way. But they did show that Wilson was prepared to make a fair and frank attempt, albeit belatedly, to meet the senators on their own ground. The conferences also indicate that the President recognized to some extent the necessity of wooing the "mild reservationists."

But the whole strategy of the conferences was poor. They involved an undue expenditure of time and energy. The same result, and possibly better results, could have been achieved if Wilson had invited the senators in small groups, with perhaps a few Democrats present.

Unfortunately also, the individual senators were forced into an awkward position. The news that they were going to the White House was heralded in advance on the front page of the newspapers. The question on the public lip was, "Will they bend the knee?" When they emerged from the White House the news hawks were there with pencil and notebook to record whether they had cravenly surrendered. The whole business savored of the naughty boy being called into the principal's office for a scolding. The natural disposition of the proud senators was to show their mettle by making up their minds in advance that they would not yield anything, and none of them apparently did. Much of this inevitable public pressure would have been removed if the senators had met with Wilson in quiet groups.

4

Informed observers generally agree that if the treaty could have been brought to a speedy vote it would have been approved with no worse than mild reservations. This is not only the judgment of present-day scholars; "bitter-ender" senators like Moses openly confessed as much when the fight was over.

The strategy of the foes of the treaty was, as we have seen, the strategy of delay. Time was on their side. The longer they kept the treaty tied up in the committee and before the Senate, the more they sent out speakers and distributed propaganda, the brighter their prospects of success. Public opinion would gradually become confused, less insistent on action, and finally somewhat indifferent to substantial changes or even outright rejection.

The "irreconcilables" were able to control time, because they were the controlling bloc on the Foreign Relations Committee. With the cooperation of Lodge, they could and did lock the treaty up indefinitely, while their orators and their propaganda were sowing doubts and winning converts. Early in the fight hundreds of thousands of copies of speeches by Lodge, Knox, Borah, and others were scattered throughout the country.

If the "irreconcilables" could control time, they had more trouble with money. A nation-wide campaign of "education" was costly, with such items as pamphlets, postage, clerical help, traveling expenses, the hiring of halls, and newspaper advertising. The game might be lost unless an adequate war chest could be scraped together.

One evening in May, 1919, a group of gloomy "bitter-enders" met at the home of Senator Brandegee. The campaign thus far had been progressing favorably, especially in the isolationist Middle West, where the powerful support of the Chicago *Tribune* and the Kansas City *Star* had been enlisted. But funds were melting away, and unless the campaign of starting backfires behind wavering senators was to be abandoned, new resources would have to be tapped.

Senator Knox suggested the name of a fellow Pennsylvanian, the multimillionaire "coke king" and art collector, Henry Clay Frick. One of the non-senatorial "irreconcilables," presumably George Harvey, who describes himself as the "delegated conspirator," journeyed to New York, where he laid the "stock" arguments before this hardheaded businessman.

When Frick heard that the United States, the richest of the nations, was going to join a League in which it could allegedly be outvoted by the other nations, chiefly its debtors, he exclaimed: "I am opposed to that. Of course I am. I don't see how any experienced businessman could fail to be. Why, it seems to me a crazy thing to do."

The aged philanthropist, who was bitterly anti-Democratic, liberally underwrote the "irreconcilable" campaign of "education," and followed it with keen interest. He died about six months later, and three days before the end, upon receiving encouraging report of progress, he smiled contentedly and pronounced it "good."

Senator Knox himself approached Andrew W. Mellon, another Pittsburgh multimillionaire and art collector, who for his services to the party was made Secretary of the Treasury and later Ambassador to the Court of St. James's. Mellon agreed to duplicate Frick's substantial contribution; and the "Battalion of Death," with two of the wealthiest "angels" in America behind it, could push on with renewed enthusiasm to ultimate victory.

The friends of the treaty, notably the League to Enforce Peace, also raised money for propaganda to support their views. But their efforts seem to have been far more open and aboveboard.

5

We must return to the meeting room of the Senate Foreign Relations Committee.

At the outset, and in pursuance of his strategy of delay, Senator Lodge read aloud the entire text of the 268-page treaty. This totally unnecessary and unedifying farce consumed a valuable two weeks, and can be explained on no other rational basis than a desire to play for time. It was unnecessary because the treaty had promptly been put into printed form, and it is fair to assume that the senators were sufficiently literate to read it themselves more rapidly than Lodge could read it to them. It was unedifying because the members could obviously study the treaty more effectively through the printed word than through the cultured intonations of their colleague.

Most of the oral reading was done before a sparse committee; some of the time only the clerk was present; and at one point on the last day the distinguished senior senator from Massachusetts was left alone to drone along before completely empty chairs. If haste had been a primary consideration, surely the learned Lodge could have completed 268 pages in less than two weeks.

Once the treaty had been read aloud, the committee arranged to protract the delay by holding public hearings, which began on July 31, 1919, and lasted to September 12, a total of six weeks. About sixty witnesses appeared, and a total of 1,297 pages of printed testimony was preserved for posterity. In a very real sense the League of Nations was drowned in a sea of words.

The hearings were ostensibly for the edification of the senators, and in some measure they undoubtedly served this purpose. But the unannounced objectives were to consume time, stir up prejudice, and further confuse the public mind. (The "confusionists" were in some ways more formidable than the isolationists.) The real purposes were betrayed at the out-

set when the committee decided to resort to the unusual ex-
pedient of public hearings.

Senator Lodge insisted that the Senate was not delaying the
treaty unduly. It had taken Wilson nearly six months, with
some thirteen hundred assistants, to draw up the pact, and
the Senate, Lodge felt, ought to be pardoned for devoting a

"Stop Playing Politics"

(From New York *Evening World*; cartoonist Cassel;
reprinted by permission)

few weeks to a study of this exceedingly complicated instrument. The President had ignored the senators while drafting
the treaty; now was their chance to find out what was in it.
Lodge complained that neither he nor anyone whom he knew
really understood it; yet Wilson was urging the Senate to
rubber-stamp an instrument of immense importance—an
instrument which would profoundly affect the foreign policy

and perhaps the very structure of the United States government.

With such fears allegedly holding them to their task, the committee went ahead with the hearings. Some of the first witnesses who appeared had been at Paris, and they were in a position to contribute first-hand information of some value. Among those who took the stand were Bernard M. Baruch (who had worked on reparations); David Hunter Miller (an architect of the League Covenant who was badgered by his inquisitors); and Secretary of State Lansing, whose sensational testimony will be discussed later.

The committee had one inflexible rule. It would permit only American citizens to testify, and this eliminated a host of aliens who were eager to argue impassionedly and interminably for their native lands. Many of the witnesses were summoned; others came at their own request. Lodge says that it was impossible to deny these people a hearing.

This statement is open to serious doubt. The committee unquestionably was empowered to reject those whom it did not want to hear, even though there was great pressure from scores of groups to have their day in court. The circumstantial evidence indicates that the committee generally favored witnesses who were likely to embarrass Wilson and the friends of the League.

The closing stages of the hearings degenerated into flagrant and irrelevant appeals to partisanship and prejudice. Former friends who had broken with Wilson were allowed to unbosom themselves. A sop was thrown to the England-haters when the committee sought to establish the British origins of the League of Nations. Ireland, too, had her inning, with a Tammany-Irish orator, among others, evoking warm and frequent applause for the cause of Hibernian freedom.

Representatives of other national or racial groups were able to find some American citizen to plead their cause, while in at least one case they remained at his elbow with promptings. There were self-appointed spokesmen for the aspirations of the Negroes, Egypt, Persia, Ukraina, China, Greece, Albania, Czechoslovakia, Yugoslavia, Hungary, Esthonia, Latvia, Lithuania (moving pictures were shown of German atrocities in Lithuania), India, and Italy (represented by the future mayor of New York, F. H. La Guardia). Sweden's claims to the Aland Islands were argued by a man who admitted that he spoke no Swedish. The height of absurdity was reached when a woman with an Irish name urged the claim of Italy to Yugoslavia's Fiume.

Lodge insists that all this could not have been avoided, for the treaty was a world treaty. But he neglects to explain how the pact related to Ireland, or India, or Egypt, or Korea, or racial equality for Negroes in the United States. It looked as though the senators thought it their duty to prevent rather than complete the treaty; to hunt mare's nests for the discrediting of Wilson while Europe starved and the world slowly crumbled to pieces.

The sapient senators sat solemnly in their seats and listened to arguments for the independence of India, as though they understood the problem and could do something about it. Neither was a valid assumption. But silent listening to various grievance mongers seemed to indicate sympathy, and this might please the Irish, Italian, and Negro voters. It was good politics, if nothing else.

6

The Senate hearings were not usually front-page copy. When the testimony was relevant to the treaty, which much of it was not, the allegations were usually old information, minor information, or relatively minor shadings of something important. There were two exceptions. One was the bombshell of William C. Bullitt which, we shall later note, burst forth spectacularly while Wilson was on his western tour. The other was the testimony of Secretary of State Lansing.

Lansing presented a rather pathetic figure. He did not shed

much light on the treaty, because he had not had much to do with it; but he did shed a flood of light on himself and his relations with Wilson. For the first time it became painfully evident that the President had largely ignored his Secretary of State.

The most startling statements of Lansing were two. He expressed the opinion that Wilson could have secured justice for China without the alleged surrendering of Shantung to Japan. This, of course, was only the Secretary's personal opinion, but it was seized upon gleefully by those who were assailing the Far Eastern clauses of the treaty.

Lansing also said that until he arrived in Paris he knew nothing of the secret pact between Japan and Britain for the division of Germany's Pacific islands. Lansing's ignorance of the secret treaties in general, and of this treaty in particular, merely added strength to the isolationist argument that the other powers were dishonest tricksters who would trade us out of our eyeteeth if we ventured to sit down with them in any League of Nations.

The net result was that Wilson's position was weakened, and he was thrown further on the defensive.

7

The breach between the President and the committee had in the meanwhile been gradually widening. In particular, Lodge and his colleagues complained that Wilson was refusing to provide them with data necessary for an understanding of the pact.

We need do no more than sketch the outlines of this part of the story. The committee requested stenographic records of the secret conferences in Paris. Wilson refused on the ground that such confidences could not be revealed without breaking faith with the governments concerned. The committee likewise requested a copy of the protest against the Shantung decision which a group of his experts had sent to the President. Wilson refused on the ground that this document reflected unfavorably on friendly governments. The committee also requested copies of the draft treaties which were then being drawn up with Austria, Hungary, Bulgaria, and Turkey. Wilson refused on the ground that this would take the constitutional function of negotiating treaties out of the hands of the Executive.

In every case Wilson's decision seems to have been fully justified on the grounds of precedent and public interest. It is highly probable that these repeated senatorial requests were made with the expectation that they would be refused, and in the hope that they would be, for the President would then appear as obdurate, uncooperative, and dictatorial. Anything to discredit Wilson.

The committee now decided on a new tack. The parade of witnesses was not providing much information; Wilson would not send over secret data of a confidential nature. It finally dawned on the solons that the man who probably knew most about the making of the treaty lived in Washington, about a mile from the Capitol. If they were really seeking information, why not go to him?

It will be remembered that Wilson, when presenting the treaty to the Senate, had announced that he was at the disposal of that body. This, as it turned out, was poor strategy, for it placed the initiative squarely in the hands of his opponents on the Foreign Relations Committee. If, at the outset, he had invited the committee to meet with him, it could not very well have refused, and he might have been able to take the offensive and start the discussion off with greater momentum.

On August 14, 1919, more than a month after the submission of the pact, Senator Lodge, speaking for the members of his committee, requested the President to meet with them, provided the proceedings were completely public. Wilson promptly and graciously acceded, and in addition invited the committee to have lunch with him. He chose August 19 as the day, ten o'clock as the time, and the stately East Room of the White House as the place.

This was the first time that a President had ever consented to meet the Foreign Relations Committee at the White House and be publicly grilled by it. The newspapers and press associations were impressed with the importance of the occasion, and nearly a hundred correspondents gathered in the corridors, with desks, typewriters, and other equipment. Relays of expert stenographers were on hand to record a verbatim account of what was revealed, and put it on the wires while it was still "hot."

On the appointed morning, the big iron gates of the White House grounds were thrown open to the senatorial inquisitors, who arrived singly or in small groups. Senator Lodge drove up in a big automobile; Borah came on foot, carrying a bulky copy of the treaty under his arm, like a schoolboy about to attend class. Only Senator Shields, a Democrat not in sympathy with Wilson's views, failed to put in an appearance.

After greeting his guests with a smile, Wilson read a brief prepared statement in which he stressed our moral obligation to ratify speedily. Then he subjected himself to about three and one-half hours of interrogation. Though slightly nervous, he was seemingly candid, quick in his responses, and in good temper, as were his questioners. Only once did he reveal a trace of impatience, for the color mounted to his cheeks when it was recalled that Secretary Lansing had testified against the Shantung "surrender." At the end of the period, the President, plainly fatigued, accompanied the senators to the luncheon room, and when the meal was over the party broke up in evident good spirits.

8

We need concern ourselves here with only the most significant aspects of Wilson's testimony.

Much of the discussion centered about Article X, which

had been pictured by its foes as an agency to beget war rather than to promote peace. Wilson made it clear that he not only regarded Article X as the "backbone" of the covenant, but that he as much as anyone was the author of it. He pointed out that since the Article was permissive in its obligations, it was morally rather than legally binding. No superbody could order us about, he said, for *in any given case we would consult our consciences and act accordingly.*

When Senator Harding suggested that we would not have to honor a moral obligation, Wilson replied, "Why, Senator, it is surprising that that question should be asked." For his part, the President regarded a moral obligation as stronger than a legal one: a person might escape legal technicalities, but he could not escape his conscience.

Senator Johnson of California, no doubt mindful of his large anti-Japanese constituency, harped on the Shantung settlement, and drew from the President the candid admission that it was not completely satisfactory. The cause of Wilson and the League was not helped when it was made to appear that the Shantung decision was in the nature of blackmail to keep Japan in the League.

Wilson also made it clear that he was willing to accept reservations of a purely interpretive nature, as long as they were embodied in a *separate resolution,* and as long as they *did not require the assent of Germany and the Allied Powers.* This was rather surprising, because only four days earlier Senator Hitchcock had come away from the White House saying that Wilson opposed reservations.

The President made a curious slip when he said that any changes in the Covenant of the League would not require the consent of Germany. He was thinking of the Reich as a nonmember of the League, rather than as a signatory of the treaty. Over in the Senate the Democratic leaders were further embarrassed, because they had been energetically taking the opposite point of view. Wilson's slip was excusable, but he further weakened and humiliated the Democratic leadership by betraying that he was not working in close harmony with it.

On the question of the secret treaties, Wilson was guilty of more than a slip. He insisted, under repeated questioning, that he had known nothing of them before going to Paris. This, as we now know, was untrue. Some have argued that he forgot, which seems improbable; that he was fatigued, as he no doubt was later in the session; or possibly that he was caught off guard. This seems hardly credible. Only two weeks before, Lansing had caused a sensation when the same question was asked him, and it is most improbable that Wilson could have failed to anticipate similar grilling.

The real explanation, which has been discussed elsewhére,* will probably remain buried in the crypt with Wilson. It seems likely that he did not want to weaken his position further by a candid admission. To have confessed that he knew all about the baleful pacts before going to Paris would no doubt have evoked embarrassing inquiry as to why he did not do more to bring about their abrogation.

Wilson had been the chief spokesman for American and Allied war aims. Yet here he was confessing that he had known nothing about the secret mortgages on the happiness of mil-lions of peoples—mortgages, as George Harvey put it, "con-ceived in sin and born of the desire for empire grabbing." The *New Republic* brutally concluded that Wilson was either an "incompetent or a liar."

9

Opinions varied as to the skill with which the President had conducted himself at the senatorial inquest. His friends, like Senator Hitchcock, went away feeling that he had been "keen and careful," and that he had upheld the Covenant effectively. Wilson had seemed filled with the subject; he had handled the questions in a masterly manner. His worshipful private

* T. A. Bailey, *Woodrow Wilson and the Lost Peace,* pp. 147–148, 347–348.

secretary, Tumulty, felt that he had "parried every blow"; that he had never been "more tactful or more brilliant in repartee."

The President's enemies found fresh confirmation of their prejudices. Lodge was forced to admit that Wilson had taken the questions, which were "rather sharp at times," in "good

"We'll Never Sign It!"

(From New York *World*; cartoonist Kirby; reprinted by permission)

part." But the incorrigible Brandegee contemptuously remarked, "What is the use of probing into an intellectual apparatus like that?"

Wilson, on his part, found fresh confirmation of his low opinion of the senatorial intellect. A few days later, at a Cabinet meeting, he remarked that "Senator Harding had a disturbingly dull mind, and that it seemed impossible to get any explanation to lodge in it."

While it is probably true that the Democratic friends of

the League came away with heightened enthusiasm, there is no evidence that a single member of the committee changed either his mind or his vote. It is also probable that the "bitter-enders" were nettled by their inability to "show Wilson up."

As far as the committee itself was concerned, the affair was a failure. But other senators, not present, read the testimony, and newspaper readers all over the country were further instructed—or confused. The Chicago *Tribune* ran a headline above the report of the conference: "U.S. ARMS AT LEAGUE'S BECK, WILSON ADMITS." The printed testimony reveals no such admission.

But all is fair in love and war. And this was war—war on Wilson.

CHAPTER SIX

THE APPEAL TO THE PEOPLE

"I am ready to fight from now until all the fight has been taken out of me by death to. redeem the faith and promises of the United States." WOODROW WILSON *at Spokane, Washington, September 12, 1919.*

1

WILSON'S DECISION to make a spectacular stumping tour across the country in behalf of the treaty was one of the most momentous decisions of his entire career, perhaps the most momentous. As it turned out, the tour was a disastrous blunder. It not only wrecked Wilson's health, but in a very real sense helped wreck the League of Nations, and with it the hopes of humanity.

The decision to make the trip is generally represented as a sudden impulse, an act of desperation, a supreme effort to build up a backfire of public opinion against the stubborn senators and thus save the treaty.

It was undoubtedly an act of desperation, but it was clearly not a sudden impulse. More than two months before returning from Paris the President stated that he expected to make a tour of the country, but he could not yet be certain that he would. There were even earlier intimations in the newspapers that he was going to barnstorm from the Potomac to the Pacific.

When Wilson reached home in July it was taken for granted that he would make his "swing around the circle." The question was not: Will he? It was: When will he? The anti-League senators were aware of his plan, and somewhat uneasy about it. Senator Moses proposed that the Foreign Relations Committee take advantage of the President's gracious offer to appear before it by requesting that he come every day at ten o'clock, and thus keep him from departing. This was a cheap trick, worthy of the "wisecracking" Moses, but it was so naked that not even the other "irreconcilables" dared push it.

2

While the general plan to swing West was no sudden inspiration, it is probable that Wilson would have spared himself such an ordeal if the fight for the treaty had been going well. Possibly he had let his intentions leak out in the first place so that he might hold the threat of a country-wide appeal over the Senate.

But the fight was not going well. The friends of the League were plainly losing ground. The results of the White House conference had been most discouraging, not only with regard to arousing public opinion, but also with regard to moving the senators. The Republican majority on the Foreign Relations Committee was now pressing forward with its plans to amend the treaty drastically.

Wilson was also distressed by growing signs of defection among his own followers in the Senate: some were betraying a friendliness for strong reservations, a few others were downright hostile to the League. The committee, moreover, had the treaty tied up, seemingly forever, and the protracted hearings were now degenerating into a Roman holiday of prejudice and passion. Some drastic and spectacular move must be made to pry the pact from the death grip of the "bitter-enders." "Seems easier to get into war than peace," gloomily remarked the *Wall Street Journal*.

The fever chart of Europe was reacting unfavorably to the exhibition of delay and impotence in the Senate. The final settlements with the other Central Powers were dragging because of the evident reluctance of Uncle Sam to jump into the international pond, certainly not without a superfluity of life-preservers. The prostrate Germans were taking heart, and there was still the alarming possibility that they might balk at going through with the final ratification of the Treaty of Versailles.

This was the discouraging predicament late in August, 1919, when friends of the treaty on Capitol Hill came to Wilson and urged him to make the contemplated tour. It was hardly necessary for them to use much persuasion; the President was already convinced that heroic measures were imperative.

Wilson, as we have seen, had indestructible faith in the power of public opinion—in democracy itself. The people

Going to Talk to the Boss
(Courtesy of Chicago *Daily News*; cartoonist Brown)

could be relied upon to judge correctly when the issues were placed clearly and truthfully before them. He had appealed over the head of Congress before, and with no little success, notably when he had built a fire under backward senators and had routed the insidious tariff lobby in 1913.

He would again appeal to the court of last resort—the court of public opinion. He would "go to the country" and arouse the people against their obstructive senators. He was tired of appealing to the better instincts of the politicians in Washington; he would go out and appeal to the source of their power, which was also the source of his power. He would keep his plea, as he wrote privately, on a strictly nonpartisan basis. Where the electorate was nation-wide, and the cause world-wide, there was no place for narrow partisanship. Yet Wilson apparently forgot that the President is the head of a great political party, and in a technical sense he can make no purely nonpolitical speeches.

Wilson was a fighter, and his Scotch-Irish blood quickened at the prospect of an open battle. It had been galling to his spirit to have to sit quietly in the White House and watch ignorant and designing men not only misrepresent but man-handle the League to which he had devoted so much of his intellect and energy. He was forced to be quiet, courteous, dignified, gentlemanly, while inwardly he was impatient, un-compromising, militant. He could now let himself go and fight for his great cause on a nation-wide stage. His imagination was fired, as Senator Hitchcock later testified, by the prospect of stirring up such a popular storm that the Senate would be forced to come to heel.

3

All these reasons for a western tour no doubt seemed plausi-ble. But even without the wisdom of hindsight it should have been evident that, barring some kind of political miracle, the President had little to gain and everything to lose by this wild venture.

Wilson, it must be admitted, was not at his best on the stump. Thoroughly at home behind the lecturer's desk, he was an effective speaker of the academic type: cold rather than warm, intellectual rather than emotional, dispassionate rather than impassionate. Men might listen to his precise prose with respect and admiration, but he lacked Theodore Roosevelt's animal heat—the capacity for arousing mass affection. People did not "go insane in pairs" over him.

The pedagogue-President had no gift for dramatizing what he had done, for presenting his deeds in their heroic aspects. He was constitutionally incapable of brutally getting down to cases, and speaking in the most concrete of terms. His mind and his speech ran naturally to abstractions—to ideals, hopes, aspirations, responsibilities, and duties.

He had no desire to resort to cheap or undignified tricks, like Theodore Roosevelt, and was temperamentally unable to do so. Time and again his friends urged him to adopt the devices of the demagogue, and his answer was, "I can't make myself over." No man of his age could. On the trip it was suggested that he "warm up a bit," pull out all the stops, and give the audiences some "sob stuff." His answer was an indignant refusal to "capitalize on the dead." Wilson was too honest to make a convincing demagogue, even if he had tried to be one. Yet he deliberately chose to get down off his high pedestal in the White House and meet the rabble-rousers on their own ground and attempt to use their own weapons—weapons which they were more adept in using than he.

Many of Wilson's foes were joined by some of his friends in saying that the President was needed in Washington rather than in the West. The treaty was not the only issue before the country: at times it seemed like a minor one. Labor was uneasy; the high cost of living seemed much closer to home than the League. Two resolutions were actually introduced in Congress by Republicans who allegedly wanted the President to stay in the capital and deal with inescapable domestic problems. Even if he returned alive and well, he would still be gone for about a month, and that was a long time for the engineer to take his hand off the throttle.

A potent argument against Wilson's going was the necessity for his staying in Washington to direct the treaty fight. He needed to keep in close touch with the Democratic leaders, something he had thus far conspicuously failed to do. He needed also to entice the "mild reservationists" into the Democratic camp, something that there was still hope of doing. It was clear to every cool-headed observer that by this time the treaty could not be approved without at least mild reservations. Then let Wilson stay in the White House, work out a compromise, and get the pact out of the way. Certainly he had compromised enough in Paris; let him compromise a little in Washington.

This was logical reasoning, and Wilson, as the event proved, would have been well advised if he had followed it. But he was evidently not convinced of the necessity of doing these things, and he seems to have had an exaggerated conception of his influence over the people.

4

A final reason against Wilson's going was the unanswerable one that he probably could not succeed even if he did succeed. In less contradictory terms, he could hardly have forced the Senate into a speedy and unreserved approval of the pact even if the results of the tour had exceeded all reasonable expectations.

Wilson had written in 1908 that the Senate was much less responsive than the House to the pressure of public opinion. This was still true. The senators are elected for a six-year term, and only one-third of them come up for reelection every two years. The next election was to be in November, 1920, fifteen months ahead.

The average senator knew that he did not have to worry unduly about his stand on the League. His term was long; the memory of the voters is short. The League would presumably be a dead issue by 1920; certainly by 1922 and 1924. New problems would arise in the meantime, some of them vitally important to the people of the individual states; and, if the senator was "right" on local issues, why need he worry about the League?

There is no reason to believe that such "bitter-enders" as Borah of Idaho and Johnson of California faithfully reflected the views of their constituents. There is ample evidence to show that a great many of the California voters were dissatisfied with their senator's stand on the treaty, and on international affairs in general. But Johnson was reelected by tremendous majorities in 1922, 1928, 1934, and 1940. He might be all wrong on the League and the World Court, but he was "sound" on such local issues as the tariff on prunes, lemons, and nuts. Besides, old-timers could not forget that he had crushed the Southern Pacific machine, and why should young whipper-snappers try to displace their hero?

There is no reason to suppose that Idaho was as isolationist as Borah. But Borah was "sound" on the wool and potato issues, and besides he was the only man of really national stature whom the state had produced. In a political sense, he was Idaho's chief export, its principal claim to national fame. He was of presidential timber, and it would be a great honor to have an Idahoan in the White House. Borah would be reelected, no matter how he stood on such seemingly unimportant things as European affairs.

Even if the senators had feared the results of Wilson's appeal many, if not most, of them were in no mood to bend the knee. If the "swing" had been started earlier, it might have been more effective; but by September the lines were drawn, and the senators had taken their stand. Tough-fibered men like Brandegee and Sherman would break before they would bend.

The supreme irony is that if Wilson had done the impossible and had defeated every Republican senator who was up for reelection in 1920, he would still have fallen short of a two-thirds vote. It is inconceivable that he overlooked this crucially important fact. Yet he may have thought that he could stir up a tremendous tidal wave of public sentiment which would roar up into the highlands of 1922 and 1924. In short, Wilson was staking everything on an upheaval which, though theoretically possible, was not at all probable.

The inescapable fact is that treaties, under our Constitution, are approved, not by public opinion, not by the President, not by the House of Representatives, not by a simple majority of the Senate, but by a two-thirds vote of the Senate. If the American people do not like this method, they are at liberty to change it. That was the system which existed in 1919, and Wilson would have done well to stay in Washington and try to effect an understanding with the only legislative agency under our Constitution empowered to approve treaties. Perhaps he would not have succeeded even then, but there was a better chance of success in the city of Washington than in the state of Washington.

This, of course, assumes a willingness on Wilson's part to accept reasonable compromise. If his mind was completely closed, then the only hope—and a slim one at that—lay in a personal appeal.

5

The best reason of all for not taking the desperate gamble of a nation-wide tour was that Wilson would almost certainly suffer a complete physical collapse. This was evident before he started; and the tragic result merely confirmed the worst fears of his close friends.

Wilson had never been physically strong. He had ruptured a blood vessel in one eye while president of Princeton University, and the doctors had recommended that he stop work. But he rose above that disability. When he came to the White House he was suffering from weak digestion and from neuritis in the arm and shoulder. His personal physician, Dr. Cary T. Grayson, prescribed a diet of raw eggs and orange juice, and had his arm and shoulder regularly baked and massaged. Wilson also followed a strict routine of recreation and exercise: he attended the theater regularly, and played golf dutifully—a conservative, down-the-middle game. Under this regimen his health markedly improved.

The events of the decade before the Peace Conference were enough to crush a more robust man. First, there were the bitter quarrels at Princeton; then the stormy two years as governor of New Jersey; the heated campaign of 1912 for the presidency; the early years of his administration when he had to drive his

reform program through Congress; the constant yawping of
the opposition; the perennial friction with Mexico; the tragic
death of his first wife; and the outbreak of the World War.
Then came the prolific vexations of neutrality; the losing
struggle to keep the nation out of war; and the final plunge
into the abyss.

During the war months Wilson conserved his strength carefully, choosing able assistants and delegating authority to
them. But at the Peace Conference the task seemed too important to delegate to others; he tried to do too much himself.
His recreation was limited to a few brisk walks and automobile rides; his diet was broken by banquets of strange and
indigestible food. He had to encounter formidable adversaries
like Clemenceau, to say nothing of showers of abuse from the
French press and backbiting within his own delegation. At
home he was nagged at by the Republican senators and the
Republican press. The volume of work at Paris was appalling.
It is no wonder that Wilson suffered a temporary breakdown
when, in April, 1919, he succumbed to a violent attack of influenza, an attack from which he may never have completely
recovered. The not-too-reliable "Ike" Hoover, the White
House usher who accompanied Wilson to France, says that he
was not the same after his illness: he began to do queer, fussy,
ungenerous little things.

Then came the trip home. Wilson expected that the Senate
would approve the treaty without undue delay, and that he
could quietly go back to the reform program interrupted by
the war. It was all a vain hope. Domestic problems allowed
him no rest; a railway strike had to be averted; a conference
between capital and labor had to be arranged. Royal visitors
were journeying to Washington. The heat was merciless.
There was no serenity in the goldfish bowl of the presidency.

The Senate, as we have noted, gave him no peace, what with
conferences and calls for data. The heat of prejudice and partisanship seemed to rise higher than that which shimmered
from the softening pavements outside the Capitol.

Wilson was a sick man before he started, and to the keen observer he looked sick. Late in July he had been forced into bed with an attack of dysentery; he was pursued by headaches, possibly premonitory warnings of a stroke. Sir William Wiseman lunched with him at the White House a few days before the ill-starred tour began, and he was shocked by the President's gray color, and by the twitching of his facial muscles.

What this haggard, tormented man needed was a vacation, not a transcontinental trip that would have taxed the strength of a "Bull Moose" like Theodore Roosevelt. He had in fact enjoyed no real vacation for several years, and in recent weeks he had been able to steal away for only a few hours during week ends on the presidential yacht.

6

Wilson's most intimate friends, including Dr. Grayson, repeatedly warned him that it would be plain suicide for a man approaching sixty-three, with hardening of the arteries and all his other disabilities, to undertake this ordeal—physical, nervous, and vocal. He was warned of the heat, the smoke, the cinders, the dust; of the interminable handshaking, the receptions, the dinners, the horrible food; of the "local committees," always demanding something for Podunk. He was warned of the dozens of speeches, and of the parades, during which he would have to stand in the back of a swaying automobile for hours at a time and wave his hat with robotlike smile at tens of thousands of curiosity seekers.

But the President had made up his mind, and to the end he was a stubborn man. He had the courage of determination and desperation. To him there was no other course; the treaty, so it seemed, was hopelessly bogged down in the Senate. To stay in Washington was to court certain defeat; to go to the country was the only chance of success. Of course there were dangers;

of course he might lose his life. But, as he told Grayson with a grim smile, "The boys who went overseas did not refuse to go because it was dangerous." To his wife he said that he could not break faith with the soldiers whom he had promised that this war was to end wars. "If I do not do all in my power to put the Treaty in effect," he said, "I will be a slacker and never able to look those boys in the eye. I must go."

In the face of his friends' opposition, Wilson developed something of a martyr complex. At one of the Cabinet meetings, when it was suggested that he might kill himself, he promptly replied that he would be willing to give up his life for the cause. He admitted to Tumulty that he was "at the end" of his "tether," but to save the world from the calamity that would flow from a rejection of the treaty, he was willing to make whatever personal sacrifice that was necessary. No man, he said, should count his own personal fortunes in such a crisis. "Even though, in my condition, it might mean the giving up of my life, I will gladly make the sacrifice to save the Treaty."

The stern Presbyterian was coming to the fore. Wilson felt, quite understandably, that he had a sacred mission. Like the early Christian martyrs he gloried in sacrificing himself for his principles.

It is well enough, when the occasion demands it, for men to die for their convictions. It is often better—as it would have been in this case—to live and work for them.

Wilson, as we have seen, was the only real leader his party had. The Democrats in the Senate were somewhat demoralized as it was; without him, they would be completely rudderless. The chief of staff does not seek the front-line trenches where he may die for his cause; he stays at the rear directing the general engagement.

The President was willing to give his life for his principles, and in a sense he did. He killed himself, and in killing himself killed the treaty in so far as the United States was concerned. It would have been better if he had been willing to give up some of the high ground he was defending, and compromise enough to save the pact. That was the only way it could have been saved.

7

The completed itinerary was not released until the eve of departure. It was evident at a glance that this was to be primarily a middle western and western trip; the West had reelected Wilson in 1916 (see map on page 336), and this was the section to which he would again appeal. The Deep South was safely Democratic and could be passed by; the East was strongly Republican and could be ignored.

The speeches had been carefully scheduled with an eye to influencing wavering senators or "irreconcilables." There were to be addresses in Reed's Missouri, in Borah's Idaho, in Poindexter's Washington, in Johnson's California. The Golden State was to be honored with nine major speeches, evidently in an attempt to correct Johnson's misrepresentations regarding Shantung and other issues.

Illinois, with its metropolis of Chicago, was deliberately avoided. There was little point in going to a state notorious for the outspokenly isolationist Chicago *Tribune;* for the blathering Chicago Mayor ("Big Bill") Thompson; for the "irreconcilable" Senators Sherman and McCormick; and for a vociferous mass of German-Americans, Irish-Americans, and Italian-Americans. The name of Wilson had already been hissed in open meeting in Chicago.

All together, there were to be about forty formal speeches, in places ranging from tents and stadia to opera houses and tabernacles, to say nothing of various unscheduled appearances on the rear of the train. The first address would be given at Columbus, Ohio, on September 4; the last at Louisville, Kentucky, on September 29.

The preliminary schedules called for a week or so of rest at the Grand Canyon of the Colorado River. But Wilson vetoed

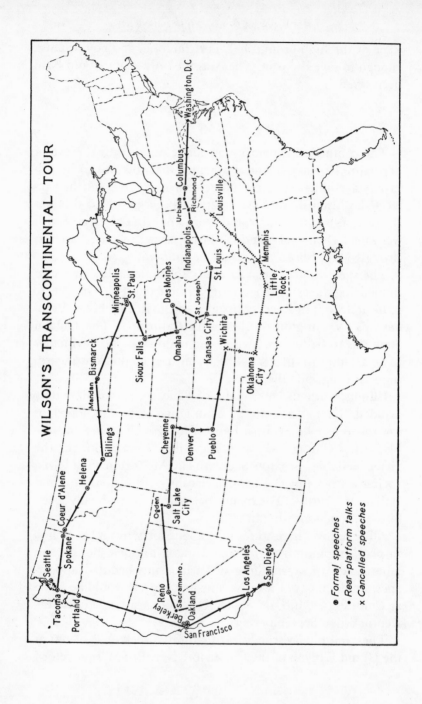

WILSON'S TRANSCONTINENTAL TOUR

● Formal speeches
• Rear-platform talks
x Cancelled speeches

Washington, D.C.
Columbus
Urbana
Richmond
Indianapolis
Louisville
St. Louis
Memphis
Minneapolis
St. Paul
Des Moines
Little Rock
Sioux Falls
St. Joseph
Omaha
Kansas City
Bismarck
Wichita
Mandan
Oklahoma City
Billings
Cheyenne
Helena
Denver
Coeur d'Alene
Pueblo
Spokane
Ogden
Salt Lake City
Seattle
Tacoma
Reno
Portland
Sacramento
Berkeley
Oakland
Los Angeles
San Diego
San Francisco

all such plans; he would not consent to even a day of vacation. As he sternly told Tumulty, he was going on a sacred crusade, and the people would never forgive him if he turned it into a sight-seeing junket.

The party was to be carried on a special train, which, for purposes of safety, was to be preceded by a pilot engine or a first section. The exact schedule was not announced until fulfilled city by city, presumably as a precaution against sabotage.

Only a few overnight stops were arranged, and the entire party was to live on whirling wheels. There were to be one baggage car, one dining car, one car for the correspondents (there were about twenty, plus the representatives of several moving picture concerns), one car for the stenographers and the Secret Service men, and one for the President. This was the last of the procession, and was called the "Mayflower," after the presidential yacht.

The wheeled White House contained sleeping accommodations for the President, Mrs. Wilson, Dr. Grayson (who kept an anxious eye on Wilson), Mrs. Wilson's maid, the President's Negro valet, and his Negro chef. A place was fitted up for a study, where the President deposited his portable typewriter. Here he consulted with his private secretary and others on matters of state.

8

The President and Mrs. Wilson arrived at the capital's Union Station at about seven P.M. on September 3, ready to board their private car. The crowd burst into hand clapping and cheers. The straw-hatted Wilson seemed to be in excellent humor, laughing and cracking jokes with the few personal friends who had come to see him off. Dr. Grayson had insisted that he rest up a few days for the ordeal, and spend a good deal of time in the open air.

But Wilson's mechanical smile was but the façade for a

troubled heart. He knew that he might crack under the strain. He knew that there would be no let-up in the cataract of current business. And when would he find time to outline those dozens of speeches, of which he had not prepared a single line?

One of the most fascinating might-have-beens of history is to speculate on what would have happened had there been then, as there was to be in a few years, a nation-wide radio hookup. Wilson had a fine voice and splendid diction. He probably would have been even more persuasive over the radio than in person. Sitting quietly in the White House, and needing only several half-hour speeches, he might in a series of "fireside chats" have informed and aroused the people, while at the same time preserving his health and strength. But this is all profitless speculation; there was no radio. Wilson had to do the job the hard way.

The train glided out of the yards to the accompaniment of no Godspeeds from the foes of the League. The "irreconcilables" had their heads together, laying plans to "trail" Wilson and wipe out whatever favorable results he might achieve. *Harvey's Weekly* railed against this "Covenanting Crusade," this "hippodroming excursion," this "tour of torment," this "cavorting and gallivanting" at the taxpayers' expense.

Wilson could expect no quarter from his foes, and he was in no mood to give any. The future lay in the lap of the gods.

CHAPTER SEVEN

THE SWING AROUND
THE CIRCLE

"The only people I owe any report to are you and the other citizens of the United States." WOODROW WILSON, *at Columbus, Ohio, September 4, 1919.*

———————

1

THE WESTWARD-SPEEDING presidential party made its first formal stop at Columbus, Ohio, on the morning of September 4, 1919. The visitors passed through streets that were crowded three or four persons deep; but there was no evidence of great interest, much less hysterical enthusiasm. The audience of some 4,000 at Memorial Hall was not so large as expected, possibly because of a morning rainfall and a local streetcar strike.

This was Wilson's first popular defense of the treaty, and he expressed pleasure at the opportunity of meeting directly with the people, the only ones to whom he owed an accounting. He drew warm applause when he praised the League as an instrument for preventing wars. Alluding to the long lines of men in khaki through which he had passed in coming to the platform, he eloquently expressed the hope that they would not have to be sent across again.

The address was well received, but as Wilson was leaving the speaker's stand a Chinese youth in the gallery jumped to his feet and shouted, "Mr. President, how about Shantung?" In the general confusion, Wilson did not hear him, and consequently made no reply.

The next speech was scheduled for Indianapolis, Indiana, later the same day, at the Coliseum on the state fair grounds. Wilson was warmly cheered on the five-mile route from the station, but the arrangements did not work out happily. There was much disorder on the edge of the crowd, where curiosity seekers who had stared at the prize bulls tried to elbow their way in for a look at Wilson.

The President was loudly cheered; but he could not project his clear voice to the confused outer edges, and many of the spectators, their curiosity satisfied, wandered off to view the blue-ribboned boars. This exodus caused a ten-minute interruption, but when order was restored Wilson could be heard clearly, and he was listened to intently. Perhaps the greatest cheer greeted his statement that the peace was severe but just.

The next stopping point was St. Louis, the home of the renegade Senator Reed, and the center of a large German-American group. All during the day Wilson received an unexpectedly enthusiastic reception, quite in contrast with the coldness of Ohio and Indianapolis, and this welcome, the warmest since his return from Paris, must have renewed his faith in the people.

The high point in St. Louis was an address that night in the Coliseum, where Wilson had been renominated in 1916. The enthusiasm of the some 12,000 people who packed themselves into the hall resembled that of a great political convention. When Wilson reached the platform, he was applauded for three minutes, and when the presiding officer predicted that the President would soon be hailed as "Wilson, the Father of World Democracy," there was a wild roar of assent.

Wilson warmed to the occasion, and with fighting words painted the choice as one between partnership in peace or isolation in arms. The United States had by the force of events been thrust into the role of a world leader for peace, and he "for one" was not a quitter (great applause). Restressing his theme that the people were being misled because they could not or would not read the treaty, he offered to send a copy to anyone who had not done so. A lusty voice shouted "Reed," to the accompaniment of applause and loud cheers.

2

With Wilson hunched over his portable typewriter, laboring on his next speech, the presidential special sped toward Kansas City, where an eager crowd of some 15,000 packed Convention Hall to the rafters. When the distinguished guest appeared, the crowd surged to its feet and gave him a mass flag salute. Stirred by this reception, the President delivered himself of a vigorous address, in which he boasted that his "fighting spirit" had been aroused.

Des Moines (Iowa), Omaha (Nebraska), and Sioux Falls (South Dakota) were all taken in stride. The enthusiasm here was more restrained, for these places were strongly Republican, the wheat harvest was on, and there was an active German element, especially in Nebraska, where "irreconcilable" Senator Norris had a loyal following.

At Des Moines, as at St. Louis, Wilson evoked the greatest demonstration when he appealed for the establishment of a new world order. At Omaha he said that he would willingly die if he thought that he stood in the path of the realization of his aims.

Three major speeches were scheduled for St. Paul and Minneapolis, Minnesota, the home state of Senators Nelson and Kellogg, two of the most respected "mild reservationists." The reception was cordial, but not wildly exuberant. Wilson emphasized the familiar themes, and in addition declared that speedy ratification would reduce the cost of living and stabilize labor relations. The newspapermen accompanying the party received the impression that while the people of Minnesota favored the treaty, they were "mild reservationists" like their senators, and did not approve a whole-hog-or-none attitude.

Then came a speech at Bismarck, North Dakota, and a rear-platform appearance across the river at Mandan, where the President was cheered by the crowd, including a group of

Indians. One wonders if these original isolationists understood the issues involved.

The train was now puffing up toward the Rockies. Thus far Wilson and his advisers had little reason to feel unduly elated.

The New Peace Conference
(Courtesy of St. Louis *Post-Dispatch*; cartoonist Fitzpatrick)

Except for St. Louis, and possibly Kansas City, there had been nothing even approaching hysterical approval. Perhaps it was pro-Germanism; perhaps rock-ribbed middle western isolationism. Certainly there was a large degree of preoccupation. One prominent member of the Omaha Chamber of Commerce confessed, "We are so busy making money that we haven't had time to worry about the Peace Treaty." The Kansas City *Times* warned, "The nation is in a hardheaded mood just now."

3

The two stops in Montana, first at Billings, and then at the capital, Helena, were marked by reverent rather than warm-hearted crowds. Scores of persons in the first audience wore mourning. Their boys had fallen in the blistering Argonne, and they had come long distances to get what comfort they could from their President. As Wilson described in touching words the sacrifices of the lads who had gone abroad, tears streamed down the weather-beaten cheeks of his hearers.

The next state was Idaho, the stamping ground of the rampageous Borah. If the presidential party approached the "enemy's country" with misgivings, these were dispelled by the ovation at the one stop, Coeur d'Alene. The generous outpouring of good will indicated that the people in this part of the state did not agree with Borah's irreconcilable position.

The same was true of Spokane, Washington, the home city of the "bitter-ender" Senator Poindexter. The people turned out in droves to greet the first citizen of the land, and some seats in the packed armory were allegedly sold by scalpers for twenty-five dollars.

At Tacoma, and particularly at Seattle, the reception was so overwhelming and unrestrained as to recall Wilson's triumphal Italian tour. The welcome was warm, genuine, Western. The West had elected him in 1916; it was seemingly still with him.

At Tacoma, some 25,000 people had gathered in the Stadium, with thousands of children in posts of honor, waving a sea of red, white, and blue flags, and singing the national anthem. Wilson's voice shook as he prayed God that these boys would never have to carry that flag into battle. On the way to the armory for the second address, the crowds became so unmanageable that Secret Service men had to hurl people back from the presidential automobile.

In Seattle, where Wilson spoke twice, the exuberance of the outpouring approached fanaticism: it was the greatest ovation thus far. Multi-colored snowstorms of confetti descended upon the visitors, while Wilson waved his silk hat. The police, aided by sturdy Boy Scouts, could scarcely hold back the throngs. A part of the enthusiasm was no doubt due to the holiday spirit in the air. The great Pacific Fleet was there to be reviewed by the Commander-in-Chief, and Mrs. Wilson remembers how impressive it was at night, bedecked with fireflies of light.

There was only one sour note in Seattle. A good many alleged I.W.W.'s were sullenly displaying printed hatbands calling for the release of political prisoners, especially the Socialist leader, Eugene V. Debs.

4

As the barometer of enthusiasm arose, the barometer of Wilson's physical and nervous reserve sank correspondingly. Those terrible headaches dogged him; well-wishers and politicians would not leave him alone so that he might snatch a moment of rest or begin work on the next speech. Mrs. Wilson and Dr. Grayson watched him furtively, apprehensively. Yet he kept up a brave front, and no doubt impressed the audiences with his vigor. But shortly after Tacoma, says Tumulty, the fatigue of the trip began to write itself plainly on Wilson's face.

The show had to go on. Portland, Oregon, was no less enthusiastic than Seattle, though perhaps lacking the mob spirit. The main speech, that in the evening, was delivered to the fortunate 7,000 among the 30,000 who had applied for tickets. Earlier the same day the party took a fifty-mile outing on the soul-refreshing Columbia River highway. Along the road cars were parked, and constant cheering accompanied the procession. A tragic automobile crash took the life of one of the most popular of the news correspondents, and seriously injured another. This did not help to relax Wilson's taut nerves.

Southward through the Cascades wound the presidential special to California, the bailiwick of the envenomed Senator Johnson. The stay in the San Francisco Bay region was spread over September 17 and 18, and embraced San Francisco, Oakland, and Berkeley. The spectacle was much the same as that in Oregon and Washington, and the streets, windows, and roofs were packed with cheering masses of humanity.

The main San Francisco speech, that in the huge Civic Auditorium, was dampened by poor acoustics and by the disorders among alleged Irish agitators. On the other side of the bay, in Berkeley and Oakland, the program went off more smoothly. Some 12,000 people jammed into the Civic Auditorium in Oakland, with half as many stranded outside. When a voice in the gallery cried, "Are we with him?" a thousand throats hurled back the reply, "We are!"

In the California addresses Wilson tried with evident success to allay the peculiar apprehensions of the people of the Golden State. To the Irish he explained that the League aided rather than hindered the cause of Ireland's freedom; to the Chinese and their sympathizers he declared that the Shantung settlement would in the long run work out to the advantage of China; to the great body of anti-Japanese Californians he gave assurances that the United States would still have sovereign control over its immigration sluice gates.

The reception in Southern California was, in the judgment of the correspondents, the high point of the trip thus far. In San Diego the main address was delivered in the Stadium, where a glass cage with an electrical device had been prepared so that the 50,000 auditors might hear.

At Los Angeles, where he spoke twice, Wilson received the now-accustomed acclaim. Yet the intrepid Covenanter was beginning to falter. Those terrible headaches were taking their toll. At the urgent insistence of Dr. Grayson, the schedule was broken in Southern California, so that Wilson might spend a few hours at a quiet resort.

Returning to Central California, Wilson made a brief, unscheduled speech at Sacramento, Senator Johnson's home town. Then the train was pointed toward the undulating Sierras and home.

The visit to California was a great success. Expecting to find audiences hostile on the Irish, Japanese, and Chinese questions, Wilson had received unprecedented ovations. Veteran newspapermen estimated that he had the state two to one for a League without crippling reservations.

The tour was a triumph, except where the results counted: the vote of Hiram W. Johnson. If anything, he was more bitter than ever. The other senator, James D. Phelan (Democrat), had been a Wilson supporter all along.

5

They were now headed for home, with the worst of the ordeal behind. Wilson was still drawing too heavily on his pitifully small balance in the bank of nature. Yet his Scotch implacability was aroused; he was so enheartened by the rousing western reception that he was beginning to talk of carrying the fight into the "enemy's country"—Senator Lodge's Massachusetts.

Nothing noteworthy happened at thinly populated Reno (Nevada) or at Ogden (Utah), though the greetings were warm. But the Utah metropolis, Salt Lake City, recalled the ovations in California. The only address was scheduled for the famed Mormon Tabernacle, which was so tightly packed with humanity that the air became stifling. Mrs. Wilson, who herself almost fainted away, soaked a large handkerchief in lavender salts and sent it up to the wilting President.

Before Wilson began to speak, all doubts as to the attitude of the Mormon Church were dispelled when a high dignitary, Heber J. Grant, besought divine inspiration for the President, and evoked a deep-throated "Amen" from the audience. Wilson then spoke vigorously against wrecking the treaty with reservations; but the effort was an exhausting one, and at the close of the address his clothes were wet with perspiration.

On to Cheyenne, and then Denver. The end was fast approaching. Wilson was making feeble jokes, saying that his constitution was gone, but that his by-laws were left. He was running on his nerve. At Denver it was doubtful, when he rose, whether he could go on. Yet he seemed to be in fighting fettle, and he struck again at Senate reservations when he insisted, "We must either go in or stay out." From the crowd came cries, "Don't worry about the Senate."

Wilson was thinner, tired-looking: to Mrs. Wilson, a sick man. Before the Denver effort she suggested a few days of rest, but he refused, saying, "No, I have caught the imagination of the people." He cheered her, or tried to, by remarking that it would soon be over, and by promising that when they reached Washington he would take a holiday. The holiday never came.

6

The address at Pueblo, Colorado, was in some respects the high point of the entire trip. Wilson's fatigue was such that he planned to speak only a few minutes. But when he appeared the entire audience rose and cheered for several minutes, and he was moved to a supreme effort. Just before he began to speak, he remarked half-jocularly to the patient pressmen who had already heard about forty of his speeches, "Aren't you fellows getting pretty sick of this?"

This last address in Wilson's public career turned out to be one of the longest of the trip, and by common consent the most moving. It was as though he recharged the batteries of his energy from his sympathetic audience. Near the close he dramatically pictured the burial places of the American boys in France, and pleaded that it should not happen again. His eyes grew damp, as did those of some of the hardened newspapermen, while tears flowed freely down the cheeks of many in his audience.

At the end he received a tremendous ovation, the memory of which probably never left him. It was a fitting climax to an inspired speaking tour, and to a world-shaking speaking career—perhaps the most memorable in history.

Pueblo was journey's end. Contrary to the Hollywood version, Wilson spoke in a new auditorium, not from the rear platform, and he did not collapse while speaking. But that night on the train was a prolonged ordeal of insomnia and excruciating headache, accompanied by unmistakable symptoms of physical and nervous exhaustion. The rest of the speeches had to be canceled.

As a physical and vocal effort the three-week tour had been tremendous: some 8,000 miles of hurried travel (from sea level to high altitudes), innumerable conferences, a dozen or so wearying parades, and thirty-six set speeches (averaging an hour in length), to say nothing of several rear-platform addresses. The wonder is that Wilson did not crack sooner.

7

We must now analyze this noteworthy series of messages at some length.

The addresses were pitched, especially the early ones, on an extremely optimistic key. Wilson made it clear that he was not arguing or fighting with any one. He was traveling to find out what the people were thinking and saying; he wanted the pleasure of seeking fresh "inspiration" from them. He was merely explaining the treaty and making a report to the people. He never for one moment doubted that the treaty would be ratified; the only thing that concerned him, he said, was the delay.

He urged his audiences to read the treaty. It was a plain document couched in plain English; he could not find a

"single obscure sentence" in it. What he most feared was ignorance rather than prejudice; and he had found much ignorance.
Critics were concentrating their fire on the most liberal and
constructive parts of the pact. He had discovered that many
people thought the Covenant consisted of one article, Article
X; and all the rest of the treaty had but a few clauses, notably
that regarding Shantung. He was doing his best to correct this
false notion, and he was surprised by the number of people
who said to him, "Why, we never dreamed that those things
were in the treaty."

Wilson realized as well as any one that the pact was not
wholly satisfactory, but he also realized that it would be poor
strategy to confess this publicly. It seemed wise to put the best
possible face on things; so he did.

The treaty was, in his judgment, a great peace, a "just"
peace, and it had been the "crowning" privilege of his life
to sign it. It was a "thoroughly American document" and a
"people's treaty," the first of this kind. It liberated oppressed
minorities, abolished secret treaties, provided a Magna Charta
for labor and for women and children; and as such it was "the
great humane document of all time."

Above all, the pact contained the Covenant of the League
of Nations, which was designed for peace and not—according
to critics—for war. In this sense it was a "disentangling alliance." The League did not guarantee that there would be no
future wars. But it made war "violently improbable" by arranging for elaborate arbitral machinery and a cooling-off
period of nine months. Would not a scheme which provided a
10 per cent guarantee against war be worth while? Yet this
was a 90 per cent guarantee.

8

Much of Wilson's time was taken up with answering the
attacks of his Senate foes. He stressed the point that at Paris

he had brought about an amendment of the League Covenant in response to their demands, and now they were complaining that they did not like the wording of the changes.

He advanced the familiar arguments to meet the charges regarding six votes to one, the Monroe Doctrine, Shantung, and the control of immigration and other domestic problems. Article X was "the heart of the treaty"; and the real danger, he correctly felt, lay not in action but in inaction, in a failure of the League to function energetically when it should.

America would not, he said, be entrapped in the League. We could always get out after serving two years' notice. But he hoped that this mighty nation would not insist on sitting timorously near the door, on the edge of its chair, with one hand on the doorknob. This did not befit a great power.

Not content with parrying arguments, Wilson presented some of his own. All this delay was but aid and comfort to the Germans, whose propaganda and whose hyphenates were behind much of the obstruction. The world was still unsettled because of uncertainty as to the support of the United States.

Isolation, he insisted, had gone forever; the processes of history and modern mechanical miracles had turned the globe into a "single whispering gallery." We could not be peaceful or prosperous in an unpeaceful and unprosperous world; we could not "disentangle" ourselves from the rest of the earth. When the next war came the United States not only would be sucked into it but would have to bear the brunt of it.

The United States, Wilson concluded, had an inescapable moral obligation to bear its share of the responsibility for world peace. He believed that the overwhelming majority of the American people favored the League; and that America would have to join sooner or later. It was just a matter of time; this nation would enter either gracefully as a charter member or disgracefully as a laggard.

9

Wilson's speeches on this tour, when read today, impress one as having been a remarkable performance, especially in view of the physical and other disabilities under which he was laboring. In elevation of tone or beauty of diction his addresses do not measure up to his finest efforts; but the occasion called for a lower tone, and extemporaneous efforts can seldom approach the precision of carefully prepared essays.

Wilson probably gave ear to the proddings of friends that he come down off his pedestal and talk plain English, for he undertook at times to speak in the vernacular. But the vernacular did not become Wilson.

Such expressions as "It gravels me" or "It sticks in the craw" were acceptable colloquially but hardly Wilsonian. At Indianapolis, Wilson declared that the League was the only conceivable arrangement for preventing war, and that those who were criticizing it, or who thought they had a wiser scheme, had better "put up or shut up." He apologized a bit for using this "common" expression, but he employed it again at Kansas City and at Omaha. At St. Louis he won great applause when he said, "You hear politics until you wish that *both* parties might be smothered in their own gas." This was not a graceful expression, nor a tactful one, because he was the titular head of one of the two great parties, and he needed its support if he hoped to win.

Even more questionable were his attacks on the Senate, which he was trying to win over. At St. Louis he said that the senators ("some gentlemen") would be "absolute, contemptible quitters if they do not see the game through." He did not say that they *were* "contemptible quitters," but that they *would be* if they failed. He also declared that unless the senators did their duty they would be "gibbeted" in the annals of mankind.

These expressions were most ill advised. If Wilson was

merely expounding, why attack the senators in this fashion?
They naturally struck back. Senator Harding said that nobody
was a "quitter" and nobody would shut up. Wilson's statements also lent themselves to misrepresentation. *Harvey's
Weekly* reported: "Yet he rushed about the country like a
howling dervish, shrieking 'Put up or shut up, you contemptible quitters, before you are hanged on a gibbet!' "

To many unfriendly critics it looked as though the President were publicly airing a private quarrel.

10

At times Wilson used mistaken tactics, or made actual errors
in tactics. To call upon great audiences to read the entire
treaty was but to offer the counsel of perfection. To call upon
them to read the French version with a French dictionary if
they could not understand plain English was to offer the
counsel of absurdity. To urge the senators, as he did at Indianapolis, to hold their own convention and draw up something
better was foolish. The senators were of no mind to hold a
convention, and they had no authority to do so. Treaty negotiation was the function of the President; treaty criticism was
the function of the Senate.

A more serious tactical error was for Wilson to admit at
Indianapolis that Article XI of the Covenant was his favorite
article (see page 385 for text). At present, he said, we had to
mind our own business; under Article XI, which permitted
friendly intervention in the affairs of others, *"we can mind
other people's business."* The logical inference was that if we
could mind other people's business those people could start
minding ours. This, of course, was gall and wormwood to the
isolationists.

Fundamentally more serious was Wilson's generally uncompromising position on reservations. A reservation which
merely quieted nerves, or which repeated in different words

what was already said, he would tolerate. But stronger reservations were too humiliating to accept. At Billings, he stated bluntly, "It is this treaty or none." At Cheyenne, as well as at Salt Lake, he declared that the Senate's proposed reservation to Article X he would regard "as a rejection of the treaty," thus implying that he would not complete ratification on these terms.

Whatever the reasons, Wilson made a number of statements which were exaggerated or erroneous. His warm advocacy of the treaty led him to say that it "has very, very few compromises in it"; that it was not "a statesman's arrangement." His conscience must have twinged a bit when he said that "forward-looking men" like Clemenceau and Orlando, who had helped him frame the pact, "spoke the conscience of the world"; their hearts "beat with the people of the world . . ."

His explanation of the six votes to one was occasionally careless. It was misleading to say, as he did in Denver, that the United States had a veto voice in the Council of the League in all cases; our vote could not be counted in our behalf if we were a party to the dispute. *Harper's Weekly* had a field day at Wilson's expense, running numerous "fillers" which read:

$$1 + 1 + 1 + 1 + 1 + 1 = 1$$

Inconsistencies or errors of fact appeared here and there, as when Wilson repeatedly put Sarajevo in Serbia instead of Austria-Hungary. But this sort of thing was relatively unimportant, except as a handle for his enemies.

Perhaps Wilson's greatest single failure was not to stress more fully and clearly what America would gain. Although less abstract than usual, he was still inclined to talk over the heads of his hearers about problems they could not understand. What they wanted to know was how the treaty affected them; or, in the immortal words of the Tammany politician, "What's in it for Mrs. Murphy and the children?"

Wilson characteristically stressed our obligations rather

than our gains. He undertook to appeal to America's unselfish self; to emphasize the duties of the strong; to demonstrate that the greatest nation must not be the master nation but the servant nation—the servant of mankind. We must not be afraid to dare new things; to take on new obligations; to measure up to our greatness.

America, as was soon to become apparent, wanted relaxation, not exertion; freedom, not responsibility; profits, not losses.

11

The apologists for Wilson insist that if he had not collapsed on the trip the Senate would have been forced to bow to the storm of public opinion. The President himself clearly shared this belief.

No one can deny that in the West, *the most thinly populated part of the country,* Wilson had succeeded in arousing lively demonstrations of enthusiasm. But there are important qualifications.

The size and exuberance of the crowds did not prove that the country was swinging to the treaty *without reservations.* Many of the people who turned out to cheer were merely curiosity seekers. Wilson had recently talked with kings; he had reordered the world. But more than that he was President; and the presidential office was entitled to respect if not reverential awe. Crowds will always turn out to see the President.

The audiences, as is almost always the case, were packed with Wilson sympathizers. Critics normally stay home and scoff; worshipers attend and approve. After Wilson's address to the St. Louis Chamber of Commerce, the New York *Times* correspondent interviewed forty or fifty of those present and found that they all favored unconditional ratification.

The length and volume of the ovations did not prove a great deal. Much of the noise was made by the "saved"; others doubtless cheered because one is always supposed to cheer the President. Others no doubt felt admiration for a "fighter" who would not submit to the Senate lying down. Also, the spirit of mob enthusiasm often takes hold of large crowds, and they cheer almost any ringing declaration. *Harvey's Weekly* was not far from the mark when it said that "some people would applaud a declamation of the binomial theorem or a proposal to repeal the Decalogue."

Using the Burning Glass on the Senate Opposition
(From New York *World*; cartoonist Kirby; reprinted by permission)

If we assume that all those who turned out and cheered for Wilson were cheering for the League, we still have not answered the question: What kind of League were they cheering for? Were they for the League as it stood; for a mildly reserved League; for a strongly reserved League; or for an amended League? This question is unanswerable, though there can be no doubt that many of the applauders favored a League with some kind of reservations.

But the question of applause is largely academic. Those who cheered could not vote on the treaty: that was to be done by the Senate. And how many senatorial votes were influenced?

It would be difficult to prove that a single vote was changed by Wilson's western appeal. It is true that a group of Democrats who had been toying with reservations lined up with the President while he was gone, but it is not apparent that the tour had any real bearing on their decision. At about the same time two other Democrats shifted over into the reservation camp.

Certainly not one of the "bitter-enders" abated his opposition. Probably Wilson's pressure tended to draw them together and further solidify their opposition. Two of the "mild reservationists," Kenyon of Iowa and Spencer of Missouri, issued unexpectedly unfriendly statements following the President's visit to their states. This further confirms the view that it would have been better to stay in Washington and attempt to win them over.

Finally, the appeal to the country gave Wilson's enemies additional ammunition to fire at him. Ex-President Taft, a friend of the League, was disgusted that Wilson should go barnstorming around the country, throwing "contemptuous phrases" at his opponents, and announcing undying opposition to effective reservations. Hostile newspapers cried, "Go back to Washington." *Harvey's Weekly* attacked Wilson for trying to be "President of the World," for setting out on his "terrifying tour," during which he unloosed the "boorish violence of his diatribes." And when the curtain fell tragically at Pueblo, the unsympathetic Harvey concluded that Wilson had "railed and raged and scolded himself into an alarming state of collapse . . ."

We have already observed that Wilson could not have succeeded if he had succeeded. The trip was not a success; it was a disastrous failure.

CHAPTER EIGHT

THE FALLEN WARRIOR

"I would rather lose in a cause that I know some day will tri-
umph than triumph in a cause that I know some day will lose."
WOODROW WILSON, *September 12, 1912.*

1

IT WOULD be an error to conclude that Wilson's tragic
breakdown was due solely to the physical strain imposed by
the tour. There were numerous other harassments—some of the
usual variety, some produced by postwar readjustment.

Domestic cares pursued the Chief Executive across the continent, and the presidential routine had to be carried on from
the perambulatory White House. Time and energy had to be
given to the approaching Industrial Conference in Washington, and to strikes, especially the steel strike.

Nor would foreign affairs stand still. The Mexican vexations continued unabated. The inflammatory Fiume problem
again blazed its way into the headlines. While Wilson was in
the Rocky Mountain area, the fanatical Italian poet, Gabriele
d'Annunzio, seized this Adriatic port for his disappointed
countrymen, and the fat was once more in the fire. Between
speeches, Wilson had to concern himself with the Fiume affair,
and even to prepare a cablegram to Paris expressing his amazement and distress that the Allied leaders should be acquiescing
in Italy's grab.

Even the Democrats in the Senate were not standing too
firm, and the Republicans were continuing their partisan
maneuvers. Senator Penrose of Pennsylvania, whose own reputation was tainted, charged on the floor of the Senate that
Wilson had improperly accepted gifts abroad valued at several
million dollars. Such vicious misrepresentations must have
been rasping to the spirit of the Princeton Puritan.

There were personal problems as well. In Los Angeles a proposed rest period was broken by a visit from Mrs. Mary H. Peck, "the butterfly of Bermuda," whom Wilson had known in happier days, and with whom he had exchanged innocuous but somewhat indiscreet letters. The tongue of scandal had smeared both. Wilson was shocked to find her a broken butterfly, completely wrapped up in her own penury and other troubles.

Only a few encouraging developments, aside from the customary ovations, interrupted the monotonous tale of toil and trouble. Not so many Democratic senators finally wobbled over into the reservationist camp as had been feared. The American Bar Association came out with an endorsement of ratification. And some 250 leaders in American life, including William H. Taft, Samuel Gompers, George W. Wickersham, and A. Lawrence Lowell, issued an appeal urging the Senate to reject the proposed Lodge amendments and ratify the treaty at once without crippling reservations.

2

While Wilson was in or near the bailiwick of Borah, doing battle for the League, William C. Bullitt (later Ambassador to France) took the stand before the Senate Committee, and did battle against the League.

The twenty-eight-year-old Bullitt was a personable man, deeply idealistic and markedly impulsive, who had been attached to the American Peace Commission in a minor capacity. He made a special trip to Russia for the purpose of clarifying relations with the Bolsheviks, but upon his return he was brushed aside by Wilson and Lloyd George. Angered by this reception, and disillusioned by the treaty, he wrote a scorching letter of criticism to Wilson, at the end of which he formally resigned. The work of peacemaking then went forward without him.

The young man was subpoenaed by the Senate committee, though he was apparently eager to come. When on the stand he offered to read freely from notes he had taken on confidential conversations in Paris, and without restraint proceeded to reveal all he knew.

The Bullitt testimony was in the highest degree sensational. The witness testified that Secretary Lansing had told him at Paris that he considered "many parts of the Treaty thoroughly bad, particularly those dealing with Shantung and the League of Nations"; that the League as constituted was entirely "useless"; that the "powers had simply gone ahead and arranged the world to suit themselves"; and that the American people would "unquestionably" defeat the pact if they "ever understand what it lets them in for."

Lansing was now on the griddle. The witty Clemenceau, who had been wounded during the Conference by an assassin, remarked: "I got my bullet at the Conference, but Lansing got his afterward." The red-faced Secretary wired Wilson, admitting that he had criticized the treaty in Bullitt's presence, but explaining that he had not meant precisely what the witness had said. Lansing thereupon offered to make a public explanation along these lines.

Wilson was profoundly distressed. The bullet had glanced off Lansing only to hit him. "My God!" he cried out to Tumulty. "I did not think it was possible for Lansing to act in this way." As nothing but a flat denial would help correct the bad impression, and as Lansing had to admit that there was a considerable measure of truth in Bullitt's remarks, a labored public explanation would only make matters worse. So the President did not give Lansing the authorization to issue a statement; hence Lansing could issue none. Wilson did not even reply to the telegram or acknowledge it.

The Bullitt business stirred international reverberations. Abroad, the loquacious ex-diplomat was freely denounced, especially in England, where he was branded a Bolshevik and a cad. At home, the foes of the League were jubilant. Whatever ground Wilson may have laboriously won thus far on his tour was now partially lost, perhaps wholly lost.

Wilson had called upon the Senate obstructionists to put up or shut up; they had put up Bullitt. *Harvey's Weekly* gleefully reported that the witness had spoken out "in meeting"; and it printed a scathing editorial under the caption, "BULLITT BLABS." Harvey also called upon Lansing to resign: how could he in good conscience continue to serve when he had admitted that the treaty to which he had put his signature was in large part "thoroughly bad"?

Some critics were inclined to view the whole mess in a somewhat more jocose vein. One southern newspaper directed attention to Lansing's statement that the American people would reject the treaty if they understood it. If that was the case, concluded this paper, "they will never reject it."

3

The Bullitt sensation was from several points of view intrinsically unimportant. Nothing new had been revealed about the treaty; and it had long been common gossip that Lansing was not in complete sympathy with the President's idealistic aspirations.

But the shock probably contributed something to Wilson's collapse, undermined public confidence in the high officials of the government, and revealed how far disillusionment would cause otherwise honorable men to go.

Bullitt did what he did deliberately, after mature reflection, and no doubt with the conviction that the public weal demanded the defeat of the treaty. Where the public weal is involved no such thing as private confidences should stand in the way—at least some people can rationalize their conduct along these lines.

If Lansing was indiscreet in talking, and Bullitt was ungentlemanly in blabbing, what shall we say of Lodge and the other Republicans who summoned him before the committee and encouraged him to talk? This in some ways was the most reprehensible part of the whole affair.

Bullitt was sneaked in as a "surprise" witness before a rump meeting of the committee, from which all Democrats were absent. If they had known he was coming, they undoubtedly would have been present, and they would have attempted to shut him off. Lodge, who was privy to all this, wrote rather lamely to his friend Henry White that Bullitt's "breach of confidence" was "his affair"; he simply turned state's evidence and insisted on reading his report of the conversations. Lodge added that Bullitt would have gone ahead and revealed all his notes, but that he (Lodge) and Senator Knox stopped him. By this time they had accumulated enough evidence; they must not make the mistake of drawing the bow too far.

Henry White always blamed Lodge for this unsavory episode. "Really," he wrote to a friend, "it requires some patience at times not to become indignant with him."

The Bullitt testimony ended the six weeks of Senate hearings. It was a fittingly disgraceful ending for a thoroughly disgraceful episode.

4

The Bullitt affair was only one of Wilson's troubles. Before him on his tour went Irish agitators, who published in the local newspapers full-page advertisements attacking the League. When he left, another advertisement (also paid for by the Friends of Irish Freedom) assailed his arguments.

Behind him, like baying bloodhounds, came several of the Senate "irreconcilables," "trailing" him from city to city. It was enough to unnerve the faltering crusader.

Most of the "Battalion of Death" stayed behind and used the senatorial sounding board, but a few went out on the stump. Poindexter made several speeches in the East, while McCormick, Borah, and especially Johnson undertook to speak in the Middle West. At some of the meetings enthusiastic listeners sprang to their feet, threw their hats into the air, and shouted approval of a smashing argument.

Wilson had avoided Chicago; it was too full of isolationists and hyphenates. The "irreconcilable" "trailers" went to the Windy City, and there held what was perhaps their most exciting meeting, with Borah, Johnson, and McCormick all speaking from the same platform. Borah was in fine fettle. He cried that Wilson had gone over to Paris preaching open covenants, and had surrendered. "Who quit?" he shouted. "Who was the quitter?"

From the crowd came the ringing response, "Wilson."

Borah referred to the hundred thousand (imaginary) men whom England was going to ask Wilson to send to Constantinople.

"Impeach him! Impeach him!" screamed the audience, many of whose members were not even American citizens.

Elsewhere Senator Johnson had a field day in exercising his tub-thumping talents. At Kansas City he cried that the League was an "infamous nostrum"; at Des Moines, "a gigantic war trust." At Lincoln, Nebraska, he shouted, "Shall American boys police the world?" At Sioux City he charged that Wilson intended to adopt a new government for the United States. Persistently and consistently he assailed Allied duplicity, Article X, and the Shantung settlement.

Many Californians were not proud of their loud-mouthed senator. In a telegram made public on September 27, over thirty prominent citizens of the state, including President Benjamin Ide Wheeler of the University of California and President Ray Lyman Wilbur of Stanford University, protested to Johnson against the tactics he was using. But the senator was not especially concerned about people at the university level; many more votes could be found among the masses.

Johnson's campaign against the League—and for his presidential candidacy—was markedly successful. His friends declared that he was running away with the nomination. Summoned back to Washington to vote for amendments to the treaty, he temporarily abandoned his trip with reluctance, insisting that if he could get "just sixty days" before the final vote the American people would make their wishes known in no uncertain fashion.

The Deadlocked Article X
(Courtesy of St. Louis *Post-Dispatch*; cartoonist Fitzpatrick)

The untamed Reed, after arousing the Senate galleries with a four-hour excoriation of the League, went out on the hustings. At Ardmore, Oklahoma, he was rotten-egged from the platform by a group of irate citizens, prominent among whom was a woman who had lost her sons in the war.

Proof is lacking, but it is reasonable to conclude that the efforts of the "irreconcilable" "trailers" to some extent canceled out the efforts of the President. Friends of Wilson complained that the conduct of the senators was unfair and unprecedented. But the United States is a democracy, and the members of Congress have as much right to free speech—even though it be ignorant speech—as the President.

It certainly would have been more dignified and perhaps more useful, as the Boston *Herald* pointed out, if both the President and the senators had stayed in Washington, subordinating prejudice and passion, discussing the issues with moderation, and seeking to reach a compromise agreement.

5

When Wilson's body finally rebelled in Colorado, it was no easy matter to convince him that the remainder of the trip must be canceled. Dr. Grayson pleaded that any other course would mean complete disaster. But the stricken man replied, through tears of pain and disappointment, "No, no, no. I must keep on."

Wilson feared that Senator Lodge would say that he was a "quitter"—perhaps a "contemptible quitter"; that he was "quitting" because the western trip was a failure. If he stopped now, it seemed as though all the ground that he had so painfully gained would be thrown away.

Until the time the train slowed down at Wichita, Kansas, Wilson still had hopes of making a public appearance. But it was not to be; instead he issued a statement to the people of Kansas. He finally yielded completely, but only after it had been pointed out to him that the trip was a great success. He had presented his case fully, and he could add nothing new in the five or so remaining speeches scheduled for the area of Kansas, Oklahoma, Arkansas, Tennessee, and Kentucky.

The plan was suggested of having Wilson seek some near-by health resort before undertaking the rest of the trip back to Washington, but Dr. Grayson decided that the quiet and privacy of the White House would be better. Grayson issued a statement announcing that Wilson's condition was not alarming; he was suffering from a nervous collapse caused by overwork and dating back to his influenza attack of April. He needed rest and quiet.

The saddened presidential party, with curtains drawn, was spirited from the Rockies to the Potomac in forty-eight hours, hardly stopping long enough to change heated engines. A crowd of the curious and the worshipful gathered at the Union Station in Washington, and the wan Wilson raised his hat automatically in response to their cheers. Worn and shaken, he was able to walk to the White House car with some show of briskness, but to the careful observer he betrayed signs of exhaustion. Though his face was drawn and haggard, he did not seem desperately ill, and his critics were further confirmed in their suspicion that he was shamming illness because the trip had been a failure.

Little sympathy was wasted on the fallen Wilson by his enemies. *Harvey's Weekly* exulted: "He went away from Washington with the edifice of his ambition quaking and trembling about him. He returns to find it in utter ruins.

"He has had his say. He has shot his bolt. He has done his worst. He is no more to be considered. Now let the Senate act."

During the three days after his return Wilson slept fitfully, wandered about aimlessly, too shaken and pain-bedeviled to work, and went for a few short automobile rides. He did not feel able to see Sir William Wiseman, a representative of the British government, who appeared with an important message; and he put off several Democratic senators who called in the hope of consulting their leader on the all-important treaty fight.

On the evening of the third day Wilson felt so much better that before retiring he vigorously read a passage from the Bible to his wife, as he had habitually done during the war. He then wound his watch, and absent-mindedly left it on the table in Mrs. Wilson's bedroom. She took it to him, and he said, "That worries me—to have left that watch there. It is not like me."

Nature was warning Wilson of more tragic things to come.

6

At about eight o'clock the next morning (October 2), Mrs. Wilson found her husband sitting on the edge of his bed, complaining of numbness in his left hand. She helped him to the bathroom, and then hurried to telephone Dr. Grayson. While still at the telephone she heard a slight noise, and rushing back she found Wilson lying on the floor unconscious. He had suffered a stroke, which thickened his speech, paralyzed the left side of his face and body, and partially incapacitated his left arm and leg until his death.

Dr. Grayson soon arrived, and shortly thereafter appeared in the hall crying (according to "Ike" Hoover), "My God, the President is paralyzed!" Other doctors were summoned, nurses were engaged, medical apparatus was moved in, and the White House became a veritable hospital. When Wilson regained consciousness, says Josephus Daniels (then the Secretary of the Navy), he extracted a promise from both his wife and Dr. Grayson that his condition, if serious, should not be made known.

For several weeks Wilson spent practically every moment on his back. The initial stroke was complicated by indigestion and a painful swelling of the prostate gland, which failed to respond to local treatment and which, on October 17, produced an obstruction of the urethra. The doctors agreed that only an operation would save the President's life.

The dilemma was a frightening one to Mrs. Wilson. It seemed as though her husband in his weakness could not survive a major operation; if there was no operation, the body would be fatally poisoned. The doctors (there were six of them) patiently explained his plight by means of diagrams, and bluntly told Mrs. Wilson that the obstruction could not be allowed to continue beyond two hours. But on her own responsibility she decided that there should be no operation.

Near the end of three interminable hours the condition cleared up, and the crisis was passed.

During these early weeks the President was a desperately sick man. Mrs. Wilson later wrote, "For days life hung in the balance." But neither the Cabinet nor the public was made fully aware of his critical condition. There was no inkling in the White House announcement that Wilson had been laid low by a stroke; it was generally believed that he had suffered a nervous breakdown, complicated by digestive and prostatic trouble. All he apparently needed was seclusion and rest.

The reasons for this deliberate deception of the public are obvious. The domestic front was in a turbulent condition, and a frank admission would have further unsettled the country. Also, a truthful statement might have led people to conclude that Wilson had become incapacitated within the plain meaning of the Constitution, and a demand for his resignation might well have reached irresistible proportions. This may have been the main reason why the President wanted his real condition concealed.

Such a lack of candor, necessary though it may have seemed, had unfortunate by-products. When truth is crushed to earth, rumors multiply. There were wild reports that Wilson was paralyzed, dead, insane. Passers-by pointed to the bars on the White House windows (put there to protect them from the ball-playing children of Theodore Roosevelt), and whispered that a madman lay behind them. Senator Moses, one of the bitterest of the "irreconcilables," wrote a letter alleging that Wilson was suffering from a brain lesion. This was so uncomfortably near the truth as to bring a denial from one of the attending specialists.

The absence of truthful bulletins no doubt accounts in part for the lack of expressions of concern from public and private bodies. While it is true that certain individuals, like Senator Hiram W. Johnson, made gracious remarks, and prayers were offered in the churches, the absence of a formal resolution of sympathy from either the House or the Senate was painfully apparent. Even as big-hearted a man as Taft could write privately that Wilson had been so intent on "hogging" all the authority that he had broken himself down. An Irish mass meeting in New York City greeted a reference to Wilson's illness with raucous laughter.

The President had earlier told Tumulty, with perhaps a touch of clairvoyance, "People will endure their tyrants for years, but they tear their deliverers to pieces if a millennium is not created immediately."

CHAPTER NINE

THE LIVING MARTYRDOM

"He fell, wounded unto death. He died . . . as much a victim
of the war as the Unknown Soldier who sleeps at Arlington."
THOMAS W. GREGORY *(Wilson's Attorney General),*
January 23, 1925.

1

THE SUPREME tragedy would have been a clouding of
Wilson's splendid mind, but this seems not to have occurred.
He was apparently able to remember and reason as well as
before the stroke, that is, for relatively short periods, then
fatigue overtook him. But while the clarity of his brain could
pass muster, it was evident to those who observed him closely
that he was not the same Wilson. He was more irritable, more
sensitive to criticism, and apt to break down in tears under
unusual emotional strain.

Prolonged illness, accompanied by pain, depression, and
permanent physical impairment, frequently affects the patient's mental fiber. A man's brain may be clear, but he may
be unable, because of his affliction, to work more than a few
minutes a day. A man's brain may be clear, but he may lack
his old energy, his emotional balance, his ability to make
speedy and sound decisions, and above all to provide that type
of vigorous leadership demanded by high executive office.

As a leader, Wilson was never the same again. Something
went out of him; his mental resiliency fled. But his Scotch
stubbornness—the will not to yield—was apparently fortified.
An unkind stroke of Fate had withered one cheek, yet he
turned the good one more resolutely than ever toward his
adversaries.

With glacial slowness the sick man got better. He was permitted to grow a beard and mustache, about which he made

feeble jokes as his strength partially returned. No one was allowed to see him during these early weeks except the doctors and nurses and Mrs. Wilson, with Tumulty hovering about in the anteroom. As the patient improved, Mrs. Wilson read him fiction and light verses, and permitted him to listen to phonograph music.

Gradually, and near the end of the third week, Wilson improved so much that he could give a few minutes to the most urgent matters of state. On October 20, he sent for some public papers; on October 21, he overruled his doctors and prepared a letter to the chairman of the Industrial Conference; on October 22, he was propped up in bed to sign four bills; on October 25, he issued a statement regarding the coal strike; on October 27, he ineffectually vetoed the prohibition enforcement bill (Volstead Act).

An unusual departure from routine came on October 30, when Wilson was allowed for a few minutes to see the King and Queen of the Belgians. The President continued intermittently to transact public business for a short time, and on November 17—a red-letter date in his recovery—he was able to recline in a wheel chair on the White House lawn for the first time since his stroke. Two days later came the momentous vote in the Senate on the treaty.

When there were setbacks, as there were, Wilson could do little or nothing; when there were good days, as there were, he might work as much as an hour or two. But it is clear that from October 2, 1919, to March 4, 1921—a period of a year and a half—the American people had only a part-time President, a shell of the distinguished statesman who returned from Paris in July. He was a sick man with a tired brain.

2

The genius of a Sophocles or a Shakespeare never created a tragedy more poignant than that of Woodrow Wilson. Elevated to a pinnacle hitherto unattained by mortal man, glimpsing the promised land of perpetual peace, he suffered physical collapse, mental aimlessness, political defeat—and lived out the rest of his days in querulous impotence. The Greek concept of nemesis—of lightning striking the proudest tree in the forest—is nowhere better exemplified.

If the President had died that night on the platform in Pueblo, it seems almost certain that the results in the long run would have been happier for all concerned. Wilson himself was a fighter; he had lived a full life; and he could have hoped for no more glorious end than to go out fighting the good fight. Ex-Senator Beveridge, one of the President's most savage critics, later remarked that, had this happened, Wilson would have eclipsed Lincoln as a martyr.

No more dramatic exit from this vale of tears could have been imagined: Wilson actually giving up his life for the League. In all probability the Senate would have been jarred —perhaps shamed—into action. Much of the partisanship would have faded, because Wilson as a third-term threat would be gone, and Vice President Marshall, a small-bored Hoosier, was not to be feared.

Marshall of course would have been President for seventeen months. Having presided over the Senate for more than six years, and knowing the temper of that body, he probably would have recognized the need for compromise, and probably would have worked for some reconciliation of the Democratic and Republican points of view. In these circumstances it seems altogether reasonable to suppose that the Senate would have approved the treaty with a few relatively minor reservations.

If Wilson had been crushed less, he might still have had his old powers of leadership, and perhaps a willingness to compromise. If he had been crushed more, either he or those near him could have accepted the inevitability of resignation with good grace. As it turned out, he could still cling to his office, without the power to lead actively and sure-footedly, but with unimpaired power to obstruct. He experienced what few men ever experience: a living martyrdom. As a dynamic political force, as a doer of great deeds, as the voice of a nation—the old Wilson died in Colorado.

The Fates were unkind to Wilson. Having set the stage for a great martyrdom, they suddenly changed their minds. If he had died, the United States probably would have entered the League, and the League might have been more successful.

But this is all speculation. Wilson did not die until 1924. He lived to attend the funeral of his successor, President Harding.

3

One of the major mysteries of this stupendous tragedy is why Wilson did not resign, or why he was not permitted to resign.

It is evident to the layman, as it must have been to the physicians, that Wilson, if he did recover, would never be more than the ghost of a President. Cerebral thrombosis is a terrible affliction, and not uncommonly recurs. The patient requires complete rest and, above all, freedom from worry and responsibility.

The presidency of the United States is a killing office, especially so since the machinery of government has become infinitely complicated. Experts were beginning seriously to doubt if a man could actually live through more than two terms, when the already crippled Franklin D. Roosevelt came along with an iron constitution and an ability to laugh off cares that would have prostrated an ordinary man. From Grant in 1877, to Roosevelt in 1941, only one man actually served two consecutive full terms; and that was Wilson, who broke before the end.

What Wilson himself thought about resignation, we shall probably never know. His natural tendency was to cling to office; he did not want to be branded a "quitter." The doctors were probably not completely candid in explaining to him the nature of his disability; to have done so might have destroyed the will to live. Wilson was probably led to believe that within a few weeks he would be nearly as well as before, and able to direct the League fight to a successful conclusion.

What all six tight-lipped doctors thought, we shall probably never know. Possibly they disagreed, as doctors will. Mrs. Wilson says that the eminent Dr. Francis X. Dercum advised against resignation, *provided* she would undertake to shield her husband from all but the most pressing business. The doctor reasoned, according to Mrs. Wilson, that resignation would weaken the patient's determination to recover, and that the country needed his leadership.

George Sylvester Viereck, who later saw a good deal of some of the principals in the drama, has an entirely different story. He says that the doctors advised resignation, but that both Wilson and his wife disregarded their advice.

The general circumstances support the Viereck version. It is possible that Mrs. Wilson does not remember accurately what Dr. Dercum told her. To the layman it seems incredible that a distinguished physician could have prescribed anything other than absolute quiet, and a complete sloughing off of all official duties. Dr. Dercum must have been naïve indeed if he thought that the country could run itself indefinitely, or that Mrs. Wilson could keep brain-disturbing decisions away from her husband, or that the country needed the leadership of a broken man.

Mrs. Wilson has been accused of a thirst for power, of a reluctance to relinquish the honor of being First Lady of the Land. It is more probable that since she knew her husband's sensitiveness on the subject of being a "quitter," and realized that his whole life was wrapped up in the fight for the League, she concluded that the shock of resignation would kill him.

This was a decision so cruel and momentous that no interested person should ever be called upon to make it. Loyalty on the one hand to a loved and stricken husband; loyalty on the other to a vexed and leaderless nation—loyalty to one person or to one hundred million persons. "Woodrow Wilson," she writes, "was first my beloved husband whose life I was trying to save, fighting with my back to the wall—after that he was the President of the United States."

4

Mrs. Wilson had to make this decision because the Constitution, in one of its few glaring omissions, gave no one else the authority. Unless this defect is remedied, a similar situation will almost certainly develop again, and possibly under circumstances even more disastrous.

The Constitution clearly states that, upon the disability of the President, the duties of the office shall devolve upon the Vice President. But who shall certify to the disability of the President? There is no answer.

Tumulty records that a few days after Wilson's collapse, Secretary Lansing called to suggest that Marshall be asked to "act in his stead"—presumably until recovery. With a great display of indignation, Tumulty replied (Dr. Grayson agreeing) that he would not be a party to any such act of disloyalty. Tumulty went further and threatened that, if anyone outside the White House attempted to certify to the President's disability, he and Dr. Grayson would repudiate such action.

To the devoted Irish secretary it seemed reprehensible that anyone should take advantage of the President's prostration, and even temporarily fill his place so that the government might function efficiently. Tumulty was willing to perjure himself for his stricken chief. Loyalty won at the expense of the public.

The position of Vice President Marshall was singularly difficult. He was being urged to declare Wilson disabled, and to force his way into the presidential office. His nerves were on edge, because he did not know at what moment he would be called upon to take over onerous new duties, and because the President's condition was carefully concealed from him. A current joke was that the Vice President had nothing to do but push the White House doorbell every morning and inquire ghoulishly after Wilson's health.

Among the President's critics there was some demand that he resign, or that Marshall seize the helm. This demand was strengthened by various rumors as to the extent of Wilson's illness. When the President recovered sufficiently to sign public documents, with a shaky hand which was steadied by his attendant, skeptics scrutinized the signature and wondered whether it was genuine. When the annual message to Congress was submitted in December, observers studied it carefully and concluded that it had not been written by Wilson at all.

Critics like the New York *Nation* remarked that Wilson treated the presidency as an hereditary monarch did his succession: it seemed like a personal possession of the Wilson family. The country was paying $75,000 for a President; it now had what amounted to a pensioned President, with someone else running the government, or the government running itself. To unfriendly observers it seemed like a dog-in-the-manger situation: Wilson could not discharge his duties, yet he would not get out (or Mrs. Wilson would not let him get out) and permit someone else to come in who could. He could not lead aggressively and effectively, but he would permit no one else to lead.

This distressing situation gave rise to various proposals for amending the Constitution so as to establish some kind of jury to determine the disability of the President, consisting perhaps of members of the Cabinet, of the Supreme Court, and of Congress. Several such proposals were actually introduced as resolutions into Congress, but nothing came of them. The American people were not properly impressed with the seriousness of the problem, even when they saw it before their faces. Perhaps some of them felt, as did the Knoxville *Sentinel*, that if Congress shall "pass upon the disability of the President . . . who shall pass upon the disability of Congress?"

5

The United States was virtually without a President for several troubled months, perhaps even longer. It was a period when of all times executive leadership of a high order was needed. Strikes convulsed the country; the treaty fight in the Senate neared its fateful conclusion; and the American peace commissioners in Paris, who were hard at work on the lesser settlements, needed presidential direction. While millions of people cried for bread and peace, the President lay inert, and the government functioned at slow motion or not at all. Events were controlling decisions, rather than decisions controlling events.

Wilson was undoubtedly incapacitated within the plain meaning of the Constitution. He was unable to discharge some of the simplest duties of his high office; or at least the guardians of the bedchamber did not feel that he was strong enough to be bothered with them. Senators could not see him about the crucial treaty struggle, but the King and Queen of the Belgians and the young Prince of Wales (who later yielded his throne for the woman he loved) were shown in for a few minutes. These conversations, of course, were but embarrassed chitchat.

While the White House remained a hospital, twenty-eight bills became law after the expiration of the ten-day period prescribed by the Constitution. Wilson presumably was too weak to sign them, or did not have the mental energy to study them and decide what action to take.

Secretary of the Interior Lane had been offered several positions paying $50,000 or more a year. He was eager to accept one of them so as to repair his shattered private fortunes. But he was unable to see the President and discuss his resignation; and he was unwilling to resign without prior consultation, lest he upset his chief emotionally, and create more wild rumors. This was as late as December 29, 1919—*nearly three full months after the complete collapse.*

An important presidential function is to receive ambassadors; in fact, they cannot officially take up their posts until they are so received. A dozen or so foreign envoys were forced to wait outside the White House gates, among them Viscount Grey of Great Britain, whose vitally important mission will be discussed later.

6

Who ran the government during the interregnum when Wilson was almost completely incapacitated? The answer seems to be that Mrs. Wilson acted as a kind of female regent and supersecretary. In a very real sense she was the first woman President of the United States; at least, she kept up the pretense of the presidency.

Though an amateur in statecraft, Mrs. Wilson undertook her difficult role with the medical advice of Dr. Grayson, and with the loyal Tumulty stationed outside the door. Her chief task was to go over the papers that came to the White House, decide which ones were so important that a decision on them could not be postponed, and reduce them to tabloid form. She would wait for an opportune time, when her husband was having one of his better days, and when Dr. Grayson would approve the intrusion of public business. Then she would present the problem to Wilson for his decision.

During these early weeks Mrs. Wilson scribbled down the President's reactions on small pieces of paper, many of which are preserved among the Wilson papers today. As the President grew stronger, he would scrawl his approval or disapproval on a document, and occasionally add a few remarks in a handwriting which became progressively less shaky.

Mrs. Wilson was undoubtedly a woman of great poise and personal charm, and she tiptoed through her role with commendable discretion. Her warm, womanly hand skillfully erected a Chinese Wall around the White House bedroom, and nursed the invalid back from the shadow of the grave.

But, much as we may admire her loyalty and devotion, we may be permitted to feel less admiration for her competence in political matters. Ill equipped and ill informed, she carried on as best she could.

Outsiders sneered about the "reigning monarch," and the "Woman who was President." She no doubt resented these implications, for in her memoirs she asserts with charming naïveté that she "never made a single decision regarding the disposition of public affairs." "The only decision that was mine," she qualifies, "was what was important and what was not, and the *very* important decision of when to present matters to my husband."

This is incredibly naïve. The proverb tells us that it matters not who writes the laws of a nation if one can only write its songs. It does not matter greatly who is President of the United States if one can decide whom he may see, when, and for how long. It does not matter greatly who is President if one can examine all executive papers, decide which are important, and present these to him in capsule memoranda, possibly not devoid of misinformation and personal bias.

The Cabinet during these fateful months was almost completely ignored, and it found out about Wilson's condition through grapevine channels. Left to its own devices, it met informally from time to time, and thus inspired some public confidence in the workings of the government.

The role of Mrs. Wilson must not be exaggerated. The government ran largely from its own momentum. When Lincoln was shot in 1865, James A. Garfield consoled an audience by saying that, even though the President was dead, "God reigns and the Government at Washington lives." In 1919 Wilson was all but dead, but the government lived. The various departments carried on their work; and that the government functioned as well as it did is a tribute to its toughness and resiliency.

7

Wilson's physical and mental condition had a profoundly important bearing on the final defeat of the treaty.

Protracted illnesses, particularly when accompanied by paralysis, tend to produce melancholy and bitterness. For many weeks Wilson had little to do but lie quietly and brood over the unkindness of Fate and over wrongs, real or fancied. It would have been strange indeed if his thoughts had not turned repeatedly to Lodge and the "bitter-enders," whose opposition had driven him forth to collapse. This may account for what seems to have been a stiffening of his already abnormal stubbornness and inflexibility.

William Allen White surmises, with much plausibility, that as Wilson lay in the White House his mind dwelt on his recent trip, and especially on the grand finale at Pueblo, where the people had seemed to want a League without reservations. But the world had kept moving; things were not as they had been at Pueblo. Wilson's dynamic leadership was gone, and public opinion and the Senate were turning more and more to a League with reservations. But this chilling fact had to be kept from the President. In his weakened condition he could not be told anything that would disturb him unduly; he might burst into tears and suffer a serious relapse. Tumulty was prompt to hasten to him with good news, as when some senator came strongly to his defense on Capitol Hill, and when the crippling amendment regarding Shantung was voted down. Wilson would smile a wan, pleased smile.

Tumulty remembers how he was warned by Dr. Grayson and Mrs. Wilson not to alarm the patient with pessimistic reports; hence he attempted to bring to Wilson "in the most delicate and tactful way" some hint of the atmosphere in the Senate. But the President, like many another man, wanted to believe what he wanted to believe, and such hints seem to have been largely lost on him.

The mail addressed to the prisoner in the White House was rigidly censored. Mrs. Wilson herself carefully sifted the correspondence so that nothing disheartening would shock the patient. H. H. Kohlsaat sent Wilson a letter late in October urging him to accept compromise reservations. Mrs. Wilson promptly returned it unopened, saying that, as she did not know the purport of his message, she assumed that it was not

As the World Sees Us!

(From New York *Evening World*; cartoonist Cassel; reprinted by permission)

important enough to bring to the attention of the President.

Colonel House addressed three important letters to Wilson, urging some kind of compromise. There was no answer, no acknowledgment. Mrs. Wilson disliked and distrusted the Colonel, and his advice did not square with what Wilson wanted to hear. It is altogether probable that these letters were never brought to the President's attention.

Henry White came to Mrs. Wilson and asked her to tell Wilson that it would be necessary to accept some reservations. She seemed disappointed, and accused White of "keeping bad company." It seems unlikely that the message ever reached the secluded President.

Wilson's collapse also deprived him of valuable consultations with the members of his Cabinet. These men were not sycophants, and they probably would have told him bluntly, if they had been permitted to do so, that the deadlock in the Senate demanded some kind of compromise. Their combined voices might have made an impression on Wilson; but they were never given a chance to speak. The first Cabinet meeting did not occur until the treaty had been rejected by the Senate for the second and last time.

Ironically enough, Wilson's personal isolation from his trained advisers and from public opinion accelerated the alarming drift toward national isolation.

8

The disability of the President left the Senate Democrats in a most awkward position.

They were without leadership. If Wilson had been completely incapacitated, they could have worked out a strategy of their own; but, since they did not know Wilson's mind, they could not. More than that, the President, before leaving on his trip, had laid down certain instructions. Until the Democratic senators heard from him again they were bound to follow those instructions, whether such orders fitted the existing situation or not.

Senator Hitchcock was in an intolerable position. Himself an acting minority leader who did not know when he might be displaced, he was trying to cooperate with a President whom he could not visit, the extent of whose disability was unknown, and who might momentarily be replaced by the Vice President. During the crucial month of October, Hitchcock did not see the President at all; during November he apparently consulted him only twice and for brief periods, just preceding the final vote.

Hitchcock, too, was forced to curse the unkindness of the Fates. He picked up what information he could about the President's true condition through the grapevine and through other private channels. That the leader of the minority, the bearer of Wilson's hopes, should have been forced into this position was not the only anomaly that the period presents.

Hitchcock despairingly told A. D. H. Smith: "Well, it looks as though the country would have to struggle along without a President, doesn't it?" And then, striking his hand on the desk, he exclaimed, "What a hopeless situation!"

CHAPTER TEN

THE BATTLE OF
RESERVATIONS

"He [Wilson] can not pass his treaty without some kind of reser-
vations and he should have seen this a month ago." SECRETARY
OF THE INTERIOR LANE, *September 11, 1919.*

I

As WILSON lay on his bed of pain, battling for his very life, the struggle in the Senate over the treaty moved into its final stages.

On September 10 the Senate committee finally relinquished the treaty from the strangle hold which it had been maintaining for the two months since July 14. The majority report, which was signed by Lodge and eight fellow Republicans, is a unique document.

Lodge denied at the outset that the committee had been unduly dilatory; surely it was entitled to a few weeks in which to consider this momentous pact. It was also handicapped by the unwillingness of the President to provide information, and by the necessity of having to ferret out data of its own. And as far as speed was concerned, how about the Allies? Great Britain had "very naturally" ratified at once (a suggestion of sinister British designs); but France, Italy, and Japan had not yet acted.

The popular clamor for haste, continued the report, was largely "artificial." It had been fomented by administration forces, by banking firms (the malign hand of Wall Street), and by the "unthinking outcry" of ignorant but well-meaning citizens who had not read the treaty beyond the words "League of Nations." Yet these were the people who were certain that the pact would bring about a beatific state of "eternal peace."

The cry that speed was necessary to restore our economic structure was just so much nonsense. Trade with Germany had already been reestablished, though on an informal basis.

The "unthinking" supporters of Wilson were crying that no amendments could be added to the treaty because such action would require a reconvening of the entire Paris Conference. This, said Lodge, was not true. The Peace Conference of Paris was still in session, working on the lesser settlements. It could be "at least as usefully employed" in considering amendments as in dividing up the booty of Southeastern Europe and Asia Minor, or handing over friendly Greeks to our enemy Bulgaria, or in seeking to shoulder off onto Uncle Sam burdensome mandates in Armenia, Anatolia, and Constantinople.

Not only was the conference in session, but the German representatives could be summoned once more to Paris. With another unseemly display of sarcasm, the report declared that "the journey is within the power of a moderate amount of human endurance . . ."

The committee then offered forty-five textual amendments, and four reservations, totaling forty-nine, the most important of which were later embodied in the well-known Lodge reservations. In general the committee amendments were designed to safeguard American sovereignty and freedom of action, and to veto a few objectionable parts of the treaty.

The Lodge group was certain that the unamended League was an alliance rather than a league, and that it was a fomenter of war rather than a preventer of war. "Unthinking" zealots were saying that the United States "must" join and "must" do this or that; they forgot that "must" was a word not to be found in the dictionary governing the intercourse of sovereign nations. No one could force us to accept this treaty as it stood, for we sought "no guarantees, no territory, no commercial benefits or advantages."

The majority report ringingly concluded: "The other na-

tions will take us on our own terms, for without us their league
is a wreck and all their gains from a victorious peace are im-
periled."

2

The six Democrats on the committee filed a minority report
which was less vigorous but no less interesting than that of
the majority.

The minority strongly urged prompt ratification without
either amendments or reservations. The long delay in committee had been totally unnecessary, it declared, because the
Republican members had known how they were going to vote
before the discussion began. Industry and commerce had suffered as a result of Senate obstructionism—an obstructionism
which was clearly out of line with American majority opinion.

It was misleading to argue, the report continued, that commerce with Germany had been resumed. Admittedly there
had been about $11,000,000 worth of trade since the Armistice
—or two cents' worth with each German per month. This was
not trade; it was a trickle.

The amendments proposed by Lodge, said the minority,
were worse than useless: they would bring about a complete
rejection of the treaty. It was true that a skeleton peace conference still lingered on in Paris; but Germany had signed,
and we had lost the power to bring her back to sign something
more. We should have to subject ourselves to the humiliation
of going as suppliants to Berlin and of begging for such terms
as our vanquished foes chose to give us.

It was both false and dishonest to say that we sought no
material gain through the treaty. The minority report listed
twelve important items, including valuable trade privileges,
the retention of 500,000 tons of seized German shipping, the
restoration of confiscated American property in Germany, and
a validation of the seizure of $800,000,000 worth of German

assets in the United States. All of these sweeping gains would be jeopardized by a renegotiation of the treaty.

The Republicans, concluded the minority, while seeking out "petty flaws" with a microscope, had nothing constructive to report. The League was the one hope of humanity, and the United States must not fail to throw its full weight behind this noble project.

Looking back on both these reports today, we cannot escape the impression that the Republican effusion was bitterly partisan, offensively sarcastic, somewhat frivolous, and largely specious. It was obviously not directed at the Senate, to which the majority was formally reporting, but at public opinion. Ex-President Taft could hardly believe that a man of Lodge's background could stoop to such "sneers" and "cheap sarcasm."

The Democratic report was also partisan, though less bitterly so, but it was badly out of line with reality in disclaiming the need for any reservations whatever. Yet on the whole it was a more honest and a more factual document.

Curiously enough, a second minority report was filed by Senator McCumber of North Dakota, the high-minded tenth Republican on the committee, who at first opposed all reservations, but who was now presenting six mild reservations. With conspicuous fairness he attacked the offensive partisanship and destructive criticism of his Republican colleagues, while censuring the Democrats for their subserviency to Wilson.

McCumber fortified the position of the Democrats when he pointed out that it would be both time-consuming and difficult to fill out again the skeleton of the conference at Paris. He opposed textual amendments on the ground that other powers would be encouraged to present additional ones of their own. On the other hand, he conceded that the purpose of some of the proposed Republican reservations was unobjectionable, though their tone was "defiant, discourteous," and "overbearing."

Altogether, the McCumber report came as a gust of fresh

air into an atmosphere fetid with partisanship, and remains a tribute to the fairness and balance of its author.

3

Before 1929, treaties were invariably debated in secret session of the Senate, unless by special vote the galleries were thrown open. The Republican majority cleverly arranged to have the Treaty of Versailles discussed in open session. The foes of Wilson realized that a public debate would give them yet another sounding board from which to hammer home their arguments and further confuse the people.

Public sentiment by this time was clearly drifting away from ratification without any reservations whatever. In July, the issue had been: ratification without reservations, or ratification with mild reservations. By September, the issue had become: ratification with reservations, or no ratification at all. As the great majority of the American people clearly favored the treaty in some form, the discussion centered on the kinds of amendments or reservations most acceptable.

The treaty as reported back to the Senate was now taken up section by section. The debate had been going on unofficially since about the previous December, and there was obviously nothing new to be said unless it was false, irrelevant, or unimportant. The senators on both sides had made up their minds how they were going to vote, and the final result could be calculated within just a few votes. Yet while Europe suffered, and the Allies marked time, and the other European settlements were delayed, and the Germans at home and abroad took heart, it seemed as though the Senate were engaged in splitting hairs and then trying to determine which pieces were the thickest.

Outright textual amendments had to be disposed of first. These were highly objectionable to the true friends of the treaty, because they would require a reopening of the negotiations not only with the Allies but also with Germany. Haggling of this kind would mean embarrassment, delay, and a further unsettling of world peace.

Scores of amendments were offered in the Senate, some of vital importance, others of no importance. Senator Sherman, an "irreconcilable," proposed an amendment that would invoke the "gracious favor of Almighty God." This was promptly objected to by Borah, who opposed anything that would seem to imply the blessing of the Almighty on "an infamous Covenant."

All the amendments were voted down by early November, principally because they would necessitate prolonged renegotiation. All were defeated by either comfortable or overwhelming majorities, except the Johnson amendment on six votes to one, which lost on October 27 by a narrow margin of 38 to 40.

The complete defeat of the amendments was a sweeping victory for the Democratic forces, and the news was doubtless enheartening to the sick Wilson. Possibly he took too much encouragement from this victory, and further developed false ideas about the needlessness of compromise.

Significantly, the victory was not won by Democrats alone. It was achieved by a solid block of Democrats (several deserted), with the assistance of about twelve "mild reservationists." The voting definitely proves that even at this late hour the "mild reservationists" were open to reason, and probably to compromise. *Nothing could better high-light the failure of the Democrats to win them over at an earlier date, or the necessity of gaining their votes if unobjectionable reservations were to be attached to the treaty.*

4

When the amendments were all rejected, Lodge presented from the Committee on Foreign Relations, on November 6, 1919, a series of fourteen reservations. In their final form these came to be known, somewhat inaccurately, as the "Lodge" reservations. (See pages 387-393 for the complete texts.)

Each one of the proposed restrictions was voted on separately, usually after debate, which in some cases was protracted. Dozens of amendments to the reservations or substitutes for them were presented by various senators, including the "irreconcilables" and the Democrats, led by Hitchcock. All such proposals lost. Only two of the fourteen reservations sponsored by the committee were defeated, but two others on different subjects were proposed from the floor and carried in their places. The Republicans, with the occasional defection of one member, voted as a compact unit for the reservations, while the Democrats, with the defection of from three to ten of their members (counting "irreconcilables" and "pairs"), voted as a group against them.

There can be no doubt whatever that a prompt and unqualified ratification by the United States would have started the treaty and the League more auspiciously, and would have caused us to appear to far better advantage in the international community. From this point of view Wilson was completely justified in opposing all qualifications. But since it was now clear that restrictions of some kind were inevitable, we may profitably examine the Lodge reservations to determine precisely how they affected the treaty.

The Lodge preamble stipulated that ratification by the United States would not become binding until three of the four principal Allied powers had accepted in writing the reservations adopted by the Senate.

As long as there were going to be reservations, much could be said in favor of this proviso. Vagueness and uncertainty are enemies of international accord. It is desirable that all parties to a compact, whether in civil or in international life, know as definitely as possible what they are undertaking to perform. Otherwise there will almost inevitably be false assumptions, friction, charges of bad faith, and perhaps an open rupture.

Yet Wilson, for quite understandable reasons, was strongly opposed to this preamble. He did not want strong reservations anyhow; but to be forced to go to the other powers, and to extort from them a solemn written statement, was humiliating in the extreme. It seemed like international bad manners, but more than that it was a confession that the President, after having drawn up the treaty, could not control the legislative body that was supposed to approve it.

So much for the preamble. The first reservation consisted of two parts, the first of which stipulated that in case of withdrawal from the League the United States would be the sole judge of whether it had fulfilled all its obligations.

This was designed to quiet the fears of nervous souls who suspected that other nations might try to hold us in the League on the pretext that we had not been faithful to our bond. Such an eventuality seemed most unlikely, for in actual practice a powerful sovereign nation is the ultimate judge of these matters. Besides, no weak League could possibly hold a great nation like the United States against its will. Since this was so, no real harm could be done by asserting the general proposition—a proposition which Wilson himself approved in the four mild reservations which he secretly prepared for Senator Hitchcock. (See pages 393-394 for text.)

The second part of the first reservation provided that notice of withdrawal from the League might be given by a concurrent resolution of Congress. A concurrent resolution, as contrasted with a joint resolution, does not require the signature of the President; nor is it subject to his veto.

Wilson was naturally much displeased by this move, for it was clearly another attempt to encroach upon the Executive in his conduct of foreign affairs. It was interpreted by the Democrats as unconstitutional, and also as a direct slap at Wilson. But, as Lodge pointed out, Wilson would not be President after March, 1921, and this limitation would be as binding upon a Republican as upon a Democratic Executive. Yet, whatever the political implications, it seems clear that the machinery set up by the United States for withdrawal would have no real bearing upon the actual functioning of the League.

5

The second reservation stabbed at Article X, and was beyond a doubt the most significant of the fourteen. If it had not been proposed, the senators and Wilson might have been able to compromise on other matters, in which case the treaty would have been ratified. The "heart" of the Covenant—Article X—was the "heart" of the difficulty.

The Lodge reservation to Article X declared that the United States "assumes no obligation" to preserve the independence or territorial integrity of any other country, or to employ the armed forces of the United States for such purpose, *unless* Congress should so provide.

We must note at the outset that the Lodge reservation did not wipe out Article X. This article could still function. The basic general obligation in the first sentence was left untouched. We *might* be willing to cooperate with other nations in employing our army and navy. But first Congress, which under our Constitution possesses the war-declaring power, would have to vote its approval. We could exercise our free choice, as the President himself had told the Senate committee, as to whether to get into the fight or not. But Wilson was unalterably opposed to the Lodge reservation because it specifically removed any *moral* obligation to exercise that free choice against the aggressor. It was, in his mind, a "knife thrust at the heart of the treaty."

It is difficult at this distance to understand why Wilson should have been determined to block all compromise, and with it the treaty, over the Lodge reservation to Article X. Actually, the more important articles which provided the machinery and the teeth of the League were left untouched or virtually untouched.

Pride of authorship, as Lodge suggests, was probably involved in Wilson's thinking. Like other successful authors, he did not care to have editors tamper with his style, and the seemingly clumsy efforts of the senators to change his literary creation were calculated to arouse great stubbornness. Lodge may in fact have had the ingenuity to concentrate his fire on Article X, rather than on the more formidable (boycott) Article XVI, because Article X was more likely to provoke the President into a politically disastrous course.

More important to Wilson, no doubt, was the idea of a *moral* obligation, which he felt was stronger than a *legal* obligation. When aggression occurred, the Council, in the words of Article X, "shall advise" as to what to do, which of course could mean much or nothing. But Wilson hoped that all the League members would be *morally* bound by the pledge "to respect and preserve" the territory and independence of all member states.

Theoretically, as was so often the case, Wilson was on sound ground. In private life a man may find a loophole in a contract; but if he is an honorable man he cannot escape a moral obligation. One of Wilson's great aspirations was to introduce into international affairs the same high standard of ethics that exists in private life among honest men.

This was a noble ideal, but like so many of Wilson's other ideals, it presupposed something for which the world was not yet ready—and may never be. The veriest amateur in diplomatic affairs knows, especially since the Munich surrender of 1938, that moral and even legal obligations may be of no real value unless they are strongly connected with self-interest.

One of the bitterest ironies of this great drama is that Wilson destroyed, or helped destroy, his dream for world peace, because he insisted upon his version of Article X—an article which meant no more than the good faith of the nations subscribing to it and the other articles.

6

The reservation to Article X, from many points of view, was unnecessary. Article X itself may have been unnecessary, as a number of distinguished international lawyers concluded, among them an American, Elihu Root, and a Frenchman, Léon Bourgeois, one of the framers of the League, the first president of its Council, and Wilson's successor as winner of the Nobel Peace Prize.

We have remarked that the unreserved Article X was vague and permissive, and that moral obligations provide a shaking foundation for world order. We should also note that no action could have been taken by the League Council to send American boys to the deserts of Arabia *unless* the vote of our representative was in the affirmative—as it almost certainly would not have been. In short, the reservation was unnecessary, except perhaps to forestall future disputes as to our good faith.

But things that are unnecessary for legal purposes are often necessary for political purposes. Ignorant and designing foes of the League had liberally sown the dragon's teeth of suspicion all over the country. There had to be a reservation to Article X as a sop to the Irish vote: American boys must never be used to crush Erin's coming revolt. There had to be a reservation to quiet nationalistic nerves: American boys must never be "hirelings" of some superstate. These fears were poorly founded, as the subsequent history of the League attests. But they were very real in 1919, and they were shared not only by Americans but by large numbers of Canadians, whose objections were later presented at Geneva.

The "strong reservationists" apparently wanted a reservation to Article X that would be sweeping enough to protect the peculiar interests of the United States, while leaving a substantial part of the article unaffected. On November 10 Senator Borah offered a reservation completely releasing the United States from any *legal* or *moral* obligation under Article

X. This attempt virtually to eliminate the disputed article was snowed under by a vote of 18 to 68, with mostly "irreconcilables" voting in the affirmative.

The Lodge adherents, whatever their motives, were evidently unwilling to kill the article completely, though that is what Wilson thought they were doing.

7

The third Lodge reservation stated that no mandate could be legally accepted by the United States except by action of Congress. This was obviously designed to prevent Wilson or some other President from taking on vexatious obligations in strange parts of the earth.

The mandate reservation, while not flattering to the President's discretion, cannot at this date be regarded as harmful. Mandates would cost money; only Congress under the Constitution may appropriate money; hence no American mandate could exist, regardless of the Executive, without the sanction of the Congress. The reservation was thus a warning to the President not to do what he probably would never have dared to do. As we shall later note, Wilson himself publicly admitted that there was no objection to a frank statement of this principle.

The fourth Lodge reservation declared that all questions pertaining to our domestic affairs were excluded from the jurisdiction, arbitral or otherwise, of any outside body. Also, the United States would be the sole judge of what were "domestic" questions.

This declaration reflected the ancient unwillingness of the Senate to submit "domestic" issues, such as those concerning tariffs and immigration, to the judgment of foreigners. In a sense the reservation was repetitious and unnecessary, for Article XV of the League Covenant (in response to Senate objections) specifically exempted questions of "domestic jurisdiction." But even though repetitious, the reservation could surely do no harm by apprising the outside world of our peculiar position on these matters. Wilson privately conceded this principle in his secret draft of the Hitchcock reservations.

The fifth Lodge reservation specifically exempted the Monroe Doctrine from the jurisdiction of the League.

This was another repetitious qualification, and in that sense unnecessary. At the behest of American and senatorial opinion, Wilson had forced an amendment into the final draft of Article XXI of the Covenant, providing that nothing in the Covenant should affect "international engagements" such as "regional understandings like the Monroe Doctrine . . ."

Lodge, Root, and others condemned these phrases as ambiguous, misleading, erroneous, and "ridiculous." The Monroe Doctrine was not then an "international engagement"; it was the *unilateral* policy of the United States. It was not then a "regional understanding"; it was *our* policy, not that of any region.

It must be conceded that Lodge and his cohorts were correct; but, inaccurate though such descriptive phrases were, the Monroe Doctrine was specifically named and specifically exempted. The famed Doctrine, like the elephant, is difficult to define but easy to recognize when seen—or rather when a situation involving it is seen.

The Lodge reservation was thoroughly unnecessary, except to give assurance to a host of Americans who set great store by the sacred shibboleth without knowing what it meant. In that sense it was thoroughly necessary. This Wilson privately conceded in his secret draft of the Hitchcock reservations.

8

The sixth Lodge reservation dealt with the "scandal of Shantung." It declared that the United States withheld its assent to the articles of the treaty countenancing this arrangement, and reserved full liberty of action in any controversy arising out of them.

This was an anticlimactic conclusion to the months of heated debate over the alleged "surrender" of Shantung province to Japan rather than to China. It was at best a futile gesture. We did not annul the arrangement; we simply refused to recognize it. The reservation would not move a single Japanese out of Shantung or a single Chinese in. Japanese policy in the Far East would run the course marked out for it, perhaps a bit more obdurately now that the senators had offended Japan by their ill informed fulminations against the "rape" of Shantung.

The reservation may have been futile, but it did salve senatorial consciences, and it did provide a sop to American opinion. With unctuous indignation we could declare that we would not be a party to this section of the settlement.

The senatorial reservation on Shantung was not without its ironical aspects. For more than twenty years the imperialistic Occidental powers—Russia, France, Great Britain, and Germany—had been carving out leaseholds and spheres of influence in China. Yet the Senate had not become unduly concerned, and silence is presumed to give consent. Now came the Japanese, who actually belonged in the Far East and who had dispossessed the Germans, and senatorial indignation boiled over.

The shade of Denis Kearney, king of San Francisco Chinese-baiters of yesteryear, must have stirred uneasily as Senator Johnson of California shed crocodile tears over the poor heathen Chinese. Certain cynics even concluded that the sapient senator was less concerned with helping China than he was with helping his presidential prospects. The New York *Evening Post* thought that he had "got all the famous hypocrites from Tartuffe to Pecksniff beaten hollow."

The blaring Borah was moving heaven and earth to stave off any world organization for peace that might get us into the broils of Europe. At the same time he was demanding that we rush headlong into the broils of the Far East in the interests of the underdog Chinese. "We have crawled and cringed long enough," he cried. "I do not anticipate war with Japan, but, if unavoidable, it might as well come now as at any other time."

Senator Johnson to the contrary, China had not lost her

The Discovery of China
(Courtesy of Brooklyn *Eagle*; cartoonist Harding)

sovereignty in Shantung to Japan, and no nation (including ourselves) could be forced under Article X to fight the Chinese in order to keep the Japanese there. German economic rights in Shantung, and not Chinese sovereignty over Shantung, had passed to Japan. The Japanese agreed to evacuate the province in due season, and did so in 1922. The best hope that China had of regaining complete control of Shantung, economic and otherwise, was to enter the League and negotiate on an amicable basis with Japan.

The loud and libelous outpourings of the senatorial "friends" of China angered the Japanese, stiffened Chinese obduracy, and made more difficult the negotiations between Japan and China leading to the final evacuation of Shantung. The Lodge reservation merely added to these difficulties. The Chinese could well pray for deliverance from their "friends" —friends who were more eager to discredit Wilson than Japan, more eager to help the party than to help China.

9

Reservations seven to thirteen inclusive (see pages 389-392 for texts) were all relatively minor, and did not interfere in any substantial way with the functioning of the League or the execution of the treaty. While somewhat ungracious in tone and suspicious in content, they were designed to reassert the primacy of the Constitution and safeguard the functions of Congress.

The fourteenth and last Lodge reservation asserted that the United States was not bound by any action of the League in which any member (with its political satellites) cast more than one vote. This was aimed at the six votes of the British Empire in the Assembly to the one for the United States.

The new six-to-one safeguard was the fruit of many proposed compromises. One bright senator had suggested that we demand forty-eight votes for ourselves—one for each state in the Union. Others urged that our vote be increased to six, while that of the British be reduced to one. (This led one commentator to propose that the vote of Idaho in the Senate be reduced in proportion to its population, and with it the vote of Borah.) Yet in the end it was decided that the British might keep their six votes, but we would not be bound by them.

Why were our fears of the British Empire so grossly exaggerated?

It was assumed that the six British votes would always be cast one way, which did not prove to be the case at all.

It was forgotten that while Great Britain had six votes in the Assembly she had only one vote in the all-important Council. This is what defenders of the League meant when they said that Britain had "six voices but only one vote." Or, as the Little Rock *Arkansas Gazette* put it, "Sort of a parallel to Hi Johnson's status in the Senate."

It was also forgotten that the United States controlled at least six votes in the Assembly through its influence over such "protectorate" nations as Cuba, Santo Domingo, Haiti, Panama, Nicaragua, and Liberia. It is probable that Washington could have "voted" these tiny countries with more consistency than London could have "voted" the component parts of the Empire.

It was also forgotten that on all decisions of substance the one vote of the United States in the Council or the Assembly could block any adverse vote by the British Empire.

There was one valid objection to the six-to-one arrangement. If we were a party to a dispute, our vote was not allowed to count in our favor, and it was conceivable, but extremely unlikely, that all six British votes would be cast against us. Yet the same was true of all other nations, and powers like Italy and France, which were more vulnerable than we, betrayed no undue suspicion.

Thus the Lodge reservation did not wipe out the six-to-one arrangement. It merely declared that in the eventuality that a decision should be rendered against us by British votes, we might refuse to be bound by it.

This of course reflected an unwholesome distrust of our associates in the world of nations. It was an affront to Canada and Australia, both of whom had sacrificed more of their sons on the field of battle than we had. We were clamoring that these highly advanced commonwealths should be denied votes while gladly conceding them to black Liberia, revolutionary Nicaragua, and (as one Canadian journal put it) "the half-caste Greaser republics of the West Indies . . ."

10

It is hard to understand how Wilson could have insisted that the fourteen Lodge reservations, ten of which concerned the League only, completely nullified the whole treaty. Most of the treaty, indeed most of the Covenant, was completely unaffected. No attempt was made to touch the European settlement. While our obligations were somewhat limited under the Covenant, the machinery of the League was left free to function. By refusing to attach any reservation whatever to some of the more important articles, including Wilson's favorite Article XI ("minding other people's business"), the Senate merely underscored its acceptance of them.

It is true that some of the reservations were of no real consequence. One even gets the impression that a few were put in to swell the number to fourteen, and thus offset Wilson's Fourteen Points. But if they were of no real consequence, why become unduly concerned about them?

It is also true that some of the reservations were completely useless—except to pacify public opinion and save senatorial face. But in this sense they were not useless.

It is also true that some of the reservations were repetitious of the Covenant. But surely no real harm could be done by saying in more words and more explicitly what the Covenant said in fewer words and less explicitly.

It is also true that some of the reservations repeated what was already in the Constitution of the United States. Colonel Bonsal, talking with Lodge about these problems, remarked, "It goes without saying." "If it goes without saying," replied Lodge rather tartly, "there is no harm in saying it—and much advantage."

It is true that Congress appropriates money and declares war. There is no harm in saying these things; in fact foreigners sometimes need to be reminded that Congress does not have to honor the commitments of the President.

It is also true that some of the reservations were tactless and offensively worded. Despite the fact that we were wealthy and powerful, they breathed an atmosphere of suspicion, as well as a determination not to be taken into camp by "slick" European diplomats. But foreign peoples had long since become used to our "shirtsleeve" tactics, and we were so rich and our support was so desperately needed that we could afford to indulge in bad manners. Nor was the reservation habit anything new: the Senate had already fallen into it in connection with other treaties.

It is also true that the reservations warned foreigners about our peculiar prejudices. Other nations no doubt had mental reservations which would have come out sooner or later; the American method at least had the merit of candor and of forestalling future misunderstanding as to our position.

Wilson thought that these few ill phrased and largely inconsequential reservations completely killed the 268-page treaty; the Republican majority professed to feel that these same reservations would save the United States from disaster. Nothing could better illustrate the distorting effect of pride, personal prejudice, prerogative, and partisanship.

A few ill chosen words, one way or another, were not going to make or break this great treaty. It was the spirit behind it that counted. If the people of the United States were unwilling to support it, the absence of reservations probably would have availed little; if the American people were willing to support it, the Lodge reservations did not prevent them from doing so.

CHAPTER ELEVEN

THE STRATEGY OF DEADLOCK

"The whole damn thing·has gotten into the maelstrom of politics, of the nastiest partisanship, when it ought to have been lifted up into the clearer air of good sense and national dignity . . ." SECRETARY OF THE INTERIOR LANE, *October 2, 1919.*

1

AS THE day for the showdown vote in the Senate neared, the burning question was: Will Wilson accept the Lodge reservations? This problem is so vital that we shall have to retrace some ground in order to put it in its proper setting.

From the very outset, as we have seen, Wilson was hostile to reservations. They meant either something or nothing. If general and innocuous, they would mean nothing, and hence were ridiculous excess baggage. If they were specific and amendatory, they would involve the humiliation of further negotiation with the Allies, and possibly the even greater humiliation of treating with our once arrogant foe. This would mean further delay, at a time when all Europe was crying for peace; and it might mean, if Germany proved refractory, a complete loss of all our material advantages under the treaty.

Wilson was convinced that to ask for special treatment would cheapen us as a nation, and put us outside the concert of powers just as clearly and definitely as rejection. The brave new League could not start off with promising momentum if we joined half-heartedly, one eye furtively on our associates, the other longingly on the exits. We ought either to go in like a great power, "scorning privileges," or to preserve a dignified aloofness. And staying aloof would both injure our commercial prospects and forfeit our world leadership.

To Wilson the Lodge reservations were cowardly and unmanly. To load ourselves down with qualifications, when not even the tiniest nations were asking for them, would make us the laughingstock of the world. If changes were to be made in the League, we could work for them after we entered, just as our states had done after ratifying the federal Constitution in 1788, and as the League members actually did in amending the Covenant.

Above all, reservations seemed to Wilson like a base betrayal —a betrayal of our honored dead, a betrayal of our war aims, a betrayal of our associates at the peace table, and a breaking of the solid front that had crushed the Prussian threat to Western civilization.

Reservations not only cut Wilson's pride in the nation; they cut his own pride as well. Pride of authorship was hurt by the proposed changes in the Covenant. Pride of prerogative was hurt by the encroachments of Congress on the Executive. Pride of leadership was hurt by an inability to get the treaty approved as signed.

There can be no doubt that personal animus and partisanship in large measure lay behind the Senate reservations. Lodge plainly hated Wilson, and was out to discredit and humiliate him. If Wilson accepted these vexatious qualifications, he would merely be playing into the hands of his archenemy.

And why should he accept such a humiliation when he did not need to? Public opinion clearly favored the League (in some form), and the people ultimately would prevail over senatorial obstructionism.

There was in Wilson a strain of the Scotch Covenanter: having made up his mind that he was right, he saw evil in any other course. Personal pride and ingrained stubbornness partially blinded him to the public weal.

2

Two days after returning home from Paris, Wilson dictated this statement to the newsmen: "The President is open-minded as to every proposition of reasonable interpretation, but will not consent to any proposition that we scuttle." In short, Wilson would accept mildly interpretive resolutions which were not a part of the treaty, and which would not involve the hazards of renegotiation.

Under such encouragement both the Democrats and the "mild reservationists" in the Senate began working on inter-pretive reservations. By mid-August it seemed as though they might be able to get together.

But suddenly Wilson struck a more uncompromising atti-tude. No doubt he was irked by the dilatory tactics of the Senate committee, and by the agitation in the Senate for out-right amendment. Whatever the reasons, he held a conference with Hitchcock on August 15, after which the senator issued a most unfortunate statement.

Hitchcock revealed that Wilson had not changed his posi-tion, but he now felt that even mild reservations "would prove tremendously embarrassing." They would betray half-heart-edness on the part of America. All this talk about reservations, said Wilson, was premature: he was not even considering them; the Democratic senators were not even to think about them.

No less significant were Wilson's views about outright textual modifications. "Both the President and I agreed," re-ported Senator Hitchcock, "that the immediate task is to see to the defeat of the proposed amendments. We've got to re-move absolutely any probability of the dotting of an 'i' or the crossing of a 't.'" Wilson also said (perhaps only half seriously) that, if the treaty was ruined by amendments, he would send Senators Lodge and Knox to Berlin to negotiate another.

Hitchcock was most indiscreet in repeating these statements, even granted that he did so correctly. Wilson was attacking amendments, not reservations; and that he was right is indicated by Republican support in the Senate. But the President's remarks were wrenched from their context. George Harvey and other partisans from then on quoted Wilson as being opposed to *all reservations,* even to the "dotting of an 'i' or the crossing of a 't.' "

The upshot was that, by mid-August, Wilson had stiffened even on interpretive reservations, his followers had become cold to the overtures of the "mild reservationists," the "mild reservationists" were unwillingly being driven into the arms of Lodge, and strong reservations were ultimately welded to the treaty.

3

On August 19, as we have observed, Wilson met with the Senate committee in their historic conference. Possibly in response to the unfavorable reaction to his interview with Hitchcock, he sounded a more conciliatory note, for he agreed to accept purely interpretive reservations embodied in a *separate* resolution.

Shortly thereafter Wilson left for his western tour, and in his speeches he took essentially the same stand. But toward the end he seemed to turn more sharply against reservations, especially at Salt Lake City, when he branded the proposed Lodge reservation to Article X as "a rejection of the Covenant." By this time he was certain that "any reservation" would have to be carried back to all the treaty signatories, including Germany.

Then catastrophe struck, and Wilson was borne back to the White House. His closing speeches on the tour, combined with his subsequent statements, gave rise to the legend that he was unalterably opposed to *all* reservations.

It is not generally known that Wilson, just before leaving

on the western trip, drafted on his typewriter four interpretive reservations which, if necessary, he was willing to accept. (See pages 393-394.) These related to Article X, the Monroe Doctrine, domestic questions, and withdrawal from the League. Wilson gave the reservations to Hitchcock and instructed him to employ them as he saw fit, but not to reveal their source. The senator used them, essentially unchanged, as the basis for four of his five reservations, but the secret of their authorship was carefully guarded for a number of years.

The confidential Wilson reservations, which related to four of the most knotty issues in dispute, are of immense importance in revealing the President's mind. They were not substantially different from the corresponding Lodge reservations, though the latter were more sweeping and more offensively worded. No less significant, the secret Wilson reservations were in essentials so close to the similar reservations being backed by the "mild reservationists" in mid-August as to raise several searching questions. If Wilson could accept his own secret reservations without violating his principles, why could he not have accepted those of the "mild reservationists"? Instead of going West when he was so near this group, why did he not remain in Washington and work out a complete understanding with them?

Up to a point Wilson's strategy was sound. It would have been folly to announce publicly that he was quite willing to accept any kind of amendment. The obvious course was for him to seem unyielding, drive as hard a bargain as he could, and then at the last moment, when there was no danger of more reservations being added, make the grand gesture of accepting the Lodge reservations as of no fundamental importance.

Wilson had played this kind of game before in securing desirable legislation, but it is a dangerous game—a game that demands that one have one's wits about one, and that one observe the play closely at every stage. During the last weeks of the fight the President was a desperately ill man, and he could not watch the maneuvering carefully. He saw darkly through the windows of his sick chamber.

Throughout the entire struggle Wilson was consistent on several counts. He would not accept amendments, and amendments were defeated. He would accept only mild reservations that were not made a part of the resolution of ratification. The Lodge reservations were not mild, and they were definitely made a part of the resolution of ratification.

Some apologists for Wilson claim that if he had not collapsed he would have compromised with Lodge. Perhaps so, but there is nothing to support such a view in his public utterances, in his private papers, or in his character.

4

By the beginning of the third week of November, 1919, the resolution of ratification was moving sluggishly toward a final vote. The Lodge reservations were being voted up, the Democratic substitutes were being voted down.

It was as plain as a pikestaff, and had been for many weeks, that the Republicans, having attached the reservations by a majority vote, could not command the necessary two-thirds vote. The only way the treaty could be approved was for the Democrats to support the Lodge reservations, or for the Republicans to abandon their program and join the Democrats in supporting the treaty without reservations or with mild Democratic reservations.

This latter alternative was plainly out of the question. The country was now demanding reservations of some kind; and the Republicans, after all their talk about "Americanizing" the treaty, could not tamely hoist the white flag. Nor could the Democrats, after all their talk about the Lodge reservations emasculating the treaty, vote with the Republicans. It was bad politics for either side to give in to the other.

Everything depended on the invalid in the White House.

He was still the leader of the Democratic party. If he told the Democrats in the Senate to vote for the treaty with the Lodge reservations, most of them undoubtedly would do so, and the two-thirds majority would be won. If he told them to vote against the treaty with the Lodge reservations, the great body of them would do so, and the treaty would be lost.

Wilson was a sick man and in no condition to direct an

It "Shall Not Pass!"

(Courtesy of Chicago *Tribune*; cartoonist Orr)

intricate parliamentary battle. The Democrats knew this, and at one point it seemed as though their strategy was to delay until the President was well enough to familiarize himself with the situation. If they could get the word of command from him, they could push off onto his bent shoulders the responsibility for their final action.

Not only was Wilson enfeebled in body and weary in mind; not only was he embittered in spirit and unstable in emotion; not only did he have false notions about the public's views on reservations (that Pueblo applause would not stop); not only was he out of touch with the currents of public opinion and with the Democratic leaders in the Senate; not only were his few informants carefully instructed to withhold news that might shock him into a relapse; but the guardians of his bedside continued to censor his mail. This, though desirable from a medical point of view, was, as we shall note, perhaps disastrous from a political point of view.

5

One of the minor tragedies of the major tragedy is that Colonel House was not available to Wilson during these crucial hours.

For over six years House's peculiar talents as an adviser and compromiser had complemented and smoothed the Scotch-Irish traits of the somewhat stiff-necked Wilson. But at the Conference the two men had appreciably drifted apart, and busybodies had widened the gap. Colonel House continued his work in Europe, and did not return to America until October 12, 1919, ten days after Wilson's stroke. House himself was seriously ill, suffering from gallstones and other ailments, and was assisted from the ship to his home in New York.

Late in October, House sent Colonel Stephen Bonsal to Washington to talk with Senator Lodge about reservations. Bonsal, though out of sympathy with Lodge's position, nevertheless found the senator courteous, considerate, and in a mood for compromise. On a printed copy of the League Covenant the scholar-politician added a few words and inserted some others, all of which constituted the minimum he would accept in the way of reservations. These were complementary, relatively inconsequential, and far less binding than the official Lodge reservations which passed a week or two later. It is clear that Lodge, at least at this stage, was more conciliatory in private than in public, that is, if he was acting in good faith and not merely jockeying for further advantage.

Bonsal promptly sent this highly important document to Colonel House, who in turn mailed it to Wilson. The Colonel packed his bags, sick though he was, expecting a summons to come to Washington and work out a compromise with Lodge. The summons never came; the letter was never acknowledged; no action was apparently ever taken as the result of it.

Possibly Wilson rejected the new proposal out of hand on the ground that Lodge was merely up to another of his tricks. Possibly the very name of the senator caused the President to react so unfavorably that he put compromise completely out of his mind. At this date he apparently still thought that he could win the battle by placing Lodge "in a hole" and by forcing the Senate to "take its medicine."

It is also possible that Mrs. Wilson or Dr. Grayson preferred to keep this disturbing document from the President. Perhaps they thought that he was not well enough to consider it—this was about November 4 or 5. Yet the previous week he had chatted with the King and Queen of the Belgians, and a few days later he had conferred with Senator Hitchcock.

If the Lodge-Bonsal document was received at the White House, as it almost certainly was, Wilson's vice-regents shouldered a grave responsibility in keeping it from him—granted that they did. If such a decision was made on the ground of the President's ill health, then this is but further proof that he should have resigned. If the decision was made on the ground that Mrs. Wilson disliked Colonel House and distrusted his advice, as we know she did, then she should have resigned along with her husband.

If Wilson received the letter, and took no action on it, whether for reasons of health or personal pique, we could want no better proof that he should have relinquished the reins of authority.

Lodge was evidently offended by this episode, as well he might have been if he had acted with sincerity. He had so far unbent as to propose a compromise which was far less drastic than the official committee reservations. For his pains he got nothing but silence.

Four days after the interview with Bonsal, Lodge introduced the reservations that bear his name, and succeeded in carrying through twelve of them.

6

Senator Hitchcock's position was still singularly difficult. He privately confessed to Colonel Bonsal, the day before the November vote, that *he and most of the Senate Democrats favored getting the treaty ratified "in almost any form."* Yet for political reasons they had to oppose the Lodge reservations: Wilson was insisting that they do so.

Hitchcock's hands were tied until he could hear from the titular leader of the party, yet the titular head of the party lay prostrate behind a shroud of darkness. To communicate with him was like trying to communicate with the spirit world.

Finally, on November 7 and again on November 17, Hitchcock was permitted to see the ailing President. The first interview came the day after the Lodge reservations were introduced, and lasted a half-hour; the second came two days before the vote on the treaty, and lasted for about an hour. Each session was carefully supervised by Mrs. Wilson and Dr. Grayson, both of whom were there to shake an admonitory finger. Hitchcock promptly gave accounts of the interviews to the press, and while they were apparently candid, they were a good deal more cheerful than those which the senator later presented in public addresses and private conversations.

During the first visit Wilson was propped up in bed, with his paralyzed arm concealed beneath the covers. Hitchcock was shocked to find that within a few weeks the President had become a white-bearded old man, though his eye was clear and his resolve strong. While Wilson was willing to accept some of the minor Lodge reservations, he would not "budge an inch" on the preamble (acceptance by the powers) and on Article X. When the senator told him that the Democrats could not muster even a simple majority for ratification with-

out reservations, the President fairly groaned, "Is it possible;
is it possible!"

Hitchcock was loath to mention Lodge's name during the
conferences: that was dangerously provocative. He could not
present both sides of the question fully and fairly: that might
shock the President unduly. He was not permitted to argue
with the patient: that might kill him. He dreaded hearing
Wilson speak, because that was final, and the door was
slammed shut on compromise.

Several years later Hitchcock publicly told of one inter-
change:

"Mr. President," I said, "it might be wise to compromise with
Lodge on this point."

"Let Lodge compromise," he replied.

"Well, of course," I added, "he must compromise also, but we
might well hold out the olive branch."

"Let Lodge hold out the olive branch," he retorted, and that
ended it for that day, for he was too sick a man to argue with in
the presence of his anxious doctor and his more anxious wife.

In the two interviews Hitchcock outlined his strategy, and
he reported to the press that Wilson had given it his full approval. The Democratic senators would unite to vote down
the treaty with the attached Lodge reservations. Then through
a favorable though questionable ruling by Vice President
Marshall, they would carry a vote to reconsider, and move for
the treaty without reservations or with the Hitchcock (Wilson)
interpretive reservations, regarding which the President had
given the Democratic leaders a free hand.

This scheme would work if enough "mild reservationists"
and others came over to make a two-thirds vote. But if it did
not work, then there would be deadlock, and the heat of public opinion (so Wilson hoped) would beat so heavily on both
the "mild" and the "strong" reservationists that they would
bolt to the Democrats and work out some kind of compromise.
But first there had to be deadlock before there could be the
kind of compromise that the Democrats would accept.

Wilson bluntly told Hitchcock on November 17 that the Lodge reservations were a "nullification" of the treaty, and that if they came to him he would pocket the whole thing. The President chose to have the treaty defeated outright in the Senate, with the Lodge reservations, rather than have to assume the responsibility for pigeonholing it himself. When Wilson was told that the Senate might adjourn while the treaty was still deadlocked, he thought that would be quite desirable. "I would like," Hitchcock quoted him as saying, "to have some of the Senators go home to their constituents while the treaty is still pending."

In short, Wilson wanted a deadlock (rather than the Lodge reservations); worked for a deadlock; and got a deadlock. He had unfaltering faith that public opinion would break the deadlock—in his favor.

7

Senator Hitchcock's strategy, as the event proved, was thoroughly bad. There is less excuse for him than for Wilson, because he was in the thick of the combat, knew the temper of the Senate, was familiar with the Senate rules, and presumably was aware of the shifting tide of public opinion.

Ominously, Lodge was saying, and in essence had long said, that if the Democrats would not take the treaty with his reservations, there would be no treaty. Its blood would be on their hands.

Lodge may have been bluffing, but he had the votes—more than a majority of them. And a majority of the Senate could block any motion to reconsider and to take up Democratic proposals. Of course the friends of the treaty still hoped that the "mild reservationists" would bolt, but these "moderates" had been treated so brusquely by Wilson that they were in no mood to help the Democrats out of the hole into which they had worked themselves. Even Hitchcock admitted that he was "taking a chance" in relying on the "mild reservationists."

Hitchcock was taking much more than a chance in counting on favorable rulings by Vice President Marshall. The presiding officer, no matter how sympathetic, could be overruled by a simple majority vote—and the Republicans commanded such a vote.

It is true, as Hitchcock planned and Wilson hoped, that there would be a deadlock if the Democrats refused to support the Lodge reservations. But it is difficult to see what good a deadlock would do Wilson's cause. The country was now weary of talk and wanted action, one way or the other. It also seems reasonably clear that by this time public opinion favored either the Lodge reservations or something rather closely akin to them.

Lodge and his fellow Republicans could not afford to yield; they would lose face intolerably. They had first sought to separate the League from the treaty, and had failed. They had next talked of rejecting the treaty outright, but that was too dangerous. They had tried direct amendments, and had been defeated. They had then added the Lodge reservations, and that was the absolute minimum. They had set out to "Americanize," "Republicanize," and "Senatorialize" the treaty; and they would lose what political capital they had gained if they finally permitted their opponents to dictate a different program.

8

As the time for the fateful vote neared, the situation in the Senate and outside the Senate was complicated in the extreme. Much time was spent in parliamentary jockeying, with the clear intent of throwing the onus for rejection on the other party. Each side was trying to stare the other down. Neither wanted to go into the next political campaign with the dead albatross of a rejected pact tied around its neck.

Lodge was saying that this was the last chance for the Democrats, and he meant it. If they rejected the treaty with his reservations, they would have no way of resurrecting it. "It may lie in the Senate inert," he promised, "but the breath of life will never be put into it again."

The "mild reservationists," angered by repeated rebuffs, were insisting that they would not clasp hands with the Democrats, and they meant it. Though restive retainers of Lodge, they were bound by pride and pledge to stand fast.

Senator Hitchcock was declaring that the Democrats would kill the treaty rather than accept the "nullifying" Lodge reservations, and he meant it. He was still awaiting final instructions from the White House as to how to vote, and the Republicans were taunting their opponents with being such rubber stamps that they could not move until they heard their master's voice. Yet on November 15, four days before final action, Hitchcock wrote to Mrs. Wilson that in the absence of definite instructions he would undertake to have his followers reject the treaty with the Lodge reservations.

The "irreconcilables" were saying that they would vote against the treaty in any form, and no one doubted that they meant it.

Of all four groups, the Democrats seemed the least dependable. The pressure was on them rather than on the Republicans. The Lodge men were proposing something concrete; the initiative lay in their hands; and their reservations seemed to a vast body of Americans like altogether sensible safeguards. The Democrats, rather than the Republicans, were cast in the role of obstructionists.

One of the nightmares of the "irreconcilables" was that the Democrats, under the pressure of this tremendous responsibility, might throw themselves at the last minute into the arms of Lodge, and the treaty would then be approved. This seemed like a very real possibility up to the time of roll call.

To the very end it seemed as though there might be some eleventh-hour compromise that would save face on both sides. It was unthinkable that on an issue of this importance the Senate should throw up its hands and confess that it was impotent. To the very end both Lodge and Wilson seem to have entertained the dual delusion that the other would give way when the showdown came.

Strong pressure was being brought to bear on Wilson to yield ground, though we do not know how much of it reached him. He had reversed himself in the past, on issues like military preparedness and woman suffrage, and the hope was still cherished that he might do so again. The Senate Democrats no doubt would have been pleased with a Wilsonian capitulation, for they were none too comfortable in the role of obstructing the only ratifying resolution that had any chance of passing.

The "mild reservationists" were scurrying about to the very last moment, seeking to bridge the gap—a gap more psychological than actual, more rhetorical then real.

Yet Hitchcock, it seems clear, did not want compromise unless such compromise was a virtual surrender by the Republicans and an adoption of the Democratic program. The Republicans did not want to do this, and they did not have to do it; so they "sat tight."

9

As the zero hour approached, various last-minute attempts were made to induce Wilson to yield or to stand fast.

Herbert Hoover, who had won world-wide fame in Belgium and as United States Food Administrator, sent a long and penetrating telegram on November 19, urging compromise, pointing out that the Lodge reservations were on the whole unobjectionable, and declaring that all these rhetorical matters paled into insignificance beside Europe's need for haste.

Senator Hitchcock seems to have brought no real pressure, either through personal interview or by letter. The nearest he apparently came was on November 18, when he sent to the White House a letter of that date from Senator Walsh of Montana, one of the most intelligent and reasonable of the Democrats. Walsh argued that even though the Lodge reservation devitalized Article X, there was still enough left in Articles XII, XIII, and XVI to provide substance and teeth for the new world organization. Hitchcock significantly added in his covering letter that *many of the Democrats held the same views as those expressed by Walsh.* In brief, these good party men, unlike Wilson, did not think that the Lodge reservations nullified the treaty, but *for the sake of party regularity they would vote as the President directed.*

Why Senator Hitchcock was not more forthright in dealing with Wilson it is not easy to say. He was not a dominating personality, he had political ambitions, and he did not want to shock the President unduly with disagreeable truths. As between the danger of killing the President and killing the treaty, he apparently preferred to take a chance with the treaty.

Incredible though it may seem, even the "irreconcilables" tried to bring pressure on Wilson not to compromise. Senator Borah and his group were desperately afraid that at the last moment Wilson would consent to the Lodge reservations, or some modification of them. The "Idaho lion" sought out Senator Swanson of Virginia, a Democratic wheel horse, and induced him to do what he could at the White House to prevent compromise. This was deliciously ironical: two men teaming up for a common end, the one because he did not want the treaty at all, the other because he wanted the treaty exactly as it was.

Close friends of Wilson, like Bernard M. Baruch, urged compromise, arguing that "half a loaf is better than no bread." Mrs. Wilson also entered the lists, for she felt that with the treaty fight jeopardizing her husband's recovery, nothing mattered but to get it out of the way, even with the hated Lodge reservations.

At the critical moment she went to the President and pleaded, "For my sake, won't you accept these reservations and get this awful thing settled?"

Wilson (according to his wife's account) stretched out his pallid hand and said, "Little girl, don't you desert me; that I cannot stand." He went on to explain that he had no moral right to accept those changes; the honor of the nation was at

"Where Do We Go from Here?"

(Courtesy of Brooklyn *Eagle*; cartoonist Harding)

stake. "Better a thousand times to go down fighting," he insisted, "than to dip your colors to dishonorable compromise."

Mrs. Wilson adds that for the first time she saw the issues clearly. Never thereafter did she plead with her husband to do what was manifestly so dishonorable.

Then, she relates, Wilson dictated his fateful message to the Senate Democrats.

10

Wilson's communication to Hitchcock, dated November 18, was without exaggeration one of the momentous documents of world history. It told the Democratic majority how they should vote, and it spelled the difference between ratification and nonratification of the Treaty of Versailles.

On the question of the Lodge reservations, Wilson minced no words: "On that I can not hesitate, for, in my opinion, the resolution in that form does not provide for ratification but, rather, for the *nullification* of the treaty. I sincerely hope that the friends and supporters of the treaty will vote against the Lodge resolution of ratification.

"I understand that the door will probably then be open for *a genuine resolution of ratification.*"

"I trust that all *true friends* of the treaty will refuse to support the Lodge resolution."

This letter was a direct slap at the "mild reservationists," whose support was not yet considered lost. They were classed as "nullifiers" and not as "true friends" of the treaty. Some of them were "true friends" of the treaty, and they were naturally angered by this tactless and unnecessary blow.

It is clear that Wilson wholeheartedly endorsed the Hitchcock strategy. First there would be deadlock, and out of the deadlock would come compromise, Wilson fondly believed, along lines that he was willing to accept. Then the way would be clear for a "genuine resolution of ratification," that is, a resolution with no more than interpretive Democratic reservations.

Wilson said nothing about pocketing the treaty if it should pass with the Lodge reservations, but the tone of the letter was so uncompromising as to reinforce his previous threats that he would.

Still strong in the faith, Wilson revealed his ingrained stubbornness, perhaps fortified by sickness and seclusion. Not fully aware of the receding tide of public opinion, he had supreme confidence in the righteousness of his cause and in his power ultimately to override the opposition, as he had done before in Congress. Angered by Lodge and his diabolically clever tactics, he permitted the pinpricks of the Republican reservations to blind him to the fact that the great structure of the treaty was virtually untouched.

Wilson was not asked to choose between a whole loaf and a half-loaf, as Baruch suggested. If those had been the alternatives, his choice would perhaps be less open to criticism. He was given three choices: a loaf with a Republican wrapper around it; a loaf with a Democratic wrapper around it (the chances were very slim); and no loaf at all.

Wilson thought he was choosing the Democratic wrapper, while apparently closing his eyes to the strong probability that he would get no loaf at all.

CHAPTER TWELVE

BREAKING THE HEART
OF THE WORLD

"The League was defeated in the United States, not because it was a League of Nations, but because it was a Woodrow Wilson league, and because the great leader had fallen and there was no one who could wield his mighty sword." THOMAS W. GREGORY *(Wilson's Attorney General), January 23, 1925.*

1

THE SCENE was Washington, the hour was noon, the day was November 19, 1919—one year and eight days after the Armistice. The Senate of the United States, with galleries packed and long lines standing out in the corridors, was convening to vote on the treaty.

The country was weary of debate; the Senate was even more weary. Several days earlier Senator Ashurst of Arizona, a Democrat, had loudly objected to further palaver. They had all made up their minds; further talk was just "making mud pies." "For God's sake," he cried, "let us all keep our mouths shut and vote, vote and only vote." (Applause in galleries.)

Last-minute maneuvers had already taken up a part of the morning. The Democrats had just met together in secret caucus, and Wilson's letter, now being published in the newspapers, was read to them. Their great President had asked them to vote down the Lodge reservations, and they would follow the leader. He had taken from their shoulders the grave responsibility of having to make this decision themselves.

The Republican "irreconcilables" had their final hour in court. Brandegee condemned the "pipe dream" of the League, and declared that he would consider himself as a "candidate for a madhouse" if he were to vote for it. Borah conceded that sooner or later the pact would no doubt be approved with reservations—"too soon" to suit him—but he wished it to be known that he still wanted no part of it. Sherman denounced the "boiling hell" of the treaty, and castigated the Covenant as the charter of an "international homicide club." He brought a ripple of laughter from the galleries when he said that he was pleased to follow the advice of Wilson and vote against the pact—the first time he had supported the administration since the Armistice.

Senator Hitchcock presented the final case for the Democrats. He went down the line to show that there was no wide gulf between his reservations and those of Lodge; in fact the Democrats could agree to most of the Lodge reservations in principle, though desiring a more tactful wording. The Republican majority, in his judgment, was using the caucus method of a political convention: presenting a group of reservations with a defiant, take-it-or-leave-it attitude. Let there be, he pleaded, the spirit of give and take; let those on the other side of the aisle who really wanted the treaty get together with the Democrats. (Applause in the galleries.)

Hitchcock's reference to the caucus method was not altogether fortunate. It was common knowledge that the Democrats had met that morning in caucus to follow the bidding of Wilson's letter. Senator Penrose (Republican) spoke up and said that "every Democrat" was "under orders from the White House." Senator Thomas (Democrat) snapped back, "I deny that." Penrose got in the last word by retorting that Thomas was the only one who could deny it.

2

The "mild reservationists" resented both Hitchcock's remarks and Wilson's tactless letter. With flushed face Senator Lenroot warmly rebutted the President's charge that the purely protective reservations were "nullification." He would resign his seat before he would consent to Article X without an adequate safeguard. Specifically, he challenged the Democrats to point out what harm there was in protecting the Monroe Doctrine and domestic autonomy.

Senator Kellogg, another "mild reservationist" friend of the treaty, was also irked by Hitchcock's last-minute appeal for compromise. This came "a little late and with bad grace." For about three months Hitchcock had been saying that there must be no substantial reservations at all; not until November 15—four days before—had he been willing to come out with any, and these did not differ essentially from those of Lodge. It was not true, declared Kellogg, that the Lodge reservations had been written by enemies of the treaty: the extreme amendments and reservations of the "irreconcilables" had all been voted down. The "mild reservationists" had long been trying to get a compromise, but the Democrats had refused to meet them halfway. "I am tired of this sort of talk," Kellogg burst out.

Senator McNary, another "mild reservationist," introduced a statement from the League to Enforce Peace, dated November 18. This highly important pressure group, with Taft at its head, had labored long and earnestly for the League of Nations. Now that the issue was clearly a League with the Lodge reservations or no League at all, it reluctantly declared itself for the Lodge reservations, except for the preamble, which it hoped could be modified so as to permit the silent acquiescence of three powers rather than to demand their written consent.

Senator McCumber, another "mild reservationist" and one of the truest friends of the treaty, had the final four minutes before the roll call. He insisted that as much compromise had gone into the reservations as was possible, while still leaving hope for a two-thirds vote. Turning to the Democrats, he pleaded with them not to retreat because they had suffered "some minor reverses." Will you bring your ship "into port," he argued, "though battered somewhat," or "will you scuttle your ship?"

3

It was now 5:30 in the afternoon, and five and one-half hours had been consumed in final debate. The Senate was impatient for action, and as McCumber took his seat cries of "Vote," "Vote," "Vote," arose from all over the chamber.

The question before the Senate was on approving the treaty with the Lodge reservations attached. The crowded galleries sat in tense silence as the roll was called, and as each senator responded to his name.

The result was then announced: 39 ayes, 55 nays. A murmur swept through the galleries. The treaty with its reservations had lost.

The Republicans (with four independently minded Democrats) had voted for the Lodge resolution of ratification. The Democrats, aided by thirteen Republican "irreconcilables," had voted as a body against it.

Then the parliamentary jockeying began. Hitchcock sprang to his feet and moved an adjournment. He evidently hoped to rally his forces before they could go over to the Republican fold and agree to some kind of compromise. His motion lost, 42 to 51. The "irreconcilables" were now back in their own camp.

Then Hitchcock sought to secure a vote on his own reservations. Vice President Marshall (evidently by prearrangement) thrice ruled favorably on his introducing them, but in each case the decision of the chair was overruled by a Republican vote.

Hitchcock's motion that the treaty be reconsidered with his reservations was next defeated 41 to 50, with the Republicans standing together.

Lodge, still in the driver's seat, then surprised the opposition by permitting another vote on the treaty with his reservations. This time he lost 41 to 51, as compared with 39 to 55 on the first vote. Three more Democrats, faced with the appalling prospect of a complete defeat of the treaty, joined the four who had already bolted.

Lodge then permitted Senator Underwood (a Democrat) to move approval of the treaty without any reservations. The motion was defeated 38 to 53, with all the Democrats (except seven) voting solidly in the affirmative, and with the "irrecon-

Nailed!

(From New York *Evening Telegram*; cartoonist Greene;
courtesy of New York *World-Telegram*)

cilables" joining all their Republican brethren (except Mc-Cumber) in opposition. This was convincing proof of what had been evident all along—that the treaty could not be approved without some reservations.

Now that the Democrats had themselves defeated the treaty with the Republican reservations attached, Lodge made good on his threat that he would permit no further compromise. And he held the whip hand. Senator Swanson (a Democrat) walked over to him and, according to one press report, pleaded: "For God's sake, can't something be done to save the treaty?"

"Senator, the door is closed," replied Lodge. "You have done it yourselves."

After further vain maneuvering, the Republican majority carried a motion to adjourn sine die, with the Democratic regulars in opposition. The latter simply could not believe that Lodge had meant what he had repeatedly said: Either his reservations or nothing. Hitchcock and his following wanted to stay and work for further compromise, even though the hour for compromise had plainly passed.

Thus ended one of the most memorable legislative days in the history of the Senate of the United States. Thus ended the first session of the Sixty-sixth Congress. The Senate had labored for more than four months over the treaty, and finally had to confess that the narrow fissure which separated the two sides simply could not be closed.

4

At first blush it appears that Lodge, the master parliamentarian and the leader of the majority, was a failure. He had been successful in getting his reservations adopted, but on the final vote he fell far short of a two-thirds majority, and substantially short of a simple majority.

Contrary to a widespread misconception, *the treaty was not defeated in November by the two-thirds rule* (though it was to be in March). Neither side was able to command a simple majority for any constructive proposal.

If Lodge was a failure in mustering adequate support for his reservations, he was also a failure in holding the thirteen Republican "irreconcilables" in line. On the crucial votes, they turned against his reservations and went over to the Democrats.

Yet this was a successful failure. Lodge had so deferred to the "bitter-enders" that, even though they deserted him on the final vote, they were with him on other issues. This was the price he had paid to keep them from splitting the party wide open.

If Lodge had really wanted the treaty, he was a failure. But there is serious doubt as to whether he actually did, and it seems clear that he was lukewarm even about his own reservations.

If Lodge did not desire the pact at all, he was a complete success. He had kept the "mild reservationists" from deserting (thanks to the ineptitude of the Democrats); he had kept the "irreconcilables" in the fold on all important issues except the final vote; and he had forced the Democrats into a corner where they had to accept his terms or nothing. And if they accepted nothing, the blame for rejecting the treaty could be thrust onto them.

Lodge did not even permit the Democrats to present the Hitchcock reservations. If he had done so, and the Republicans had voted them down (as they certainly would have done), then the onus would have been shifted from the backs of the Democrats to those of the Republicans. Lodge no doubt thought that the Democrats, when faced with their horrible dilemma, would break and come over to him. But he seems not to have cared a great deal whether they broke or not: either way, the Republicans would make political capital.

Lodge was also a complete success in so far as general party harmony was concerned. Chairman Hays, of the Republican National Committee, was in Washington during the closing days of the fight, collaborating with Lodge at every step. He was apparently not unhappy over the result.

The "bitter-enders" were deliriously happy. Borah proclaimed the result "the second winning of the independence of America," and the "greatest victory since Appomattox." Fearing a momentary defeat through a Democratic bolt, the "irreconcilables" had won a resounding triumph for obstructionism. A group of them met for supper that night with some "strong reservationists" at the home of Mrs. Alice Roosevelt

Longworth. The treaty-scramblers ate scrambled eggs, cooked by Mrs. Harding.

The Republican regulars were not unhappy; they had jockeyed the Democrats into a politically disadvantageous position. Mrs. Longworth found that, now it was all over, they seemed as pleased as the "irreconcilables."

The "mild reservationists" were acutely unhappy, but their anger was directed at Wilson for his stubbornness and at the Democrats for their servile loyalty, rather than at Lodge.

So the Republicans were one big united family. That Lodge should have achieved this result, in the face of serious difficulties, is a tribute both to his skill and to the unwitting collaboration of Wilson and the Democratic minority.

5

Two of the Republican groups require more extended consideration.

The "bitter-enders" have been and still are savagely condemned for their alleged insincerity. They voted to attach the Lodge reservations; then they voted them down.

There is far more to the story than this. The "irreconcilables" did not want any part of the treaty. They did not believe that any reservations, however stringent, could make a silk purse out of a sow's ear. But since the great majority of the Senate favored the treaty in some form, it seemed highly probable that in the end the pact would be approved with some reservations. The aim of the "bitter-enders" was to tack on as drastic reservations as they could get, so that, if and when the treaty was adopted, American interests would have the maximum of protection. In this sense the "Battalion of Death" was sincere in supporting reservations.

The "irreconcilables" have also been blamed for the single-handed defeat of the treaty. Even today one reads how one-sixth of the membership of the Senate forced its will upon the other five-sixths.

This is a perversion of both figures and facts. The thirteen Republican "bitter-enders" alone could not have defeated the treaty. It takes 33 votes (one-third plus one of the full membership) to accomplish this result. The Democrats in many ways were more important. If they had voted for the treaty with the Lodge reservations, *instead of combining with the "irreconcilables,"* the Senate would have approved the pact (on the first vote) 81 to 13, or with 19 votes to spare.

Speaking broadly, there were more important "irreconcilables" than those in the "Battalion of Death." Lodge was an "irreconcilable" in that he insisted on his reservations or nothing. Hitchcock was an "irreconcilable" in that he and his following insisted on nothing rather than the Lodge reservations. Wilson was in some ways the most important of all the "irreconcilables." He insisted that the treaty be ratified on his terms, or not at all. There was too much irreconcilability all around.

When it came to the actual voting, the "mild reservationists" were in some respects more important than the "bitter-enders," and the fact that they have been largely overlooked testifies to the power of noise. We have repeatedly observed that these "middle-grounders," had they been won over by the Democrats, could have voted down the Lodge reservations, and then voted through the milder Democratic reservations. Perhaps the Republican regulars would have defeated the treaty so reserved, but if they had done so the blame for obstructing ratification would have been placed squarely on them rather than on the Democrats.

When the Senate adjourned, two of the "mild reservationists," Kellogg and Nelson, issued a joint statement declaring that they had done all they could to bring about ratification with adequate safeguards for the United States. "As a matter of fact," they concluded, "the Republicans Americanized the treaty and the Democrats killed it."

Privately, the "mild reservationists" expressed themselves more emphatically. Senator Colt exclaimed to A. D. H. Smith: "This is not good politics. It is not good Republican politics.

It is not good Democratic politics. It is not patriotic. It is un-American. We are losing sight of what we have been fighting for . . ."

With tears in his eyes Senator Kenyon of Iowa, another "mild reservationist," told A. D. H. Smith: "I am ashamed and disgusted. I cannot continue a member of a body which can be so small. If this is politics, I'm out of it. I'll get out as soon as I can."

In 1922, two years before the end of his term, Kenyon resigned his seat for the federal bench.

6

Senator Hitchcock and his colleagues prided themselves on having played a creditable role: they had gone down with their colors flying. They had put the odium for defeat, they felt, on the Republicans.

In point of fact their strategy was inexcusably bad. Hitchcock had counted on favorable rulings that were not sustained, on "mild-reservationist" support that was not forthcoming. He could not even muster a majority vote to get his own reservations before the Senate. All this, as we have noted, could have been confidently predicted.

Hitchcock afterward confessed that the one thing he did not foresee was that the Republicans would force an immediate adjournment. He was counting on a deadlock and continued discussion, with public opinion and the logic of the situation forcing his opponents to bend the knee. This strategy, as Hitchcock should have anticipated, also backfired.

The Democratic minority leader also failed to hold his ranks intact; four Democrats broke over on the first vote and seven on the second. Even so, his record was better than that of Lodge, who lost thirteen "irreconcilables." When it was all over, Hitchcock told a reporter, after pointing to the (temporary) division in the Republican ranks, "I think we made a pretty good showing."

It now seems reasonably certain that if it had not been for the rigid bonds of party regularity, more than seven Democrats would have bolted, probably enough to make a two-thirds majority. But held together by partisan loyalty, and specifically directed by Wilson, the Democrats voted the treaty down, in the confident hope that there would still be a chance to "Democratize" it.

The Democrats, now the minority party, recognized the absolute necessity of keeping their ranks solid, of standing behind their great President, and of facing the campaign of 1920 with an unbroken front. The newspaper reporters noted that Postmaster General Burleson, the political wheel horse of the Cabinet, was conferring with Democrats on the floor of the Senate during the day of the voting, presumably beating the waverers into line.

The great majority of the Democrats no doubt wanted the treaty; but for partisan reasons they could not accept the Republican reservations. So they voted the whole thing down. The "bitter-enders" wanted neither the reservations nor the treaty, so they voted the whole thing down. If the "irreconcilables" were insincere, what shall we say about the Democratic regulars?

7

To criticize Wilson is ungracious but necessary. He was a sick and secluded man, poorly advised by Hitchcock.

The President was still counting on an upsurge of public opinion to break the deadlock and bring about ratification with mild Democratic reservations. The upsurge did come, but it had to be more than an upsurge: it had to be an earthquake. Nothing less than that would have forced the Senate to act against its will.

Wilson might have yielded to anyone but Lodge; but to Lodge he could not yield. One evening before the final vote, Senator Watson was at Lodge's home, and he expressed the fear that Wilson might suddenly accept the Republican reservations, and then the United States would be in the League. Lodge replied with a confident smile that Wilson's hatred of him was such that the fear was utterly groundless. Watson demurred that this was a rather "slender thread on which to hang so great a cause."

"A slender thread!" Lodge scornfully replied. "Why, it is as strong as any cable with its strands wired and twisted together."

The longer the struggle continued, the more a refusal to yield became a sacred principle, both on the part of Wilson and on that of Lodge. Warm friends of the treaty, like ex-President Taft, cursed the stubbornness of the "mulish enigma" in the White House.

Wilson's Secretary of Agriculture, David F. Houston, concedes that the President was stubborn, but he asks, were not Borah and Johnson and Brandegee also stubborn?

What the apologists for Wilson often fail to see is that it was not Wilson's responsibility to be as stubborn as or more stubborn than the "bitter-enders." They might with good grace play a purely negative role. His task was to keep things moving, to get measures adopted. His executive leadership was at stake, and here, whatever the reasons, he failed. Deadlock was not to his credit; compromise and achievement would have been.

The champions of Wilson still argue that there was no point in his accepting the treaty with the Lodge reservations, because the three requisite Allied powers would not have approved them. We shall consider this whole problem later, but for the present we may note that these powers were never given an opportunity to accept or reject. This tremendous responsibility the President deliberately took upon himself.

If Wilson had advised his faithful followers to vote with the Republicans, then the problem of acceptance would have been placed squarely in the laps of the Allies. If these powers had rejected our terms, then the position of the Democrats would have ·been immeasurably strengthened, for they could have gloated that this was what they had predicted all along. If the

Allies had accepted our conditions, then we should have been in the League, with reservations which were of no real consequence, and which the Senate subsequently could have softened or eliminated.

The defenders of Wilson also insist that, if he had accepted the Lodge reservations, then Lodge would have screwed on more, until Wilson would have been forced to balk. This contention is no doubt sound for the early stages of the fight, but it falls to the ground when we consider the vote on the final day.

All Wilson had to do at the eleventh hour was quietly to instruct the Democrats to vote for the resolution of ratification with the Lodge reservations incorporated. Had he done so, the resolution would unquestionably have carried. Lodge might conceivably have moved a reconsideration so as to screw on more reservations; but such a gesture would have been so flagrantly obstructive that the Republicans probably would not have dared support it. Besides, the "mild reservationists" almost certainly would have joined with the Democrats to block any such transparent trick.

The fact that the "irreconcilables" were desperately afraid of a last-minute bolt by the Democrats to the Lodge reservations is final proof that the "screw-on" argument is flimsy.

8

We come now to a crucially important point which renders much of the preceding discussion purely academic.

Before his collapse and after his collapse—in private letter, White House interview, and public speech—Wilson made it clear, both explicitly and by indirection, that if the treaty came to him with the odious Lodge reservations attached, he would simply pocket it and not go through with ratification.

We cannot be certain that he would have carried out this threat, because he did not permit the treaty to get to this stage. But it seems likely that he would have done so. He was a stubborn man; he bitterly resented Lodge's tactics; his fighting spirit was aroused. And the events following his collapse strengthened his obduracy.

The outcome, at any rate, was a sad commentary on the functioning of the democratic process under our Constitution. More than 80 of the 95 or 96 members of the Senate professed to favor the treaty in some form, yet they could not muster even a simple majority vote for any constructive proposition. It was legislative impotence at its worst.

A. D. H. Smith relates that a Japanese correspondent for two important newspapers sat next to him in the Senate press gallery on the final day. He continued laughing to himself, quietly and politely. "It iss so fonny," he kept repeating. "It iss so fonny. Why do they do thiss so fonny? You excuss'? But I muss' laugh."

It is fruitless and to some extent childish to try to apportion blame, particularly in exact percentages. The situation was exceedingly complex, shot through with personal pride, prejudice, and partisanship. Much of the final debate was devoted to the possible effects of the Senate's action on the fortunes of both parties—to the battledore and shuttlecock of trying to leave the onus on the other side.

The "bitter-enders" were to blame for thinking that the unfledged League would destroy the United States; the "mild reservationists" were to blame for not overlooking the snubs of Wilson and the Democrats; Lodge and the "strong reservationists" were to blame for their stubbornness and blind partisanship; Hitchcock and the Democrats were to blame for their bad strategy and servile loyalty; Wilson was to blame for his insistence on the whole loaf or none.

If the senators could have foreseen that their vote would mean the eventual defeat of the treaty, and the probable ruin of man's noblest scheme for world peace, they might well have acted differently. But they—at least the Democrats—did not believe that this was the end. We can hardly blame them and Wilson for not having been soothsayers.

There comes to mind the remark of a Frenchman at the time of the French Revolution: "I do not blame anyone. I blame the situation."

9

The Senate had gone home, but the aftertaste lingered. The sorry exhibition of partisanship and impotence made a profound impression, not only at home but abroad.

Strangely enough, the newspapers and other media for expressing public opinion seem not to have been unduly concerned as the momentous vote approached. The debate had been too long dragged out; other diversions had come up, including John L. Lewis' coal strike. The wearied public found it difficult to appreciate the rhetorical difference between the reservations which in Democratic eyes would save the treaty and those which in Republican eyes would save face.

Another distraction was the approaching holiday season; a tremendous splurge of Christmas shopping struck the large cities in November. One enterprising merchant caught the spirit of the hour when he advertised in the Philadelphia *Public Ledger:*

TREATY OR NO TREATY
EVERYBODY MUST HAVE
NEW WINTER CLOTHES

When the results of the voting were announced, the anti-League press naturally broke into extravaganzas of rejoicing. The editorial in the anti-League Boston *Transcript* (Republican) began, "Thanks be to God which giveth us the victory," and went on to rejoice over the defeat of "the evil thing with a holy name." Hearst's Boston *American* reached even dizzier heights:

The treaty is dead!
Thanks and congratulations and felicitations.

Thanks to God, who rules the affairs of peoples and directs the destinies of nations.

. . . .

These are great days for the republic—glorious, gallant, splendid, wonderful days!

They will live forever in the annals of the American people.

. . . .

Thank God, I am an American.

Sober anti-League journals, like the liberal New York *Nation,* were generally pleased over the result, though the *Nation* regretted that the treaty had not been rejected outright on the ground that it was a base betrayal of Wilson's ideals and an unjustifiable imposition on Germany.

A large group of Republican newspapers, many of them genuinely lamenting the result, were disposed to blame Wilson rather than Lodge. The New York *Sun* (Independent Republican) thought that the tragic farce was due to a surrender of American sovereignty in the unreserved treaty, and to Wilson's arrogance in trying to override the Senate.

Ex-President Taft, writing in the Philadelphia *Public Ledger,* blamed Wilson for a failure to effect an early compromise, and for his fatuous belief that by a frontal attack on the Republicans he could reduce a plain majority against the treaty to a two-thirds majority for it. Privately Taft boiled against both Lodge and Wilson, who continued "to exalt their personal prestige and the saving of their ugly faces above the welfare of the country and the world."

The Philadelphia *North American* (Progressive Republican) declared that Wilson had been consistent: his arrogance and unyielding nature had killed the treaty. The New York *Tribune* (Independent Republican), in an editorial entitled "Infanticide," concluded that Wilson was willing to sting his own to death rather than consent to coguardianship. The Boston *Transcript* felt that the responsibility should rest squarely on those Democratic senators who had docilely followed White House bidding.

10

Many sorrowful Democrats bemoaned "the greatest tragedy since the crucifixion of the Saviour of Mankind." Dyed-in-the-wool Democratic newspapers were especially bitter, and they heatedly denied that the fault was Wilson's. The New York *World*, an indefatigable champion of the League, blamed the result on Lodge's "rule-or-ruin" policy. He could not get his reservations through, so he would not let anyone else have the treaty. If partisanship and personal vanity had been subordinated to national needs, agreement would have been speedy.

The Peace Dove That Got Away
(Courtesy of Chicago *Daily News*; cartoonist Brown)

The St. Louis *Post-Dispatch* (Independent, with Democratic leanings) struck the same note under the heading, "THE SENATE'S DISGRACE." The treaty had not been considered on its merits: personal vanity, resentment, malice, and partisanship had brought disaster. Lodge had demonstrated that he could ruin but not rule. If he ran again for the Senate, his platform should be, "He kept us out of peace."

The Atlanta *Constitution* (Democratic) bitterly blamed "a little coterie" of Wilson-haters in the Senate, while the St. Louis *Star* (Independent) was especially savage with the "mild reservationists"—a name which was "a synonym for a plain coward." These men, of all the members of the Senate, merited the "greatest contempt," for "they went the farthest in violating the dictates of conscience."

To other newspapers the issue was not one of simple black and white. The Cleveland *Plain Dealer,* a prominent Independent Democratic paper, thought that both sides were to some extent at fault. The Lodge men were partisan, but the Democrats went to their fall with their eyes wide open. Compromise had been essential from the beginning, and much easier at the beginning than later. Wilson should have recognized at the outset that ratification on his terms, and only on his terms, was an impossibility. Or, as the Boston *Globe* (Democratic) put it, the great fault of the administration lay in not making a timely and genuine attempt at compromise.

The Philadelphia *Public Ledger,* an Independent journal with strong Republican sympathies, felt that the result was a blow at boasted American efficiency; we were discredited in the eyes of the world. Personal vanity and party prejudice were to be found on both sides. Wilson had snubbed the senators, including the "mild reservationists," and they had sunk a stiletto of hate into his sick body.

Other newspapers made much of the fact that only 64 votes were needed for ratification, and 81 Senators had voted for the treaty in one form or another. Surely the sweet reasonableness of compromise—the very basis of our democratic process—would ultimately triumph. The American people were disgusted with an exhibition of partisanship and wounded vanity which left the world in despair.

Many journals declared that the nation wanted peace and the treaty, not deadlock. Public opinion would not let the matter rest in suspense. The Senate sorely mistook the temper of the people if it thought that this was the end. Compromise was still possible, and compromise we must have. Let both Wilson and Lodge retreat from their high ground; let Wilson unbend; and let the Republicans soften the tone if not the substance of their reservations.

So argued the more reasonable editorial commentators.

11

Across the Atlantic, the British were disturbed, but on the whole they seem to have viewed the partisan impotence of the Senate with sorrow rather than with anger. They had been left in the lurch, but they would carry on and count upon the sober second thought of the United States to bring ratification.

The French were profoundly alarmed by the turn events had taken. Obsessed with a passion for security, and relying on the powerful military support of the United States, they condemned American politics, and felt keenly the bitterness of betrayal.

The attitude of the more important French journals toward the Lodge reservations is highly significant, particularly in view of the repeated statements by Wilsonians that the Allies would never accept them. The Paris *Liberté* favored a treaty with reservations rather than none at all. The influential *Journal des Débats* had held all along that, if slightly modified, they did not contradict the spirit of the treaty. The powerful *Temps,* which often spoke for the Foreign Office, took the same line; it believed that the Lodge reservations merely set forth restrictions which would in practice exist anyhow.

By December, and in the face of increasing German arrogance, the *Temps* thought the reservations wise, and to the best interests of France. The French would accept them as they were; the British would probably want to negotiate further over the preamble.

Italy was far less disturbed than France. She was acutely dissatisfied with her meager share of the spoils; she still had unrealized Adriatic aspirations. The withdrawal of America would weaken the concert of powers, and leave Italy in a position to push her demands with greater vigor, as she did.

The shocking decision of the Senate cooled very appreciably the enthusiasm of the recent European neutrals for the League of Nations. They felt that without the powerful participation

of the United States the new world organization would be weak
and fangless.

In China, every single one of the four hundred vernacular
newspapers was reported as having commented favorably on
the refusal of the Senate to "swallow" the "Shantung surrender."

In Japan, the press showed much less concern. It naturally
could not applaud the Shantung reservation, but was inclined
to dismiss it as of no real effect. On the whole, Japanese opinion seems to have regretted the blow to world order administered by the United States.

12

The German reaction to the tragic farce in Washington was
confused and somewhat restrained. A great host of Teutonic
treaty-haters regarded rejection by the Senate as a "tremendous
moral victory"—a step toward final repudiation, as it no doubt
was. Yet those who were hoping for the blessings of speedy and
permanent peace were not sure that any good would come of
America's defection.

The Germans now claimed that the desertion of the United
States altered the fundamental character of the treaty which
they had signed. They had approved it with the understanding
that America would accept membership on the various commissions (including the all-important Reparations Commission); and they had counted on American fairness and disinter-
estedness to soften the execution of the pact. They therefore
requested a modification of the treaty; but the Supreme Council in Paris turned a deaf ear to all such pleas. The fact is that
the Germans would have had to sign anyhow, Senate or no
Senate.

Certain German journals charged that the United States, by
entering the war and blocking all possibility of a negotiated
peace, had turned Europe into a scrap heap. The Americans

had a moral obligation to help pick up the pieces; yet, now that they found they could not keep their tempers long enough to agree on terms of ratification, they were quitting the game and turning their backs on Europe as though it were a pesthouse.

The American desertion no doubt contributed substantially to the further deterioration of the European and Near Eastern situation. In early December, when the Allies attempted to assess damages for Germany's suicidal destruction of her fleet at Scapa Flow, a genuine crisis developed, the worst since June. The Berlin government refused for a time to sign the protocol necessary to make the Treaty of Versailles effective, and it was generally believed that this new flash of defiance was encouraged by the action of the Senate.

Thus the United States continued in the uncertain twilight zone between peace and war. Our material gains under the treaty were left in doubt and perhaps in jeopardy; we were not free to extend credits to Germany, or to resume trade relationships with her. We had impaired our prestige, abdicated our leadership, and had left the world in confusion and despair.

CHAPTER THIRTEEN

THE BIRTH OF A SOLEMN REFERENDUM

"Personally, I do not accept the action of the Senate of the United States as the decision of the Nation." WOODROW WILSON, *Jackson Day letter, January 8, 1920.*

1

THE SENATORS scattered to their homes for a brief vacation prior to the opening of the second session of the 66th Congress, on December 1, 1919. The treaty was left behind, suspended in mid-air. The mountain had labored for more than four months, and had not even brought forth a mouse.

Two days after the last futile vote, Lodge issued a statement to the press, throwing the blame on Wilson and declaring that the reservations were simple, direct, American. There was no more room for compromise. "I wish," Lodge asserted, "to carry those reservations into the campaign." In a word, let the people decide between simple Americanism and overweening Wilsonism.

This was an ominous note indeed. Senator Borah had long been urging that the question be thrust into national politics; Senator Johnson had already begun his bid for the presidency on the treaty issue. But the Republican leaders, not sure about the temper of the country, did not relish the prospect of having to defend themselves against the charge of being treaty-killers. So why not make one more attempt at compromise, and clear the explosive issue away?

Senator Hitchcock publicly rebuked Lodge for his latest maneuver, and declared that the Massachusetts senator was thinking more of politics than of patriotism. Reservations were inevitable, admitted Hitchcock, but they must be framed by the friends of the treaty for the purpose of securing its ratification, and not by the enemies of the treaty for the purpose of engineering its defeat.

Hitchcock appears not to have seen Wilson during the week or two immediately after the crucial vote. The press reported that the senator was invited to the White House, but that the appointment was canceled because of the President's ill health.

The senator nevertheless continued to keep Wilson informed—or at least he continued to address letters to the White House. On November 22 he wrote that the result was not defeat but deadlock: surely it would be possible to work out a compromise among the great majority who professed to favor the treaty. On November 24 he expressed the hope that something might be done with the "mild reservationists," a number of whom were most eager for a settlement. Hitchcock believed that the Democrats could still win, *provided they made concessions which were substantial* but which would leave the League in good working order.

This last assumption was no doubt correct. But it would have been better if the Democrats had made "substantial" concessions before the "mild reservationists" had been driven into the unwelcome embrace of Lodge. Above all, would Wilson ever consent to "substantial" concessions?

2

What were the shattered President's reactions to the Senate debacle?

Mrs. Wilson hesitated to bring him the disheartening news; she feared that the shock might cause a relapse. Finally she went to the bedside and gently explained the situation. Wilson lay there quietly for a few moments, and then said: "All the more reason I must get well and try again to bring this country to a sense of its great opportunity and greater responsibility."

While Wilson lay prostrate, physically unable to lead and temperamentally unable to retreat, Colonel House sent him two highly significant letters, dated November 24 and November 27, 1919. House advised that Wilson, having discharged his duty, leave the responsibility for further action at the door of the Senate. The Democratic senators could be instructed to secure as mild reservations as possible, but in the end to vote for ratification with reservations. Wilson could then dump the whole business on the doorstep of the Allies. If they accepted, Wilson's conscience would be clear; if they refused, his position would be vindicated. If they insisted on further negotiations, these could be undertaken. In any event, the treaty would be put into operation, and Wilson's great Covenant would live.

This scheme seems to have been the only practicable course that could have saved face all around. It was in fact supported by President Polk's way of handling the Oregon treaty of 1846.

Neither of House's two letters was answered or acknowledged. There is good reason to suppose that Mrs. Wilson did not permit her husband to see them. There is also good reason to suppose that Wilson, in his sick stubbornness, would have rejected this advice even if he had been permitted to see it.

3

As the dead line for the annual message to Congress approached, Wilson's feeling of helplessness was further borne in on him. He was physically unable to appear in person, as he had proudly done at the opening of every December session since 1913. He was also physically unable to prepare the lengthy document. The various heads of departments submitted memoranda, which Tumulty dovetailed together, and the whole thing was read to the President and slightly revised in the light of his criticism.

The message, as usual, was received sympathetically by the Democrats, critically by the Republicans. Much of it was obviously not of Wilson's composition. It was devoted almost exclusively to domestic affairs; there was only one vague allusion to the delay of the peace settlement. Many Republicans regarded this as a studied insult.

The ensuing debate over the authorship of the message revived rumors that the President was crazy. It seemed desirable that someone, aside from his intimates, look into the bedchamber and tell the country candidly what was going on.

An excuse was provided by the Mexican muddle, which had reached a crisis after the seizure for ransom of William Oscar Jenkins, United States consular agent at Puebla. Senator Fall of New Mexico pressed a resolution in the Foreign Relations Committee for the appointment of a subcommittee of two to wait on the President, ostensibly to discuss Mexican affairs with him, but actually to discover if his mind was clear. After a heated debate in the committee, the resolution passed by six Republican votes to five Democratic votes.

The two men appointed for this ungracious mission were Hitchcock and Fall. The latter was personally offensive to Wilson. He was a leading "irreconcilable," with a florid manner and with an affectation for the garb of a prosperous frontiersman—clothing which he ultimately exchanged for the more drab habiliments of the penitentiary. His reputation in Washington was unsavory, so much so that it was believed (without foundation) that he actually tore back Wilson's bedclothes to see how much of the invalid was left.

Wilson had been up that morning (December 5), but he was now propped up in bed, in a shaded corner of the room, and clad in a dark brown sweater. Fall brazenly entered with the embarrassed Hitchcock, and after washing his hands with invisible soap in invisible water, smirked, "Well, Mr. President, we have all been praying for you." "Which way, Senator?" shot back Wilson.

The interview lasted forty minutes, and the President bore up well. He seemed to be the brightest and most self-possessed person in the room. Mrs. Wilson hovered near by with a pencil and pad in her hand (this provided her with a good excuse for

not shaking the oily palm of Fall), and scribbled down a summary of the discussion. In the midst of the session, by one of
those dramatic coincidences which occasionally occur, the news
was brought in that Consular Agent Jenkins had been released.

The whole affair was something of a triumph for Wilson: he
had dispelled all doubts as to his sanity. Hitchcock emerged
smiling; and even Fall admitted that the President was able to
handle the Mexican situation. Wilson apparently enjoyed the
episode, which, far from causing a relapse, had something of
a tonic effect.

Nearly three months later, Wilson spoke to Secretary Houston about the "smelling committee" which had come over to
find out whether "he was all there or not." He had been angered by Fall's unctuous reference to prayer. "If I could have
got out of bed," he declared, "I would have hit the man. Why
did he want to put me in bad with the Almighty?"

4

As the "smelling committee" prepared to leave the sickroom, Hitchcock inquired about the future of the treaty. Wilson's reply showed that he had not budged from his earlier
position: the responsibility for the pact, he said, had been
shifted to the shoulders of others (the Republicans), and he
was content to let it rest there awhile.

In the week that followed, Wilson showed marked improvement, and by mid-December he was dressing himself and hobbling around with a cane. These encouraging symptoms of
recovery may have increased his belligerency, for on December 14 a most uncompromising official statement came from
the White House. Sharply rebutting the rumor that the President was preparing to make a conciliatory gesture toward the
Republicans, the declaration continued: "He has *no compromise or concession of any kind in mind,* but intends, so far as
he is concerned, that the Republican leaders of the Senate shall
continue to bear the undivided responsibility for the fate of

the treaty and the present condition of the world in consequence of that fate."

Wilson was evidently still hoping that the righteous wrath of an outraged public opinion would force the Republicans to accept his terms.

The country continued to be concerned over the inability of Wilson and his antagonists to unbend. "Let us take counsel together," the New York *Tribune* (Independent Republican) imagined Wilson saying; "and my idea of counsel is for you to sign here." The Philadelphia *Public Ledger* (Independent Republican), referring to both Wilson and Lodge, declared that each of these gentlemen "must come down from his high horse and get his feet on the ground and face the situation."

Even the Democratic senators were reported to be resentful at Wilson's unyielding statement. It put the party in an unreasonable light before the country, and branded the Democratic senators as traitors if they should turn against their great leader and even consider compromise.

The unfavorable reaction to this latest gesture of defiance made no impression on Wilson, assuming of course that he got some inkling of it. Writing to Senator Hitchcock (through his wife) on December 19, and responding to the overtures of Senator Glass at about the same time, he elaborated his unyielding views.

It would be a serious tactical mistake, Wilson insisted, for the Democrats *to propose* anything; any proposition must come from those senators who had defeated the treaty. Absolute inactivity on the part of the Democrats would be better than mistaken initiative. *No proposal or even intimation of compromise and concession should come from the Democratic side.* Surely there was enough parliamentary skill and ability among the Democrats to force the Republicans to vote on the treaty as it stood, or propose some new course regarding it.

The cloistered President was clearly in an unbending if not belligerent mood. He still failed to see that no amount of technical skill and maneuvering would overcome a hostile majority.

5

While Wilson lay secluded in his darkened bedroom, his brain concocted one of the wildest schemes imaginable. It finally took shape in the form of a document, clearly prepared late in January, 1920, which lies unsuspected among his private papers.

This striking statement was couched in the form of a public appeal, and was directed, as was his ill omened Congressional appeal of October, 1918, to "My Fellow Countrymen." It was unthinkable, Wilson said, that we should withdraw from the concert of enlightened nations. Germany was still technically at war with us; she was open to Bolshevist intrigue; she was raising her head in arrogance because of our desertion of the Allies. None of our war aims could be realized without the treaty and the Covenant.

All this, Wilson continued, was not what the American people desired. He knew that the overwhelming majority wanted the treaty, for he had found abundant confirmation of this view in his "recent" visit to seventeen states. (That "recent" visit had taken place about four months before, and Wilson was unwilling or unable to recognize the subsequent shifts in public opinion.) Yet he was not believed when he said that a majority of the people favored the treaty. It was assumed that he was no longer their spokesman, and that he no longer enjoyed the confidence which they had expressed when they reelected him in 1916.

There was, concluded Wilson, only one way to settle the dispute: direct reference to the voters of the country. Regrettably, the Constitution provided no machinery for such a referendum; but he had devised a method which was both legal and feasible, and he hoped that it would receive public support.

He thereupon boldly challenged all senators who had obstructed the Democratic program in the recent voting—a long list of them was specifically named—to resign their seats and seek immediate reelection on the issue of that record.

Wilson then solemnly promised that if all these senators, or a majority of them, were returned, he would resign the Presidency. Vice President Marshall had in this case agreed to follow suit. The office of President would then devolve upon the Secretary of State, and Wilson would invite one of the Republican leaders to accept that post. (Presumably Secretary Lansing would be induced to resign, or would be dismissed.)

This utterly fantastic scheme was finally pigeonholed, possibly at the insistence of Wilson's most intimate advisers. There was not the slightest prospect of its succeeding. The President completely misjudged the temper of men like Senators Shields and Borah, both of whom had more than four years left in their terms, if he thought that they would bow themselves out of the Senate at his behest. For that matter, would any of them resign? And even if they should, there could be no special elections under the constitutions of many of the states: the governors would have to appoint successors. Yet would the incumbents be reappointed?

The abortive January appeal is remarkably revealing of Wilson's mental processes. It spotlights his lifelong fondness for the parliamentary form of government, and his desire to engraft that form upon the American presidential system. It betrays his inability to shake off the appeal habit, which had backfired disastrously since October, 1918. It underscores his stubbornness, and particularly his quite understandable vindictiveness toward the senators. It shows that the applause of Pueblo was still ringing in his ears, and that he was interpreting that applause to mean no compromise when, as a matter of fact, the country clearly wanted compromise.

6

While Wilson was still toying with the idea of a public demand for the resignation of senators, he decided upon a step which, though less sensational, was more disastrous.

The occasion was the annual Jackson Day dinner in Washington, when the Democrats gathered ostensibly to honor one of their patron saints, the Hero of New Orleans, but actually to sing their own praises and promote their own political fortunes. These annual gatherings were not always love feasts; the fighting spirit of the indomitable Andrew Jackson seemingly brooded over the banquet hall.

Some little while before the memorable dinner, it was made known that the President, though unable to appear, would send over a statement to be read. No inkling was given as to its contents, and the tongues of political wiseacres wagged overtime. No doubt the document would be a ringing challenge to Wilson's senatorial enemies; possibly it would announce his determination to accept a third term and carry on the battle for four more years. The demand for tickets became so overwhelming that the original banquet hall had to be supplemented by another.

The Jackson Day letter—a fourteen-hundred-word document—was edited by some of Wilson's advisers, including Secretary Houston, who found so many errors in the original draft that he could not believe that the President had anything to do with its composition. Houston's corrections were generally accepted, but even the final product, while undeniably Wilsonian in ideas and spirit, was so unlike Wilson in style that it was generally believed to have been prepared for him by other hands.

The letter was addressed to Homer S. Cummings, chairman of the Democratic National Committee, and a spellbinder of considerable ability. On the night of the banquet he read it to a sympathetic audience, which interrupted him time and again with "the wildest enthusiasm."

Wilson declared that America had abdicated spiritual leadership, and that the world had come to dire straits as a result of our dallying. He simply could not believe that the country wished to remain outside the concert of powers which was organizing the League, and he refused to accept the action of the Senate "as the decision of the nation."

He had long asserted that the overwhelming majority of the American people desired ratification, and this impression had been "recently" confirmed by his western tour. He still had no objection to purely interpretive reservations accompanying the act of ratification, but he could not accept those that made it uncertain whether we had "ratified or rejected." We could not rewrite the treaty. We had to *"take it"* without changes which altered its meaning, or *"leave it"*; and if we left it we should have to face the "unthinkable task" of making a separate peace with Germany.

Wilson concluded by saying that his own assertions as to popular approval were not being credited. So, if there was any doubt as to the views of the people, the clear way out was to submit the treaty issue to the voters, and "to give the next election the form *of a great and solemn referendum* . . ."

This appeal was typically Wilsonian in that the President's statement unfortunately left the door wide open for misconstruction. Wilson did not appeal unqualifiedly, as many thought, for "a great and solemn referendum." This was merely implied; it was the only way out "if"—and this was a big "if"—there was any doubt as to what the people thought.

It is a striking fact that some of the ideas and actual phraseology of the Jackson Day letter were taken over from the unissued appeal for the resignation of senators.

7

William Jennings Bryan, the "Peerless One" and three-time nominee of the Democratic party, attended the Jackson Day jamboree. His relations with Wilson had been somewhat strained since his resignation from the Cabinet in 1915 over the *Lusitania* issue, and it was widely believed that he was piqued because Wilson had not taken him to Paris as a peace commissioner. (Wilson had in fact summarily dismissed this suggestion.) Bryan still had a large and worshipful popular following (more Democrats had voted for him in 1896, 1900, and 1908 than had supported the victorious Wilson in 1912), and despite his lack of success at the polls, he was no fool as a politician. He had learned a good deal the hard way.

Like Wilson, Bryan had at first opposed reservations, thinking quite logically that it was better to join the League and work for amendments later. But he was now convinced that the crippling effect of the Lodge reservations was much overestimated, and that without reservations there could be no ratification.

Bryan found himself strongly in disagreement with Wilson's Jackson Day letter, and after it was read he sprang to his feet to express objections in that once magnificent voice. All this talk of a "solemn referendum," he insisted, was complete folly. It was merely delaying the issue; and in the nature of things a presidential election could not be a referendum on a question of foreign policy. The thing to do was to work out a compromise, and get the vexatious issue out of the way before it completely wrecked the party. In a democracy the majority should rule, and the Democrats were merely placing themselves in the position of a filibustering minority.

Bryan's eloquent objections were not too favorably received. The audience was pro-Wilson, and it could not applaud the Commoner for putting ratification with reservations above party loyalty. When he asked if the Democrats could afford to "gamble" on getting control of the Senate and postponing the issue for fourteen months, cries arose of "Stand by the President!" "Stand by the President!" Others yelled, "Go on, Bryan." " 'Ray for Wilson." People jumped up all over the room, while Chairman Cummings impotently thumped his gavel.

There was sound if unpalatable advice in Bryan's unwelcome remarks. He had tried in the campaign of 1900 to get a solemn referendum on imperialism, but the issue had got tangled up with the trusts, free silver, Bryanism, and a host of

Who's Driving?

(Courtesy of Chicago *Daily News*; cartoonist Brown)

other domestic problems. Bryan's words were deserving of respectful attention; after all, he had acquired a good deal more experience than anyone else in losing presidential elections.

8

The Republican party chieftains, as earlier noted, were somewhat reluctant to take the treaty into the uncertainties of a presidential canvass. One exception was Lodge. He had urged that the issue be settled at the ballot box, and it is possible that his challenge had, in part, provoked Wilson into asking for a "solemn referendum."

The "irreconcilables" were overjoyed at the turn affairs had taken; Wilson was playing directly into their hands. Senators Borah and Johnson not only expressed delight—Johnson openly and defiantly accepted Wilson's challenge. The "bitter-enders," with their talents for confusing and distorting issues, could hope for nothing better than fourteen more months in which to plant doubts in the public mind. They could hope for nothing better than to pose as the champions of nationalism versus internationalism, as saviors of the Republic from the machinations of some horrendous superstate.

The Republican and liberal press was on the whole sharply critical of Wilson. Senator Capper's paper, the Topeka *Capital* (Republican), was sure that the President's letter had "spilled the beans" to such an extent that not even his own party leaders were behind him. Elsewhere Wilson was widely condemned for his obduracy. Already some promising compromise negotiations had started in the Senate, and it was feared that the President's obstinate attitude would put an end to them.

Other critics, like the New York *Nation*, pointed to an apparent inconsistency in Wilson's position. He had come home saying that there must be the utmost haste in ratification; speedy action would end labor troubles, revive business, and cure many of the world's ills. Six months had passed since the President returned demanding hot haste. Now he was proposing a scheme which meant postponing the issue until November, and then to the inauguration of the new government the following March—a total of at least fourteen months.

Republican journals rather generally felt that the spirit of Andrew Jackson had guided too closely the pen of Woodrow Wilson. Public opinion, they felt, was demanding a reasonable compromise, and acceptance of that compromise by the President.

9

The Democrats were sharply divided in their reaction to Wilson's appeal for a "solemn referendum." The pro-Wilson

phalanx lined up squarely behind their chief, among them
Senators Hitchcock and Underwood, both of whom desired
Wilson's support for the Democratic senatorial leadership. In
loyal Democratic circles Bryan was regarded as a "sorehead"
who had forsaken principle for expediency, and who was making this "grandstand" gesture in the hope of capturing his
fourth presidential nomination. "Mr. Bryan is indeed a hardy
quadrennial," opined the Philadelphia *Public Ledger* (Independent Republican).

Elsewhere in Democratic ranks there was widespread but
rather grudging support of Bryan. Senators Myers of Montana
and King of Utah openly declared that it would be a great mistake to make the treaty a party issue: Wilson would have a
desperate fight on his hands which would break the ranks of
the Democrats.

An impressive number of Democratic newspapers, some of
them hitherto foursquare in their support of Wilson, declared
that Bryan had sensed more accurately the temper of both the
party and the country. Among them were journals like the New
York *Times,* the Brooklyn *Eagle,* the Hartford *Times,* the
Dallas *News,* and the Montgomery *Advertiser.* The country
was already sick of the much-debated issue, and the thing to do
was to compromise and clear it out of the way. The Democratic
party would cut its own throat if it went before the country
opposing adequate reservations to preserve American sovereignty.

Some of the Democratic newspapers concluded that Wilson
was much too bullheaded, and that there could be no true
referendum in the fiery furnace of a national election. Compromise was the essence of democracy, and a majority of the people
wanted a give-and-take adjustment. The Democratic Hartford
Times went so far as to say that Wilson, through his Jacksonian
opposition to conciliation, was putting himself in the same
category as the Senate "irreconcilables," Brandegee and Borah.

All this was meat for the Republicans. Their editors and car-
toonists had a field day, and again the hawklike features of the

Peerless One sprang into prominence. The Republicans had feared that Johnson and Borah would split the party wide open; instead it looked as though Bryan would split the Democrats wide open and, reversing the tables of 1912, enable the Republicans to win "in a walk."

Bryan in subsequent statements denied that he had broken with Wilson; he differed from him only in method and not in purpose. He could not allow the Democrats in the Senate to go to the country and stand on their record; delay was a "disgrace," and he would not permit his party "to commit this crime" of filibustering until November while the world slipped into the abyss of anarchy.

10

The Jackson Day letter was one of the most reverberating in a long series of Wilsonian blunders. In some ways it was Wilson's worst. It is true that he reaffirmed his willingness to accept mildly interpretive reservations; but many more people doubtless read comments on the letter than the letter itself, and these interpreters made Wilson appear more uncompromising than he actually was. Even so, his position was so unyielding as to cost him the support of many of his most loyal and influential followers.

The letter also had a depressing effect on several attempts at compromise in the Senate which had made promising headway since December. Inasmuch as Wilson preferred a popular referendum to a surrender, why should his faithful followers try to compromise? Push the issue off into the next election, and if things did not go well the reproach could rest on Wilson's frail shoulders. Or, as the Brooklyn *Eagle* put it, the "Congressional motto seems to be, 'Never put off until to-morrow what you can postpone until after election.'"

Clearheaded students of the American political scene shared Bryan's view that it would be impossible to get a referendum on the treaty in a national election. As in the 1918 Congressional elections, Wilson was asking for an electoral mandate when there could be none. The treaty issues were themselves confused; they would be further confused by local issues.

The Cincinnati *Enquirer* (Democrat) concluded that the people were not competent to decide such a complicated ques-

Why Wait Till 1920!

(From New York *Evening World*; cartoonist Cassel; reprinted by permission)

tion. The obvious lack of any machinery for recording a referendum on the treaty issue prompted Senator France of Maryland (Republican) to suggest a resolution providing for a poll on this single issue. Nothing of course came of it. The New York *Evening Post* (Independent) hit the nail squarely on the head when it declared: "To throw the Treaty into the campaign would bring about, not 'a great and solemn referendum,' but a great and solemn muddle."

The situation was further complicated by one inescapable fact which Wilson seems to have ignored all along. It was not mathematically possible for the Democrats to win enough Senate seats in 1920 to command the necessary two-thirds vote. By 1922 it might be possible; but by that time Wilson would presumably be gone, and the issue long since decided.

But would Wilson be gone by 1921? He had not yet declared himself out of the running, and his demand for a referendum in 1920 high-lighted himself as the logical standard-bearer in a cause for which he had already broken his body but not his spirit. This, of course, revived all the fears of the Republican Wilson-haters.

*   *   *

Meanwhile the Allied powers and Germany had come to final terms, and the formal ratifications of the Treaty of Versailles were exchanged in Paris, two days after the reading of the Jackson Day letter. America, the most powerful of them all and a co-author of the pact, was not represented. The bells of London pealed in honor of the peace, but they pealed dismally. The people were not unduly excited. The future did not look bright with America drifting further and further away from the entente which had won the war and which could have guaranteed the peace.

CHAPTER FOURTEEN

COMPROMISE WITHOUT CONCESSION

*"The Anglo-Saxon idea of Government is founded on the prin-
ciple of compromise. No public official can have his own way all
the time."* EX-PRESIDENT TAFT, *January 16, 1920.*

1

THE AMERICAN people have long preened themselves on
their Anglo-Saxon genius for compromise, and their historical
scroll bears the names of such immortal compromisers as Henry
Clay and Daniel Webster. Yet both Wilson and the senators
had been unable to tread in these illustrious footsteps. We had
become the laughingstock of the world, and our vaunted Constitution was seemingly on trial before the bar of international
opinion. American sentiment was plainly disgusted with the
political dodges of both Democrats and Republicans.

A number of distinguished political and educational leaders
urged compromise, among them Taft, Wickersham, Lowell,
and Hoover. An appeal from the League of Free Nations Association urged the President to accept the necessary reservations
and get the treaty into operation; he had done his duty, and any
responsibility for reservations would rest with their authors,
not with him. Among the signers of this appeal were Cardi-
nal Gibbons, David Hunter Miller (Wilson's chief assistant in
framing the Covenant at Paris), Dr. Isaiah Bowman (one of the
leading American experts at Paris), and Ray Stannard Baker,
director of the American Press Bureau in Paris, and destined to
be Wilson's able and sympathetic biographer.

Various other groups and organizations, during December
and January, petitioned for speedy ratification. The League
to Enforce Peace continued its widespread propaganda; uni-
versities, church groups, and labor organizations added their

voices to the swelling chorus. Business and banking leaders pressed for action, among them the mighty J. P. Morgan, whose advocacy evoked new blasts against Wall Street from Borah and others.

Mass meetings of aroused citizens insisted on some kind of agreement. Newspaper editorials, letters to the editor, and letters and telegrams to the senators added to the growing demand. If the rising tide of ink could float the treaty through the Senate, ratification seemed a certainty.

The high point of this pressure agitation came in mid-January and February. On January 13, 1920, the spokesmen for twenty-six organizations, representing twenty to thirty million people, waited on both Lodge and Hitchcock, urging ratification in such form as would not require renegotiation. On February 9, a committee representing twenty-six organizations, with a total membership of fifty million, memorialized both the President and the Senate to compromise their differences. This committee was unable to see any real distinction between the Lodge reservation on Article X and the Hitchcock reservation, the latter of which Wilson was prepared to accept.

This tremendous ground swell was an impressive tribute to the power of public opinion, and to its ability to secure action (if not results) when it makes up its mind that something must be done.

2

When the senators returned to Washington in December, 1919, after having taken a bath in local opinion, the atmosphere on Capitol Hill seemed highly favorable to compromise. There was general agreement that the corpse of the treaty should be brought in for a post-mortem examination, and that an effort should be made to breathe life into it. The Democrats were hopeful that some kind of adjustment could be worked out; the "mild reservationists" were receptive to compromise; and the rank and file of the Republicans seemed agreeable to changes in the Lodge reservations, provided there was enough of the original left to enable them to claim some credit for having "Americanized" the pact.

Outwardly, Lodge was as completely deaf to concession as Wilson. On the eve of the reassembling of Congress he declared that his reservations were the "irreducible minimum," and that any immaterial changes were "foolish and needless." If the President wanted ratification, he would have to accept the Lodge reservations as they stood. The senator was confident that his view reflected that of public opinion, and he was still quite ready to drag the issue into the election of 1920.

Privately, Lodge said that the treaty had been "killed by Wilson," who had been a "marplot from the beginning." The senator was tired of having Taft and others urge him to give ground. "Why," he asked, "do they not put their pressure on Wilson and make him yield?" Lodge thought that the next move was up to the President, but the senator did not think him capable of making a move; his condition was no doubt worse than the White House bulletins indicated.

Neither Wilson nor Lodge would give an inch, and each thought that the next move was up to the other. In such circumstances there can be only disagreement or complete surrender, with an intolerable loss of face to one of the antagonists.

Throughout the month of December various and complicated attempts at compromise were pressed in the Senate. Hitchcock, evidently nettled by all this shilly-shallying, accused Lodge of consulting with the "irreconcilables," who did not want the treaty at all, while declining to consult with the Democrats, who did want it. Lodge curtly replied that this was because the votes of the opposition party were not their own but (inferentially) Wilson's. When the Democrats sprang angrily to their feet to resent this insult, Lodge withdrew his remark. Yet there was enough truth in it to hurt.

The "mild reservationists," who wanted the issue cleared

away before the election, were much displeased with Lodge's obstinacy, and late in December they began to hold conferences among themselves. It was alleged that they were preparing to revolt against Lodge's leadership unless he would make some conciliatory moves. The "irreconcilables," who wanted the issue thrown into the election, were openly threatening to desert the Massachusetts senator and filibuster if he attempted to compromise. Senator Johnson was reported hurrying back to Washington to "stiffen Lodge's spine."

Lodge was evidently back with his tightrope act. If he yielded, the "irreconcilables" would push him off; if he did not, the "mild reservationists" might push him off. The way of both the transgressor and the party leader is hard.

3

If Lodge's position was difficult, that of Hitchcock was hardly less so. Various Democratic senators were bringing pressure to bear on him to yield, and by January 3, 1920, the press could report that four of them were giving signs of revolting from his leadership. Even such stalwart Wilsonian journals as the Cleveland *Plain Dealer* were saying, "Concession there must be, and the first move toward concession must come from the Democratic side."

Yet Hitchcock could not compromise unless Wilson would compromise; with Wilson refusing to make concessions, Hitchcock was not permitted to see him in order to persuade him of the necessity of making concessions. On December 31, six weeks after the rejection of the treaty, the senator was allowed to consult Tumulty for half an hour, after Tumulty had talked with Wilson. This kind of one-way negotiation was highly unsatisfactory, though Hitchcock bravely told the newsmen late in January that he had not seen the President and did not need to see him.

On January 5, 1920, the senator wrote Mrs. Wilson a candid

and somewhat pathetic letter. The thing to do, he said, was to win over the dozen or so moderate Republicans, with at least eight additional recruits. Once this was done, the treaty could be sent to Wilson, Lodge or no Lodge, with reservations that the President might accept. Yet to do this meant concessions, and thus far Hitchcock had "little encouragement" from the President to make them.

Wilson's answer to all such pleas (assuming that he saw them) came in his unflinching Jackson Day letter. He stood exactly where he had stood all along, only he was now suggesting that the issue be tossed into politics.

The Jackson Day letter, while no doubt providing some of the Democratic die-hards with justification for standing pat, spurred the movement for compromise among certain of their associates. These men felt the sting of public opinion, and recognized the folly of trying to solve the problem by pushing it off to the next election. The way things were drifting, neither side could claim political credit from postponement.

4

All this pulling and hauling in the direction of compromise resulted in only one development that seemingly had any real prospect of success. This was the bipartisan conference of senators, which met between January 15 and 30, 1920, apparently at the instance of Senator Owen of Oklahoma, a Democrat.

The group gathered in the committee room of the Foreign Relations Committee, and consisted of four Republicans and five Democrats. The Republicans were New of Indiana, Lenroot of Wisconsin, Kellogg of Minnesota, and Lodge of Massachusetts. None of the true "irreconcilables" was appointed, though Hitchcock regarded Kellogg as the only genuine compromiser of the lot.

The Democrats were Hitchcock, Walsh of Montana, Mc-

Kellar of Tennessee (later involved with the TVA), Simmons of North Carolina, and Owen of Oklahoma. It was unfortunate that such an interested party as Lodge was present, for it seems clear that his heart was not in compromise, and that he was just going through motions for the sake of party harmony and as a sop to public opinion. In any event, this was apparently the first time since the treaty rejection on November 19 that the leaders of the opposing groups were able to get their feet together under a table for full discussion.

The meetings were supposed to be held in secret, but this did not prevent the press from reporting developments in some detail. The "middle-ground" Republicans applied spurs when they threatened, unless the conferees moved rapidly, to call up the treaty and begin the debate all over—a repetitious performance which nobody really welcomed.

The high point of the bipartisan conferences came on January 23, 1920. On that day the "bitter-enders" learned that the conferees were nearing agreement on the points in dispute, and particularly that Lodge was about to break the log jam by working out a compromise with Senator Simmons on Article X.

Borah seized his telephone and summoned a group of "bitter-enders" to his office for a council of war. As the Idaho senator told the story to the present writer in 1937, they selected Moses, as the member of the group who had the most "nerve," to go over to Senator Simmons' office and haul Lodge out of his secret conclave.

Moses soon triumphantly returned with Lodge, who stood there pale and nervous. (Borah had never seen a man look so scared in his life.) Lodge protested, "Can't I discuss this matter with my friends?"

Borah spoke up, "No, Cabot, not without telling your other friends!"

Lodge leaned against the wall for support. "Well," he finally said, "I suppose I'll have to resign as majority leader."

"No, by God!" burst out Borah. "You won't have a chance

to resign! On Monday, I'll move for the election of a new majority leader and give the reasons for my action."

After a prolonged session, Lodge agreed to end his dickering with Senator Simmons on Article X, and the "irreconcilables" thereafter congratulated themselves on having by the narrowest of margins rescued the Republic from complete disaster. Senator McNary, a "mild reservationist," told the present

"Teacher, It Can't Be Done!"

(Courtesy of Dallas *News*; cartoonist Knott)

writer in 1937 that he had in his safe-deposit box a copy of the Simmons compromise resolution with interlineations in the handwriting of Lodge.

The details of Borah's dramatic story were no doubt improved by him with repeated telling. But this much is certain: the bipartisan meeting scheduled for the next day was postponed, and Lodge allegedly told his colleagues that he would never compromise on principle. On January 26, when the bi-partisan committee met again, Lodge was reported to have declared that there could be no concessions on the reservations regarding the Monroe Doctrine and Article X.

On January 30 the meetings broke down completely. Steps were thereupon taken to call up the treaty and to restart the verbiage mill on the floor of the Senate.

Hitchcock flatly announced that definite progress had been made when the conferences were broken up by the "irrecon-cilable" uprising. The committee had tentatively agreed upon a changed preamble and upon all the reservations except those relating to Article X, the Monroe Doctrine, and one or two minor matters. Agreement on Article X was in sight when the end abruptly came.

The assertions of Hitchcock were heatedly and categorically denied by Republican members of the committee, and the upshot is that only a few things emerge with clarity. There was a bipartisan conference; it did discuss certain concessions and tentatively agreed to set them down. Article X was the big stumbling block. The "irreconcilables" did threaten to go on the warpath, but it may be doubted whether agreement was as near as they feared or as near as Hitchcock wishfully thought.

It is also clear that Lodge would go so far as to make certain concessions, such as watering down the preamble and permit-ting withdrawal from the League by a joint rather than by a concurrent resolution of Congress. He was apparently willing to change the phraseology of his reservation on Article X, but he seems never to have been prepared to concede that there was a moral obligation, which was the kernel of the whole controversy.

5

On January 31, 1920, the day after the breakdown of the bipartisan conferences, the London *Times* published a docu-

ment written by an eminent British statesman which had a
vital bearing on the struggle for compromise. Behind th·
statement lies an extraordinarily interesting story.

Some weeks after Wilson had returned from Paris in an
unbending mood, Colonel House and others in London urged
Viscount Grey of Fallodon to undertake a special mission to
the United States with the purpose of putting the President
in a more reasonable frame of mind. Grey was the logical man
for this delicate assignment, for he was by common consent
one of the greatest living Englishmen, and one for whom Wilson had expressed deep admiration.

The ostensible purposes of the mission were to discuss the
Irish question and the increasingly ominous naval race between Britain and America. But there can be little doubt that
the real object was to bring about a breaking of the treaty deadlock. Britain already had a competent minister ad interim in
Washington, and she was able to draw upon a large and well-
trained diplomatic corps for men to handle routine problems.

Grey was nearing sixty, and in 1916 had retired from active
service as Foreign Secretary, weary and in ill health. The world
had grown morally dark for him in 1914, when war came
despite his best efforts to avert it; the world was now growing
physically dark, for he was losing his sight. It is perfectly clear
that this man, broken in health and spirit, who delighted in
the woodlands and bird calls of his home, would not come out
of retirement and undertake a strange mission to a strange
land unless he was convinced that this was an extraordinary
task which only he could perform.

With a twilight world gathering around him, Grey reached
New York the day after Wilson collapsed at Pueblo and began
to enter a twilight world of his own. Grey's rank was that of
ambassador on special mission, but he could not become an
official envoy until he had presented his credentials to a President who was unable to see anyone. So the noble Briton had
to content himself with marking time, pending Wilson's recovery, and during this period he undertook to inform himself

by consulting with senators from both parties, and by trying to absorb all points of view.

Viscount Grey was an experienced diplomatist, and he seems to have moved with great caution. He was reported to have said that he remembered very well the fate of Lionel Sackville-West, the British minister who in 1888 was dismissed by President Cleveland for writing an indiscreet letter interfering with American politics.

6

Wilson did not receive or even see Grey. At first it was clear that he was unable to; but as the weeks wore on, and various visitors appeared at the White House, the suspicion developed that the President did not want to meet him. After about three months of heel-cooling the special ambassador went home, with little to show for his experience but the American point of view and an operation on his eyes which may have postponed the final curtain of darkness.

It seems certain that Wilson was physically able to receive Grey by early January, the time of his departure. A dozen or so visitors had been admitted to the White House, including the Fall "smelling committee." If Wilson could have seen the senatorial inquisitors for forty minutes on December 6, he surely could have seen Grey for a half-hour a month or so later.

Henry White, a Republican and a retired professional diplomat of much experience, privately defended Wilson. He wrote that there were a dozen or so traditionally jealous foreign envoys waiting to be officially received, and their noses would have been put out of joint if the President had singled out Grey for special consideration. This is no doubt true; but Britain was such a great power, and the issues involved were so world-shaking, that Wilson would have been justified in giving offense to a few protocol-bound diplomats.

The President did not even have to go through the boresome routine of receiving Grey with great formality. All the customary flummery doubtless meant nothing to the distinguished statesman. All he wanted was a chance to relay his message, and he could have done this just as well—perhaps better—in a half-hour of informal conversation.

The suspicion is not easily quieted that Wilson did not want to see Grey—or perhaps Mrs. Wilson did not want him to. The real purpose of the special envoy's mission was common knowledge; and the President, who conceived of himself as fighting a holy crusade against the forces of evil, did not want to be talked into what he regarded as base surrender. Grey had moreover been giving a receptive ear to the senators on both sides. Secretary Houston relates that at a dinner in Washington he overheard Grey commenting sympathetically to Lodge on the senator's handling of the treaty. It is likely that such reports got back to Wilson. In his eyes even listening to Lodge was probably a serious offense, as it no doubt was to Houston, who may easily have exaggerated Grey's approval of the senator.

Dr. Grayson later remembered that an indiscreet attaché of the British embassy had been criticizing the President and spreading silly stories about Mrs. Wilson. Wilson attempted to have him removed, but there were objections and delays. Perhaps the President blamed Grey for this failure to secure prompt and satisfactory action.

There is one other disquieting explanation. It is possible that the President's bedside guardians did not like Grey, and that they did not permit Wilson to see him, or persuaded Wilson that Grey's mission was not really important. Mrs. Wilson confesses that she disliked Sir William Wiseman, of the British Embassy, and that it gave her pleasure when the President, just before his disastrous stroke, declined to see him.

If Wilson refused to receive Grey for reasons of health, this is but further proof that he should have resigned. If he refused to see him for reasons of personal pique, or because he was under the influence of advisers with petty spirits, the same conclusion seems warranted.

A final possibility—and the one most creditable to Wilson —is that he hesitated to stir up the anti-British elements in the country by appearing to fall under the influence of Grey. While there is admittedly some force in this argument, it is also true that the Irish and other England-haters were already arrayed against the League; and it is difficult to see how they could have become much more vocal.

7

Grey reached England on January 13, but refrained from public comment until January 31, when it became clear that the promising bipartisan negotiations in the Senate had collapsed. He doubtless had concluded that a premature statement would complicate the controversy by arousing resentment against outside meddling. His medium of expression was a lengthy letter in the London *Times* of January 31, 1920.

This able document is of the highest importance, and deserves much more emphasis than it has yet received. It is the report of a distinguished man, respected for his fairness and objectivity, who had come with the detached point of view of a foreigner, who had listened to the senatorial debates, and who had considered the problem from all angles.

Grey made it evident at the outset that he was speaking as a private individual in the hope of clarifying for the British people the much-misunderstood position of America. Outsiders must be patient and tolerant, he said, for the Senate was an independent body, and its refusal to approve the treaty was not evidence of repudiation or bad faith. While it was true that politics—the curse of all democratic legislative bodies —had entered into the struggle, partisanship was not the sole or even the main cause of deadlock over the League. More vital in Grey's judgment was the persistence of the isolationist tradition, with its fear of foreign entanglements. Also important was the conflict between the executive and the legislative—a conflict which was inevitable under our Constitution.

Without the United States, Grey continued prophetically, the League would lack moral force, and would become merely a league of victorious Allies. Without a real League the old order would return, and America would again be sucked into the European maelstrom. If the United States entered the League as a *willing* partner with *limited* obligations (reservations), this was much better than as an *unwilling* partner with *unlimited* obligations. The proposed reservations were admittedly material qualifications, but those persons who were experienced in statecraft knew that expected dangers often never arise. Hence these reservations might never have to be invoked, and they probably would not weaken the League nearly so seriously as was feared. It would therefore be a mistake to spurn the cooperation of the United States simply because strings were attached to it.

By implication Grey accepted the fourteen reservations, except one. The British dominions, he insisted, could not be deprived of their vote in the Assembly. They would in effect *all* be debarred from voting on an issue that arrayed *one* of them against the United States; and there was no objection to the United States' having more than one vote. But this whole problem could no doubt be solved by amicable negotiation between the two powers.

8

If the Grey letter created a profound impression in England, it was a front-page sensation in the United States. One of the strongest Wilsonian arguments had been that the other powers would reject the Lodge reservations. Now Grey, after presumably consulting the British Cabinet, was saying in effect that the mightiest of our former associates would accept them.

Some of the senators professed no great surprise. They reported that Grey when in Washington had secretly shown them a cablegram from Prime Minister Lloyd George stating that Great Britain would accept reservations. This, they alleged, was the basis for Republican confidence that the Allies would not balk at our terms.

Lodge and his following were jubilant: the props had been completely knocked out from under Wilson and his "subservient" senators. What, the "strong reservationists" insisted, are we waiting for? Why not pass the Lodge reservations without further delay?

The "bitter-enders" like Johnson and Borah were much less happy. Borah found in the Grey letter complete justification for all his fears. Grey admitted that the League was a sharp departure from American tradition—which was what the "bitter-enders" had been contending all along. Grey confessed that once we were in the League the weakening effects of the "American reservations would not be felt in practice"— which merely confirmed the "irreconcilable" suspicion that the Lodge reservations did not erect safeguards enough. Grey conceded that the League could not work without the United States. Hence, declared Borah, the Allies were admittedly bankrupt; they were merely seeking a rich and gullible partner who would carry all the burdens.

The Democrats were crestfallen, and their eyes instinctively turned to the White House for guidance. The Grey letter was clearly in the nature of an appeal to the American people over the head of their ailing President, however much it might be disguised as a simple report to the British public. Such appeals are not regarded as good diplomatic form; ambassadors have been bundled off home for less. But Grey could not be bundled off home; he was already home. He could not be dismissed; he had never been officially received. Yet it was felt that he had been guilty of a breach of etiquette, for he was still technically a special ambassador on leave of absence.

The Republican critics of Wilson remembered that during

the Paris Conference he had appealed over the heads of the Italian authorities to the Italian people. It was ironical indeed that the tables should now be turned. The unrelenting *Harvey's Weekly* poked another sharp jab at the President when it said that not even the League of Nations went so far as to prevent a freeborn Briton from writing to the London *Times* without the consent of Woodrow Wilson.

9

Wilson's inward reactions to the Grey letter were cloaked in official silence. It was reported in the press that he was very angry, and had drafted a rebuke to be secretly presented at Downing Street. The curious were partly satisfied when, on February 5, the White House issued a statement through Tumulty declaring that Grey had acted without consulting the President, and without even letting the President know his views.

The Wilson papers permit us to lift one corner of the veil of secrecy. Among them lies an undated note, written in Mrs. Wilson's hand and evidently dictated by Wilson or prepared at his direction as a White House release. It states that the President was as much surprised as the public by Grey's extraordinary attempt to influence both the Senate and the executive. If, the release concludes, Grey had undertaken to issue such a statement while still ambassador in Washington, his government would speedily have been asked to recall him.

Wiser counsels evidently prevailed, and this stinging reprimand was not published. It would have come with poor grace indeed from one who had less than a year before publicly appealed to the Italian people. It would have seemed a futile act of spite against a man who was not and never had been an official British agent in the United States, and who had not been permitted to convey his message to Wilson. Grey may in fact have been speaking not so much to the British and the American people as to the recluse in the White House.

Downing Street was put in an awkward position. Outsiders naturally took it for granted that Grey would not have made public so important a statement without consulting the British government and perhaps that of France. Prime Minister Lloyd George flatly told the American ambassador that there was no truth in the charge that Grey had shown a cablegram from him to the senators. Lloyd George wanted Wilson to know that he had no knowledge of the Grey letter' until he read it in the London *Times*. (The Prime Minister may or may not have been telling the truth; his reputation for veracity was not good.)

In the same interview Lloyd George made one striking declaration regarding the Lodge reservations. As long as the other powers were not *expressly required to agree to American conditions,* it was up to the United States to determine what restrictions it desired to lay down. Unlike Grey, Lloyd George (if we may believe him) did not even object to the six-to-one reservation.

This statement casts a flood of light on the question of whether or not the Allies would have accepted our terms. Lloyd George's one objection was met when the preamble to the Lodge reservations was amended in March so as to provide for silent acquiescence rather than specific approval.

Even private official utterances like those of Lloyd George were probably rare. Governments have long since discovered that it is dangerous to try to influence pending legislation in foreign countries. But it is highly significant that Lloyd George's views were essentially those of the Grey letter, which probably reflected the general attitude of the British government, and which may well have been framed in informal collaboration with it.

10

The British press welcomed the reverberating letter as on the whole clarifying the situation. The editor of the London

Observer would go even further than Grey: Let the Americans bring over a whole shipload of reservations, with the understanding that they would apply to the other members of the League as well. The London *Morning Post* said that Grey was really proposing that America be allowed to enter the shallow end of the pool, and then gradually work toward the middle.

"Come on In, It Isn't Deep!"

(From St. Louis *Star*; cartoonist Tuthill; courtesy of
St. Louis *Star-Times*)

The uproar on both sides of the ocean gave leading French journals like the *Temps* and the *Journal des Débats* another opportunity to repeat what they had been saying for many weeks. Better the United States with reservations than no United States at all. Inasmuch as these newspapers reflected official opinion, it was assumed that the French government would raise even fewer objections than the British.

Grey, it now seems clear, put his finger on one very fundamental truth. There are always more possibilities than actualities in this world. If one enters an organization with reservations designed to meet every possible contingency, those reservations tend to be forgotten with the passing of time.

The worst fears of those who shied away from the League were proved ridiculous by the event. If Uncle Sam had entered the pool at the shallow end, he no doubt would shortly have found himself moving toward the middle. Ahd when he discovered that the water was not shark-infested, he probably would have ignored the reservations or repealed them. At all events the League would have got off to a far better start with Uncle Sam in the shallow end of the pool, even though loaded down with life preservers.

The upshot of the Grey letter was to strengthen Lodge, throw the Democrats further on the defensive, and portray Wilson as needlessly perverse. If the European nations, who were far more vulnerable than we, did not think that the Lodge reservations crippled the League, then why should Wilson continue to insist that they did?

CHAPTER FIFTEEN

THE NEW
WOODROW WILSON

"I shall always believe ratification would have been possible if Wilson's health had not given way; when that tragedy occurred, not even his best friends could exercise any considerable influence on him." SENATOR GILBERT M. HITCHCOCK, *December 7, 1922.*

1

As THE Senate, under the lash of public opinion, prepared to call up the treaty on February 10, 1920, and renew the seemingly interminable debate, Wilson began to reveal increasing evidences of a marked improvement in health.

The terribly twisted, sunken expression on his face was smoothing out. Gradually more motion returned to his withered arm, and he was able to hobble around more vigorously on his blackthorn cane, which he whimsically called his "third leg." Much of the time he spent in the sun in a wheel chair near the south portico of the White House. The Washington correspondent of the Chicago *Tribune* found him there, hooking his cane to a post, swinging his chair around in a semicircle on the stone flagging, and exclaiming delightedly, "See how strong I am getting!"

By February 10 Wilson's recovery had progressed so far that Dr. Hugh Young of the Johns Hopkins Hospital, one of the attending physicians, could reveal through a reporter for the Baltimore *Sun* that Wilson had suffered an attack of cerebral thrombosis. This rather unusual departure from ordinary professional ethics may have been prompted by the White House, for the doctor's report (assuming that he was correctly quoted) was far more optimistic than the facts seem to have warranted.

By February 19 it could be announced that the President was

at his desk every day at 9:30 in the morning; but how much work he could do was problematical. And on March 3, Wilson went for an hour's motor ride—the first such outing in five months.

2

Politically minded Joseph P. Tumulty had repeatedly urged Wilson to prepare a statement that would expedite the compromise negotiations then being undertaken in the Senate. The President finally acquiesced when on January 26 he sent a letter to Hitchcock, and appended a note (in Mrs. Wilson's hand) saying that it might be published at the senator's discretion. Hitchcock held it back until the eve of the renewal of the debate, and then released it.

At the same time that Wilson sent the statement he returned a proposed compromise on Article X which had been debated by the bipartisan committee. He conceded in the letter to Hitchcock that he could not object to its substance, because he, like the senators, was under oath to observe the Constitution. But he found the form "very unfortunate." Any statement asserting that the United States declined to assume any obligations "unless or except" would "chill" our relationship with the other great powers in maintaining world peace.

Wilson went on to explain that his criticism was happily not all negative. He had gone over the five Hitchcock reservations again (he had drafted the first four), and he was glad to report that he could "accept them as they stand."

In concluding, Wilson affirmed that he had no reason to doubt the good faith of our recent associates; that he hoped the reservation regarding withdrawal from the League would provide for a joint Congressional resolution (which could be vetoed); and finally that he could see no objection to stating that the United States would not accept a mandate without the authorization of Congress.

This letter, though somewhat conciliatory in tone, was not

calculated to promote compromise in the Senate. While conceding the obvious point on the mandates, Wilson stood just where he had stood all along. He would tolerate interpretive reservations, such as those of Hitchcock, but he would go no further. This was where he had been back in November, and even in July. He apparently would not even accept a reservation to Article X that was unobjectionable in substance but "chilling" in tone.

If Wilson stood just where he had stood all along, the country and the Senate did not. Much water had flowed down the Potomac since the previous July. It takes two to make a compromise, just as it takes two to make a quarrel, and if neither Wilson nor Lodge would retreat an inch there could be no real hope of adjustment.

3

Wilson's new access of vigor, and the strengthening of his inflexible attitude, were sensationally high-lighted in mid-February by a public rupture of relations with Secretary of State Lansing.

On February 7, Wilson peremptorily wrote Lansing and asked if it was true that he had been calling Cabinet meetings. Lansing answered that he had frequently summoned the Cabinet in informal conferences during the past months. The members had regarded such gatherings as useful and necessary, and they had not believed that they were acting contrary to Wilson's wishes. Lansing thereupon volunteered to resign if by so doing he could relieve the President of embarrassment.

Wilson bluntly replied that he was much disappointed by the reasons which Lansing gave for usurping authority. The Cabinet could take no official action without the President; hence there was no point in having meetings. Wilson went on to say that these acts of insubordination merely deepened the distrust which he had begun to develop at Paris regarding the noncooperation of Lansing. He would therefore accept the

Secretary's resignation, and would endeavor to find a successor whose mind would run along more closely with his.

Lansing vigorously defended himself in his rejoinder of February 12. He denied that he had usurped authority; insisted that the Cabinet meetings had been necessary and proper; and contended that he would have been derelict in his duty if he had not called them. He had been planning to resign for a long time. He had wanted to at Paris, but had delayed doing so because he had thought it unwise to comfort the enemy and weaken the President's hand by advertising dissension within the ranks. He had wished to leave after the President's collapse, but that would have further shaken confidence in the government. Now that his services were no longer wanted, he could resign with a feeling of "profound relief." This no doubt was true; Lansing had too long been forced to choose between disloyalty and dishonesty.

The next day Wilson formally accepted Lansing's resignation, at the same time conveying best wishes for his future success and recalling most pleasantly "our delightful personal relations." But conspicuously absent was the customary appreciation of Lansing's long and laborious public services.

The President was evidently in an unforgiving mood. When Tumulty remonstrated that in the existing state of public opinion it was the wrong time to do the right thing, Wilson shot back from his invalid's chair, with a flash of his old fire: "Tumulty, it is never the wrong time to spike disloyalty. When Lansing sought to oust me, I was upon my back. I am on my feet now and I will not have disloyalty about me."

4

The publication at Wilson's instance of the correspondence between him and Lansing caused a reverberation throughout the country. The nation was left amazed and regretful at what seemed to be an unbecoming fit of temper.

Wilson remained serene throughout it all. To his secretary he remarked with a smile in his eye, "Well, Tumulty, have I any friends left?" "Very few, Governor," was the reply. Wilson then remarked that the whole thing would blow over in a few days, and that the country would turn against a Secretary who had put his signature to a treaty and then had come home to testify against it.

The country, though shocked, was hardly surprised. Rumors of friction between Wilson and Lansing had long been current, especially after the Bullitt testimony, and the Secretary had actually been forced to deny reports of resignation. It was Wilson's published explanation for his action, rather than the action itself, which deeply disturbed the public. The very fact that the President should have had the correspondence published, evidently thinking that it would vindicate him, is further proof that something had happened to his soundness of judgment.

Mrs. Wilson, with her woman's intuition, claims that she urged him not to send the letter as written, because it did not expose Lansing's more serious acts of disloyalty. To request his resignation because he had summoned the Cabinet would make the President "look small." But Wilson brushed aside her objections.

Most of the friends of Wilson were eloquently silent. Some of the newspapers that had defended him through thick and thin were openly critical. The loyal New York *World* (Democratic) remarked that the President is not obliged to give reasons for evicting a Cabinet officer, but when he does give them, they should be complete. It seems clear at this distance that Wilson would have appeared to better advantage if he had shown Lansing the door for alleged incompetence in handling Mexican affairs, rather than for usurping authority. As long as he was going to give reasons, they should have been good ones, whether the real ones or not.

Several other members of the Cabinet sprang to the defense of their colleague when they testified that they were equally guilty in arranging for meetings. In the public eye Lansing became something of a martyr, especially among those unfriendly to Wilson. His chief sin had apparently been to do his duty and serve the country in difficult circumstances. Lansing remained something of a martyr until he published his book about a year later, and then it became evident that he should have left much sooner than he did.

Discerning observers knew that Cabinet meetings in the absence of the President were not altogether without precedent, and that, Wilson to the contrary, such meetings could be useful in promoting an exchange of information and in making informal decisions. Besides, it was extremely desirable that public confidence in the government be bolstered. Lansing conferred a great favor on Wilson, for which he was ill repaid, by arranging for Cabinet sessions; otherwise public opinion might have risen up in its might and demanded the resignation of the incapacitated President and the installation of Vice President Marshall.

5

The unfortunate public quarrel with Lansing raised even more serious questions about the President's candor and his physical and mental health.

Wilson did not say in his letter that he had just heard of the unauthorized Cabinet meetings. He merely asked Lansing if the report was true, the implication being that he had but recently learned of them. This, as we now know, was false. At the very first meeting, that of October 6, Dr. Grayson appeared and (according to Secretary Houston) reported that Wilson was irked because of this evidence of independent action.

It was common knowledge that the Cabinet had met about twenty-five times. If, the public felt, Wilson had not until very recently had any hint of this, then an investigation had better be started to find out who was running the government.

Less defensible in some eyes was the arbitrary and even dictatorial tone of Wilson's letters. "That thrombosis," jocu-

larly observed one southern newspaper, "evidently has not
affected the President's kicking foot." The Secretary of State,
whatever his shortcomings, occupies what is commonly regarded as the most distinguished appointive administrative
post in the United States—a position second in importance only
to the Presidency. Lansing had served long and diligently in

Dropping the First Mate

(Courtesy of St. Louis *Post-Dispatch*; cartoonist Fitzpatrick)

the Department of State, and his reward was to be dismissed
as brutally as if he had been an insolent filing clerk.

If Wilson's friends were speechless or openly distressed, his
enemies enjoyed a field day. Even more moderate critics regretted that he had not appeared to better advantage. *Harvey's
Weekly* cried that the President had gone completely "mad."

It was widely felt that this latest exhibition of Wilsonism
went far beyond mere petulance; perhaps it was the result of

the thrombosis. The President's position seemed to be the dog-in-the-mangerish one that he would not tolerate having anyone share his authority. If he could not run the Cabinet, then the Cabinet should not run at all.

The real reason for Lansing's dismissal seems to have been an explosion of pent-up wrath against an associate who over many months had seemed insubordinate and downright disloyal. But the public reactions to the incident have been analyzed at length because they had an important bearing, hitherto unemphasized, on the final stages of the treaty fight in the Senate. The press teemed with such adjectives as "uncandid," "querulous," "petty," "pettish," "peevish," "petulant," "jealous," "ungenerous," "uncompromising," "egotistical," "overbearing," and "arrogant."

Enemies of Wilson were further embittered. Even some senators who were friendly to the treaty remarked privately that they would not yield a point and promote compromise, because compromise was impossible with a mentality which had become childishly unreasonable.

6

The headlines of February 26 announced that Lansing's successor would be Bainbridge Colby, a New York lawyer with considerable oratorical and literary talents. The resulting roar of criticism, from both Democrats and Republicans, approached in volume and vigor that which had greeted the dropping of Lansing.

Colby was rather generally known as a brilliant but erratic figure. He had been a Republican; he had bolted to the Progressives in 1912; but he had supported Wilson in 1916. There was some doubt as to whether he really was a Democrat; there was more as to his emotional balance. He was totally without experience in diplomatic matters, as most of our new Secretaries of State are; but the American people will excuse inexperience before they will instability.

The Democrats were quietly angry. Were there not enough of the faithful who had toiled in the vineyard for twenty or thirty years, without having to reach over into Republican ranks and come out with a turncoat Progressive? Frank L. Polk, who had served capably as Acting Secretary of State and who had headed the American Peace Commission in Paris after the return of Wilson, was widely regarded as the logical choice. Granted that his health would have permitted him to accept, he would have been an excellent appointment. But Wilson, who according to Dr. Grayson was worrying himself sick over the problem, did not react favorably to Polk's name.

Senator Lodge and his Foreign Relations Committee went over Colby's qualifications with a fine-toothed comb, and even haled the nominee before them. Lodge defended his conduct by saying that with the President broken in health, with the Vice President unwell, and with the Secretary of State next in line, it was necessary to be cautious. The Senate finally though belatedly confirmed the nomination.

The selection of Colby was so incredible that political experts racked their brains to guess its inner meaning. The New York *Nation* said that the appointment further demonstrated Wilson's unfitness to serve. The *New Republic* guessed that, since the treaty was to be thrown into the campaign, Wilson wanted an able speaker to take the stump in its behalf.

The reasons for the choice, otherwise inexplicable, seem to have been largely personal. Wilson wanted a man whose mind would "run along" with his; those of Lansing and Bryan had run in contrary directions. Wilson wanted a man who was loyal; Colby was worshipfully loyal. Colby was an idealist, like Wilson, and a gifted speaker who could represent Wilson in public. Finally, Colby could write beautiful prose. This was probably a large part of the answer. Wilson admitted to Dr. Grayson that as a result of his disability he would be unable to draft public papers with his former facility, and he needed someone to help him.

7

The scandal of Lansing's dismissal was still the talk of the nation when Wilson hurled another bombshell, which had international repercussions. On February 16 the press carried the summary of a note which the Department of State, clearly with the collaboration of Wilson, had recently sent to Rome, Paris, and London. In it the President objected in the strongest terms to a proposed settlement of the Fiume controversy with Italy in a manner contrary to the strong moral position already taken by the powers.

Wilson stingingly rebuked the Allies for going behind his back and drawing up an arrangement which flew in the face of every principle for which we had recently fought. The American people were fearful, Wilson declared with undeniable truth, of being inveigled into the unjust bargains of Europe, and this latest exhibition of chicanery provided the most "solid ground for such fears."

Then Wilson laid down his ultimatum. If the Allies would not carry through the just proposal already accepted by Britain, France, and the United States, the President "must take under serious consideration" the question of withdrawing the Treaty of Versailles from the Senate, and of leaving the Allies to carry out the settlement without our support.

To European peoples this sounded like dictatorial talk. The Liberal *Westminster Gazette* (London), while admitting that Wilson had justice on his side, felt that his tone recalled "a European monarch of the eighteenth century . . ." The French press was mightily aroused by the prospect of being left completely in the lurch, and denounced Wilson as an autocrat who outdid the Russian tsars. Back in America, the isolationist Washington *Post* chuckled, "Paris is puzzled about the stand of the United States in world affairs, and so is the United States."

Two more Wilsonian notes followed, somewhat more conciliatory in tone and context, but the controversy dragged on for many more months. We need concern ourselves here only with the effect of this Adriatic flare-up on the fortunes of the treaty.

Wilson's ultimatum undoubtedly injured the prospects of treaty ratification. The "irreconcilables" saw in the whole unsavory affair abundant confirmation of their worst fears. If such an exhibition of treachery was typical of our future associates in the League, then why not wash our hands of the whole wretched business? Perhaps the most common reaction of the press was that we should never have become involved in the first place.

The hyphenates, especially Italian-Americans, were again in full cry, with F. H. La Guardia of New York (the future "Little Flower") a leader of the pack. The Italians in distant San Remo did some renaming of streets: Corso Wilson became Corso Fiume.

The whole affair did not make for a sweet spirit of compromise in the Senate. This latest outburst of temper on the part of Wilson indicated that he was not in a state of mind to come anywhere near halfway. If the Adriatic snarl was a fair sample of European trickery, then there was all the more reason for attaching strong reservations to the treaty. And if the President was going to withdraw the whole thing, what was the point in trying to sew little patches of reservations on a useless garment?

In the Lansing affair Wilson was technically right; no President should be saddled with a Cabinet member whom he does not want. In the Adriatic affair Wilson was morally right, as he so often was. But in both cases his timing was poor. The main task was to conciliate the Senate and facilitate compromise, not to inject new distractions and antagonisms. Both the Lansing and the Adriatic showdowns could have been postponed a few weeks, until the treaty was approved. Then dismissals and ultimata, if necessary, would have been in order.

CHAPTER SIXTEEN

THE LAST CHANCE

*"So far as the United States Senate is concerned, the dead of this
war have died in vain." New York* WORLD, *March 20, 1920.*

1

WHILE WILSON was purging his Cabinet and laying down
the law to the Allies, the senators were languidly moving
toward a reconsideration of their previous action. Finally, on
February 9, the Senate formally voted to reconsider the treaty,
and the members entered upon a rehash of their old arguments with little evident relish. Vice President Marshall
weariedly remarked to the news correspondents, "Boys, why
don't you just take your files on this treaty debate and print
them over again?"

Yet an atmosphere of optimism pervaded the capital: this
time the treaty must not be allowed to fail. Even the "irreconcilables" were privately conceding defeat. One of them remarked that, now they had "raised all the Cain possible," he
would not be surprised to see most of them voting for ratification. Borah sneered that the only essential difference between the Lodge and Hitchcock reservations to Article X was
the difference between "unless" and "until," and with all his
oratorical talents he poured scorn upon the heads of the
"unlessites" and the "untillites."

Senator Hitchcock was revealing an auspicious willingness
to compromise. Lodge, on his part, agreed to accept the bipartisan conference changes on nine of the original fourteen
reservations. But the stumbling block was a more satisfactory
reservation regarding Article X. Hitchcock emphatically declared that the new proposal of both Lodge and the "mild
reservationists" was worse than the original. By February 17

the Democratic leader was deeply discouraged; he feared that "we may come out at the same hole we went in."

Hitchcock openly blamed the Republicans. The Democrats, he complained, had agreed to accept two versions of a reservation on Article X which came so close to the original Lodge reservation that many senators could see no real difference between them. Whereupon the irrepressible Borah summed the situation up neatly: The Democrats had come nine-tenths of the way toward compromise; they were admitting that the remaining one-tenth amounted to little or nothing. Then why not, after having gone this far, go the whole way?

2

The Senate at first moved with gratifying speed. Between February 21 and March 7 it adopted or revised eight of the fourteen so-called Lodge reservations.

The withdrawal reservation was approved as it stood (45 to 20), with Lodge vainly trying to secure a joint resolution of Congress, *as Wilson desired,* rather than a concurrent resolution.

The reservation declining to accept a League mandate without the consent of Congress carried by the overwhelming vote of 68 to 4. Wilson had conceded that there was no real objection to this.

The reservation on Shantung was changed (48 to 21), as the Democrats had urged in the bipartisan conferences, to a more tactful version, with the words "China" and "Japan" omitted.

These three reservations all received a two-thirds vote, quite in contrast with the narrow margins of November. Strong Democratic support was mustered for all of them, which indicated that Hitchcock would be unable to hold his followers completely in line on the final vote. Nevertheless a feeling of hopelessness overtook the Senate by the end of February. The "irreconcilables" were voting the reservations on, as before, but they would vote against the whole thing at the end, and

barring a surrender by Wilson they would be joined by enough
Democrats to defeat the treaty.

The blast that chilled the Democrats, and indirectly the
Republicans, came from the White House. About the last
week in February, Senator Glass of Virginia (Democrat) was

Can't Even Remove the Victim
(Courtesy of Brooklyn *Eagle*; cartoonist Harding)

delegated to visit the convalescing President and ascertain
whether he would pocket the treaty if it should be approved
with the Lodge reservations. Wilson emphatically told Glass
that he would, according to a newspaper account which is
confirmed by their private correspondence. This being the
case, why waste more time?

Late in February, Hitchcock told the reporters that he expected the present attempt at ratification to fail, but he was "quite confident" that there would be another one which would succeed. This was incredibly purblind. Only by the grace of a tidal wave of public opinion were the Democrats having their second chance; such tidal waves would not roll up indefinitely. Henry White talked with Hitchcock and was vexed by his "light and airy way" of referring to the treaty, and of expecting that another deadlock would force the Republicans to yield.

Hitchcock's confidence may have been bolstered by Borah, who was declaring that he intended to present a strong anti-League plank at the coming Republican convention, and bolt the party if it was rejected. The prospect of another Republican schism was highly tempting to the Democrats. Why should either Hitchcock or Wilson yield too much in the way of compromise and get the League issue out of the way, when there was this high political premium on continued deadlock?

3

During the first week in March the debate over reservations was alternately listless and heated. The "bitter-enders" were again cheerful. Everywhere there was a feeling that the treaty white elephant should be dragged from the Senate floor and pushed into the coming campaign. There seemed to be no other way to get rid of it.

Yet the debate ground on, to the amusement of well-filled galleries. Having made up their minds to kill the treaty, the senators could not decide on a prompt and decent burial. Borah baited the Democrats by charging that they would all finally surrender and be in there voting for the Lodge reservations at the end. This naturally hardened Democratic resistance, as did the rumor that the President, if his followers surrendered, would head a third party in the approaching campaign and ruin their chances of reelection.

Lodge was at his wit's end. He had endorsed most of the changes which the Democrats had pushed in the bipartisan conferences, and had succeeded in getting some of them adopted. But the "irreconcilables" were threatening to bolt if he gave ground on Article X; the "mild reservationists" were threatening to bolt if he did not; and the Democrats were under orders from the White House to vote down whatever was agreed upon. On March 4 Lodge flared up and said that since the Democrats seemed unwilling to support some of the amendments which they had presented in the bipartisan conferences, he would offer no more. He solemnly admitted for the first time that the treaty had "fallen by the wayside."

Yet to the very end a few of the faithful never gave up hope that some compromise might be worked out on the reservation to Article X. Senator Simmons of North Carolina (a Democrat) was one of these, and he enlisted the support of Senator Watson (a Republican), who in turn secured the assent of Lodge to a part of the plan.

Simmons was anxious to talk with the President about his proposal. On or about March 5 (the letter is undated), Hitchcock wrote directly to Wilson urging that Simmons be called to the White House, and giving reasons why. At the bottom of this letter is a brief notation in the writing of Mrs. Wilson, presumably dictated by the President and sent on to Hitchcock. The note curtly said that it would be folly to undertake individual interviews. (Wilson was probably thinking of the fruitless conferences with individual senators back in July.)

The upshot was that Senator Simmons and his fellow compromisers were not permitted to see Wilson, and Senator Watson records that Simmons was much vexed. The President was probably vexed, too: why should people be constantly bothering him about compromising on Article X, especially since he had already made it clear that he would not compromise?

Wilson's Olympian seclusion from the Senate during these critical days is puzzling. Senator Glass, a warm friend, seems to have been the only one whom he did consult, though others were reported as anxious to see him. There can be no doubt that he was physically able to talk with individual senators, and might have done so if his mind had been open and if he had realized the importance of keeping in touch with developments in the Senate. Evidently Wilson had reconciled himself to the rejection of the treaty, and looked forward to a triumphant vindication at the polls.

4

The President fired another verbal bombshell, on March 8, 1920, when he addressed a communication to Senator Hitchcock setting forth his objections to the Lodge reservations. The letter was in the nature of a reply to Hitchcock's request that Wilson see Senator Simmons and one or two of his colleagues.

No devitalizing reservation to Article X, Wilson insisted, would be acceptable, for Article X was a moral obligation—a sacred pledge to our gallant boys. Without this article we should get nothing out of the war but regrets for having gone in. Either we should enter the League fearlessly, accepting responsibility for world leadership, or we should retire "as gracefully as possible" from the concert of powers.

Wilson went on to say that at Paris he had run afoul of "militaristic" forces, particularly those of France, and they had fought Article X. The Lodge reservation would be a victory for them.

The President further explained that "practically every so-called reservation" was a "rather sweeping nullification" of the actual terms of the treaty. He had heard of "reservationists" and "mild reservationists," but he could not understand the difference between "a nullifier" and a "mild nullifier." In concluding, Wilson expressed the wish that Hitchcock would communicate these views to his fellow Democrats in the Senate for their guidance. In brief, reject the Lodge reservations because they nullified the treaty.

This letter is one of the most striking that Wilson ever wrote. In his discussion of Article X he soared again into the empyrean idealism of his Fourteen Points and other war addresses. But he was clearly out of touch with reality. Some of the things he said were no doubt true but they would not get the treaty approved. It was, for example, a gross exaggeration to assert that practically every one of the proposed reservations was in effect a sweeping nullification of the treaty.

The letter disclosed not only a stubborn mind, but a closed mind. By the day that Wilson wrote these instructions, *about half of the Lodge reservations had not yet been voted upon* (including that to Article X), and in general they were the less important ones. The others were still taking shape, and were subject to amendment. The reservation to Article X was still being hammered out, and at the time Wilson sent the letter there was still a lively hope of some kind of compromise along the lines of the Simmons-Watson proposal. Yet Wilson *vetoed all the rest of the reservations without even waiting to see what they were going to be.*

5

The reverberations from this March letter were both national and international.

The wavering Democrats were beaten back into line by the crack of the Wilsonian whip. Most of them, especially those up for reelection, did not care to go before the voters and admit that they had defied the sickbed wishes of their great President.

Some of the more reasonable Democrats, like Owen of Oklahoma, were forced to choose between Wilson and Lodge, and they sadly chose Lodge. Owen openly announced that he would fall in behind any leadership that would take us into the League, with or without reservations.

The "mild reservationists," who had not completely abandoned hope of a compromise on Article X, were again slapped in the face. They were branded as "nullifiers," when in their judgment they were trying to save the treaty from a stubborn zealot who would destroy it.

The "irreconcilables" were delighted. Senator Brandegee, "overjoyed and exultant," hastened with a copy of the letter to Mrs. Alice Roosevelt Longworth. It meant that the angered "mild reservationists" would stand with the "bitter-enders" in voting reservations onto the treaty. Senator Moses sacrilegiously rejoiced that he, an "irreconcilable," had been united in the holy bonds of "political wedlock" with Senator Kellogg, a "mild reservationist," by the Reverend Woodrow Wilson.

The "Lodge reservationists" were now more determined than ever to carry through their program with dispatch, and dump the dead treaty on Wilson's doorstep. Lodge snorted that the President's letter contained some "delightful" passages, especially on French militarism and imperialism. He rose in the Senate several days later to explain that he had meant this sarcastically.

The French were stunned by the attack upon their militarism. Wilson had promised them security through the League and the Security Treaty. The League was dying; the Security Treaty was dead. Could France be blamed, after this betrayal, for building up a strong system of alliances and trying to safeguard herself against future aggression?

The French Ambassador in Washington, Jules Jusserand, promptly sent a note of remonstrance to Acting Secretary of State Polk, who forwarded it to Wilson. The President replied on March 15 that he resented Jusserand's rushing in, and expected Polk to have a frank and firm talk with him. Wilson evidently was piqued because Jusserand was piqued. The same trace of asperity that had crept into the Lansing and Adriatic notes again had come to the surface.

Across the Atlantic, the French press flared forth in anger. It was shocking to learn that Article X had been devised to hold France in check. It was hypocritical for America (who had not reduced her armaments) to blame France (after betraying her) for maintaining large armies. Some of the less moderate French journals referred to the maunderings of a sick man. The Paris *Midi* said bluntly, "The American nation is directed by an idiot." The Paris *Matin* quoted *Harvey's Weekly* as saying, "No, Mr. Wilson has not become insane; *he* is just as he always was."

The London *Globe*, the first English paper to break silence, wondered if Wilson was now physically or temperamentally capable of dealing with a complicated international situation which demanded give-and-take. His illness had aroused the sympathy of the whole world; his recent petulant outbursts elicited "a certain degree of sympathy for the United States."

6

On March 8, the day that Wilson wrote his disturbing letter, the weary senators, convinced of the futility of what they were doing, unanimously adopted a motion to limit debate. Most of the remaining reservations were rapidly carried through, all of them by lopsided if not overwhelming votes, all of them with some Democratic support, and one of them without debate. The six-to-one reservation, in revised form, was approved 57 to 20, *with 17 Democrats supporting it.*

By March 10 the crisis was approaching on Article X. There were rumors that the Simmons-Watson proposal might yet win enough votes. Even Lodge alarmed the "irreconcilables" by presenting a watered-down version of his own reservation, though he admitted he had changed the phraseology and not the basic principle. Senator Reed then told the story of the boy who was fishing for suckers: when they would not bite, he merely reversed the same worm on the hook, saying, "Oh, these are just fish I'm after; they don't know much."

Senator Hitchcock took the trouble to send the new Lodge reservation to the White House about March 12 with a note (undated) saying he assumed it would be unacceptable. Wilson curtly noted on the bottom of the page that the senator was quite right, and returned it. The "irreconcilables," by threatening dire things, were finally able to force Lodge to accept an amendment to his revised reservation on Article X which, if anything, made it more sweeping. In this form it was adopted on March 15 by a vote of 56 to 26, *with 14 Democrats voting for it.*

The irate Senator Simmons taxed Lodge with twice having surrendered on Article X when agreement was in sight, and with twice having entered into an alliance with the "irreconcilables." Lodge replied that the Republican senators had been "endeavoring to act together." Then, with an acid thrust at Wilson, he added: "We cannot conduct matters on this side of the aisle as they are conducted on that side. *We have no one to write us letters."*

Simmons snapped back that no one had to write Lodge letters. All that was necessary was for Borah, the leader of the "irreconcilables," to "tell" the Massachusetts senator what to do.

Borah then spoke up for the "irreconcilables" to say that they were standing foursquare with Wilson in seeking "to defeat the treaty." "There is just as much of an understanding between the President of the United States and myself as there is between the Senator from Massachusetts and myself."

7

On March 18, appropriately enough the day after St. Patrick's Day, an astonishing development occurred. Senator Gerry of Rhode Island, a stalwart Democrat, proposed a fifteenth reservation putting the Senate on record as favoring self-determination and independence for Ireland.

This was the acme of legislative absurdity. Ireland was completely irrelevant to the subject matter of the treaty. The fourth Lodge reservation warned other powers to keep out of our domestic concerns, and now we were rushing headlong into those of Britain. Such an indefensible irrelevancy would give Wilson complete justification for pocketing the entire treaty, even assuming that he would not have done so anyhow. Finally, the British would be strongly impelled to object to the Irish reservation and perhaps defeat or delay final ratification.

It was crystal-clear by this time that the only chance of securing ratification lay in the Lodge reservations. The last-minute Ireland dodge was but a transparent trick by the Democrats to make the preceding fourteen reservations so offensive that not even the Republicans would vote for them. The regular Democratic senators apparently did not want agreement, and they preferred to take their chances in the coming campaign, unless they were allowed to put the stamp of their own interpretation on the treaty. From now on the Democrats were hardly in a position to accuse the "irreconcilables" of bad faith in voting for reservations with the plain intent of later voting them down.

Lodge frantically sought to wriggle out of this diabolically clever trap. He finally proposed a recess so that he might rally his demoralized ranks. But the outspoken Ashurst of Arizona (Democrat) cried out in piercing tones against further delay. The Senate, he shouted, should either take this treaty in a pair of tongs and drop it into the Potomac, or ratify it without more palaver or delay, for the people were heartily tired of it. This sally brought such a tremendous outburst of applause from the packed galleries that not even the stern hammerings of the presiding officer could check it.

The Irish reservation carried by the close vote of 38 to 36, with the "bitter-enders" and *over half the Democrats present voting for it,* among them men like Hitchcock who had consistently opposed the Lodge reservations. Such are the mutations of politics.

Just before the final vote, on March 19, the Senate adopted without record vote a Lodge amendment to the preamble of the original reservations. This provided for silent acquiescence

by all the Allied powers, rather than explicit written acceptance by three of the major four. (It will be remembered that
Wilson had strongly objected to the original reservation because it required written consent.)

By this time it was hardly accurate to speak of the "Lodge"
reservations. That regarding Ireland was vehemently opposed
by the Massachusetts senator. Others had been revised to meet
Democratic objections and had received strong Democratic
support, notably the preamble, the Shantung reservation, and
the League-expense reservation. Lodge seemingly was willing
to yield more than this but was repeatedly beaten back by the
"bitter-enders." Generally speaking, the revised Lodge reservations (except for that on Ireland) were more tactful, less likely
to wound foreign sensibilities, and more carefully worded.

Throughout the debate Hitchcock consistently presented
substitute reservations, and was as consistently voted down. A
careful analysis of his proposals shows that in principle, if not
in phraseology, they differed little if any from the corresponding ones of Lodge. The difference was not so much between
tweedledum and tweedledee as between Democratic political
face and Republican political face. Throughout the debate,
repeated and unabashed references to the impending campaign again demonstrated that the curse of party politics was
ever present.

8

As the hour again approached for the crucial vote, it was
apparent that the tide of public opinion, even within Democratic ranks, had begun to turn strongly against the uncompromising President. This was quite in contrast with November, when Wilson had radiated something of the aura of a
martyr. But the Lansing and Adriatic affairs, combined with
the peremptory letter to Hitchcock, had caused the President
to appear in a less lovely light.

When it became clear that the choice was either a reserved

treaty or nothing, all but the most partisan and stubborn shrank from the terrifying responsibility of giving the country and the world nothing. Men like Herbert Hoover, William Jennings Bryan, and ex-President Taft begged Wilson not to throw away nine-tenths of a loaf because he could not get the whole loaf. Personal friends of the President added their voices to the swelling chorus.

Highly significant was the defection in March of a number of the most influential Democratic newspapers. The Cleveland *Plain Dealer* turned a somersault and reluctantly declared for the Lodge reservations. The Brooklyn *Eagle* was sadly urging the senators to ignore the President and vote their own convictions. The powerful New York *World,* an unflagging defender of the League, now belittled the Lodge reservations, and while insisting that Wilson was right in principle, admitted that on occasion every statesman must yield to expediency. The President's position, from this point of view, was "weak and untenable."

The Louisville *Courier-Journal,* which carried on the violently outspoken tradition of "Marse Henry" Watterson, had long been, like the other Democratic newspapers, a foe of reservations. It now reversed itself and urged ratification on "the best terms possible." The St. Louis *Post-Dispatch* (nominally Independent, though strongly Democratic in its leanings), had supported the treaty all along with great vigor. It now parted company with Wilson because he was "endangering the cause"—and the cause was greater than any man or any party.

9

It was in this changing atmosphere that, on March 19, 1920, the Senate prepared for the final vote. The galleries were jammed; the air was electric; but the excitement was less tense than in November. Barring some kind of miracle or last-minute shift, the treaty would be rejected.

Several of the senators took the floor to make their final

arguments. Among them was Senator Walsh of Montana, who contributed one of the few really impressive speeches of the entire debate. He would reluctantly vote for reservations, partly because the influence of Article X had been exaggerated, but primarily because there was no alternative.

The zero hour had now arrived. The question was on agreeing to the resolution of ratification with the Lodge reservations incorporated. With stentorian tones the clerk began to call the roll. Three of the first four Democrats turned against Wilson and voted for the treaty. Then came the name of Senator Culberson of Texas, a Democrat who had grown gray in the service and who was high in the esteem of his colleagues. If he too voted "Yea" he might touch off a Democratic stampede. His face was perplexed, but after a moment's hesitation he voted "Nay." (Later in the street he turned to a friend, and after speaking in the highest terms of Walsh's speech, remarked, "You know, for a minute in there I didn't know how to vote.")

The roll call continued. Some of the Democratic stalwarts stood fast; others deserted. Then came the name of Hitchcock. If he voted with Lodge, he might yet start a stampede among the remaining Democrats. But he remained true to Wilson's leadership and voted "Nay." (Some years afterward he told Dr. Nicholas Murray Butler that he was the man who had really defeated the treaty, at "virtually the command" of Wilson. "It was," Butler reports him as saying, "the mistake of my life.")

When the votes were all tallied, the count stood 49 to 35, which meant that the treaty, *though commanding a simple majority this time,* lacked seven votes of the necessary two-thirds. Twenty-one Democrats went over to the Lodge camp, but twenty-three remained loyal. If seven of the twenty-three had followed the others, the treaty would have carried. Thus twenty-three old-line Democrats, acting at the behest of the uncompromising Wilson, joined with the "bitter-ender" Republicans to bring about the second and final defeat of the treaty.

The "irreconcilable" Brandegee turned to Lodge and said, "We can always depend on Mr. Wilson. He never has failed us."

10

Once the treaty was rejected, the Senate passed the customary motion (47 to 37) to return it to the President. No effort was made, as in November, to approve the treaty without reservations, or with the Hitchcock reservations. All this was regarded as completely hopeless.

Yet a feeble attempt was made to reconsider the vote of rejection. It was generally felt that such a motion would be acceptable, once the wheel-horse Democrats had stuck by their guns and Wilson long enough to salve their consciences and stay in the good graces of their constituents. The loyal Democrats could then support a motion to reconsider, and leave the final decision up to the President.

The press reported that the administration Democrats had worked out a "deal" with the "mild reservationists" to carry a vote to reconsider. Senator Robinson (Democrat) actually made such a motion. Senator Watson moved to table it, but this maneuver lost 43 to 34, with the "mild reservationists" joining the Democrats.

The president of the Senate pro tempore (Senator Cummins of Iowa, Republican) thereupon declared the Robinson motion to reconsider out of order. He expressed misgivings as to the soundness of his ruling, and plainly invited an appeal from the decision of the chair. If such an appeal had been made, the loyal Democrats doubtless would have combined again with the "mild reservationists" to declare the Robinson motion in order, and there would have been a final chance to save the treaty. Incredible though it may seem, *not a single one of those who professed to favor the treaty with reservations,* either Republicans or Democrats, *rose to challenge the chairman's questionable ruling.*

Then Lodge came forward. He said that since some of the senators obviously wanted another chance to vote, he would propose unanimous consent for a motion to reconsider, and in this way give the Democrats one more opportunity to approve the treaty with his reservations. But Hitchcock flatly

Entirely Unadoptable

(Courtesy of San Francisco *Chronicle*; cartoonist Bronstrup)

objected to unanimous consent, and Lodge's last attempt to revive the pact had to be dropped. The Treaty of Versailles was never again formally considered in the Senate of the United States.

It is clear that, if those Democrats who voted against the treaty had really wanted a second chance, they could have had it. The conclusion must be that they did not want it. The twenty-three loyal Democrats were standing so steadfast that another roll call would obviously have been a waste of time. Wilson was insisting that he would rather have the treaty thrown into the tumult of politics than have it approved with the Lodge reservations; so the administration Democrats, for whatever reasons, gave their crippled leader what he wanted.

As before, the "irreconcilables" met at the home of Mrs. Longworth for a victory supper. But the affair was not a great success; they were all tired and suffering from the feeling of an anticlimax. "For weeks," says Mrs. Longworth, "it was really comic how we missed having the League to fight about."

Bright and early the next morning after the final vote, the secretary of the Senate appeared at the White House Executive Offices with the big bound volume of the official treaty, wrapped securely in brown paper and tied generously with red tape. The President had personally presented it to the Senate for approval; the senators could not agree on a resolution of ratification, so they were sending it back.

The next move, as Lodge explained, was up to the President. If he wanted to resubmit the treaty, the Senate would treat it as new business. If he wanted to toss it into the campaign, then the Republicans would gladly meet him on the hustings.

CHAPTER SEVENTEEN

THE SUPREME
INFANTICIDE

*"As a friend of the President, as one who has loyally followed
him, I solemnly declare to him this morning: If you want to kill
your own child because the Senate straightens out its crooked
limbs, you must take the responsibility and accept the verdict of
history."* SENATOR ASHURST *of Arizona (Democrat),*
March 11, 1920.

1

THE TREATY was now dead, as far as America was concerned. Who had killed it?

The vital role of the loyal Democrats must be reemphasized.
If all of them who professed to want the treaty had voted "Yea,"
it would have passed with more than a dozen votes to spare.
If the strait-jacket of party loyalty had not been involved, the
necessary two-thirds could easily have been mustered.

In the previous November, the Democrats might have voted
against the treaty (as they did) even without White House
pressure. But this time pressure had to be applied to force them
into line, and even in the face of Wilsonian wrath almost half
of them bolted. On the day of the final balloting the newsmen
observed that two Cabinet members (Burleson and Daniels),
possibly acting at the President's direction, were on the floor
of the Senate, buttonholing waverers. The day after the fateful
voting Hitchcock wrote Wilson that it had required the "most
energetic efforts" on his part *to prevent a majority of the Democrats from surrendering to Lodge.*

Desertion of the President, as we have seen, is no light offense
in the political world, especially when he has declared himself emphatically. Senators do not ordinarily court political
suicide. Wilson still had the patronage bludgeon in his hands,

and having more than a trace of vindictiveness, he could oppose renegade senators when they ran again, and in fact did so.

Many of the loyal Democrats were up for reelection in 1920. They certainly were aware of the effects of party treachery on their political fortunes. They knew—or many of them knew —that they were killing the treaty; they made no real effort to revive it; they must have wanted it killed—at least until after the November election.

One striking fact stands out like a lighthouse. With the exception of Hitchcock of Nebraska, Johnson of South Dakota, and Thomas of Colorado, *every single one of the twenty-three senators who stood loyally with Wilson in March came from south of the Mason and Dixon line.* Only four of the "disloyal" twenty-one represented states that had seceded in 1860–1861. At the polls, as well as on the floor of the Senate, decent southern Democrats voted "the way their fathers shot." As between bothersome world responsibility on the one hand, and loyalty to President, party, section, and race on the other, there was but one choice. Perhaps world leadership would come eventually anyhow.

Democratic senators like Walsh of Montana and Ashurst of Arizona were not from the South. When the issue was clearly drawn between loyalty to party and loyalty to country, their consciences bade them choose the greater good. Ashurst had gone down the line in supporting Wilson; but several days before the final vote he declared, "I am just as much opposed to a White House irreconcilable as I am to a Lodge irreconcilable."

2

A word now about public opinion.

In March, as in November, more than 80 per cent of the senators professed to favor the treaty with some kind of reservations. All the polls and other studies indicate that this was roughly the sentiment of the country. Yet the senators were unable to scrape together a two-thirds vote for any one set of reservations.

The reaction of many newspaper editors, as before, was to cry out against the shame of it all—this indictment of the "capacity of our democracy to do business." We had astonished the world by our ability to make war; we now astonished the world with our "imbecility" in trying to make peace. How could we blame other countries for thinking us "a nation of boobs and bigots"? The Louisville *Courier-Journal* (Democrat), referring to our broken promises to the Allies, cried that we stood betrayed as "cravens and crooks," "hypocrites and liars."

Partisan Republican newspapers loudly blamed the stiff-backed Wilson and his "me-too" senators. Two wings of "irreconcilables"—the Wilsonites and the "bitter-enders"—had closed in to execute a successful pincers movement against the treaty. The New York *Tribune* (Independent Republican) condemned the "inefficiency, all-sufficiency and self-sufficiency of our self-named only negotiator," Woodrow Wilson. If the treaty died, said the *Tribune*, the handle of the dagger that pierced its heart would bear the "initials 'W. W.' "

If Republicans scolded Democrats, Democrats scolded Republicans. Lodge and his cheap political tricks were roundly condemned, and the general conclusion was that "the blood of the Treaty stains the floor of the Republican wigwam." A few of the less partisan Democratic journals openly conceded that Wilson's obstinacy had something to do with the final result. William Jennings Bryan asserted from the platform that this "most colossal crime against our nation and the civilized world in all history" made his "blood boil." He began a vigorous campaign against the two-thirds rule in the Senate. "A majority of Congress can declare war," he cried; "it ought to be as easy to end a war as to begin it."

The leading liberal journals, as before, were sadly happy. They rejoiced that the result would clear the way for a renovation of the treaty, but they regretted that the pact had been defeated as a result of partisanship rather than as a result of the betrayal of Wilson's promises.

An impressive number of the more discerning editors deplored the fact that the issue was now in the dirty hands of

"He Did It!"

(Courtesy of Los Angeles *Times*; cartoonist Gale)

politicians. An electoral referendum, it was felt, would merely confuse the issue; such a canvass could not possibly reveal anything more than was already known, namely, that *an overwhelming majority of the people wanted the treaty with some kind of reservations.*

3

Is it true that the invalid in the White House really strangled the treaty to death with his own enfeebled hands?

It is seldom that statesmen have a second chance—a second guess. They decide on a course of action, and the swift current of events bears them downstream from the starting point. Only rarely does the stream reverse itself and carry them back.

In November, Wilson had decided that he wanted deadlock, because he reasoned that deadlock would arouse public opinion and force the Senate to do his bidding. The tidal wave of public opinion did surge in, and Wilson got his second chance. But he threw it away, first by spurning compromise (except on his terms), and then by spurning the Lodge reservations.

There had been much more justification for Wilson's course in November than in March. In November he was sick, secluded, was fed censored news, and was convinced by Hitchcock that the strategy of deadlock was sound. In March, he was much improved in health, far less secluded, more in touch with the press and with the currents of opinion, though probably still not enough. He consulted even less with the Senate, presumably because he had made up his mind in advance to oppose the Lodge reservations. In November, there was a fair possibility of reconsideration; in March, it was clear that the only possibility lay in making the League an issue in the coming campaign. Wilson, with his broad knowledge of government and politics, should have seen that this hope was largely if not completely illusory. Perhaps he would have seen it had he not been blinded by his feeling for Lodge.

The evidence is convincing that Wilson wanted the issue cast into the hurly-burly of politics. He could not accept Lodge's terms; Lodge would not accept his terms. The only possible chance of beating the senator—and this was slim indeed—was to win a resounding mandate in 1920.

Yet this strategy, as already noted, meant further delay. At

Paris, the feeling at times had been, "Better a bad treaty today than a good treaty four months hence." Europe was still in chaos, and increasingly in need of America's helping hand. Well might the Europeans cry, "Better a treaty with the Lodge reservations today than a probable treaty without reservations after the election." Or as Dr. Frank Crane wrote in *Current Opinion*, "It is vastly more needful that some sort of League be formed, *any sort*, than that it be formed *perfectly*." (Italics Crane's.)

Yet Wilson, for the reasons indicated, could not see all this clearly. Four days after the fatal vote he wrote Hitchcock, praising him for having done all in his power to protect the honor of the nation and the peace of the world against the Republican majority.

Mrs. Wilson, no doubt reflecting her husband's views, later wrote, "My conviction is that Mr. Lodge put the world back fifty years, and that at his door lies the wreckage of human hopes and the peril to human lives that afflict mankind today."

4

To the very end Wilson was a fighter. When the Scotch-Irish in him became aroused, he would nail his colors to the mast. He said in 1916 that he was "playing for the verdict of mankind." His conception of duty as he saw it was overpowering. He once remarked that if he were a judge, and it became his duty to sentence his own brother to the gallows, he would do so—and afterwards die of a broken heart.

It is well to have principles; it is well to have a noble conception of duty. But Wilson, as he became warmed up in a fight, tended to get things out of focus and to lose a proper sense of values.

The basic issue in 1920 was the Hitchcock reservations or the Lodge reservations. Wilson accepted those of Hitchcock while rejecting those of Lodge, which, he said, completely nullified the treaty and betrayed his promises to the Allies and to the American dead.

This, as we have seen, was a gross exaggeration. Minds no less acute than Wilson's, and less clouded with sickness and pride, denied that the Lodge reservations completely nullified the treaty. To the man in the street—in so far as he gave the dispute thought—there was little discernible difference between the two sets of reservations. How could one decry statements which merely reaffirmed the basic principles of the Constitution and of our foreign policy? To a vast number of Americans the Lodge reservations, far from nullifying the treaty, actually improved it. This was so apparent to even the most loyal Democrats in the Senate that Wilson could barely keep them in line.

In the final analysis the treaty was slain in the house of its friends rather than in the house of its enemies. In the final analysis it was not the two-thirds rule, or the "irreconcilables," or Lodge, or the "strong" and "mild reservationists," but Wilson and his docile following who delivered the fatal stab. If the President had been permitted to vote he would have sided with Borah, Brandegee, Johnson, and the other "bitter-enders"—though for entirely different reasons.

Wilson had said that the reservation to Article X was a knife thrust at the heart of the Covenant. Ironically, he parried this knife thrust, and stuck his own dagger, not into the heart of the Covenant, but into the entire treaty.

This was the supreme act of infanticide. With his own sickly hands Wilson slew his own brain child—or the one to which he had contributed so much.

This was the supreme paradox. He who had forced the Allies to write the League into the treaty, unwrote it; he who had done more than any other man to make the Covenant, unmade it—at least so far as America was concerned. And by his action, he contributed powerfully to the ultimate undoing of the League, and with it the high hopes of himself and mankind for an organization to prevent World War II.

5

The preceding dogmatic observations are of course qualified by the phrase, "in the last analysis."

Many elements enter into a log jam. Among them are the width of the stream, the depth of the stream, the swiftness of the current, the presence of boulders, the size of the logs, and the absence of enough lumberjacks. No one of these factors can be solely responsible for the pile-up.

Many elements entered into the legislative log jam of March, 1920. Among them were isolationism, partisanship, senatorial prerogative, confusion, apathy, personal pride, and private feuds. No one of them was solely responsible for the pile-up. *But as the pile-up finally developed, there was only one lumberjack who could break it, and that was Woodrow Wilson.* If at any time before the final vote he had told the Senate Democrats to support the treaty with the Lodge reservations, or even if he had merely told them that they were on their own, the pact would almost certainly have been approved. So "in the last analysis" the primary responsibility for the failure in March rested with Wilson.

What about Lodge? If the treaty would have passed by Wilson's surrendering, is it not equally true that it would have passed by Lodge's surrendering?

The answer is probably "Yes," but the important point is that Lodge had far less responsibility for getting the treaty through than Wilson. If Lodge had yielded, he probably would have created a schism within his ranks. His ultimate responsibility was to keep the party from breaking to pieces, and in this he succeeded. Wilson's ultimate responsibility was to get the treaty ratified, and in this he failed. With Lodge, as with any truly partisan leader, the party comes before country; with the President the country should come before party, though unhappily it often does not.

It is possible that Wilson saw all this—but not clearly

enough. He might have been willing to compromise if his adversary had been any other than Lodge. But so bitter was the feeling between the two men that Wilson, rather than give way, grasped at the straw of the election of 1920.

Lodge did not like Wilson either, but he made more of a show of compromising than the President. He actually supported and drove through amendments to his original reservations which were in line with Wilson's wishes, and he probably would have gone further had the "irreconcilables" not been on his back. He fought the crippling Irish reservation, as well as others supported by the "bitter-enders." Finally, he gave the Democrats a fair chance to reconsider their vote and get on the bandwagon, but they spurned it.

If Lodge's words mean anything, and if his actions were not those of a monstrous hypocrite, he actually tried to get the treaty through with his reservations: When he found that he could not, he washed his hands of the whole business in disgust.

The charge is frequently made that, if Wilson had yielded to his adversary, Lodge would have gleefully piled on more reservations until Wilson, further humiliated, would have had to throw out the whole thing.

The strongest evidence for this view is a circumstantial story which Secretary Houston relates. During a Cabinet meeting Wilson was called to the telephone, and agreed to make certain concessions agreeable to Lodge. Before adjournment the telephone rang again, and word came that Lodge would not adhere to his original proposal.

This story is highly improbable, because Wilson attended no Cabinet meetings between September 2, 1919, and April 13, 1920. By the latter date, all serious attempts at compromise had been dropped; by the earlier date the treaty was still before the Senate committee, and the Lodge reservations, though in an embryonic stage, were yet unborn. But, even if the story is true, it merely proves that Lodge veered about, as he frequently did under "irreconcilable" pressure.

In March, as in November, all Wilson had to do was to send

over Postmaster General Burleson to the Senate a few minutes
before the final vote with the quiet word that the Democrats
were to vote "Yea." The treaty would then have passed with
the Lodge reservations, and Lodge could hardly have dared
incur for himself or his party the odium of moving to reconsider for the purpose of screwing on more reservations. Had
he tried to do so, the "mild reservationists" almost certainly
would have blocked him.

6

A few days after the disastrous final vote, Wilson's only comment to Tumulty was, "They have shamed us in the eyes of
the world." If his previous words said what he really meant,
he was hardly more shamed by the defeat of the treaty than by
the addition of the Lodge reservations. In his eyes it all
amounted to the same thing.

If the treaty had passed, would the President have been willing to go through with the exchange of ratifications? Would
he not have pocketed it, as he threatened to do prior to the
November vote?

Again, if Wilson's words may be taken at their face value,
this is what he would have done. He had not backed down
from his pre-November position. His Jackson Day message
and his letter to Hitchcock made it unmistakably clear that
he preferred the uncertainties of a political campaign to the
certainties of ratification with the Lodge reservations. The
addition of the indefensible Irish reservation provided even
stronger justification for pocketing the entire pact.

It is probable that some of the loyal Democrats voted as they
did partly because they were convinced that Wilson was going
to pigeonhole the treaty anyhow. From their point of view it
was better that the odium for defeat should seemingly rest on
Lodge rather than on their President. It also seems clear that
Wilson preferred, as in November, to have the blood of the
treaty on the Senate doorstep rather than on his. As he wrote

to Secretary Colby, on April 2, 1920, the slain pact lay heavily on the consciences of those who had stabbed it, and he was quite willing to have it lie there until those consciences were either awakened or crushed.

Yet it is one thing to say, just before Senate action, "I will pocket the treaty." It is another, after the pact is approved and sent to the White House, to assume this tremendous responsibility. The eyes of the world are upon the President; he is the only man keeping the nation out of the peace which it so urgently needs; he is the one man standing in the way of the rehabilitation which the world so desperately demands. Public pressure to ratify in such a case would be enormous—probably irresistible.

Some years later Senator Hitchcock said that in the event of senatorial approval Wilson would possibly have waited for the November election. If he had won, he would have worked for the removal of the Lodge reservations; if he had lost, then the compulsion to go through with ratification would have become overpowering. By November more than six months would have passed, and by that time Wilson might have developed a saner perspective.

But this is all speculation. Wilson gave orders that the treaty was to be killed in the Senate chamber. And there it died.

7

One other line of inquiry must be briefly pursued. Is it true, as some writers allege, that the thirty-odd Allied signatories of the original treaty would have rejected the Lodge reservations when officially presented? We recall that under the terms of the preamble these nations were privileged to acquiesce silently or file objections.

One will never know the answer to this question, because Wilson denied the other signatories a chance to act. But it seems proper to point to certain probabilities.

One or more of the Latin American nations might have objected to the reservation regarding the then hated Monroe Doctrine. Yet the Monroe Doctrine would have continued to exist anyhow; it was already in the Covenant; and these neighboring republics might well have swallowed their pride in the interest of world peace.

Italy probably would have acquiesced, and the evidence is strong that France would have done likewise. The Japanese could not completely overlook the Shantung reservation, but it was generally recognized in their press as meaningless, and for this reason it might have been tolerated, though not without some loss of face. It is noteworthy that the most important Japanese newspapers regretted the Senate stalemate as an encouragement to world instability, particularly in China.

Great Britain probably would have been the chief objector. The reservation on Ireland was highly offensive but completely innocuous, for the British lion had long endured Irish-American tail-twistings in pained but dignified silence. The reservation on six-to-one was a slap at the loyal and sacrificing Dominions, but it did not mean that their vote was to be taken away. Moreover, the contingency envisaged by this proviso was unlikely to arise very often, and in the long run would doubtless have proved inconsequential.

In sum, there were only two or three reservations to which the outside powers could seriously object. If they had objected, it is probable that a satisfactory adjustment could have been threshed out through diplomatic channels. For when it became clear that only a few phrases stood between the United States and peace, the dictates of common sense and the pressure of public opinion probably would have led to an acceptable compromise. If the Senate had refused to give ground in such a case, then the onus would have been clearly on it and not on Wilson.

The World Court is a case in point. In 1926 the Senate voted to join, but attached five reservations, four of which were accepted by the other powers. By 1935 a compromise was worked out on the fifth, but an isolationist uprising led by William

Randolph Hearst and Father Coughlin turned what seemed to be a favorable vote in the Senate into a narrow defeat for the World Court. The one-third minority again triumphed, with the aging Borah and Johnson and Norris and Gore still voting their fears and prejudices.

But the World Court analogy must not be pressed too far. In 1920 Europe was in a desperate condition; the only real

The Accuser

(From New York *World*; cartoonist Kirby; reprinted by permission)

hope for a successful League lay in American cooperation. Unless the United States would shoulder its obligations the whole treaty system was in danger of collapse. In 1926 the powers could afford to haggle over the World Court; in 1920 there was far less temptation to haggle while Europe burned. The European nations were under strong compulsion to swallow their pride, or at the very worst not to drive too hard a bargain in seeking adjustment.

But this again is pure speculation. Wilson never gave the

other powers a chance to act on the reservations, though Colonel House and others urged him to. He assumed this terrific responsibility all by himself. While thinking that he was throwing the onus on the consciences of the senators, he was in fact throwing a large share of the onus upon his own bent shoulders.

8

What were the reactions of our recent brothers in arms on the other side of the Atlantic?

The British viewed the Senate debacle with mixed emotions. The result had been a foregone conclusion, and there was some relief in having an end to senatorial uncertainty—at least this stage of it. Some journals were inclined to blame the two-thirds rule; others, the unbending doctrinaire in the White House. The London *Times* sorrowfully concluded that all the processes of peace would have to be suspended pending the outcome of the November election.

The French were shocked, though hardly surprised. The Paris *Liberté* aptly referred to the state of anarchy existing between the executive and the legislative in America. Other journals, smarting under Wilson's recent blast against French militarism, blamed the autocrat in the White House. "At the most troubled moment in history," gibed the Paris *Matin*, "America has a sick President, an amateur Secretary of State, and no Treaty of Peace. A President in the clouds, a Secretary of State in the bushes, and a treaty in the cabbage patch. What a situation!"

But the French did not completely abandon hope that America might yet honor her commitments. Meanwhile they would keep their powder dry and pursue the militaristic course which widened the growing rift between Britain and France, and which proved so fatal to the peace of Europe in the 1930's. The French finally became disgusted with German excuses (which were probably encouraged by America's defection), and in April, 1920, the month after the Senate rejected the treaty, their tanks rumbled into the Ruhr and occupied several German cities as hostages for reparations payments. Bullets were fired, and some blood was shed. This was but a dress rehearsal for the catastrophic invasion of the Ruhr in 1923.

The action—or rather inaction—of the United States had other tragic consequences. It encouraged German radicals in their determination to tear up the treaty: they were finding unwitting collaborators in Senator Borah and President Wilson. It delayed by many months, as British Foreign Secretary Curzon openly charged, the treaty with Turkey, thus giving the "Sick Man of Europe" (Turkey) a chance to prove that he was the "Slick Man of Europe." It held up the economic and moral rehabilitation of the Continent, and even hampered the work of relief then going forward. It further disillusioned the liberals of Europe and others who had clung to Wilson as the major prophet of a new order. It gave new comfort to the forces of disorder everywhere. It left the United States discredited, isolated, shorn of its prestige, and branded as a hypocrite and renegade. It marked the first unbridgeable rift in the ranks of the victorious Allies, a coalition that might have kept the peace. Instead they now went their separate ways, perhaps not as enemies, but certainly no longer as close friends. The United States was the first to break completely away.

America—and the world—paid a high price for the collapse of the treaty-making process in Washington. We are still paying it.

9

One final question. Who won after all these months of parliamentary jockeying?

Lodge the master parliamentarian had not won—that is, if he really wanted the treaty with his reservations. As in November, he was unable to keep the "irreconcilables" in line on the crucial vote, and he was unable to muster a two-thirds majority. He finally had to confess failure of leadership, except in so far as he prevented a schism.

The Republican party had not won. Lodge had avoided a serious split with the "bitter-enders" by knuckling under when they laid down the law. But the Republican leaders did not

Strange Bedfellows

(From St. Louis *Star*; cartoonist Chapin; courtesy of St. Louis *Star-Times*)

really want the issue in the campaign, and they had made strong efforts to keep it out. Now it was on their hands to cause them no end of embarrassment.

Wilson had not won. He has been praised for having kept the party ranks intact, and for having retained undisputed leadership of his following. But the Democrats in the Senate split 21 for the treaty to 23 against it, and that is hardly holding one's followers in line. Wilson lost irreparably because he did not get his treaty, even with reservations, and because he was doomed to lose again by insisting on a referendum where there could be no referendum.

The Democrats had not won. The treaty issue had caused a serious rift in the Senate, and Bryan, who was still a great leader, was on the rampage. Except for Wilson and some of his "yes men," there were few Democratic leaders who wanted this troublesome issue catapulted into the campaign. Yet there it was.

The United States had not won. It had won the war, to be sure; but it was now kicking the fruits of the victory back under the peace table. We had helped turn Europe into a scrap heap, and now we were scrapping the treaty. We were going to stand by the Allies—with our arms folded. We were throwing away the only hope of averting World War II.

The real victor was international anarchy.

CHAPTER EIGHTEEN

ADVANTAGES
WITHOUT OBLIGATIONS

*"A separate peace with the Central Empires could accomplish
nothing but our eternal disgrace . . ."* WOODROW WILSON, *at San
Francisco, September 17, 1919.*

1

THE POPPIES were now growing for the second spring on
the graves of American boys in France. Other American boys
were helping keep the watch on the Rhine. Millions of men
all over the world were under arms, and brother was still killing brother. The fine ideals of ending war and establishing a
lasting peace seemed now but hollow mockery. As the Los
Angeles *Times* cynically observed, "It is quite impossible to
tell what the war made the world safe for."

The first meeting of the Council of the League of Nations
had convened at Paris on January 16, 1920, in response to an
invitation issued by President Wilson. The American delegate
was conspicuously absent, and the presiding officer, Léon
Bourgeois, regretted the absence of the United States. Without the active participation of the freshest and most powerful
of the nations, the League was getting off to a wobbly start.
Men had no real confidence in what they were doing.

In America, the "irreconcilables" pointed to the tramping
hordes of men in Europe, and said: "Aha, we told you so.
Wilson's League is powerless to prevent war!" The friends of
international cooperation rejoined that some of these clashes
antedated the birth of the League, and that one should not expect a babe in swaddling clothes to go forth and do battle with
Mars. To internationally minded persons the weakness of the
League was a challenge to make it stronger; to nationally
minded persons the weakness of the League and the disorders

in Europe were unanswerable arguments for staying out of
the whole mess.

It seems never to have dawned upon the isolationists, then
or later, that their obstruction had prolonged and worsened
the chaos in Europe, that a strong League might have been
able to deal with some of the current disorders, and that the

On the Outside Looking In
(Courtesy of Los Angeles *Times*; cartoonist Gale)

chief handicap of the League at this stage was the refusal of
the United States to join it. We had dealt the League a crippling blow; yet we stood on the sidelines and loudly blamed it
for being a cripple.

Interest in the League began to fade rapidly in America
during the spring of 1920; there were actually expressions of

relief when the treaty was unloaded at the White House door. A few of the faithful still nourished the hope that the President might return the pact to the Senate. But it was evident to everyone with postadolescent acumen that such a move would be useless unless Wilson was willing to give ground, and plainly he was not. He had unalterably decided to appeal from the Senate to the sovereign people.

The secluded invalid in the White House could contemplate with serenity the eight-month wait until November, and the twelve-month wait until the following March. But others were more impatient. When the leaders of both parties stopped accusing each other of having blocked the treaty, they realized that no matter where the blame lay, the country was still technically at war, and would continue to be until some legal action was taken to end it.

The United States was still suffering economically from its uncertain status. The complaints of American bankers and exporters were increasing in volume and vigor; we could not even station consular officials in Germany. Several score of wartime measures were still on the statute books, and some of these were hobbling American industry. Plainly something drastic had to be done to cut the Gordian knot.

2

The only alternative to further costly delay seemed to be for Congress to declare peace by a simple majority vote, just as it had declared war by a simple majority. This, of course, would anger Wilson, but he had in large measure brought it on himself.

The separate-peace resolution, which had been seriously considered since the November rejection of the treaty, was a curious admixture of practicality and politics. It was practical because it would merely declare a state of peace which everyone knew existed, while freeing the hands of business enterprise. It was excellent politics, because everyone knew that Wilson would veto it. This would put him and his henchmen further "in the hole." He had "kept us out of peace," it could be charged, by blocking treaty ratification; he would now keep us out of peace by blocking the only other way out—a Congressional resolution. Some of the Republican members of Congress were reported to be saying quite openly that partisanship was the primary purpose of the maneuver. The proposed resolution was obviously designed to make politics rather than peace.

The first separate-peace resolution was introduced in the House by Representative Porter, a fellow townsman of the "irreconcilable" Senator Knox. It was reported from the Foreign Affairs Committee by a strictly party vote. The floor of the House then became a verbal bullfighting arena, for the Democrats showed much heat during the fifty or so speeches on the proposal. Representative Pou of North Carolina cried that it was a "bastard resolution" designed to embarrass the President, a "damnable plot" to discredit Wilson. Representative Kitchin of North Carolina attacked the scheme with such vehemence that he collapsed and suffered a stroke of paralysis.

Nothing daunted, the Republican steamroller in the House pushed the resolution through on April 9, by a vote of 242 to 150. Virtually all of the Republicans, joined by a scattering of Democrats, voted in the affirmative.

The Senate produced a somewhat different resolution, framed by Senator Knox, working hand in glove with Lodge. It provided (1) for a repeal of the war declarations against Germany and Austria-Hungary and for a declaration of peace; (2) for a retention by the United States of *all the advantages accruing to it under the Treaty of Versailles.* This resolution was also reported from committee by a purely partisan vote.

The aging Senator Knox supported his proposal with vigorous words, and he was listened to intently, for his speech was regarded as one of the opening guns in his presidential boom. He declared that although we were actually at peace the President, "with stubborn irresponsibility," kept us in a state of technical war so that he might coerce the Senate into accepting his terms. The only war then existing was the war which Wilson was waging "against American citizens and American industry."

After acrimonious debate, and after the usual charges and countercharges about keeping the nation out of peace, the Knox resolution passed on May 15 by a count of 43 to 38. Only one Republican voted against it; all the others, aided by three Democrats, voted for it. Among them was Reed of Missouri, who cried with his usual intemperance but with unusual accuracy, "Nobody outside of a lunatic asylum believes unqualified ratification possible."

3

The Knox resolution differed in some particulars from that already passed by the House. The usual procedure would have been for the two measures to go to a conference committee; but this would have taken so much time that the completed draft could not have been laid on the President's desk before the Congress disbanded for the Republican convention in Chicago. To avoid such delay the House hastily took over the Knox resolution and adopted it verbatim.

This was politics of the crassest kind. The Republicans not only wanted to put Wilson "in the hole," but they wanted to do it on the eve of the convention. The Democrats of course might have obstructed the Knox resolution by filibustering tactics, but they failed to do so. The press reported—and this seems plausible—that Wilson sent word to the Democratic minority not to delay the resolution. Homer S. Cummings, who was in close touch with the White House, declared that the President was just as willing to make the separate peace resolution an issue as he was the League and the treaty.

Wilson did the expected. His veto message of May 27 was a ringing document, reminiscent of the old Wilson and his burning idealism. Ignoring the fact that he had himself threatened a separate peace in his Adriatic note, he decried such a course as dishonorable and ignoble. It "would place ineffaceable stain upon the gallantry and honor of the United States."

The Democrats applauded Wilson's stirring message; when it was read in the House the prolonged cheer from the Democratic side was led by ex-Speaker Champ Clark. The Republicans, on the other hand, defended their position by saying that Wilson had left them no alternative.

Liberals throughout America were scandalized not so much by the declaration of peace as by what they regarded as the cool effrontery, indecency, and moral degeneracy of claiming all the advantages of the treaty without assuming a single obligation. The Europeans, it was felt, were completely justified in all the unpleasant things they were saying about us; henceforth, said the New York *Nation*, no honorable American could hold up his head in a foreign land.

Everyone knew that Wilson would veto the Knox resolution. He did. Everyone knew that the Republicans could not scrape together enough strength in either house to override his veto by a two-thirds vote. They did not. The vote in the House (May 28) was 220 to 152, or substantially short of the requisite number.

The Republicans were happy. They could further pillory Wilson as the only real obstacle in the road to peace. The blame, they said, was now on the Democrats; the Republicans had made every possible effort to bring hostilities to a formal end. Significantly, Republican leaders like Will H. Hays, who had tried to keep the peace issue out of politics, were now welcoming it. They sensed that the drift of public opinion was to their side.

Wilson and the Democrats on the other hand were not displeased. They felt that, far from being forced "into a hole," they had allowed the Republicans to fall into a pit of their own digging. During the war the very suggestion of deserting the

Allies and making a separate peace had been enough to bring expressions of anguish even from Senator Lodge. If the Republicans could go into the campaign shouting, "He kept us out of peace," the Democrats could cry back, "The Republicans will bring us disgrace, ignominy, and dishonor."

It seems reasonably clear that Wilson welcomed a chance

Peace by Resolution!

(From New York *Evening World*; cartoonist Cassel; reprinted by permission)

to veto the Knox resolution. He wanted the election of 1920 to be a "solemn referendum" on the treaty. If he signed the separate peace proposal, he would dampen the burning issue. If he vetoed it, he would bring into even sharper relief the clash of views between himself and his foes.

4

By the late spring and early summer of 1920 Wilson was much improved in health. He was able to hold a Cabinet meeting on April 13, the first since he departed for his tragic tour in September.

Secretary Houston's diary etches a vivid picture of the occasion. The President looked "old, worn, and haggard"; one of his arms hung useless. His jaw tended to drop to one side as he spoke, and his voice was weak and strained. He attempted to keep up a brave front for a few minutes, feebly cracking jokes. Then there was painful silence; he would not or could not take the initiative. One member brought up the railroad situation, and Wilson seemed to have difficulty in keeping his mind fixed on it. Dr. Grayson peered in anxiously through the door several times, as if to suggest that the President should not be worn out with prolonged discussion. Finally, after about an hour, Mrs. Wilson appeared, looking rather disturbed, and suggested that they had all better go. They went.

The next meeting was held two weeks later. Houston was pleased to note that Wilson looked much better, and took a more vigorous part in the discussion.

Symptomatic of Wilson's improvement was his more active interest in Armenia. On May 22 he accepted an invitation from the powers to arbitrate its boundaries, though there were many who questioned his fitness for such a task. Two days later he submitted a special message to Congress urging it to grant him authorization to assume the mandate over Armenia.

Sentiment throughout the country seems to have been strongly if not overwhelmingly opposed to shouldering this strange burden. It is true that the Armenians wanted us; that we had missionary interests in Armenia; that it was to our advantage to stabilize the Near Eastern situation and prevent another world war; and that we had a moral obligation to help others less favored than ourselves. But on the other hand the mandate would cost hundreds of millions of dollars (at a time when taxes were high), involve tens of thousands of boys (at a time when they were homesick), and drag us into the quarrels of the powers (at a time when we were in a mood to stay out).

The suspicion was not easily quieted that Uncle Sam was being "played for a sucker." Britain had made off with Palestine and Iraq, and France with Syria. This left Armenia, poor in natural resources but rich in the possibilities of trouble and expense. It was a persimmon rather than a plum, for if it had been a plum the Allies, it was believed, would have kept it themselves. One Chicago paper was sure that Armenia would not find a desirable foster parent "until she discovers oil or something."

We wished the Armenians well, but we wished them well at a distance. We hoped the resilient Sick Man of Europe would stop butchering them; we sympathized deeply with them in their troubles; we would send missionaries; we would dole out some bread; but that was all. We were not our brother's keeper—especially on other continents.

A final argument against the Armenian mandate—at least in Republican ranks—was that Wilson wanted it. On June 1 the Senate soundly rebuffed him when it rejected his request, 52 to 23. The close-knit Republican phalanx, joined by 13 Democrats, constituted the majority, while the opposition came from a solid block of undying Democrats. The vote seems roughly to have reflected public sentiment.

Why Wilson invited this species of humiliation on the eve of the nominating conventions is not easy to explain. (The Republican platform condemned him roundly for his action.) He could easily have ascertained by a few discreet inquiries what the outcome would be. Possibly he felt that the Republicans, by spurning the Armenian proposal, would appear to even poorer advantage in the coming campaign. Certain it is that by this time he had set his heart on the mandate, and perhaps he was hoping for some kind of miracle.

5

Before either the Knox resolution or the Armenian mandate was killed, Wilson showed his fighting spirit in another statement.

Senator Chamberlain of Oregon, a prominent Democrat, was running for renomination in the primaries of his state. Wilson, it is safe to assume, had no great love for him. The senator had in 1918 undertaken a most embarrassing investigation of the alleged ineptitudes of the War Department, and he had been one of the Democrats who had forsaken the President in the March voting.

Chamberlain's chief rival for the Democratic nomination, H. G. Starkweather, was running on a platform which endorsed the Treaty of Versailles without any reservations whatever. One of Starkweather's leading backers, G. E. Hamaker, conceived the idea of asking Wilson if it was important to nominate candidates pledged to no reservations.

Wilson's telegraphed reply, which was promptly published, left no doubt in anyone's mind. It condemned the Lodge reservations as dragging us into the depths of dishonor, and it inferred that no reservations whatever would be the ideal arrangement. It reechoed the unquenchable idealism and uncompromising tone of the speech in Pueblo.

The telegram caused much fluttering in the political dovecotes. Senator Chamberlain could hardly fail to conclude that it was a vindictive outburst aimed at him, though Tumulty denied that it was directed at any local situation. Other Democratic senators who had bolted in March were up for reelection, and they could derive no comfort from Wilson's stern message.

It seems obvious that Wilson was shooting at larger game than the Oregon primaries. There was already some talk among the Democrats of pledging the party to compromise on reservations in the approaching nominating convention. The Oregon bombshell would rout such traitors. There was also a growing tendency to praise the bolting Democrats as sensible people. The Oregon ultimatum would brand them with dishonor and make personal allegiance to Wilson the supreme test. In short, the telegram would clear away the mists gathering about the League issue, and bring it back into the clear light of day.

Various Democratic groups registered varying reactions. Senator Thomas of Colorado resented the tarbrush of dishonor. Senator Reed condemned the no-reservation policy as political suicide. Every member of the Senate, except six, he declared, had voted for at least one of the Lodge reservations. Bryan, then in Florida, blamed Wilson for blocking majority rule, and opined that the secluded President was denied information "essential to sound judgment and safe leadership." But the faithful Senator Hitchcock concluded that a majority of the Democrats would applaud the Oregon telegram.

The Republicans were more nearly unanimous. Some of their newspapers praised the Democratic bolters for their good sense and statesmanship. These senators, they said, were unwilling that "the test of faith in democracy shall be faith in Wilson." Ex-President Taft called Wilson "the greatest obstructionist in Washington. He desires to destroy all if he cannot get all."

The "irreconcilables" likewise applauded. Senator Johnson remarked that at least Wilson was consistent in opposing reservations. Senator Moses declared that "once more the President has shown that he is our best friend."

There could be no doubt whatsoever about Wilson's stand as the date for the two great conventions approached. He wanted a "solemn referendum" on the paramount issue of the League. He would scuttle his own ship before he would surrender. It was neck or nothing.

CHAPTER NINETEEN

A TALE OF TWO
CONVENTIONS

*"What a hell of a condition the land is in politically. Cowardice
and hypocrisy are slated to win, and makeshift and the cheapest
politics are to take possession of national affairs."* EX-SECRETARY
OF THE INTERIOR LANE, *October 28, 1920.*

1

EARLY IN June, 1920, like long lines of ants hastening to
a giant anthill, the delegates to the Republican convention
began to converge on the windy city of Chicago.

The Old Guard senatorial oligarchy was everywhere in evidence, and firmly in the saddle. Lodge, partly as a reward for
his services in blocking a "Wilson treaty," was made both
keynoter and permanent chairman. (In the latter capacity he
made two highly arbitrary rulings to help the cause of the
oligarchy.) Senator Watson was named chairman of the subcommittee which framed the platform; and associated with
him were Borah and two other senators. Nine senators were
active candidates for the Presidency. Senator ("Boss") Penrose
was seriously ill in his Pennsylvania home, but he kept in touch
with the proceedings by private wire. The New York *Times*
pointedly referred to the convention as "government of the
Senate, by the Senate, and for the Senate."

The "irreconcilables" were there to make the most of their
"nuisance value." Borah loudly announced that he would bolt
the party if the convention declared for the League in any
form. Senator Johnson, the darling of the hyphenates and a
leading candidate, took the polyglot city by storm. He was
going to see that there was no "pussyfooting" or "sulking" on
the League issue. He appeared with Borah before a giant crowd
in the Auditorium Theater, and after the strongly pro-German

and pro-Irish ovation had died down, he declared for no straddling.

The Old Guard was mortally afraid of Borah and particularly of Johnson, who was an experienced bolter. He had left the party to run with Roosevelt on the ill-fated "Bull Moose" ticket in 1912, thus insuring victory for Wilson. It had all happened in this same city of Chicago, and it must not be allowed to happen again.

On June 8, 1920, the convention opened tamely, dutifully, mechanically. The slender and bewhiskered Senator Lodge appeared to deliver the keynote address, clad in black cutaway, white vest, and black tie. With crisp and cultured accents he read for over an hour from a manuscript, employing a minimum of gestures, but now and then smiling smugly at one of his phrases.

The speech was a prolonged "hymn of hate" against Wilson and Wilsonism. The President had twice kept us out of peace, declared the orator, by spurning first the Lodge reservations, and then the Knox resolution. "Mr. Wilson and his dynasty, his heirs and assigns, or anybody that is his, anybody who with bent knee has served his purposes, must be driven from control," cried Lodge, to the accompaniment of approving handclaps.

The address was not regarded as a great success. It was the uninspired and uninspiring utterance of a weary and cynical politician. Only a few passages evoked enough applause to stir the hot air of the convention oven. A few Republican apologists blamed the lack of enthusiasm on the advent of prohibition and the consequent increase in the price of hard liquor from six to nine dollars a pint.

Yet the keynote speech struck the keynote: anti-Wilsonism. This was both the dominant theme and the cohesive force in the convention as well as in the Republican campaign. "Make an end of this Wilson" were the words everywhere heard on delegates' lips.

2

The platform was the most ticklish business of all. The problem was to prepare a League plank so vague that the "irreconcilables" would not be driven out of the party, and so ambiguous that even the League advocates and "mild reservationists" could stand on it. Every man could be his own interpreter. "Harmony at any price" was the actual if unproclaimed slogan of the convention.

The subcommittee that drafted the platform not only contained four senators (two of them "irreconcilables"), but it worked closely with Senator Lodge, Senator Brandegee (an "irreconcilable"), George W. Pepper (the successor to the dying Senator Penrose), and ex-Senator W. Murray Crane of Massachusetts, a sick man who died four months later. Crane wielded considerable influence, and he insisted that the convention declare for the treaty with reservations. This seems to have been, as Lodge privately conceded, the wish of the great majority of the delegates and of the people.

But a declaration for reservations would drive the "irreconcilables" berserk. It would also cause the Republicans to appear as the tail to Wilson's kite. They would be conceding that the President was 95 per cent right, and that all they wanted to do was to renovate the remaining 5 per cent. In politics one must never admit that one's opponent is even 2 per cent right.

Lodge flared up against ex-Senator Crane's proposal. He threatened to lay down his gavel, take the floor, and fight against his own reservations if the committee took any such action. Wilson must be beaten and the party kept united, even at the cost of consistency.

After the committee had wrangled for three days and two nights, the deadlock was finally broken when one of ex-Senator Elihu Root's associates produced a compromise formula which the elder statesman had earlier prepared. (Root was then on his way to Europe for the purpose of organizing the World Court.) After a bitter fight in the committee, this compromise was adopted.

It was a masterpiece of ambiguity. It excoriated the treaty which Wilson had signed at Paris; it commended the senators for doing their duty and refusing to be his rubber stamps. Nothing was said specifically about the League; nothing about reservations to the League, though the Senate, inferentially, was praised for having voted through the Lodge reservations. Instead there was a mumbo jumbo about "international justice," "international association," and "general international conference." The first two paragraphs of the plank seemed to promise international cooperation, the next four paragraphs seemed to take it away, like the small print in a fraudulent contract. All one had to do was pick one's favorite paragraphs and be happy.

The platform was read to the perspiring delegates by Senator Watson, but he raced through the manuscript with such haste and inaudibility that it was impossible to hear all he was saying. Yet the delegates cheered happily. They knew that a rift had been avoided, and that all they had to do was to pick their paragraph.

The "irreconcilables" were delighted; they applauded the platform as meaning that there would be no League whatever. At all events they were determined to fasten their interpretation upon it. Again they had won a signal victory for minority rule; again they had blackjacked the majority into submission.

The Republican friends of a League with qualifications were less happy, but there was nothing in the platform which forbade reservations, and the reservationists were more determined than ever to work for them. Besides, the rest of the platform denounced Wilsonism, and this was eminently satisfactory.

Professional Democratic politicians like Senator Hitchcock were reported as highly pleased; the Republicans had played squarely into their hands by straddling on the "great issue."

Even William Allen White, a member of the drafting committee, frankly described the League plank as a "Pandora's box of seemingly contradictory propositions," worthy of Machiavelli at his best. It was indeed a superb example of a collection of words which made sense but not meaning.

3

The Senate oligarchy had by a narrow margin scraped over the platform reef. The next task was to pick a safe and manageable candidate.

General Leonard Wood and Governor Frank O. Lowden of Illinois were the two leading candidates, but their chances (whatever they may have been) were killed when it was learned that money had been spent too plentifully or too indiscreetly in their behalf. Senator Johnson had the third largest number of delegates, and he had enjoyed considerable success in the primaries. His rabble-rousing tactics had proved effective among isolationists and hyphenates, and his opponents had managed to split the pro-League vote. But he was too independent, too headstrong, too much of the bull-in-the-canebrake. The Senate oligarchy wanted no part of him: they could never forget his apostasy in 1912.

Senator Knox, another "irreconcilable," had a brief hour of notoriety; but he was too old and too sick. (His weak heart sputtered out the next year.) President Nicholas Murray Butler of Columbia University commanded a modest amount of support, but the country was weary of internationalists and professor-presidents.

The candidacy of Senator Warren G. Harding was hardly taken seriously by the public, and scarcely more so by the senator himself. He had run unimpressively in the primaries (even in his own state), and only the prodding of his wife and designing "friends" kept him from closing his forlorn headquarters in Chicago.

But the bosses were eyeing the statuesque senator far more

seriously than the senator was eyeing himself. He came from Ohio, which commanded many electoral votes. He was a regular politician with his hand on the rail of the escalator. He was not one to kick over the apple cart; weak of will and befuddled of mind, he would take orders from his cronies in the Senate oligarchy. He was "sound" on the League issue, having voted for strong reservations. While it is true that he had few if any original ideas, and no real force of character, these were not necessary; the oligarchy would provide the ideas and the momentum. He was admittedly a colorless party hack with low mental visibility, and without executive experience; but the times, as Senator Brandegee remarked, did not demand "first-raters."

Harding looked like a statesman; he was the perfect "stuffed shirt." He had made few enemies. He could make meaningless speeches of the bowwow variety with a great deal of noise and even more unction. He had been preaching the gospel of "normalcy," and although this word was not then in general currency, it was what the people wanted. They were tired of "moral overstrain" under Wilson; they would warm to a good, red-blooded, "average" American from the Middle West who would let them till their cornfields in peace without trying to take on all the burdens of the world.

The people were tired of the cold academic aloofness—the "highbrowism"—of Woodrow Wilson. No one ever accused Harding, the small-town newspaperman, of "highbrowism." He could set type in his newspaper plant; pitch horseshoes behind the house; and play poker of an evening with "the gang." He was a "regular fellow" who could be counted on to "go along" and be "one of the boys." Big, handsome, affable, plausible, he was "just folks"—"folksy," as one admirer put it. He loved dogs (he brought "Laddie Boy" to the White House); he loved people and liked to clasp their hands in his warm palm; he was a great backslapper and "first-namer." He liked to please every one, and he was unusually successful as a conciliator of differences.

4

As the Senate cabal expected and planned, General Wood and Governor Lowden cut each other's political throats, and the convention became deadlocked. The temperature was mounting; the hotel bills were mounting; the impatience of the delegates was mounting.

Then the Senate clique took hold, with George Harvey one of the mainsprings, though he was not a senator, not even a delegate, and nominally still a Democrat. After dinner on that humid Friday night (June 11) they met with him in the "smoke-filled" Room 404 of the Hotel Blackstone. It was an informal gathering, and lasted for a number of hours, with various persons wandering in and out—among them at least eight senators. They canvassed all the possibilities, and finally came to the unofficial conclusion that Harding was the most "available" of the possible candidates.

There was one hitch. Rumors had begun to go the rounds that the handsome but flabby Harding had become involved in some scandal which might prove damaging to the ticket. The dazed senator was called in and asked, man to man and before God, if there was anything in his "past life" which would endanger his candidacy. Harding was silent for a moment, and then he asked to be alone. After having stepped into an adjoining bedroom for about fifteen minutes, and after having presumably wrestled with his conscience and communed with his Maker, he came back and said firmly: "Gentlemen, there is no such reason."

(Seven years later Miss Nan Britton published her sensational book, *The President's Daughter,* alleging that a child had been born to her of which Harding [then Senator] was the father.)

The "smoke-filled room" took Harding at his face value, the whispered word was passed along, and the convention sweatily stampeded to the enemyless Harding on the tenth ballot.

The senatorial soviet had planned to nominate Senator Lenroot of Wisconsin for the vice presidency. Senator Hiram W. Johnson had indignantly announced that he would take no second-fiddle consolation prizes; he would have no single

On the Same Platform

(Courtesy of Dallas *News*; cartoonist Knott)

heartbeat between him and the presidency. (If he had been willing to stoop so low he would have satisfied in 1923 his consuming ambition to be President.) The senatorial cabal was pushing the Lenroot nomination through when the boss-ridden delegates suddenly took the bit in their teeth and stampeded to "Silent Cal" Coolidge, governor of Massachusetts. "Silent Cal" had recently talked himself into national prominence by issuing a smashing denunciation of the Boston police strike, albeit somewhat belatedly.

The delegates wearily pulled on coats over their wilted shirts, and entrained for home with a prolonged sigh of relief rather than a whoop of enthusiasm. They had avoided a split on the platform and a split on the candidate. Victory was in the bag.

The selection of the rubber-stamp Harding was something of a shock to the country. As George Harvey later testified, "He was nominated because there was nothing against him, and because the delegates wanted to go home." He was a respectable mediocrity—or at least a mediocrity. And that mediocrity was what nominated him; ability in Chicago was suicidal. The Republicans must have been confident of victory to reach so far down into the sack for their standard-bearer. People were saying that the country was so "fed up" on Wilsonism that all the opposition had to do was to nominate a "rag baby" or a "yellow dog." They nominated Harding.

Editorial reactions were varied. The Chicago *Tribune* (Independent Republican) regarded Harding as a "four-square American" who had worked his way up from the "humblest beginnings." The liberal Springfield (Massachusetts) *Republican* thought the nominee the "feeblest" Republican candidate since 1876, when the bewildered Grant bowed himself out. The New York *Times* (Democratic), usually more restrained, branded Harding as "the fine and perfect flower of the cowardice and imbecility of the Senatorial cabal." The liberal New York *Nation* dismissed him as "a colorless and platitudinous, uninspired and uninspiring nobody," who was but an errand boy of the Old Guard, put forward "like a cigar-store Indian to attract trade."

5

The nomination of a wooden-Indian candidate on a patchwork platform presented the Democrats with an enviable opportunity. But it was doubtful whether they would capitalize on it, for they were torn with doubt and dissension, and completely without aggressive leadership.

A strong majority of the Democratic conventions in rock-ribbed Democratic states endorsed either President Wilson or his administration or his stand on the League of Nations. But in other states the situation was badly confused by local politics, prohibition, Anglophobia, and resentment against Wilson's leadership. The Tammany-mottled New York state convention adjourned without endorsing the administration; the Democrats in the Rhode Island convention (many of them with Irish names) unanimously adopted a plank opposing Article X of the League Covenant.

The Georgia Democratic convention flatly refused to endorse the administration, and the primaries were, superficially at least, a rebuke to Wilson. Attorney General Palmer, who supported the President on the treaty, ran third; Thomas E. Watson, who condemned both Wilson and the League, polled the largest vote. One of his reported slogans was that "Woodrow Wilson should be in prison and Eugene V. Debs in the White House." Yet the situation in Georgia was so complicated by local feuds that one must not try to read too much into these primary election results.

The confusion in the state primaries was closely connected with another and more important puzzle. One of the chief embarrassments of the Democrats during these preconvention months was speculation regarding a possible third term for Wilson. Did he really want it? Was he angling for it? Would he take it if offered? Was he physically able to serve? Would the country permit a violation of the sacred two-term tradition?

It is incredible that Wilson—the pathetic shadow of a once great leader—should have been eyeing a third term. But the circumstantial and direct evidence points so strongly in this direction that the riddle must be given some attention.

Several months before his collapse, Wilson seems definitely to have made up his mind to retire. He assumed, of course, that the treaty would be ratified, and the League started off under the most favorable auspices. There would be no reason or excuse for his arranging to have himself "drafted."

Then why did he not publicly renounce any designs on a third term? As we have seen, the Republicans were suspicious of him, and this was one of the basic reasons why they could not permit a "Wilsonized" League to go through. We have earlier noted that in May, 1919, so influential a newspaper as the Springfield *Republican* urged him to declare himself out of the picture. But Wilson, for reasons that may never be known, turned aside this suggestion.

After his tragic collapse and the first defeat of the treaty, there was more excuse for a third term, but the flesh was obviously too weak. Here and there one could find some support for Wilson, but conspicuously not in the South. On March 25, 1920, Representative Humphreys of Mississippi delivered a speech against the third term which elicited tremendous applause from both Democrats and Republicans.

Still Wilson did not declare or even hint that he was out of the running. His Jackson Day letter and his other public utterances completely ignored the question, and by ignoring it emphasized it. Indeed, if the League was going to be the burning issue in the election of 1920, was not Wilson the logical candidate?

Wilson's supporters intended to run him in the Georgia primary, but under the law the candidate had formally to file. A request that the President comply with the law met with stony silence from the White House, and his candidacy had to be dropped.

In the spring of 1920 the *Literary Digest* undertook an extensive poll of the voters in an attempt to ascertain their preferences for the presidency. It is significant that Wilson, despite his known physical disabilities, was highly regarded by the Democratic rank and file. He placed behind his son-in-law, ex-Secretary McAdoo, but well ahead of the other three leading Democratic aspirants.

6

On June 15, 1920, three days after the adjournment of the Republican convention, a striking development occurred. Possibly encouraged by the nomination of a "bungalow-minded" Harding on a shilly-shally platform, Wilson decided to take more decisive steps. He arranged for a three-hour interview with Mr. Louis Seibold, Washington correspondent of the New York *World,* one of the most powerful Democratic newspapers in the country.

Wilson was confident that the Republicans were cooperating in making the coming campaign a "solemn referendum" which would result in a Democratic victory. He dictated letters with his old-time decisiveness, observed Seibold, made decisions unwaveringly, and signed papers "with the same copper-plate signature." The reporter found that Wilson had gained twenty pounds, and that his face was not much changed, except for lines of suffering. He was still a bit lame, but—and this was a revealing touch—his leg did not drag so badly as that of General Wood, who had led on the early balloting in Chicago.

After Seibold had talked for about two hours to Wilson, and had loitered about to see him sign papers decisively and make decisions unwaveringly, the two men and Mrs. Wilson attended a White House showing of a "Bill" Hart western "thriller." (During these tedious days Wilson looked forward with juvenile delight to the frequent exhibition of films by what he called his "movie doctor.")

The Seibold interview, which was published on the morning of June 18, was a front-page sensation, and subsequently won for its author a coveted Pulitzer prize. That same afternoon the news "broke" that McAdoo, the leading Democratic contender for the nomination, had withdrawn from the race. He denied that he had done this with the prior knowledge of Wilson, but if he did bow himself out to clear the way for his father-in-law, he could not very well have revealed his hand so early in the game.

On the next day, George W. Harris, a leading Washington photographer, spent an hour with Wilson taking a series of photographs of the revitalized President. Harris later told reporters that Wilson looked fine, "better than I had expected. But the pictures speak for themselves."

The photographs were released on June 21, a week before the Democratic convention in San Francisco, and in time for the Pacific Coast newspapers to print them. It was reported that they would show a new and dynamic Wilson. The picture that was published in the San Francisco *Chronicle* on June 27 (the day before the convention opened) was taken from the unparalyzed right side, and shows Wilson decisively signing a document.

7

It is difficult to believe that all these developments were unrelated to the approaching Democratic convention. Newspaper correspondents do not ordinarily interview the President alone; they do not ordinarily interview a sick President for three hours; and after the interview is over they do not ordinarily hover about, gazing at the President while he signs documents and transacts other business.

All this does not prove—though some newspapers concluded as much—that Wilson was pulling wires for a third nomination. But it seems to indicate that on the eve of the Democratic convention he was eager to appear before the country as substantially recovered and able to discharge with old-time energy the duties of his high office.

Not only did Wilson refuse to declare himself out of the race, but he steadfastly declined to throw his support to any of the candidates. A sense of delicacy forbade any statement as long as his son-in-law, McAdoo, was in the race. To have come out for him would have savored of nepotism; to have come out for someone else would have savored of disloyalty.

But McAdoo had now withdrawn. If Wilson wanted a candidate who would faithfully carry out his ideals, why did he not back the most promising of the lot? He had not scrupled to support the program of Senator Chamberlain's opponent in Oregon. Why should he decline to do so when the issue was fundamentally the same but the scale of action much larger? Is it possible that Wilson did not issue a statement favoring someone else because he really favored himself?

On June 10 Postmaster General Burleson told Senator Glass (according to the latter's diary notes) that in his judgment the President wanted another nomination. Earlier the same day Dr. Grayson confided to Glass that Wilson "seriously" contemplated a third term, but that such an ordeal "would kill him." Six days later Grayson again expressed to the senator the "greatest anxiety about [the] President's third term thoughts," for the exactions of the campaign alone would "probably kill him." Yet the faithful doctor believed that Wilson's sole concern was for the League; if reelected, he would resign after the adoption of the Covenant. Tumulty, records Glass, shared Grayson's concern about a third nomination.

As the zero hour for the convention approached, Wilson closeted himself with some of the Democratic leaders. Homer S. Cummings, the keynote speaker, conferred with the President for about two hours, and then told reporters that Wilson approved his address. (Cummings remembered in 1929 that the President had expressed no preference for a candidate.)

Senator Glass, author of the Wilson-approved Virginia Democratic platform and Wilson's preference for chairman of the platform-drafting committee, was at the White House for about an hour, and this visit multiplied third-term rumors. But subsequent events, taken in connection with the senator's diary notes, indicate that Glass was there primarily to discuss the League of Nations plank. Wilson handed him a copy of a proposed plank on Armenia, and hoped that it would be included in the platform.

Later that day (June 19) both Dr. Grayson and Tumulty saw Glass off on the convention-bound train, and were anxious to know whether Wilson had said anything about a third term.

"Are You in the Race, Woodrow?"

(Courtesy of Brooklyn *Citizen*; cartoonist Norris)

The senator replied in the negative. Grayson again begged Glass to save the "life" and the "fame" of the President from "the juggling of false friends."

Even more mysterious were the comings and goings of Secretary of State Colby. He was an accomplished orator, and an inspiring convention speaker. We know that at Wilson's insistence, and apparently as a last-minute arrangement, he consented to go out to San Francisco as a delegate from the

District of Columbia—something that Secretaries of State do not ordinarily do. We also know that the President wanted him to be chosen permanent chairman of the convention.

It is possible that Wilson planned to have, or hoped to have, Secretary Colby seize the opportune moment, present the President's name to the convention in a stirring speech, and engineer a stampede for a third nomination.

The third-term movement was not sentimental but serious. Wilson, as already noted, ran well in the *Literary Digest* poll. Moreover, the hardheaded Wall Street operators reported on June 30, two days after the San Francisco convention opened, that *Wilson had taken the place of the favorite in the betting*.

Perhaps Wilson was merely seeking to control the convention. Perhaps he wanted no more than a courtesy nomination, which would have been flattering to anyone in his position, and which could easily have been declined. But it seems as though he were more than receptive to a nomination of some kind. He did not say one word in public to discourage a move in this direction. He probably was not thinking in terms of personal glory: he had had enough of that. But he may have concluded that he was the only man who had the prestige and vision to consummate his great dream.

8

Late in June, bands of train-weary Democrats were disgorged from ferryboats leading to the hill-crested city of St. Francis by the Golden Gate. This was the first and last great national nominating convention west of the Rockies.

It was a motley group, and the delegates in their persons emphasized the fact that during these years the most important elements in the Democratic party were the Solid South and the political machines of the northern industrial centers. There were three factions fighting for control: the Wilsonites, the Bryanites, and the bosses of the northern cities—Murphy of

Tammany Hall, Taggart of Indiana, and Brennan of Illinois. If the Chicago convention had its Senate bosses, the San Francisco convention had its Irish bosses.

The Republicans had fought their fights in Chicago, but they had concealed them pretty well behind the walls of smoke-filled rooms. The Democrats fought violently in public. The Irish bosses made no bones about what they were after. They wanted no more of Wilson and his ideals; they wanted a Democratic edition of Harding (a man who would "take orders"); and they wanted "booze." They and their crimson-nosed henchmen, liberally besprinkled with hoarse-throated Irishmen, detested prohibition, and they demanded as "wet" a plank and as "wet" a candidate as would float. They also wanted a declaration in favor of Irish independence.

The Wilsonites won only a partial victory in organizing the convention. Cummings, the keynote speaker, was there to present a Wilson-endorsed address. Senator Glass, likewise fresh from the White House, was made chairman of the platform drafting committee. But the convention choked on Colby as permanent chairman. The Senate bloc was finally able to shake off White House domination and select Senator Robinson of Arkansas.

Just as the formal sessions were opening, a beflagged and illuminated portrait of Wilson was dramatically unveiled, and it touched off an eighteen-minute demonstration. The New York delegation, possibly fearing a stampede for the President, sat in sullen silence among the 10,000 cheerers. Whereupon young Franklin Delano Roosevelt and a colleague seized the state standard from protesting Tammany hands, and after a fist fight and a football rush, carried it into the aisle with the other demonstrators.

When order was restored, Cummings, the keynoter, presented with great vigor and militancy the Wilson-endorsed speech. The President, he shouted, had been "physically wounded" by his enemies, just as Lincoln, Garfield, and McKinley had been. Wilson was not opposed to reservation but to "nullification." The League was the paramount issue; and "the only trouble with the treaty is that it was negotiated by a Democratic President [applause]."

The Republican platform, Cummings shouted, was a "masterpiece of evasion." [Cries: "Go to it. Hit 'em again. That's the stuff."] He called the roll of the nations who had joined the League, and asked if his audience wanted to hear the list of those who had not joined. "Yes, yes, tell us," came from all parts of the floor. "Revolutionary Mexico, Bolshevist Russia, unspeakable Turkey, and—the United States of America." [Tremendous roar.]

9

The first big fight was in the committee that framed the platform. The three most knotty problems were "booze," Ireland, and the League. Prohibition was neatly sidestepped, and an innocuous plank was adopted on Ireland. But the League was a different matter.

After an exhausting all-night session, the committee finally agreed upon a compromise. Senator Glass had presented the rather general formula which Wilson had approved: "We advocate the immediate ratification of the treaty without reservations which would impair its essential integrity." But Senator Walsh of Massachusetts, one of the Democratic near "irreconcilables," was able to add a qualification, *"but we do not oppose the acceptance of any reservations making clearer or more specific the obligations of the United States to the League associates."* (Senate reservations even pursued Wilson to San Francisco!)

After this reservation carried, Senator Glass and Secretary Colby, making a virtue of necessity, declared that the whole statement was in accord with Wilson's position. This may well be doubted. The platform now endorsed reservations that would define our "obligations"—which was essentially all that the Lodge reservations did, or all that their authors claimed they did. "Reservation" or "nullification" depended somewhat on who was doing the reserving or nullifying. In short, the Democratic plank opened the door to the Lodge reservations, or something akin to them.

This augured poorly for a clean-cut "solemn referendum." Strong reservations were permissible under the Chicago platform, by indirection; they were permissible under the San Francisco platform, by interpretation. The two pronouncements were not so very far apart after all.

The bleary-eyed Senator Glass, his voice husky from the all-night debate in committee, undertook to read the 8,000-word platform to the assembled convention. The League was given the place of honor, and those of the delegates who could hear waved flags and cheered lustily. The others cheered also. As Glass droned on for two hours, many cried "Louder." Someone shouted, "Let somebody read it who knows how." "Let Bryan read it." The plank for woman suffrage evoked a ten-minute cheer, and the band struck up, "Oh, You Beautiful Doll."

The crowd was eagerly waiting to hear the silver-tongued Bryan, who was there to seize demon rum by the throat in what was probably his last great convention speech. As he began, a foghorn voice in the audience shouted, "Grape-juice." The Commoner pleaded eloquently for the abolition of the two-thirds rule in the Senate, and for the ratification of the treaty with necessary reservations. This part of his address was well received. But when he argued for a dry plank he was booed by the thirsty Tammanyites.

After an eight-and-one-half-hour debate on the floor, all proposed amendments to the platform were defeated. Bryan, as usual, got many cheers, but not enough votes.

10

The nominations and the balloting were the next major tasks. Wilson continued to keep his hands off the candidates; his chief concern was apparently for the League. After the favorite sons had been eliminated, the contest settled down to a three-cornered struggle among McAdoo, the unfavored son-in-law, Attorney General Palmer, who had recently treated the country to an obscene orgy of red-baiting, and the "wet" Governor Cox of Ohio, who was from a politically important state and who was not closely identified with Wilsonism.

The Cox men were indefatigable. They had brought along a glee club which made the galleries ring with:

> Ohio! Ohio!
> The hills send back the cry,
> We're here to do or die!
> Ohio! Ohio!
> We'll win with Cox or know the reason why.

The parched Irish bosses killed off the "dry" McAdoo. He was too close to the White House (he was sneeringly dubbed the "Crown Prince" at a time when the German Crown Prince was most unpopular), and he had been too niggardly in doling out patronage plums while Secretary of the Treasury. Cox won on the forty-fourth ballot.

The vice-presidential nomination went by acclamation to the thirty-eight-year-old Assistant Secretary of the Navy, Franklin Delano Roosevelt. He was handsome, personable, intelligent, and was an able speaker. He was also a member of the administration (a sop to Wilsonians), an Easterner (to offset Cox), from New York (with its great block of electoral votes), anti-Tammany, and progressive. It was felt that his liberal views might seduce Progressive Republicans from the reactionary Chicago ticket. *Harvey's Weekly,* which was sparing of compliments to anyone associated with Wilson, remarked: "Mr. Roosevelt deserves to go far in public life, and will, even though he does have to suffer defeat next fall."

The exhausted delegates packed their bags without any general feeling of satisfaction. Even the League plank had turned·out to be something of a straddle, though far clearer than its Republican counterpart. Cox was a boss-dictated nominee, the first one in many years. The convention had completely evaded the issue which was to it personally the most burning: "booze." Bryan shook the wicked dust of San Francisco off his feet, sadly remarking, "My heart is in the grave."

11

Wilson could hardly have been overjoyed. His plans had partially miscarried. Colby had not become permanent chairman; his personally drafted Armenian declaration was watered down; even the League plank was "weasel-worded." How could there be a "solemn referendum"?

It was an open secret that Cox was the most objectionable of the leading candidates to Wilson. McAdoo and Palmer had both been a part of the administration and outspokenly enthusiastic about the League. Cox had been neither. When Senator Glass had mentioned his name at the White House on June 19, Wilson had broken in, "Oh! you know Cox's nomination would be a joke."

Yet Wilson could hardly blame anyone but himself. During the balloting repeated messages had come to the White House, pleading for support for one candidate or another. But Wilson turned a deaf ear. He would lean over backward to the very end.

When the Cabinet members who had been at the convention returned to Washington, Wilson was reported to be cool toward them. Something had gone wrong. There had been much cheering for the President's portrait, but not even a complimentary nomination. He had received only two votes, and those on the twenty-second ballot.

Wilson's private papers reveal that on July 2, the crisis of the convention, Secretary Colby wired the White House in *secret code*. He had been conferring constantly with Wilson's friends; it was definitely a Wilson convention. None of the other candidates could break the deadlock. Colby thereupon proposed, unless otherwise definitely instructed, to take advantage of the first opportune moment, move a suspension of the rules, and place Wilson's name in nomination.

A telephoned reply which has not been preserved came from the White House, and on the strength of it Colby, as reported in his code telegram of July 4, summoned the Democratic leaders into a council of war. All those present, except Colby, regarded the move for a third nomination as most unwise. Wilson, for various reasons, could not command the necessary support in the convention, and his failure to do so would promptly though unfairly be seized upon as proof of anti-League sentiment among the Democrats.

The evidence is convincing that Wilson seriously considered accepting a third term. But it was obvious to the hardheaded Democratic leaders that the two-term tradition, if broken at all, could not be broken by an invalid.

CHAPTER TWENTY

THE GREAT AND SOLEMN MUDDLEMENT

"Cox will be defeated not by those who dislike him but by those who dislike Wilson and his group." EX-SECRETARY LANE, *September, 1920.*

1

FOR THE first two weeks or so after his nomination, Governor Cox seems to have had no strong desire to make the League the paramount issue. The people were tired of hearing about it; it was "old stuff." But on July 18 he and Roosevelt made a pilgrimage to the White House, and they came away fired with new zeal. Publicly, Cox announced that he was in complete accord with Wilson; privately, he told Tumulty that no one could talk with the crippled idealist about the League without becoming "a crusader in its behalf."

Cox and Roosevelt have been blamed for going to the White House and permitting themselves to fall under the Wilsonian spell and the Wilsonian liability. If they had stayed away and soft-pedaled the League, could they not have won on domestic issues alone?

The answer is that the Democrats, after nearly eight years in office, were on the defensive. Negation was not enough. They had to have some positive issue. The only important one available was the League, and it seemed to offer a real prospect of victory.

Such was the general atmosphere when Cox, on August 7, appeared before some 50,000 persons at the Dayton Fair grounds to deliver his speech of acceptance. With his collar rapidly wilting, he stood squarely for the League with such clarifying (not devitalizing) reservations as were necessary. "I am ready to go in," he cried, to the accompaniment of such shouts as "That's the way to talk, Jimmy!"

Cox then took the stump in one of the most ambitious barnstorming tours on record, one which carried him 22,000 miles and brought him before an estimated 2,000,000 people. He gestured vigorously, stamped his foot emphatically, and called spades spades, crooks crooks, and liars liars. He declared that this was "no pink tea campaign," "no pillow fight." When accused by Republicans of "getting rough," he cried that they had hit Wilson "below the belt"—"a sick man in his sickroom." Now they were squealing because someone was punching back.

Cox, in spite of the injection of idealism at the White House, did not really make the League the paramount issue until the last few weeks of the campaign. During much of the canvass he emphasized the alleged "slush" fund. The Republicans, he charged, were raising $30,000,000 by high-pressure methods to "buy" the election. He called Republican Chairman Hays a liar, and branded the two chief Republican money-raisers as the "Gold Dust twins." The Republicans were distinctly annoyed by such "barroom talk"; they were convinced that Cox was no gentleman. The subsequent Senate investigation did not arouse the voters from their apathy, especially when it was revealed that the money-getters were using the techniques of the Y.M.C.A. and the Red Cross.

Cox was constantly "assailing" other things besides "slush," among them the *Saturday Evening Post,* the Senate oligarchy, and the "wobbles" of Harding. He assailed the Republicans for charging that he was "wet." He would enforce the law; besides, as he truthfully pointed out, Harding owned stock in a brewery. The noble referendum—the great spiritual crusade—was clearly degenerating into something ignoble and unspiritual.

2

During the last three or so weeks of the campaign Cox struck a more lofty note when he strongly emphasized the League. He had some little difficulty in explaining Article X to Irish and German audiences, and the wind was almost completely taken out of his sails when, on October 25, the distinguished Frenchman, Léon Bourgeois, one of the framers of the League, announced that Article X did not amount to much anyway. Why were the Americans making all this fuss? The really vital articles could be found elsewhere.

In the face of the drift away from Article X, Cox himself "wobbled." He announced in his Madison Square Garden speech that he now favored a reservation stating that the United States assumed no obligation to defend other members of the League *"unless approved and authorized by Congress in each case."*

Here we find Cox cheerfully cutting out the moral obligation from Article X—the moral obligation on which Wilson had insisted all along, and on which all compromise had been wrecked. Cox's position was now essentially that of Lodge on Article X. Charles Evans Hughes caustically remarked that before the week was out the Democratic candidate would be running on the Republican platform.

Franklin Delano Roosevelt was only slightly less energetic than Cox. He barnstormed from coast to coast for 18,000 miles, making many vigorous speeches and gaining some fruitful political experience. He betrayed no little naïveté when he promised that if Cox were elected the treaty would be ratified in sixty days. He blundered badly at Butte, Montana, when he said (or was quoted as saying) that the United States would really control about twelve votes in the League Assembly; that while Assistant Secretary of the Navy he had himself controlled two Caribbean republics (Haiti and Santo Domingo); and that he had written the new constitution of Haiti himself. When

Harding made an issue of this statement, Roosevelt heatedly denied having said the part about the votes. But all this was relatively minor; to the very end the Democratic nominee fought vigorously for the League and against "League Liars."

Theodore Roosevelt, Jr., son of the famed Rough Rider, was sent out by the Republican high command to "trail" his Democratic cousin. "Little Teddy" did some "assailing" on his own. In Wyoming he spoke to a thinning band of Rough Riders, and sneered at the Democratic degeneracy of Cousin Franklin: "He is a maverick—he does not have the brand of our family."

There can be no doubt that the Democrats, especially Cox, put on a fighting campaign which in its closing stages suggested a crusade. But all this did not appeal to the temper of the people. They were tired of crusades; they wanted repose. They did not want to arouse themselves again to noble deeds; they had done so once, and the results had been most disillusioning.

There was more than a grain of truth in the observation that in this campaign more enthusiasm was generated on the speakers' platform than was aroused in the audiences.

3

The Republicans adopted a completely different strategy. They did not need to embark upon a holy crusade; they did not have to prod a nation that wanted only repose. All they had to do was to stand on their ambiguous platform, be all things to all men, and wait for the tidal wave of reaction against Wilsonism to wash them into the White House.

Harding was a seasoned campaigner, whose statesmanlike profile appeared well on the stump. He had a magnificent voice and a superb string of meaningless and mangled words. He exuded amiability and love for his fellow man. He liked nothing better than to go out to the people, spread his muscular arms, and—as he put it—"bloviate," which he could do with considerable success.

But Harding's managers—"masters," Cox called them—did not want their "stuffed shirt" to go out on the stump. They wanted to keep him at home in Marion, Ohio, where he could run a small-town front-porch campaign, in the McKinley tradition. There his talents for glad-handing could be exercised to their full. There he could read carefully prepared little "straddles," censored if not written by his "masters."

Out on the stump Harding might betray himself. He might reveal that his "bungalow" mind did not measure up to his statesmanlike shoulders. His great gush of "bloviating" words might, through some horrible mischance, mean something definite. It was much too dangerous.

There were two opposing factions in the Republican party, and Harding was in the middle. "Irreconcilables" like Senator Johnson tried to interpret his words to mean that he would wash his hands completely of the nefarious League; pro-Leaguers like Taft tried to interpret his words to mean that he would take us into some kind of pasteurized League. The harassed Harding was shoved back and forth between the two factions like a giant pushball.

If the Republicans took liberties with the truth in misrepresenting the views (such as they were) of their confused candidate, the Democrats took liberties with the truth in attacking a Republican straw man. Their strategy was to say that the Republicans were unalterably opposed *to any kind of League.*

The Republicans, for their part, had a different straw man. They insisted that the Democrats were for the "Paris League," or the League "just as Wilson brought it back from Paris." (Few persons with any political discernment were now expecting that there could ever be senatorial approval of an unreserved League.)

So while the Democrats belabored the straw man of No League Whatsoever, and the Republicans belabored the straw man of Unreserved League, the two Republican factions propped up their straw-man candidate and promised that he would lead them in opposite directions at the same time.

For most of the campaign Harding sat benignly on his front porch at the Mecca of Marion, being "folksy" to the numerous bands of front-porch pilgrims. He clasped the hands of representatives of various walks of life, and when the Chicago "Cubs" appeared, he donned a glove and dexterously caught a half-dozen pitches from the great Grover Cleveland Alexander, appropriately remarking that our "one-man team" had "muffed domestic affairs badly," and had then "struck out at Paris."

4

July 22, 1920, was a gala day in Marion, Ohio; Warren G. Harding was to deliver his speech of acceptance. The crowds poured in, among them a Columbus glee club which sang lustily:

> We'll throw out Woodrow and his crew,
> They really don't know what to do.

Marion's favorite son stood before 30,000 of the curious and admiring, clad in cutaway coat, purple tie, and striped trousers, and spoke for an hour and a half, while his collar and cuffs grew limp, and his voice grew husky. For an hour and a half he wobbled all over the spacious Republican platform. He rejected the League of Nations (though not completely); hinted vaguely at a substitute Association of Nations; and asserted that we would help in international affairs (but in our own way).

Harding's most important front-porch speech was that of August 28, in which he vaguely sketched his ideas for the Association of Nations. He did not outline clearly what he had in mind, probably because (as he admitted one month later) he was "without specific program about an Association of Nations."

The Democrats promptly attacked "Harding's False Teeth Proposal." There was only one association of nations, and that was the League. It was actually functioning, and had a roster of some thirty members. These countries were all bound by Article XX of the Covenant to make no other compacts. It was ridiculous to suppose that all the other nations would abandon a going concern and stampede to an Association of Nations which did not even exist in the sterile mind of Harding.

Harding's Way Out of the War
(Courtesy of St. Louis *Post-Dispatch*; cartoonist Fitzpatrick)

Late in September, the Republican high command decided to run the risk of permitting their candidate to go out and "bloviate." Cox was putting on too dynamic a campaign; Harding had better venture forth and show his statuesque profile. At Des Moines, Iowa (October 7), the confused senator made the mistake of coming out flatfootedly about the League. He was quoted as saying: "I do not want to clarify these obligations; I want to turn my back on them. *It is not interpretation, but rejection that I am seeking.*"

Senators Borah and Johnson let out a whoop of delight. Up

to this time, they had been pouting or campaigning half-heartedly; now they were in the fight with both fists. Johnson went out on the stump to shout that Harding had never been ambiguous, that he had never wavered, and that he had been foursquare against the League all the time.

Cox was delighted also, remarking, "Now he's against the League, I'm for the League." "Evidently," sneered Cox, "Harding has been pulled over into the 'irreconcilable camp' by 'Brother Borah.' "

The angry protest among pro-League Republicans against the Des Moines blunder apparently frightened Harding into appearing more friendly toward the League. Cox seized glee-fully upon this unexpected advantage, and counted up his opponent's alleged fourteen wobbles on the issue, both as senator and as candidate. Actually, in most of his speeches Harding condemned the "Paris" or "Wilson" League, while conceding that an amended League was within the range of possibilities. His most consistent theme in the closing weeks of the campaign was that when elected he would summon to Washington the "best minds" of the country, male and female, Republican and Democrat. (There would be no more "one-mannism.") His task would be to harmonize divergent views and, with these "best minds," work out some kind of associa-tion of nations or even a reconstructed League.

Wobble though he did, Harding could hardly be accused of having uttered one friendly sentiment about the League *as then constituted*. On the contrary, he said some very bitter things about it ("a stupendous fraud"), while not slamming the door on salvage operations. He seems to have felt that his chief task was to sit on the fence, keep the "irreconcilables" reason-ably quiet until after election, and then work out something in line with majority wishes. This led the Grand Rapids *Press* to observe: "There are two sides to every question, and even if there were three we believe that each of our splendid Ohio candidates for President could be on all of them at once."

Harding walked down a tortuous path, with Hiram W.

Johnson holding one hand and William H. Taft the other.
Both men claimed that they held the controlling hand. That
Harding could do this, and keep a semblance of peace within
the family, while at the same time commending himself to the
electorate, was no mean political achievement.

One of the Republican campaign slogans was, "Let's have
done with wiggle and wobble." It could better have been applied to the Republicans themselves.

5

On October 14, one of the most striking documents in American political history was given to the press. It was an appeal
to the public, signed by thirty-one eminent people (mostly
Republicans), later joined by twenty-five more. The list was
an impressive one, containing the names of Root (who drafted
it), Hughes, Hoover, and a distinguished group of educators
and other public men. Here were the brains and conscience
of the Republican party.

The gist of this curious document was that the alternatives
in the campaign were the (straw-man) *unreserved* Wilson
League or a *modified* Harding League. No matter what Harding said, the United States under his leadership would enter a
reserved League of Nations. This assertion was unique in that
it virtually proclaimed, under the most respectable auspices,
that Harding was a liar, or he did not know what he was saying,
or he could be controlled by the elder statesmen after election.

Root's biographer reveals that the real purpose of the
declaration was to bolster Harding's backbone, particularly
after his Des Moines wobble, by trying to force him out of the
camp of the "irreconcilables." The statement was probably
also designed to stop the alarming desertion of prominent pro-
League Republicans to the Cox banner, and to prevent the inevitable Harding victory from being interpreted as a decisive
mandate against the League.

Some of the arguments set forth in the appeal were thoroughly dishonest, and worthy of a shyster rather than Elihu Root. But the logic of the situation was such as to give the statement much plausibility. A case could be made out as follows.

The Republican party, which probably had a majority of the "best minds," had long stood for international cooperation; the Republican Senate had tried to get us into the League with the Lodge reservations, but had been blocked by Wilson. Cox, even if he won, could not get the treaty through. The Republican platform did not preclude a League, and while Harding had admittedly been blowing both hot and cold, he had twice voted for the League, and he conceded the possibilities of an amended League. Regardless of what he was now saying, when he came to high office the force of circumstances would compel him to accept a reserved League. He would then see that the League was operating hopefully, and that the other nations would not accept his vague association.

Harding was known to be a weak character. He would fall under the spell of the "best minds," and they would lead him and the country into a revised League. After the election, Dr. Frank Crane concluded in *Current Opinion:* "There have been Presidents elected on the strength of what they promised before election; *this one was elected in the belief that he will not keep his promise.*"

The appeal of the Illustrious Thirty-one undoubtedly had a great though undeterminable influence. It was primarily useful in enabling a large number of pro-League Republicans to salve their consciences and justify their natural desire not to leave the party.

The Democrats and some pro-League Republicans vigorously condemned this specious appeal. Harding was too amiable a character; he would say "Yes" to those who got to him last. If he could be counted on to consort with Hughes and Taft and Root and Hoover, all might be well. But the Senate oligarchy had nominated Harding, and he knew it. These men were his associates; they spoke his language; and he would be grateful to those who had befriended him. The Senate oligarchy would get to him last, *and they were not friends of international cooperation.*

One pro-Leaguer pointedly remarked that to support Harding on the ground that he would take us into the League was like "supporting the Devil in order to get to Heaven."

"Let Not Thy Left Hand Know What Thy Right Doeth"

(Courtesy of New York *Times*; cartoonist Marcus

6

President Wilson naturally could not make an active contribution to the campaign, though he evidently watched it with much interest. About September 17 he sent a check for $500 to the Democratic campaign chest, announcing that he wanted to make this contribution as a private in the ranks. This touched off a Match-the-President Fund, which met with considerable success.

In the closing weeks of the campaign, Wilson, in his feeble

way, became more active. Evidently displeased with the emphasis on "slush" and with the misrepresentations of Article X as a war pledge, he issued an appeal on October 3, beginning with the familiar, "My Fellow Countrymen." He pleaded for a vindication of the nation's honor, and for a repudiation of the "gross ignorance" and "impudent audacity" of those who were urging a policy of "defiant segregation." We had to keep faith with those nations which were anxiously awaiting our verdict, and with the boys who were sleeping "beneath the sod of France." He rejoiced that the election was to be "a genuine national referendum," in which the people would deliver a "solemn mandate" to the politicians.

But the President's most dramatic personal effort came on October 27, when he received and addressed a delegation of fifteen prominent pro-League Republicans. Seated in a wheel chair, and reading from a manuscript in a voice so thick and a tone so low as to be almost inaudible, he pleaded that we go through with our moral obligation to finish the job. His voice betrayed deep emotion as he referred to our fallen heroes. Possibly as an offset to Cox's last-minute wobbling and to Léon Bourgeois' startling disclaimer, Wilson stressed Article X as the redemption of our pledge that Germany should not be allowed to break loose again. He feared that the real issue in the campaign had become obscured by partisanship (which was no doubt true), but he was sure that the nation had never been called upon to return a more solemn referendum.

The delegation went away saddened and shocked. This was Wilson's first public appearance since Pueblo. He had occasionally met with his Cabinet, and now and then outsiders had seen a muffled figure speed by in an automobile. It was evident either that Wilson had suffered a severe setback or that his condition had been reported by Seibold and others in too optimistic a vein. The latter explanation is probably the correct one.

On the eve of the balloting, Wilson sent his congratulations to Cox, expressing admiration for his courageous efforts. He could hardly have been pleased with the candidate's emphasis on "slush," or with his fatal wobble on Article X. Probably Wilson was trying to keep up a brave front in the interest of the greater good.

7

The closing days of the campaign were marked by two scandalous developments.

The venomously anti-Wilson *Harvey's Weekly* published a sacrilegious burlesque of a famous painting by Raphael which satirized both Cox and the League. The Republican leaders immediately made what shamefaced amends they could, but this unseemly sneer at the Catholic faith undoubtedly dampened the enthusiasm of thousands of Democratic Irishmen who were flocking over to Harding's banner because of Article X.

For some little while the rumor had been spread by word of mouth and by pamphlet that Negro blood coursed through the veins of the handsome Harding. Several days before the election a professor in an Ohio college was dismissed because of his alleged connection with the preparation of pseudogenealogical tables, and the whole affair, though discussed by the press in veiled terms, was a sensation.

Either one of these developments might have been enough to ruin Harding in a close election. Wilson, of course, had nothing to do with either; in fact he rebuked Tumulty, who was overjoyed at the appearance of the Negro-blood scandal, by saying that the campaign would be fought out on principle, not on backstairs gossip. But it is a sardonic commentary on Wilson's appeal for a "solemn referendum" that the whole sorry mess should have degenerated in the last days to a crass appeal to religious and racial antagonisms.

As the American people prepared for their quadrennial tramp to the polls, the result seemed a foregone conclusion to all but purblind partisans and professional Pollyannas. The straw votes all pointed one way; and despite the "Coxsureness" of the Democrats, the Wall Street betting odds were ten to one for Harding. It was not a question of who was going to win; it was just a question of how big the Republican plurality would be.

Election Day dawned for some 26,000,000 voters. Wearied of Wilson and Wilsonism, sated with idealism, disillusioned and morally dulled, bewildered by the various "wobbles" of the candidates, bored by the protracted debate and deadlock over the League, preoccupied with domestic problems, and fondly hoping for a return of "the good old days," the electorate rose up in its sovereign might and cast 16,152,000 votes for the apostle of "normalcy"—an unprecedented plurality of more than 7,000,000 votes. This was a popular vote of 60.35 per cent, a figure not equaled since Washington's day, not even by the extraordinary vote-getting ability of President Franklin D. Roosevelt. Cox failed to carry even his own state and his own district. Harding won Tennessee, the first state of the Secession since Reconstruction days to bolt over to the Republican column. It was not a landslide, remarked Tumulty, it was an "earthquake."

Long-term Democratic governors, congressmen, and senators were smothered beneath a blizzard of ballots. The Republicans increased their majority in the Senate, and the "irreconcilable" Brandegee and Moses (though running behind Harding) were triumphantly returned. The "Battalion of Death" was now stronger than ever.

It was not a "solemn referendum"; it was an awe-inspiring cataclysm.

8

The kind of crusade that Wilson hoped for never came. Enthusiasm was conspicuously lacking. An unusually large percentage of the eligible voters (among them newly enfranchised women) did not even bother to go to the polls. Many people openly said that it made no real difference who won. Cox was for the League with reservations; Harding (so the Illustrious Thirty-one promised) would get us in with reservations.

There was also a vast amount of dissatisfaction with each of the standard-bearers. Both candidates straddled, obscured the issues, stirred up offensive irrelevancies, or raked over dead ashes. There was little that was clear-cut. *Current Opinion* felt that the result was a victory for "General Grouch," while the New York *Nation* concluded that Harding was elected "by disgust."

Further evidence of disgust and protest is to be found in the remarkable showing of the Socialist candidate, Eugene V. Debs. As an involuntary guest of the federal government in the Atlanta penitentiary, Convict No. 2253 polled over 900,000 votes, the best showing quantitatively that the Socialists have ever made. Part of the Debs vote was certainly a protest against keeping men in prison for merely talking, but some of it was undoubtedly a protest against the "devil's choice" presented by Cox and Harding.

While the stunned Democrats shoveled the last clods on their dead hopes, the Republicans were hardly less stunned by their prodigious plurality. In the face of such a tremendous social phenomenon, it was impious to gloat. Warren G. Harding, who had made a poor showing in the three spring primaries which he had entered, was chastened rather than boastful.

But within a short time the spell wore off, and Republicans began to sense what they might do with their victory. Wilson had asked for a "solemn referendum." Cox had come out for the League; Harding had criticized the League (though the Illustrious Thirty-one said he did not really mean it). The Republicans had won by a stupendous plurality. Did they not have a solemn "mandate" to inter the League?

It is the time-honored privilege of the winner to place whatever interpretation he cares to on the result. His opponents

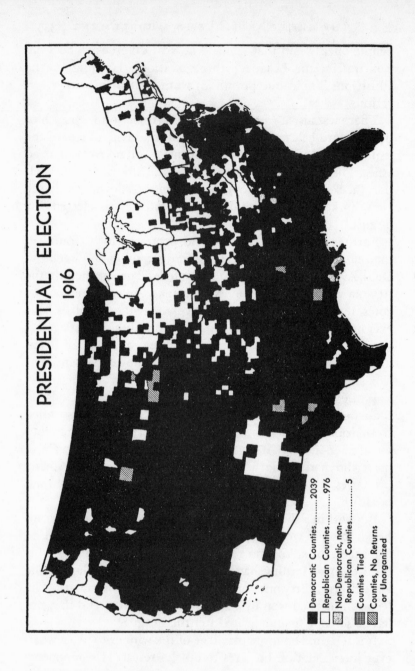

PRESIDENTIAL ELECTION
1916

Democratic Counties........2039
Republican Counties........976
Non-Democratic, non-
Republican Counties.........5
Counties Tied
Counties, No Returns
or Unorganized

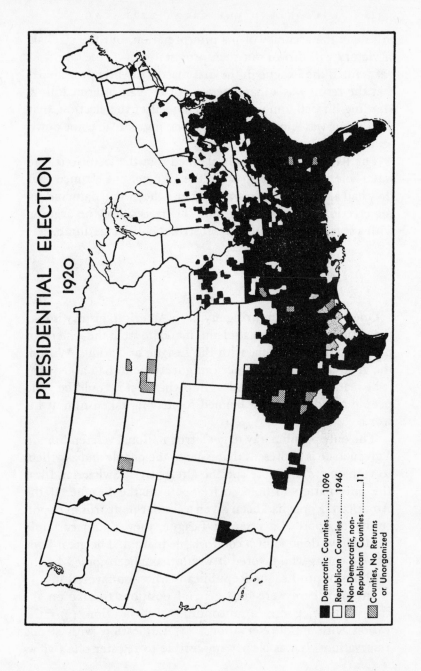

PRESIDENTIAL ELECTION

1920

Democratic Counties........1096
Republican Counties........1946
Non-Democratic, non-
Republican Counties........11
Counties, No Returns
or Unorganized

will deny the accuracy of his interpretation, but the cymbals of victory will drown out such protestations. Those who had not wanted the League in the first place stridently proclaimed that the result was a mandate against foreign intermeddling. Harding himself announced, two days after the election, that the League was "now deceased." It was now safe to come down off the fence.

The Republicans not only claimed that the victorious vote was a solemn mandate to scrap the League, but claimed that they had a mandate to do anything else they wanted, including the erection of a high tariff wall. There is simply no arguing with a seven-million plurality. It strikes politicians dumb.

9

One of the most enduring myths in American history is that the election of 1920 was a solemn mandate from the American people to have no traffic with the League of Nations. Wilson, the great authority on American government, had asked that it be made a referendum, thus implying that it could be. The people could hardly be blamed for having taken him at his word.

The only possible way to get a true national referendum on a given issue is to present that issue to the people and ask them to vote on two or more specific alternatives. Switzerland was the only nation to hold such a poll on the League. If the American people had been given a similar nonpartisan opportunity to approve a *reserved* League, they almost certainly would have done so by a comfortable margin. The great body of Democrats who favored it would have been joined by the millions of pro-League Republicans who also favored it.

In 1920 there were four general positions to take on the treaty: (1) rejection; (2) unconditional ratification; (3) ratification with mild reservations; (4) ratification with strong reservations. It was clearly impossible to register one's views on four questions by voting for one of two major candidates, one of whom "wobbled" at the end, and the other of whom publicly admitted that he did not know what he had in mind, while the best brains of his party announced that, regardless of what he had in mind, he did not mean what he said.

Even if the candidates had taken clear-cut positions on the League, there still would not have been a referendum, because the League was by no means the only issue, though it was clearly the most talked-about issue. Aside from purely local problems, there were about a hundred issues or subjects for discussion, ranging from the Armenian mandate to the tariff on California lemons.

The Republicans concentrated their fire on Wilsonism ("one-mannism," autocracy, extravagance, meddling with business, dreamy internationalism), and the sins of the war government (heavy taxes, the railroad muddle, civil liberties, the price ceiling on wheat). The Democrats emphasized the treaty, but also progressivism versus reaction, with special attention to the Senate oligarchy and the "smoke-filled" room. To say that the final vote was a clear mandate on any one of the scores of issues involved is plainly absurd.

There is even some doubt as to whether the League was the leading or "paramount" issue. Various leaders on both sides said contradictory things at different times. To Taft, "Wilsonism" was paramount; to Bryan, prohibition was paramount. Cox at one time made "slush" the leading issue; Roosevelt at one time said progressivism was the "big" issue, though both men shifted back to the League. Harding wobbled over the many issues, though perhaps talking most about Wilsonism and world organization. A few prominent newspapers like the Portland *Oregonian* (Independent Republican) said that the League was not an issue at all: it was (or should be) completely nonpartisan. The Newark *Ledger* (Independent) insisted that no red herring of foreign policy should blind us to more pressing domestic problems. The Socialist New York *Call* scoffed that, as an issue, the League was as "vital as a dead cat in a gutter."

One of the issues in the campaign was,' "What is the paramount issue?"

10

The elementary facts are these. Several million congenital Republicans and several million congenital Democrats (especially from the Solid South) were going to vote the straight party ticket, no matter who the candidates were or what the alleged issues might be. These voters were partisans by birth, race, heredity, habit, environment, conviction, and even by marriage. There is little reason to suppose that the Democrats would have won if Cox had declared flatly against the League and Harding had declared flatly for it.

Senator Reed of Missouri, a violent Democratic opponent of the League who had been snubbed and booed by the delegates in San Francisco, voted for Cox, and displayed his marked ballot to prove it. Did this mean that he was voting for the League which Cox was advocating? Not at all. His vote was a victory not for the League but for party regularity.

William Jennings Bryan, who had been hooted and jeered at by the convention, more or less sulked in his tent. Yet he announced that he had voted for the personally "wet" Cox against the personally "wet" but politically "dry" brewer, Harding. What was this a mandate on?

Pro-League Republicans were presented with a horrible dilemma, especially if they were "big business" Republicans as well, and desirous of fattening under a protective tariff. Should they bolt the party and vote their consciences against their pocketbooks? An impressive number did bolt, and no doubt tens of thousands of others would have done likewise if they had not been able to ease their consciences by the ambiguities of the platform, of the candidate, and of the Illustrious Thirty-one. George W. Wickersham, favoring the League but distrusting the motley crew of Democrats, said that there was nothing to do but "to retire to private life and cultivate roses."

When the tidal wave of votes poured in, the Hearst press and other isolationist newspapers raucously proclaimed that Wilson had asked for his solemn referendum and he had got it in no uncertain terms. The League was dead.

Washed In by the Waves

(From New York *World*; cartoonist Kirby; reprinted by permission)

But other newspapers, among them the most discerning and well balanced journals in the country, soberly denied that there had been a mandate on the League. The great majority of informed observers interpreted the vote as evidence of a revolt against Wilsonism, and of a desire for some kind of change.

This was undoubtedly true. The results were a victory that

could not be explained in purely political terms. The magnitude of the pluralities even in normally Democratic areas was evidence of something hardly less than a social or psychological upheaval. Cox *lost* New York City by about 440,000 votes; Governor "Al" Smith, running for reelection on the same ticket, *carried* the city (though narrowly losing the state) by some 320,000 votes. This was partly evidence of Smith's personal popularity, and perhaps of an Irish bolt from the national ticket, but it is unmistakable proof of a protest against Wilsonism and all that it implied.

The crippled Wilson, not the dynamic Cox, was running in 1920. The result was not a vote for Harding, but a vote against the minority party and Wilson—a Wilson who was made the whipping boy for all that had gone wrong during the previous eight years, both at home and abroad. In addition to the rank and file, countless thousands of disappointed and embittered Irish-Americans, German-Americans, and Italian-Americans vented their spleen at the polls. One English observer summed it up when he said that the crucial question had been, "Are you tired of this Administration?" And the answer was, "By God, we are!"

If there was any mandate it was in the mighty shout from the people to throw the minority party out of power.

11

Many of the pro-League journals denied that the outcome was a solemn referendum; they simply could not accept the results as final, for if they did the League would be lost. Some of these protestations were no doubt of the "sour grapes" variety. If Cox had won, the friends of the League would have claimed a mandate. But the fact remains that *long before the election,* scores of men in both parties had urged that the issue be kept out of the campaign because it was impossible to secure a true referendum.

Wilson's final blunder—and in some ways the most costly of all—was to insist that there be a referendum when there could be none. Deep in his heart he must have known this; but so great was his devotion to the League, and so unshakable was his faith in the people, that he was prepared to take this chance. Taft was right when he insisted that it was grossly unfair to condemn the League to death in a test which might well prove fatal and which was certain to be misleading.

Wilson's hopes and cause were buried beneath some 16,000,-000 votes. If he had kept the issue out of the campaign by judicious compromise, the United States almost certainly would have entered the League. Yet he insisted on the impossible. Catastrophe struck, and the champions of the League were never able to disentangle the remains of Wilson's brain child from the wreckage.

CHAPTER TWENTY-ONE

THE FINAL CURTAIN

*"The carrying out of that promise [an association for peace] is
the test of the entire sincerity, integrity and statesmanship of the
Republican party."* HERBERT HOOVER, *October 9, 1920.*

1

THE TREMENDOUS tidal wave that washed in Harding
should have come as no surprise to Wilson. The signs all
pointed so clearly in one direction that his friends tried to
cushion the inevitable blow. On the very day of the election
the Cabinet members met, but in response to their warnings
Wilson insisted: "The American people will not turn Cox
down and elect Harding. A great moral issue is involved." As
ex-Secretary Lane later noted, "Such faith, even in oneself,
is almost genius!"

When the election returns poured in, Wilson took the
shock unflinchingly. To Tumulty he remarked simply, "They
have disgraced us in the eyes of the world." At the next Cabinet
meeting Wilson looked worried; but he expressed concern, not
for himself, but for the distraught world.

A host of admirers addressed letters to the White House,
urging Wilson not to be downhearted; he had fought the good
fight, and the people were proud of him. To his daughter
Eleanor he wrote that no harm had been done to him or to
anything essential; but he was distressed because the country
now had to face a period of great trial. Symptomàtic of a heavy
heart was his request that Secretary Colby draft the annual
Thanksgiving proclamation; while Wilson bore no resentment, he found it difficult to frame a proper statement.

The outspoken Bryan publicly called upon Wilson to appoint Harding his Secretary of State, and then resign along
with Vice President Marshall. But Wilson ignored such ap-

peals. Strong as was his admiration for the parliamentary system, he was unwilling to carry his convictions through to their logical conclusion. He had asked for a vote of confidence, and he certainly had not got one, whatever it was. But he stayed on to the bitter end.

The sands of the final weeks inexorably drained out. Tumulty submitted a draft of the last annual message to Congress, which Wilson edited in his own hand; Secretary Baker was called upon to write a veto message. Occasionally, Wilson would meet visitors, but he could not shake hands with them because his left arm was useless and his good arm had to support him on his cane. Senator Carter Glass, who was seeking an interview, wrote to Wilson in jest about a newspaper report to the effect that the President had refused to shake hands with Lodge because of his "third leg." Wilson replied rather sharply that it made him very cross that so good a friend as Glass should associate himself, even in fun, with Senator Lodge.

The last days were brightened somewhat by the news that Wilson had been voted the Nobel Peace Prize (about $40,000) in recognition of his heroic efforts to establish a new international order. This coveted honor brought a flood of congratulatory letters and telegrams.

Harvey's Weekly awaited the demise of the Wilson administration with satirical impatience. Week after week, with devilish iteration, it ran fillers: "Only 237 Days More"; "Only 230 Days More"; and so on. In the issue of February 26, 1921, it could gleefully announce, "Only 144 Hours More!"

The last Cabinet meeting was a painful experience for all present. When asked what he was planning to do in retirement, Wilson replied (no doubt thinking of the troublesome Theodore Roosevelt) that he was "going to try to teach ex-Presidents how to behave." But, he added, one difficult thing for him to have to endure was "Mr. Harding's English." At the very end, following a touching tribute from his associates, his lips trembled, tears rolled down his cheeks, and he choked out, "God bless you all."

On inauguration day, Wilson rode bravely to the Capitol with the incoming President. The contrast was striking: Wilson stooped, trembling, pallid; Harding square, strong, and bronzed. At the Capitol the President was waited upon by a Congressional committee which, through the voice of Senator Lodge, asked if there were any final communications. As if pulling himself together for a final effort, Wilson turned to his bitter foeman and in icy tones said: "I have no further communication. I would be glad if you would inform both Houses and thank them for their courtesy—good morning, sir."

The ceremony ended on this chilling note. A few minutes later the reign of normalcy began.

2

Upon retirement Wilson went to live in a recently purchased house on S Street. He had chosen Washington for his home largely because he was planning to write a book, and he wanted to be near the rich resources of the Library of Congress. He actually completed only the dedicatory page—a touching tribute to his wife. His total literary output consisted of a two-page article which appeared in the *Atlantic Monthly,* and for which he received three hundred dollars.

Needing additional income, Wilson proposed to ex-Secretary Colby that they form a law partnership. Colby acquiesced; offices were opened in both New York and Washington; but Wilson went to his desk only once. The partnership was in fact more hampered by Wilson's moral strength than by his physical weakness: he flatly refused to accept cases growing out of his connection with the government. His honor and his prestige were not for sale, even though one fee of $500,000 had to be rejected. From an ethical standpoint such standards are in the highest degree admirable; but Colby had to eat, and the partnership was dissolved. This was the final irony. Disliking the law and lawyers, and having failed early in life as a lawyer, Wilson ended his career as an unsuccessful lawyer.

The routine at S Street was quiet and secluded. Wilson spent much of his time resting, reading and being read to, and dictating answers to a heavy correspondence. A few of these letters betrayed the crotchets of a sickly and elderly man, and they were suppressed by those who were caring for him. He enjoyed automobile rides and attendance at the theater, where his appearance was invariably greeted by gratifying applause. He received an ovation when he appeared briefly in a procession preliminary to the dedication of the tomb of the unknown soldier at Arlington, in November, 1921, and rode to the White House on the day of Harding's funeral, in August, 1923. On his last birthday, his sixty-seventh, a group of admirers touched him deeply when they presented him with a handsome Rolls Royce limousine, painted in Princeton colors.

Wilson more than kept his promise to show how ex-Presidents should behave. He refrained from criticizing publicly either the bad English or the bad government of Harding, though there was much to condemn in both. But he did thrust his hands into state politics, and among other things wrote letters designed to defeat for reelection both Senator Reed and Senator Shields, two of the Democratic "irreconcilables" who had not supported him on the League. Privately, he criticized Senator Underwood of Alabama for cooperating with the Republicans in carrying through their separate peace and their Washington Conference program. "If Underwood is a Democrat," he remarked to a friend, "then I am a Republican."

Weakened though he was, and failing rapidly, Wilson still regarded himself as a leader not only of the Democrats but of liberals everywhere. He met with the Democratic chieftains, and laid plans for making the election of 1924 a true referendum on the League. He did not want the defeated Cox to carry the banner again; and when Tumulty conveyed a message purporting to come from Wilson which was construed to be an endorsement of Cox, the devoted ex-secretary was dropped from the throne of grace.

Late in 1923, just a few months before his death, Wilson

seriously considered serving as United States senator from
New Jersey. Evidently he thought himself stronger than he
was, and his chances for complete recovery far better than they
were. But considerations of health, combined with the trial of
having to associate with senatorial minds, caused him to
abandon the whole idea. As he told James Kerney, they
"haven't had a thought down there in fifty years." He added
that he had a temper, and if he were to go to the Senate, he
"would get into a row with that old Lodge, who no longer
counts for anything."

3

A procession of visitors, distinguished and otherwise, journeyed to the S Street shrine. The grizzled Georges Clemenceau,
associate and antagonist of peace conference days, paid his respects, and was so distressed by what he saw that he canceled
a dinner invitation for that evening.

Lloyd George, both an adversary and a supporter at the peace
table, also came and tried to get Wilson to repeat some of the
limericks which had amused them at Paris. One impression
that the distinguished Briton carried away was the ex-President's enduring bitterness against the then French Premier,
Raymond Poincaré. "He is a cheat and a liar!" burst out
Wilson.

Viscount Cecil, faithful collaborator on the League of Nations Commission in Paris, also put in an appearance. To him
Wilson exclaimed: "We are winning! Don't make any concessions." In other words, the League should not offer to accept
such reservations as the United States might care to propose.
This was as late as April 20, 1923.

Wilson's steadfastness in the faith seems to have been unshakable. It was perhaps his strongest trait, while at the same
time his greatest weakness, for it led to self-deception. He
believed that the people would soon see the light; they had
merely been misled by false Republican prophets. He wrote to

Rabbi Wise (July 11, 1923) opposing any cooperation with the League of Nations *except on the basis of full membership.* A partial cooperation might damage the prospects of complete participation. To the very end Wilson was a whole-loaf man.

Shortly before the curtain fell, Wilson surprised his friends when he told them (according to Josephus Daniels), "I am not

Afraid of His Own Shadow!

(From New York *Evening World*; cartoonist Cassel;
reprinted by permission)

sorry I broke down." He went on to explain that as it turned out the American people were thinking their way through to their own decision, "and that is the better way for it to come." This may be the key to his unwillingness to compromise on the Lodge reservations, and to his demand for a "solemn referendum."

The day before Armistice Day, 1923, Wilson undertook the ordeal of giving a brief address over the radio—his first and last experience with the microphone. He was in an enfeebled condition, and the unperfected radio of those days did not produce the best results. Yet he managed to stir up another hornets' nest abroad when he condemned both Italy and France for having made "waste paper" of the Treaty of Versailles. (Privately he told James Kerney that he "would like to see Germany clean up France . . .") But with even-handed justice, Wilson condemned the "great wrong to civilization" resulting from our "cowardly and dishonorable" withdrawal into a policy of "sullen and selfish isolation."

The next day—Armistice Day—a worshipful crowd came to S Street for the purpose of honoring Wilson. He hobbled out onto the porch for his last public appearance, and made a few appropriate remarks. The band then struck up "How Firm a Foundation," and the aging Covenanter, as though moved by the grand old hymn, interrupted to add:

I am not one of those that have the least anxiety about the triumph of the principles I have stood for. I have seen fools resist Providence before, and I have seen their destruction . . . That we shall prevail is as sure as that God reigns. Thank you. [Great and long-continued applause.]

Early in February, 1924, it became known that the intrepid spirit of the great idealist was about to take flight. Scores of the faithful gathered outside the house, and kneeling in the snow they kept their chilly vigil day and night. Amazing as were the demonstrations of esteem accorded Wilson in France and Italy, they seem hollow when compared with this last meed of devotion. It was an unprecedented tribute to courage, sincerity, vision, and a stern sense of duty.

Wilson died on February 3, 1924—on God's Holy Day. The last whispered words that Dr. Grayson heard were, "I am ready."

4

Turning from the sublime to the scandalous, we must consider briefly some of the high lights of the Harding administration.

The photogenic new President partially redeemed his promise to gather about him the "best minds." His Cabinet contained some of the "best minds" in the country, notably those of Charles Evans Hughes and Herbert Hoover, both of whom had signed the appeal of the Illustrious Thirty-one. It also contained some of the worst minds, including ex-Senator Albert B. Fall (who later served a term in the penitentiary), Harry M. Daugherty (who was brought to trial but was saved by two hung juries), and Edwin Denby (who was so incredibly stupid that responsible people did not seriously think he was implicated in the Teapot Dome "steal"). The goings-on of some of the Harding appointees gave much point to a current quip: The difference between George Washington and Warren Harding was that while Washington could not tell a lie, Harding could not tell a liar.

The hope was still cherished, not only in America but in Europe, that Harding would redeem the assurances of the Illustrious Thirty-one and take definite steps toward international cooperation. But, as the Scripture tells us, no man can serve two masters. During the campaign Harding had clasped both devils and angels to his broad bosom. Now he had to make a choice, and it seems clear that he was swayed by his "masters" and by the awesomeness of the 7,000,000 plurality. Harding seems to have become convinced, after hearing the Republican politicians repeat the refrain endlessly, that the election was truly a mandate against the League, and that it would be politically disastrous to touch the issue even with a ten-foot pole.

In his inaugural address, Harding did not even mention the

League by name, though it had been the leading issue in the recent election. In his first message to Congress he stated bluntly that America would have nothing to do with the League; in one of his last speeches he said that the issue was as "dead as slavery." The Association of Nations died a quiet death—granted that it had ever fuzzily existed in the brain of Harding.

The isolationist newspapers and the partisan Republican press did not even wish the League well. These journals sneered at its successes and jeered at its failures, as if to prove that they had been right in opposing it. Letter after letter from the League Secretariat lay unanswered in the files of the Department of State. It seemed unwise politically even to acknowledge communications from a League which had seemingly been rejected by a 7,000,000 plurality. But public opinion became aroused when it found out what was happening, and in September, 1921, the State Department daringly acknowledged the receipt of these communications, without, of course, committing the country to anything. Some of our early notes for the League were timorously routed through the Swiss and Dutch governments. Beware of 7,000,000 votes!

5

Frightened though it was by the League, the Harding administration did pull itself together long enough to make a separate peace with our technical enemies. In July, 1921, Congress declared peace; and late in August, *nearly three years after the Armistice,* the United States negotiated treaties of peace with Germany, Austria, and Hungary. In these pacts it was stipulated that this country, while not ratifying the treaties originally negotiated with those nations, "shall fully enjoy" *all of the advantages and privileges flowing therefrom.* All three pacts were promptly approved by the Senate.

Thus the Harding administration kept faith with the boys who had thought they were giving their lives in a holy crusade.

The regime of normalcy retreated into a policy of "sullen and selfish" isolation. Immigration barriers were erected against the destitute of Europe; tariff barriers were erected against the products of an industrially shattered Europe which could not pay its debts to us except in goods.

But the conscience of the Republicans was not greatly troubled. Only one of the Illustrious Thirty-one made any real public protest against the betrayal of the electorate, and he was President Lowell of Harvard University. The two signers in the Cabinet did not resign in protest: both held their posts well into the Coolidge administration, and the available record does not show that they took energetic steps to prod Harding into a redemption of the promises they had made for him.

With the League spurned, and the Association forgotten, Harding was under some moral obligation to show that he meant well toward the outside world. The result was the Washington Disarmament Conference of 1921–1922, which was acclaimed by Republicans as a safe substitute for the League. Not only was the Conference almost completely illusory in its long-run disarmament results, but it also interfered seriously with the disarmament program of the League of Nations.

Harding died with scandals beginning to break all about his befuddled head; death was a merciful refuge. We had exchanged a President who was physically sick for one who was morally sick, and one result was to prove that there could be worse things than a cripple in the White House.

Charity begs us to drop the curtain here; Truth insists that we record certain brutal conclusions.

The Senate oligarchs betrayed the country when they nominated Harding, knowing that he was weak and suspecting that he was immoral.

The Illustrious Thirty-one betrayed the country when they

vouched for Harding, and then did nothing effective to force him to redeem their promises.

The Republican chieftains betrayed their party not only by backing Harding, but by wishfully interpreting the results of the election as a mandate against the League, and by acquiescing in Harding's timorous policy of do-nothingism. This gross

"A Banner with a Strange Device"
(Courtesy of Brooklyn *Eagle*; cartoonist Harding)

betrayal of the party and of the country was not soon to be forgotten; in the campaign of 1944 it was repeatedly brought up in an attempt to prove that a Republican administration under Thomas E. Dewey could not be entrusted with the high responsibilities of peacemaking.

The voters betrayed their obligation to their country and its obligations to the world when they elected a spineless and double-talking candidate.

Harding betrayed his party, his country, and the world, when he permitted his administration to fall into the hands of thieves, and when he turned his back upon that international cooperation which he had ringingly—and perhaps sincerely—promised.

CHAPTER TWENTY-TWO

THE GREAT BETRAYAL

"If ye break faith with us who die,
We shall not sleep, though poppies grow
In Flanders fields."

JOHN MCCRAE

1

WILSON HAS been savagely denounced for having made commitments at Paris which the American people were ultimately unwilling to honor.

The truth is that only the President was in a position to make such pledges for the nation, and that the assurances which Wilson gave were in line with his war addresses, which the people either had warmly applauded or had seemingly accepted. Wilson erred not so much in making commitments—for commitments of some sort had to be made—as in assuming that the same high degree of wartime idealism would continue indefinitely after the signing of the peace.

But whoever was at fault, the unwillingness or inability of the United States to carry through the promises made in its behalf was catastrophic.

(1) One result was a betrayal of the League of Nations. The newly formed organization was crippled at birth when this nation, the most powerful of its sponsors, left it an orphaned waif on the international doorstep. With the United States in a position to hamstring the boycotts of the League—the League's most potent economic weapon—the other countries had little faith in what they were doing. While preaching peace they prepared for war. They could not hope to carry through a successful disarmament program as long as the United States would have no traffic with them. Under the League ideal there were to be no neutrals: either one was for

the League, or one was against it. By not being for it, the United States was against it.

It is possible of course that the League would have proved a failure even with our participation. But that is speculation. It is a demonstrable fact that the League was weakened and demoralized at the outset by the defection of the mightiest of the nations.

(2) Another result was a betrayal of the Treaty of Versailles —or better, the Truce of Versailles. This pact became a different treaty as a result of our desertion, and a much harsher one. Wilson had counted on the Covenant—the "heart" of the treaty—to soften its punitive features and provide a forum for wronged peoples. But the treaty could not work unless the "heart" worked, and the League could not work unless we worked with it.

The two chief instruments for giving flexibility to the Treaty of Versailles were the League of Nations and the Reparations Commission. We spurned the one, while declining representation on the other. The all-important commission then fell under the domination of France, although at Paris it had been assumed that the United States would use its great influence in the direction of moderation. The result of our withdrawal was that Germany was saddled with an impossible reparations burden, which unsettled Europe (and America) economically for more than a decade, contributed to the coming of the Great Depression, and helped prepare the path for Adolf Hitler.

The same sad story must be told elsewhere. The commission for the administration of the Saar was to have been headed by a high-minded American historian, but it fell under the influence of a nationalistic Frenchman, who was made no less nationalistic by fears growing out of the retirement of the United States. This was the sort of thing that Lloyd George had in mind when he said that the great failure lay not in the Treaty of Versailles but in the failure of the powers to carry out its provisions in the manner intended. To this tragic result the United States, by mere abstention, contributed powerfully.

(3) Another result was a betrayal of the Allies. The United States, by seceding from the victorious Allied coalition, made the first major breach in an alliance which might have·kept the peace. In so doing, we indirectly joined with our former enemy, Germany, against the Treaty of Versailles. If the original entente had been kept intact, Hitler today might be ranting in the beer halls of an unbombed Munich.

Our sins were sins of omission; the sins of Britain and France were sins of commission. But our failure to stand by our associates gave them justification in their own minds for blaming us for many of their ills, and provided a plausible excuse for not acting together resolutely in the face of their common dangers.

(4) Another result was a betrayal of France. Suffering from a security psychosis, the French were stunned by our renunciation of the League, of the Treaty of Versailles, and of the Security Treaty. The resulting state of "jitters" was largely responsible for harsh measures against Germany, particularly the disastrous invasion of the Ruhr in 1923, all of which further aroused German nationalism and provided combustibles for demagogues like Adolf Hitler.

(5) Another result was a betrayal of Germany. The Treaty of Versailles, as noted, became a different treaty from the one which the Germans had thought they were signing. One of the Fourteen Points was a League of Nations—presumably a potent, *world* League of Nations. It was partly on the strength of such a promise that the Germans laid down their arms in 1918. But through our defection the League was condemned to anemia, and at the outset it became essentially a European league, in large part aimed at Germany, rather than a world league with the United States as a moderating member.

(6) Another result was a betrayal of liberal opinion the world over, not only in England, France, and America, but also in Germany. The black eye given German liberalism helped

undermine faith in the Weimar Republic and smoothed the way for Adolf Hitler and other apostles of oppression.

(7) Another result was a betrayal of American boys who had died, and of American boys yet unborn. Those who had died had been assured that their lives were being expended in a war to end wars; those yet unborn had to go over and do the job—a bloodier job—all over again.

(8) Another result was a betrayal of the masses everywhere, particularly the unredeemed minorities who through Wilson had been promised a better world.

(9) Another result was a betrayal of our humanitarian, missionary, and educational interests not only in Europe, but particularly in the Near East. Our retirement from the scene delayed the Near Eastern settlement, and infused new life into the Turks, with resulting disaster to the Armenians and other peoples for whom we had something of a moral responsibility.

(10) Another result was a betrayal of the legitimate interests of American merchants, manufacturers, bankers, and investors. We adopted a policy of ostrichism: trying to play the role of a debtor nation when we were now a creditor nation; seeking to eat our cake and have it too; raising high tariff and other barriers. In so doing we contributed heavily to the economic ills of Europe in the 1920's and 1930's, which in turn prepared the foundations of the Great Depression, which in turn brought in Adolf Hitler.

(11) Another result was a betrayal of America's responsibility to assume that world leadership which had been thrust upon her. First of all, there was a kind of *noblesse oblige*—an obligation to help the less fortunate. Secondly, there were the dictates of both selfishness and common sense—of playing an active role so as to safeguard our interests and prevent our being dragged into World War II. Instead, we cravenly retreated, while our prestige sank to a new low in Europe, the Far East, and Latin America. Instead of trying to control events, we left ourselves at the mercy of events which inexorably drew us again into their vortex.

(12) Another result was a betrayal of the nation's plighted word and of good faith in international dealings. The world will be long in recovering completely from the shock of our desertion in 1919–1920. The cooperation of the United States had been indispensable for victory; it was no less indispensable for a victorious peace. We achieved the one gloriously; we botched the other ingloriously. Henceforth other nations, in laying their plans for a world order, must choose not what they think is desirable but what they think the political situation in America will permit the Senate to accept. All this makes for world instability, and militates against that maximum of international cooperation which might otherwise be possible.

The moral is that the ill effects of broken pledges are worse than those resulting from no pledges at all. If our government is so unworkable that we cannot carry through commitments which the President makes and a majority of the people want to honor, then we had better warn other nations in advance, so that they can count on only limited American cooperation —or no cooperation at all.

(13) Another result was a betrayal of our clear moral obligation to finish the job. If we had stayed out of the war in 1917, Europe would have worked out something different if not better—perhaps a negotiated peace. By throwing our power into the balance, we brought victory to one side and prostration to the other, all the while creating problems which we were morally bound to help solve. Vice President Marshall pointedly remarked that we were like the man who rushed into his neighbor's house to beat off a burglar, and then rushed back home, leaving the victim bleeding to death on the floor.

It ill became the United States to sit self-righteously on the side lines during the 1920's and 1930's and blame the Europeans for not solving their problems, when some of those problems would never have been created if we had stayed out altogether, or had not turned away from the plow when the furrow was only half completed.

(14) Another result was a betrayal of the American people. An overwhelming majority of our citizens clearly wanted the League—at least with some reservations. Wilson's instincts were sound when he vainly sought to find some way by which the people might express their will through their government. But our method of approving treaties is so antiquated, illogical, undemocratic, and unworkable that the American people had no mechanism through which to implement their desires. And Wilson's own inflexibility, as we have noted, tightened the deadlock.

The Gap in the Bridge

(Reproduced by permission of the Proprietors of *Punch*)

In 1919 and in 1920, the American people were willing to forsake the ancient path of isolation, at least with reservations. By the 1930's they were in a different mood, because by that time they saw that the League (which they had helped condemn to impotence) was a failure in preventing aggression by a major power.

This long and disconcerting list of "betrayals" does not necessarily mean that our withdrawal was solely, or even primarily, responsible for all the ills that befell Europe from 1919 to 1939. But it does mean that the United States cannot escape a very considerable share of the blame for what happened.

2

At the conclusion of the volume *Woodrow Wilson and the Lost Peace,* certain general principles were set forth regarding peacemaking. It now seems proper to list a few maxims relating to peace-ratifying and peace-executing.

(1) Politics, in so far as possible, should be kept out of foreign affairs. Nothing should be more nonpartisan than international relations, because what is good for one party is presumably good for both parties and the entire country. This, of course, suggests the counsel of perfection: politics is a bacillus which laughs at three-mile lines. Yet we should never wantonly throw a delicate issue on foreign affairs into the turbulence of a political campaign. The result is certain to be misleading and possibly disastrous. We must seek senators to match our mountains—men who will put the good of the country above the good of the party; who will put the advancement of humanity above the advancement of self. We should select senators and members of the House as much (if not more) for their position on foreign affairs as for their position on domestic affairs: the two, as we shall note, are inextricably intertwined.

(2) The two-thirds rule in the Senate should be eliminated. It is the refuge of the filibusterer, the obstructionist, and the devotee of minority rule, all of whom are foreign to a true democracy. This antique restriction adds immeasurably to clumsiness and deadlock in the treaty-ratifying process. In March, 1920 (though not in November, 1919), it was directly responsible for the defeat of the treaty.

(3) A postwar slump in idealism is inescapable in the cold, gray dawn that follows victory. The urge to return to a normalcy that can never be again is age-old; the growth of distrust in one's allies, once the common cause is won, is inevitable. The peacemakers should never lose sight of these things when

they come to design the temple of the future, and not try to attain the unattainable.

(4) Perfectionism is impossible in this workaday world. Our statesmen and our people, whether fashioning treaties of peace or fashioning new world organizations, should seek what will work—not what seems ideally desirable. The League was not perfect. It was, said one critic, only half a League—but it was half a League onward. Even today, after more than a century and a half of experience—our Constitution is far from perfect; yet we have changed it and are changing it.

(5) Compromise may be as essential in peace-ratifying as in peacemaking. Certainly this was true in Washington during 1919-1920. A stubborn refusal to compromise when the people demand compromise not only is undemocratic but may, as it did in 1920, lead to the defeat of the entire treaty.

(6) Sovereignty is a sacred cow tied across the path of international cooperation. It conjures up all kinds of unwarranted fears. But an impairment of sovereignty—of national freedom of action—is a characteristic of treaties entered into on a free and friendly basis. Broadly speaking, a treaty is a promise to give up, in return for something else, that which we would ordinarily do. The United States has entered into hundreds of international agreements, but our sovereignty is essentially unimpaired.

(7) Effective international cooperation demands a price. That price is the yielding of some small part of our freedom of action—our sovereignty—so that we may, through preventing international disorders, enjoy greater freedom of action. The good things of life may be free, but peace is not one of them. One of the supreme follies of the American people in the post-Versailles years was to demand rights, while shunning responsibilities. We found ourselves in the immoral and disastrous position of seeking all the immunities, privileges, and advantages of riding in the international boat, while refusing to pull the laboring oar of liabilities, responsibilities, and costs.

(8) An excess of suspicion—a Yankee horse-trading trait—

is a barrier to international cooperation. Peace can be preserved only among men of good will, for it is a blessing which
rests not so much on paper pacts as on attitudes of mind. Peace
can no more be maintained by parchment than sobriety can
be maintained by constitutional amendments.

In 1919 we were the most powerful and secluded of the great
nations, yet we acted as though we were the weakest and most
vulnerable. Rich though we were, we feared that we might be
asked to contribute one cent more than our proper share;
powerful though we were, we feared that a few thousand of
our soldiers might be sent abroad to prevent ten million from
following them. We confessed by our conduct that our representatives were not intelligent enough to sit down at the same
table with those of other nations, even though we had the
highest stack of chips and most of the high cards.

If we enter a world organization for peace, eyeing our colleagues distrustfully and momentarily expecting them to try
to "put something over on us," then failure is inevitable. There
is usually more to be gained through an excess of confidence
than through an excess of suspicion.

(9) Domestic affairs are but the obverse side of the shield
of foreign affairs. In the 1920's the American people fatuously
sought to crawl into a hole and pull the hole in after them.
But they discovered to their sorrow—or at least some of them
did—that immigration barriers, tariff walls, reparations payments, and foreign debts all stir up international reverberations. World depressions leap lightly across international
boundaries; bumper wheat crops in the Argentine and Australia bring impoverishment to American farmers. The wars
of Europe and Asia have an ugly and inexorable habit of becoming our wars.

(10) It is better to desert one's associates before the peace
is drawn up than after. In 1919 we forced the Europeans to
adopt a kind of treaty they would not have adopted if we had
stayed out. Then we left them in the lurch and loudly condemned them because they could not make our kind of peace

work. If we are unwilling or unable to ratify and help execute a world peace, then we owe it to our associates to say so, in order that they may draw their plans accordingly.

(11) Isolationism as a physical fact is dead (granted that it ever existed), even though the isolationists are not. The desire to draw apart and mind one's own business is entirely natural and often commendable. But on this shriveling planet such an ideal is impracticable. With new inventions annihilating both time and distance, the Atlantic Ocean today is far smaller than the Aegean Sea was in the day of Pericles. It is now "One World," and we cannot secede from it. This whirling ball has now become so small that an international quarrel anywhere becomes our business. Wilson recognized all this, and it explains why he fought to the death for his ideal.

Since 1689, there have been nine world wars, and the American people have been drawn into *every single one of them*. This disconcerting fact lends much force to the truism that the only sure way for us to keep out of a great world conflict is to prevent its outbreak. If we are unwilling to recognize that we are a part of this planet, and if we are not utter fools, *we had better start preparing for the next world war right now.*

(12) Power creates responsibilities. The United States has become so wealthy and so powerful that, whether we do nothing or something in regard to an international organization, our influence will be felt for good or ill, positively or negatively. Aloofness merely accelerates the chaos which will inevitably engulf us. As long as this power exists, and as long as it will be felt one way or the other, elemental common sense commands us to direct it actively into channels which will be most helpful to the rest of the world and indirectly to ourselves.

(13) The United States, as the richest of the powers, has as vital an interest in world peace as any other nation. Another world war may bankrupt us. In 1919 we prided ourselves on not asking for anything at the peace table—in spurning reparations which we did not need and mandates which we did not

want. But we did have an enormous material stake, *and that was in making the peace last.* Because it did not last we were forced to incur a debt of over $200,000,000,000 and mobilize a force of over 11,000,000 men. Compared with this colossal outlay, the cost of making a world order operate would be nothing.

False Security

(Courtesy of Denver *Rocky Mountain News*; cartoonist Cory)

(14) American opinion must be educated to its responsibilities in international affairs. If a new world organization is to work, we as a people must have a better appreciation of our long-run interests and our long-range responsibilities. One of the most formidable barriers to international cooperation is the pursuit of the immediate, short-run advantage to the exclusion of the less immediate but more profitable longer-run advantage. Unless man is willing to labor for the interests of

all (which are his long-run interests); unless he is prepared to avoid the selfish short-run gain which hurts his neighbor and indirectly himself; unless he can assume that most people are decent human beings striving toward a common end—then we might just as well start preparing to go back into the jungle and up into the trees. *There can be no long-range peace without a long-range view.*

3

A few final observations.

Should the United States have ratified the treaty and joined the League? In the face of the evidence herein presented, there can be only one answer. We had very little if anything to lose—perhaps the trivial expenses of the League; and everything to gain—possibly a preventing of so-called World War II. No nation was ever trapped in the League, as our isolationists feared: Japan got out, Germany got out, Russia was thrown out. Where the possible losses were so negligible, and the probable gains so tremendous, the United States, as Wilson repeatedly pointed out, was more than justified in taking the chance.

Would the results have been essentially different if we had joined the League?

The conclusions here must of course be more speculative. But it seems clear that some kind of "slump in idealism" would have come sooner or later, and it may legitimately be doubted whether, when the pinch came, the United States would have provided adequate support for the League of Nations. The events of the 1930's would seem to support such a view, but we must remember that the set of circumstances then encountered might not have come into being if we had joined the League in the first instance.

General Jan C. Smuts said that not Wilson but "humanity" failed at Paris. This is a striking statement that has little meaning, in part because the real failure came after Paris. If a horseman spurs his mount at a twelve-foot brick wall, who is responsible for the ensuing accident: the horse that fails to make the jump, or the rider who has attempted an impossible feat?

A horseman must know his horse and its limitations; a statesman must know his people and their limitations, as well as the limitations of foreign peoples. Otherwise he is not a statesman. He must not set for his people impossible goals, however desirable they may be in the abstract. He must train public opinion by gradations for the new tasks—not try to shoot Niagara all at once. He must educate the people in advance for the responsibility which he is asking them to shoulder. Otherwise, even though they may temporarily take on the burden, they are likely to find it too wearisome and cast it aside.

Wilson engineered a revolution in our foreign policy when he undertook to lead the American people out of the path of isolationism into that of effective world cooperation. Yet the isolationists, aided by the circumstances set forth in this book, were able to effect a counterrevolution, and take us back into the old paths. But it is possible that this counterrevolution would have come within a few years anyhow; the people were not yet fully ready for a major departure.

The great Covenanter was eternally right in recognizing that isolationism was but a mirage, and that the next war would surely drag us in, and that the new organization for peace had to be based upon justice for all. The stakes were enormous; they were worth giving one's life for. He failed in part because he seems not to have realized that his was a dual task: making a peace and changing a national—perhaps a world—psychology.

Wilson was the greatest of the neutral statesmen, the greatest mediator, the greatest war leader, the greatest peacemaker, the greatest tragedy, and the greatest disappointment. Reaching for the stars, he crashed to earth.

But his was a magnificent failure, and in some ways a successful failure. Wilson once said, "Ideas live; men die." His ideas have lived. The Wilsonian tradition has been kept alive, and countless thousands of men and women have vowed that we shall not make the same mistakes again. We shall know better how to do it next time. We know better our limitations and those of other peoples, for we have before us the successes and failures of the League. We know better what machinery will work, and what will not. We know that a League without teeth is little better than a debating society.

We must never forget that there are two phases to a war: the fighting duration, and the peace duration. Partly because men did not recognize this, the Treaty of Versailles became an armistice, and the postwar era a prewar era. Only a handful of statesmen can actually draw up a treaty of peace. *But in a democracy every citizen can actively participate in its ratification and in its execution.* Upon him rests a sacred obligation not only to do so but to do so intelligently. The record is there for him to read, and he should read it—*with due regard for changed conditions.*

We do not want to have to do the ghastly job a third time.

BIBLIOGRAPHICAL NOTES

INTRODUCTION

THIS BOOK, like its predecessor,' *Woodrow Wilson and the Lost Peace,* is to some extent a synthesis and largely an interpretation or reinterpretation of certain basic facts. It contains more significant new data than the earlier volume; hence the Bibliographical Notes are somewhat more fully documented. Footnotes are not included in the text, primarily because it should be reasonably clear to the specialist after examining these Notes where the material in question may be found.

Public opinion was even more vitally important in peace-ratifying than in peace-making, and for this reason more emphasis is placed upon it than in the preceding volume. The New York *Times* was followed throughout, and for specific periods use was made of the various other newspapers herein listed. The periodical press was most helpful, including the *Independent,* the *Outlook,* the *New Republic,* the New York *Nation,* the *Review of Reviews,* and particularly *Harvey's Weekly, Current Opinion,* and the *Literary Digest.*

Although the already-exploited House Papers at Yale University were of some value, the significant manuscript discoveries were made in the Ray Stannard Baker Collection, the Lansing Papers, the Hitchcock Papers, and particularly the Wilson Papers—all in the Library of Congress.

In the bibliographies and notes that follow, the full citation is given the first time only; thereafter the shortened form. Where quoted material appears in italics, both in the notes and in the text, these have been inserted by the present writer, unless otherwise indicated.

CHAPTER ONE

THE RETURN OF THE
MESSIAH

FOR THE events connected with Wilson's return, see the relevant issues of the New York *Times;* also Alice R. Longworth, *Crowded Hours* (New York, 1938), pp. 285–286; David F. Houston, *Eight Years with Wilson's Cabinet* (Garden City, N.Y., 1926), II, 4–6. Joseph P. Tumulty, *Woodrow Wilson As I Know Him* (Garden City, 1921), is useful, but the historian must use with caution all reports of conversations with Wilson reproduced verbatim from memory. The texts of Wilson's two speeches appear in Woodrow Wilson, *War and Peace: Presidential Messages, Addresses, and Public Papers* (1917–1924), eds. Ray Stannard Baker and William E. Dodd (2 vols., New York, 1927), I, 532–535, 537–552.

PUBLICATION OF THE TREATY. Wilson's views on the publication problem were expressed to the Council of Four on May 17 and June 12, 1919 (Minutes of the Council of Four, Wilson Papers, IX–C). See also R. S. Baker, *Woodrow Wilson and World Settlement* (Garden City, 1922), I, 158; Allan Nevins, *Henry White* (New York, 1930), pp. 449, 452–453; Claudius O. Johnson, *Borah of Idaho* (New York, 1936), pp. 236–237; Philip C. Jessup, *Elihu Root* (New York, 1938), II, 396–399. Root's role during the treaty fight was a devious one. Though an outstanding friend of international collaboration, he worked closely with the Senate Republicans in planning a program of reservations, and either wittingly or unwittingly played into the hands of the obstructionists.

WILSON'S GENERAL ATTITUDE. On Wilson's state of mind, particularly regarding the Senate, both before and after his return, see Wilson to Lansing, May 24, 1919; Wilson to Tumulty, June 14, June 16, 1919 (Wilson Papers, IX–A). Also Tumulty to Wilson, May 26, 1919 (in *ibid.*); Stephen Bonsal, *Unfinished Business* (Garden City, 1944), pp. 48, 58–60, 153; Charles Seymour, *The Intimate Papers of Colonel House* (Boston, 1928), IV, 487; Herbert Hoover, *America's First Crusade* (New York, 1942), p. 63; Henry Cabot Lodge, *The Senate and the League of Nations* (New York, 1925), chaps. VII, IX; David Lawrence, *The True Story of Woodrow Wilson* (New York, 1924), p. 269; C. T. Thompson, *The Peace*

Conference Day by Day (New York, 1920), p. 415; W. Stull Holt, *Treaties Defeated by the Senate* (Baltimore, 1933), pp. 272–276. The incident recorded by Butler appears in N. M. Butler, *Across the Busy Years* (New York, 1940), II, 197–201. The time element in this situation is not altogether clear. Especially useful is John McCook Roots, "The Treaty of Versailles in the United States Senate," a manuscript Senior Honors Thesis (1925) deposited in the Widener Library, Harvard University. The author interviewed a number of the surviving participants (including Hitchcock, Taft, Glass, and Borah), and was given access by Senator Borah to the confidential minutes of the Senate Foreign Relations Committee.

THE SECURITY TREATY WITH FRANCE. For the text of the treaty and Wilson's message of presentation, see *Cong. Record,* 66 Cong., 1 sess., pp. 3310–3311. For general backgrounds and bibliography, consult T. A. Bailey, *Woodrow Wilson and the Lost Peace* (New York, 1944), pp. 230–237, 357–358. Also Robert Lansing, *The Peace Negotiations* (Boston, 1921), chap. XV; Wilson's press interview, July 10, 1919 (Wilson Papers, II–C); and Lodge, *op. cit.,* pp. 152–156. For the sympathy of certain anti-League leaders with the idea of the treaty, if divorced from the League and limited in time, see Allan Nevins, *op. cit.,* p. 450; Claude G. Bowers, *Beveridge and the Progressive Era* (Boston, 1932), p. 507; Jessup, *op. cit.,* p. 401; and particularly the leading article in *Harvey's Weekly,* Aug. 9, 1919, pp. 1–2.

CHAPTER TWO

THE PARADE OF PREJUDICE

M U C H O F the material used in this chapter has been drawn from the contemporary press, both newspaper and periodical. The general background for the period may be best found in F. L. Allen, *Only Yesterday* (New York, 1931), and Mark Sullivan, *Our Times,* vols. V, VI (New York, 1933, 1937). There is also some sketchy general material in Roger Burlingame and Alden Stevens, *Victory*

Without Peace (New York, 1944); in David Loth, *Woodrow Wilson: The Fifteenth Point* (Philadelphia, 1941); and particularly in W. E. Dodd, *Woodrow Wilson and His Work* (Garden City, N.Y., 1922). The viewpoint of the isolationists is set forth in C. O. Johnson, *Borah;* in C. G. Bowers, *Beveridge;* and in W. F. Johnson, *George Harvey* (Boston, 1929).

THE LIBERALS AND THE TREATY. Probably the best source consists of the files of the *New Republic* and the New York *Nation*. See Oswald G. Villard, *Fighting Years* (New York, 1939), and the same author's sketch of Herbert D. Croly (the *New Republic*'s editor) in the *Dictionary of American Biography*, XXI, Supplement One. The influence of J. M. Keynes' book, *The Economic Consequences of the Peace* (New York, 1920), can hardly be overestimated. The *New Republic* not only published parts serially, but sold a cheap edition to its subscribers. On May 15, 1919, five minor members of the Peace Commission wrote to Joseph C. Grew, severely criticizing the treaty and in some cases threatening to resign. They were Adolf A. Berle, Jr., Joseph V. Fuller, Samuel E. Morison, George B. Noble and John Storck (Lansing Papers, vol. 43). William C. Bullitt's sensational letter of resignation, dated May 17, 1919, is in this file. On the question of resignations, see Robert Lansing, *Peace Negotiations*, pp. 274–275; the New York *Nation*, Feb. 21, 1920, p. 224.

CHAPTER THREE

THE PALL OF PARTISANSHIP

THE GENERAL backgrounds of partisanship are well set forth in D. F. Fleming, *The United States and the League of Nations, 1918–1920* (New York, 1932); in W. S. Holt, *Treaties Defeated by the Senate,* chap. X; and in J. M. Roots, "The Treaty of Versailles." See also W. E. Dodd, *Woodrow Wilson;* P. C. Jessup, *Elihu Root;* C. G. Bowers, *Beveridge;* H. F. Pringle, *The Life and Times of*

William Howard Taft (New York, 1939), vol. II; David Lawrence, *Woodrow Wilson;* and Alice R. Longworth, *Crowded Hours.* On the rebuffing of Wood and Roosevelt, see Hermann Hagedorn, *Leonard Wood* (New York, 1931), vol. II; and H. F. Pringle, *Theodore Roosevelt* (New York, 1931).

THE THIRD-TERM ISSUE. For the documentation of this episode, and the further elaboration of it, see pp. 409–411. David Lawrence, early in 1919, wrote for the London *Times* that the League cause in the United States would be strengthened if divorced from a third term. Wilson, Lawrence says, cabled to Tumulty from Paris, asking whether he should renounce a third term; Tumulty replied that this was unnecessary. About a year later, when Lawrence published a story setting forth these developments, he noted evidence of White House displeasure. (Lawrence, *Woodrow Wilson,* pp. 299-300.)

SENATORIAL ASPIRANTS FOR THE PRESIDENCY. Republican senators who were mentioned more or less prominently, or actually nominated, were: Johnson, Knox, Poindexter, Lenroot, Harding, Sutherland, France, Capper, and Borah. The Democratic senators were Underwood, Hoke Smith, Pomerene, Sheppard, Simmons, and Hitchcock. Senators Calder and Lenroot were well regarded for the Republican vice presidential nomination.

CHAPTER FOUR

THE CAVE OF THE WINDS

USEFUL BACKGROUND accounts appear in D. F. Fleming, *The United States and the League of Nations;* in W. S. Holt, *Treaties Defeated by the Senate;* in C. A. Berdahl, *The Policy of the United States with Respect to the League of Nations* (Geneva, 1932); in H. B. Learned, "The Attitude of the United States Senate Towards the Versailles Treaty: 1918–1920," in H. W. V. Temperley, ed., *A History of the Peace Conference of Paris* (London, 1924), vol. VI, chap. V; in J. M. Roots, "The Treaty of Versailles";

and in G. A. Finch, "The Treaty of Peace with Germany in the United States Senate," *American Journal of International Law,* XIV (1920), 155–206. See also J. E. Watson, *As I Knew Them* (Indianapolis, 1936), by a "strong reservationist" Republican senator from Indiana; Allan Nevins, *Henry White;* P. C. Jessup, *Elihu Root,* vol. II; H. F. Pringle, *William H. Taft,* vol. II; Alice R. Longworth, *Crowded Hours.* Considerable ephemeral material exists on the "irreconcilables," but two books must be particularly mentioned: C. G. Bowers, *Beveridge* (ex-Senator Beveridge was closely associated with the "irreconcilables"); and C. O. Johnson, *Borah,* a high-grade campaign biography, written in close collaboration with the senator. On Lodge the most revealing work is the senator's apology, H. C. Lodge, *The Senate and the League.* See also, Stephen Bonsal, *Unfinished Business;* Allan Nevins, *op. cit.;* William Lawrence, *Henry Cabot Lodge* (Boston, 1925), a most sympathetic account; and the most recent biography, Karl Schriftgiesser, *The Gentleman from Massachusetts: Henry Cabot Lodge* (Boston, 1944), which presents the conventional interpretation of Lodge's wickedness in the treaty fight. See also the revealing account in Fleming, *op. cit.,* chap. XIX.

THE SENATE GROUPS. It is difficult, if not impossible, to make accurate statements regarding the exact composition of the various Senate groups throughout the entire fight. Their personnel changed from time to time; and in each classification there were marginal senators who fluctuated back and forth. This was notably true of the "mild reservationists" and the "strong reservationists." The Democratic regulars were on the whole constant, as was the "Battalion of Death," but even here there was a marked contrast between these two groups in the November and the March voting. See particularly W. S. Holt, *Treaties Defeated by the Senate,* p. 296.

CHAPTER FIVE

THE STRATEGY
OF STRANGULATION

On packing the committee see H. C. Lodge, *The Senate and the League;* J. M. Roots, "The Treaty of Versailles"; David Bryn-Jones, *Frank B. Kellogg* (New York, 1937); D. F. Fleming, *The United States and the League of Nations.* On the conferences with individual senators, consult Lodge, *op. cit.;* J. E. Watson, *As I Knew Them;* and Hitchcock's speech of Jan. 13, 1925 (Nebraska Historical Society). On the Senate Committee hearings, the best source is *Sen. Docs.,* 66 Cong., 1 sess., no. 106. See also Fleming, *op. cit.;* Lodge, *op. cit.;* Allan Nevins, *Henry White;* W. S. Holt, *Treaties Defeated by the Senate.* The official record of the White House conference appears in *Sen. Docs.,* 66 Cong., 1 sess., no. 76; the correspondence between Lodge and Wilson leading up to it is published in the New York *Times,* Aug. 16, 1919. See also Lodge, *op. cit.;* J. P. Tumulty, *Woodrow Wilson As I Know Him;* and David Lawrence, *Woodrow Wilson* (Lawrence apparently was there).

SENATORIAL INVITEES TO INDIVIDUAL CONFERENCES. As the Wilson papers show, the President, on July 16, invited Jones of Washington, Colt of Rhode Island, Nelson and Kellogg of Minnesota, Kenyon of Iowa, Capper of Kansas, and McNary of Oregon. On July 19, he invited McLean of Connecticut, Cummins of Iowa, Calder of New York, Edge of New Jersey, Newberry of Michigan, Page of Vermont, and Norris of Nebraska. On July 29, he invited Watson and New of Indiana, Keyes of New Hampshire, Lenroot of Wisconsin, Fernald of Maine, Harding of Ohio, and Dillingham of Vermont. The New York *Times* reported that in addition to these, McCumber of North Dakota, Sterling of South Dakota, and Spencer of Missouri were invited, though carbon copies of the invitations were not found in the Wilson Papers. Lodge's list, *op. cit.,* p. 157, is somewhat inaccurate. Twenty-four in all seem to have been invited.

THE UNSUMMONED WITNESSES. On August 13, 1919, Borah and Johnson sent a letter to Lodge saying that it was "absolutely essential" to have the testimony of Bliss, White, House, Williams, Hornbeck, Young, Bullitt, Ferguson and Millard—all experts at Paris. Bullitt was subpoenaed by a strict party vote of 9 to 7, and all the others, except Bliss, House, and White, without roll call. The last-named three were still at work with the Paris Conference, and to have brought them home would have involved a serious interruption of their labors. When Borah moved that the committee subpoena these three, the vote was 8 to 9, with Harding and McCumber defeating the motion by shifting to the Democrats. (Roots, *op. cit.*, pp. 56–57, from committee minutes.) For plans to summon House, who arrived home in ill health after the hearings ended, see Stephen Bonsal, *Unfinished Business*, pp. 272–274; Charles Seymour, *House Papers*, IV, 505–506.

WILSON'S REFUSAL TO PROVIDE DATA. Two letters of Wilson to Lodge on this subject are printed in *Sen. Docs.*, 66 Cong., 1 sess., no. 106, pp. 252–253. The letters regarding secret data and the draft treaties were sent by Wilson to Lodge on Aug. 8 and Aug. 28, 1919, respectively (Wilson Papers, II–C). Lodge later complained that Wilson provided only two of the many documents requested by the committee (*op. cit.*, p. 167). He further complained that the treaties with Poland and France, as well as the Rhine protocol, which were all parts of the treaty with Germany, were first secured from documents laid before the British and French legislative bodies.

CHAPTER SIX

THE APPEAL TO THE PEOPLE

ON THE origins of the trip and Wilson's health, see D. F. Fleming, *The United States and the League of Nations;* J. P. Tumulty, *Woodrow Wilson As I Know Him;* Edith Bolling Wilson (Mrs. Woodrow Wilson), *My Memoir* (Indianapolis, 1939); and G. S.

Viereck, *The Strangest Friendship in History* (that is, of Wilson and House—New York, 1932); and Irwin Hood Hoover, *Forty-two Years in the White House* (Boston, 1934). Although Hoover had unusual opportunities for observation, he is unreliable; he apparently knew nothing of Wilson's pre-Conference ill health. On this general subject, see the record of Dr. Grayson's interview with Ray Stannard Baker (Feb., 1926), Baker Collection. See also the Hitchcock speech of Jan. 13, 1925 (Nebraska Historical Society). Secretary of the Navy Josephus Daniels, who was a first-hand witness, says that Wilson did not regard the trip as a strain; it would be a pleasure and a relief to meet the people and speak from a heart so full of the subject (*The Life of Woodrow Wilson* [Philadelphia, 1924], p. 327). Perhaps Wilson was whistling in the dark —granted that Daniels remembers correctly. In any event, this evidence differs from that found elsewhere. For Wilson's evident expectation that the White House Conference with the senators would prove more fruitful, see Lansing to House, Aug. 21, 1919, Lansing Papers, vol. 45. On Wilson's determination to keep politics out of the tour, see Wilson to E. F. Goltra, Sept. 3, 1919, Wilson Papers, II–C.

THE SENATE AND THE ELECTION OF 1920. The number of seats to be filled was 32: 17 Democratic and 15 Republican. If the Democrats had retained all 17 (which they did not) and had captured all 15 (which they did not), they would still have been 2 short of a two-thirds majority. In addition, certain of their members, such as Reed, Gore, Shields, Smith of Georgia, and Walsh of Massachusetts, could not be counted on to support Wilson's position.

ORIGINS OF THE SWING AROUND THE CIRCLE. Mrs. Wilson in *My Memoir*, p. 273, and Tumulty in *op. cit.*, pp. 434, 438, both indicate that the trip was the result of a sudden impulse; also D. F. Houston, *Eight Years with Wilson's Cabinet*, II, 20. Yet as early as February, 1919, when Wilson was in the United States on his return trip, the press announced that he was going to swing around the circle on his final return. (New York *Times*, Feb. 25, 1919. See also earlier rumors from Paris in *ibid.*, Jan. 15, 1919.) Wilson's cablegram to Tumulty of May 2, 1919, announcing his intention of going, is printed in Tumulty, *op. cit.*, p. 546. On June 13, 1919, Thomas W. Lamont wrote to Wilson from Paris that the plans for the trip should then be announced, so that the people would get into a fever of expectation (Wilson Papers, IX–A). On June 17, 1919, the New York *Times* stated that the plans were in full swing; Wilson hoped to go to Washington, Idaho, and California, the states of the "irreconcilable" Poindexter, Borah, and Johnson. The next day the *Times* reported a White House spokesman as announcing that Wilson planned a three-week swing in July, shortly after addressing Congress. The same journal also divulged the news that the senators would make plans to "trail" him as soon as they got the itinerary. On June 24, 1919, the *Times* confirmed the same general announcement. At his press conference on July 10, 1919, two days after returning to Washington, Wilson said that he could not make any announcement about the projected trip: he had been home only long enough to see the terrible table in his study piled high with documents (Wilson Papers, II–C). For the proposal of the Foreign Relations Committee to prevent the trip by demanding a daily conference, see New York *Times,* July 12, 1919. For further talk of the trip, consult *ibid.,* July 26, 28, 30, 1919.

CHAPTER SEVEN

THE SWING AROUND THE CIRCLE

THE ADDRESSES on the tour are published in Woodrow Wilson, *War and Peace,* vols. I and II. For the incidents on the trip, consult the New York *Times.* A good running account appears in D. F. Fleming, *The United States and the League of Nations;* a superficial narrative, in R. Burlingame and A. Stevens, *Victory Without Peace.* See also Robert E. Annin, *Woodrow Wilson* (New York, 1924). Valuable intimate glimpses may be found in Edith B. Wilson, *My Memoir;* in J. P. Tumulty, *Woodrow Wilson As I Know Him;* and in David Lawrence, *Woodrow Wilson.*

THE SITUATION IN WASHINGTON. Rudolph Forster (White House Executive Clerk) wired to Tumulty (Sept. 8, 1919) Senator Pittman's enthusiastic comment on the success of the tour. Yet on Sept. 22 Guy Mason telegraphed from Washington to Tumulty at Reno that the "mild reservationists" and Lodge had come to terms, and had been joined by some Democrats. However, on Sept. 24 Hitchcock informed Tumulty by wire that the situation had not materially changed in the Senate. He advised postponing a discussion of reservations until Wilson returned, because Johnson and Borah would oppose any compromise. They wanted, Hitchcock thought, to throw the issue into the presidential campaign. (Telegrams in Wilson Papers, II–C.) For the announcement of Ashurst and several other wavering Democrats that they would support Wilson foursquare, see New York *Times,* Sept. 26, 1919. See also Thomas W. Lamont to Wilson, June 13, 1919, for advice as to how to conduct the trip (Wilson Papers, IX–A).

WILSON'S SPEECHMAKING ERRORS. For a hypercritical analysis of the speeches, see William Bayard Hale, *The Story of a Style* (New York, 1920), chap. IX. The author, an estranged Wilsonian, stresses the President's infelicities of style; his geographical errors in relation to Serbia, Poland, Rumania, and Persia; and his various contradictions as to the causes of the war. On this point, see also O. G. Villard, *Fighting Years,* p. 469. It is clear from these speeches that Wilson's thinking on the situation in 1917 changed under the impact of his exalted objectives. See T. A. Bailey, *Woodrow Wilson and the Lost Peace,* pp. 330–331. Wilson also made careless statements as to the American origins of the League, as to the ease with which the Covenant was inserted in the treaty, and as to the incorporation of American ideas into the pact (Woodrow Wilson, *War and Peace,* II, 95, 121, 122, 398). Near the start of the tour he said that German rights in Shantung were promised Japan in order to induce her to enter the war. The secret agreement in question actually was negotiated in 1917, some three years later. After Senator Norris had directed his attention to this misstatement, Wilson acknowledged his mistake. (Fleming, *op. cit.,* p. 347.) There were many other errors, contradictions, or arguable statements of more or less minor importance, some of which were inevitable under the circumstances.

CHAPTER EIGHT

THE FALLEN WARRIOR

ON WILSON'S collapse, three published accounts have been left by occupants of the White House: Edith B. Wilson, *My Memoir;* J. P. Tumulty, *Woodrow Wilson As I Know Him;* and I. H. Hoover, *Forty-two Years in the White House.* Of these accounts, Mrs. Wilson's is the most trustworthy; Tumulty's, the least trustworthy, at least on this general subject. Tumulty says that Wilson was stricken with paralysis on the trip, which is not true, and which is the basis for many of the erroneous accounts on the subject. See also the daily White House bulletins as printed in the New York *Times,* and the account of an interview with Dr. Hugh H. Young (an attending physician from Johns Hopkins) which appeared in the Baltimore *Sun,* Feb. 10, 1920, and was reprinted in the New York *Times,* Feb. 11. The present writer also had access to the data, oral and written, which Dr. Grayson later gave Ray Stannard Baker (Baker Collection).

For backgrounds, see the general works previously cited, including the biographies of Wilson. Some material on German-Irish propaganda appears in G. S. Viereck, *Spreading Germs of Hate* (New York, 1930).

THE BULLITT AFFAIR. The testimony is published in *Sen. Docs.,* 66 Cong., 1 sess., no. 106, pp. 1161–1297. The facts regarding Bullitt's subpoena appear in J. M. Roots, "The Treaty of Versailles." For Lodge's connection with the affair, see Allan Nevins, *Henry White,* pp. 462–467. Lansing's published apology is in his *Peace Negotiations,* chap. XIX. Lansing's telegram to Wilson of Sept. 16, 1919, reproduced in part by Lansing (pp. 270–271), appears in full in the Wilson Papers, II–C. Lansing seems to have been vacationing at Henderson Harbor, New York, and the Acting Secretary of State wired him on Sept. 13, saying that everyone in Washington, including the press men, felt that Bullitt's conduct was reprehensible; the Acting Secretary himself felt that some kind of denunciation was necessary. A notation at the bottom of this telegram, dated Sept. 15, records that on this day the Acting Secretary telephoned from Washington to say that Senator Hitchcock believed that silence was best unless Lansing wished to issue an absolute denial. But Hitchcock thought that Lansing could give him a statement on behalf of the treaty which could be used in case the opposition began to exploit the Bullitt testimony improperly. Lansing did send a personal and confidential telegram to the Acting Secretary (undated). All these Bullitt materials appear in the Lansing Papers, vol. 46. The clippings which Lansing preserved show that the British and the French were greatly disturbed, and that there was much speculation as to Lansing's imminent resignation and his succession by Undersecretary of State Frank L. Polk.

CHAPTER NINE

THE LIVING MARTYRDOM

THE MOST revealing book is Edith B. Wilson, *My Memoir*. See also J. P. Tumulty, *Woodrow Wilson As I Know Him*, and I. H. Hoover, *Forty-two Years in the White House*, for personal glimpses. T. R. Marshall, *Recollections of Thomas R. Marshall* (Indianapolis, 1925), is not very helpful. For accounts by those who made direct or indirect contacts with the White House, see G. S. Viereck, *The Strangest Friendship in History;* Stephen Bonsal, *Unfinished Business;* David Lawrence, *Woodrow Wilson;* and A. D. H. Smith, *Mr. House of Texas* (New York, 1940). Bits of information appear in H. H. Kohlsaat, *From McKinley to Harding* (New York, 1923), pp. 220, 223; Allan Nevins, *Henry White*, p. 481; A. W. Lane and L. H. Wall, eds., *The Letters of Franklin K. Lane* (Boston, 1922), pp. 325, 330; and James Kerney, *The Political Education of Woodrow Wilson* (New York, 1926), pp. 429, 434.

PRESIDENTIAL DISABILITY. For an able discussion of this problem, consult Edward S. Corwin, *The President: Office and Powers* (2nd ed., New York, 1941), pp. 51–56, 333–339. There is much material here relevant to Wilson's collapse. Corwin thinks, as others thought, that he was plainly disabled within the meaning of the Constitution. The current view was that the initiative lay with Marshall in taking over. For proposals to correct this defect in the Constitution, see D. F. Houston, *Eight Years with Wilson's Cabinet*, II, 39–40; New York *Times*, Feb. 19, 20, 21, 27, 1920.

CHAPTER TEN

THE BATTLE OF RESERVATIONS

THE THREE reports from the Senate committee appear in *Sen. Reports*, 66 Cong., 1 sess., no. 176. The debates and voting on the various reservations may best be followed in the *Congressional Record*, although G. A. Finch, in the *American Journal of International Law*, XIV (1920), 155–206, has a convenient digest. See also W. S. Holt, *Treaties Defeated by the Senate* (note the useful tabulations of votes); H. C. Lodge, *The Senate and the League;* D. F. Fleming, *The United States and the League of Nations;* and Dexter Perkins, *Hands Off: A History of the Monroe Doctrine* (Boston, 1941).

THE HARMFUL EFFECT OF RESERVATIONS. The tendency has been to accept Wilson's conclusion that the reservations "nullified" the entire treaty. This uncritical view has recently been elaborated by Ruhl J. Bartlett, in *The League to Enforce Peace* (Chapel Hill, N.C., 1944), pp. 162–166, although the League to Enforce Peace itself conceded (*ibid.*, p. 154) that its purposes could be accomplished by the Covenant with the Lodge reservations. For an elaborate and masterly analysis demonstrating for the State Department (Mar., 1920) that the effect of the reservations had been much exaggerated, see David Hunter Miller, *My Diary at the Conference of Paris* (21 vols., New York, 1924–1926), XX, 569–593. Miller, who had been at Paris, and who probably knew as much about the League as any other man, later testified, "for as far as the Lodge reservations made changes in the League, they were of a wholly minor character, they left its structure intact, and they would have interfered with its workings not at all." (E. M. House and Charles Seymour, eds., *What Really Happened at Paris* [New York, 1921], p. 424). Fleming, *op. cit.,* chap. XVII, follows the lengthy Miller memorandum rather closely in his analysis. Gen. Tasker H. Bliss (one of the American commissioners in Paris) prepared a penetrating memorandum along the same lines for Secretary Lansing, dated Jan. 21, 1920 (Lansing Papers, vol. 50). Another able statement, anonymous but apparently written by an American diplomat, appears in the New York *Times,* Dec. 16, 1919; see also the analysis of the League of Free Nations Association, in *ibid.,* Dec. 7, 1919. Taft and Hoover both recognized that the effect of the Lodge reservations had been much overplayed (Taft to Hitchcock, Nov. 15, 1919, Hitchcock Papers; Hoover to Wilson, Nov. 19, 1919, Wilson Papers, File VIII, vol. 6). Similar views were expressed by Henry White, one of the American Commissioners at Paris (Allan Nevins, *Henry White,* p. 480), and by President A. Lawrence Lowell of Harvard University (Stephen Bonsal, *Unfinished Business,* p. 280). See also the remarks of Senators Lenroot and McCumber, on Nov. 19, 1919, and Senators Lenroot, Pomerene, and especially Walsh of Montana, on Mar. 19, 1920 (*Cong. Record,* 66 Cong., 1 sess., pp. 8771–8773, 8786; *ibid.,* 2 sess., pp. 4574–4577, 4578–4585.

Covenant of the League of Nations

(THE PORTIONS BEARING MOST DIRECTLY ON THE RESERVATIONS FIGHT)

Article I

. . . .

Sec. 3. Any Member of the League may, after two years' notice of its intention so to do, withdraw from the League, provided that all its international obligations and all its obligations under this Covenant shall have been fulfilled at the time of its withdrawal.

Article V

Sec. 1. Except where otherwise expressly provided in this Covenant or by the terms of the present Treaty, decisions at any meeting of the Assembly or of the Council shall require the agreement of all the Members of the League represented at the meeting.

. . . .

Article VI

. . . .

Sec. 5. The expenses of the Secretariat shall be borne by the Members of the League in accordance with the apportionment of the expenses of the International Bureau of the Universal Postal Union.

Article VIII

Sec. 1. The Members of the League recognize that the maintenance of peace requires the reduction of national armaments to the lowest point consistent with national safety and the enforcement by common action of international obligations.

Sec. 2. The Council, taking account of the geographical situation and circumstances of each State, shall formulate plans for such reduction for the consideration and action of the several Governments.

Sec. 3. Such plans shall be subject to reconsideration and revision at least every ten years.

Sec. 4. After these plans shall have been adopted by the several Governments, the limits of armaments therein fixed shall not be exceeded without the concurrence of the Council.

. . . .

Article X

Sec. 1. The Members of the League undertake to respect and preserve as against external aggression the territorial integrity and existing political independence of all Members of the League. In case of any such aggression or in case of any threat or danger of such aggression the Council shall advise upon the means by which this obligation shall be fulfilled.

Article XI

Sec. 1. Any war or threat of war, whether immediately affecting any of the Members of the League or not, is hereby declared a matter of concern to the whole League, and the League shall take any action that may be deemed wise and effectual to safeguard the peace of nations. In case any such emergency should arise the Secretary-General shall on the request of any Member of the League forthwith summon a meeting of the Council.

Sec. 2. It is also declared to be the friendly right of each Member of the League to bring to the attention of the Assembly or of the

Council any circumstance whatever affecting international relations which threatens to disturb international peace or the good understanding between nations upon which peace depends.

Article XII

Sec. 1. The Members of the League agree that if there should arise between them any dispute likely to lead to a rupture, they will submit the matter either to arbitration or to inquiry by the Council, and they agree in no case to resort to war until three months after the award by the arbitrators or the report by the Council.

Sec. 2. In any case under this Article the award of the arbitrators shall be made within a reasonable time, and the report of the Council shall be made within six months after the submission of the dispute.

Article XV

. . . .

Sec. 8. If the dispute between the parties is claimed by one of them, and is found by the Council, to arise out of a matter which by international law is *solely within the domestic jurisdiction* of that party, the Council shall so report, and shall make no recommendation as to its settlement.

. . . .

Article XVI

Sec. 1. Should any Member of the League resort to war in disregard of its covenants under Articles 12, 13, or 15, it shall *ipso facto* be deemed to have committed an act of war against all other Members of the League, which hereby undertake immediately to subject it to the severance of all trade or financial relations, the prohibition of all intercourse between their nationals and the nationals of the covenant-breaking State, and the prevention of all financial, commercial or personal intercourse between the nationals of the covenant-breaking State and the nationals of any other State, whether a Member of the League or not.

Sec. 2. It shall be the duty of the Council in such case to recommend to the several Governments concerned what effective military, naval or air force the Members of the League shall severally contribute to the armed forces to be used to protect the covenants of the League.

Sec. 3. The Members of the League agree, further, that they will mutually support one another in the financial and economic measures which are taken under this Article, in order to minimize the loss and inconvenience resulting from the above measures, and that they will mutually support one another in resisting any special measures aimed at one of their number by the covenant-breaking State, and that they will take the necessary steps to afford passage through their territory to the forces of any of the Members of the League which are co-operating to protect the covenants of the League.

Sec. 4. Any Member of the League which has violated any covenant of the League may be declared to be no longer a Member of the League by a vote of the Council concurred in by the Representatives of all the other Members of the League represented thereon.

Article XXI

Sec. 1. Nothing in this Covenant shall be deemed to affect the validity of international engagements, such as treaties of arbitration or regional understandings *like the Monroe Doctrine,* for securing the maintenance of peace.

Article XXII

Sec. 1. To those colonies and territories which as a consequence of the late war have ceased to be under the sovereignty of the States which formerly governed them and which are inhabited by peoples not yet able to stand by themselves under the strenuous conditions of the modern world, there should be applied the principle that the well-being and development of such peoples form a sacred trust of civilization and that securities for the performance of this trust should be embodied in this Covenant.

Sec. 2. The best method of giving practical effect to this principle is that the tutelage of such peoples should be entrusted to advanced nations who by reason of their resources, their experience or their geographical position, can best undertake this responsibility, and *who are willing to accept it,* and that this tutelage should be exercised by them as Mandatories on behalf of the League.

. . . .

The Lodge Reservations

(Those of November, 1919, appear unindented; those of March, 1920, were exactly the same, except that the italicized and bracketed passages were deleted, and the indented passages were added. Such comments as appear in footnotes are in addition to those in the text of this book. For originals, see *Cong. Record,* 66 Cong., 1 sess., p. 8773; *ibid.,* 2 sess., p. 4599.)

Resolved (two-thirds of the Senators present concurring therein), That the Senate advise and consent to the ratification of the treaty of peace with Germany concluded at Versailles on the 28th day of June, 1919, subject to the following reservations and understandings, which are hereby made a part and condition of this resolution of ratification, which ratification is not to take effect or bind the United States until the said reservations and understandings adopted by the Senate have been accepted [*by an exchange of notes as a part and a condition of this resolution of ratification by at least three of the four principal allied and associated powers, to wit, Great Britain, France, Italy, and Japan:*]

> as a part and a condition of this resolution of ratification by the allied and associated powers and a failure on the part of the allied and associated powers to make objection to said reservations and understandings prior to the deposit of ratification by the United States shall be taken as a full and final acceptance of such reservations and understandings by said powers:

1. The United States so understands and construes article 1 that in case of notice of withdrawal from the league of nations, as provided in said article, the United States shall be the sole judge as to whether all its international obligations and all its obligations under the said covenant have been fulfilled, and notice of withdrawal by the United States may be given by a concurrent resolution of the Congress of the United States.

2. The United States assumes no obligation to preserve the territorial integrity or political independence of any other country [*or to interfere in controversies between nations—whether members of the league or not—under the provisions of article 10, or to employ the military or naval forces of the United States under any article of the treaty for any purpose, unless in any particular case the Congress, which, under the Constitution, has the sole power to declare war or authorize the employment of the military or naval forces of the United States, shall by act or joint resolution so provide.*]

> by the employment of its military or naval forces, its resources, or any form of economic discrimination, or to interfere in any way in controversies between nations, including all controversies relating to territorial integrity or political independence, whether members of the league or not, under the provisions of article 10, or to employ the military or naval forces of the United States, under any article of the treaty for any purpose, unless in any particular case the Congress, which, under the Constitution, has the sole power to declare war or authorize the employment of the military or naval forces of the United States, shall, in

the exercise of full liberty of action, by act or joint resolution so provide.

3. No mandate shall be accepted by the United States under article 22, Part 1, or any other provision of the treaty of peace with Germany, except by action of the Congress of the United States.

4. The United States reserves to itself exclusively the right to decide what questions are within its domestic jurisdiction and declares that all domestic and political questions relating wholly or in part to its internal affairs, including immigration, labor, coastwise traffic, the tariff, commerce, the suppression of traffic in women and children and in opium and other dangerous drugs, and all other domestic questions, are solely within the jurisdiction of the United States and are not under this treaty to be submitted in any way either to arbitration or to the consideration of the council or of the assembly of the league of nations, or any agency thereof, or to the decision or recommendation of any other power.

5. The United States will not submit to arbitration or to inquiry by the assembly or by the council of the league of nations, provided for in said treaty of peace, any questions which in the judgment of the United States depend upon or relate to its long-established policy, commonly known as the Monroe doctrine; said doctrine is to be interpreted by the United States alone and is hereby declared to be wholly outside the jurisdiction of said league of nations and entirely unaffected by any provision contained in the said treaty of peace with Germany.

6. The United States withholds its assent to articles 156, 157, and 158 [regarding Shantung], and reserves full liberty of action with respect to any controversy which may arise under said articles [*between the Republic of China and the Empire of Japan*].

7. [*The Congress of the United States will provide by law for the appointment of the representatives of the United States in the assembly and the council of the league of nations, and may in its discretion provide for the participation of the United States in any commission, committee, tribunal, court, council, or conference, or in the selection of any members thereof and for the appointment of members of said commissions, committees, tribunals, courts, councils, or conferences, or any other representatives under the treaty of peace, or in carrying out its provisions, and until such participation and appointment have been so provided for and the powers and duties of such representatives have been defined by law, no person shall represent the United States under either said league of nations or the treaty of peace with Germany or be authorized to perform any act for or on behalf of the United States thereunder, and no citizen of the United States shall be selected or appointed as a member of said commissions, committees, tribu-*]

nals, courts, councils, or conferences except with the approval of the Senate of the United States.] [1]

No person is or shall be authorized to represent the United States, nor shall any citizen of the United States be eligible, as a member of any body or agency established or authorized by said treaty of peace with Germany, except pursuant to an act of the Congress of the United States providing for his appointment and defining his powers and duties.

8. The United States understands that the reparation commission will regulate or interfere with exports from the United States to Germany, or from Germany to the United States, only when the United States by act or joint resolution of Congress approves such regulation or interference.[2]

9. The United States shall not be obligated to contribute to any expenses of the league of nations, or of the secretariat, or of any commission, or committee, or conference, or other agency, organized under the league of nations or under the treaty or for the purpose of carrying out the treaty provisions, unless and until an appropriation of funds available for such expenses shall have been made by the Congress of the United States.[3]

Provided, That the foregoing limitation shall not apply to the United States proportionate share of the expense of the office force and salary of the secretary general.

10. [*If the United States shall at any time adopt any plan for the limitation of armaments proposed by the council of the league*

---

[1] This reservation was minor as far as the functioning of the League was concerned. It further betrayed postwar senatorial suspicion of the Executive. It was primarily a matter of internal administration; such details were left to the jurisdiction of the individual member states.

[2] This was relatively minor. The situation referred to was most unlikely to arise, and if it did the American representative in the Council could cast his veto vote. But the reservation would clear us of charges of noncooperation should such a contingency occur. As a matter of fact the problem never arose; the powers handled the reparations question themselves.

[3] This also was minor, and almost completely unnecessary. No appropriations can be lawfully made under our Constitution without Congressional approval. The reservation was a sop to certain imaginative senators who feared that our annual share of the League expenses might run into hundreds of millions of dollars, and who feared that the League would accuse us of bad faith if the President did not immediately provide the money. As a sedative to such nervous senators, and as a possible preventive of foreign criticism, the reservation was not wholly pointless. But it was ungracious, for it implied that unscrupulous foreigners might in some way commit the United States, the wealthiest of nations, to pay more than its just share of the League expenses.

of nations under the provisions of article 8, it reserves the right to increase such armaments without the consent of the council whenever the United States is threatened with invasion or engaged in war.] [4]

No plan for the limitation of armaments proposed by the council of the League of Nations under the provisions of article 8 shall be held as binding the United States until the same shall have been accepted by Congress, and the United States reserves the right to increase its armament without the consent of the council whenever the United States is threatened with invasion or engaged in war.

11. The United States reserves the right to permit, in its discretion, the nationals of a covenant-breaking State, as defined in article 16 of the covenant of the league of nations, residing within the United States or in countries other than [*that violating said article 16, to continue their commercial, financial, and personal relations with the nationals of the United States.]* [5]

such covenant-breaking State, to continue their commercial, financial, and personal relations with the nationals of the United States.

12. Nothing in articles 296, 297, or in any of the annexes thereto or in any other article, section, or annex of the treaty of peace with Germany shall, as against citizens of the United States, be taken to mean any confirmation, ratification, or approval of any act otherwise illegal or in contravention of the rights of citizens of the United States.[6]

[4] This, theoretically, was of major importance. But actually any disarmament plan adopted by the League probably would have contained such escape clauses, as was true of the naval disarmament treaties of the 1930's. Article 8 of the Covenant clearly provided for a reconsideration of all disarmament plans "at least every ten years." Even if such safeguards had not been provided, there can be little doubt that the United States, or any other nation similarly situated, would have taken matters into its own hands anyhow. The reservation was useful in that it would have cleared us of charges of bad faith had we been forced to increase our armaments in the face of aggression.

[5] This, actually, was not of great importance. A League boycott against, say, Japan would not have been critically weakened if the United States had continued trade with Japanese outside Japan. But, theoretically, the reservation was unfortunate, because it weakened in principle the concept of international sanctions.

[6] This was designed to permit American citizens to seek redress in American courts for injury sustained by seizures under the Alien Property Custodian. It was relatively unimportant, and probably unnecessary. No real harm was done by inserting it.

13. The United States withholds its assent to Part XIII (articles 387 to 427, inclusive) [International Labor Organization] unless Congress by act or joint resolution shall hereafter make provision for representation in the organization established by said Part XIII, and in such event the participation of the United States will be governed and conditioned by the provisions of such act or joint resolution.[7]

14. [*The United States assumes no obligation to be bound by any election, decision, report, or finding of the council or assembly in which any member of the league and its self-governing dominions, colonies, or parts of empire, in the aggregate have cast more than one vote, and assumes no obligation to be bound by any decision, report, or finding of the council or assembly arising out of any dispute between the United States and any member of the league if such a member, or any self-governing dominion, colony, empire, or part of empire united with it politically has voted.*]

Until Part I, being the covenant of the League of Nations, shall be so amended as to provide that the United States shall be entitled to cast a number of votes equal to that which any member of the league and its self-governing dominions, colonies, or parts of empire, in the aggregate shall be entitled to cast, the United States assumes no obligation to be bound, except in cases where Congress has previously given its consent, by any election, decision, report, or finding of the council or assembly in which any member of the league and its self-governing dominions, colonies, or parts of empire in the aggregate have cast more than one vote.

The United States assumes no obligation to be bound by any decision, report, or finding of the council or assembly arising out of any dispute between the United States and any member of the league if such member, or any self-governing dominion, colony, empire, or part of empire united with it politically has voted.

15. In consenting to the ratification of the treaty with Germany the United States adheres to the principle of self-determination and to the resolution of sympathy with the aspirations of the Irish people for a government of their own choice adopted by the Senate June 6, 1919, and declares that when such government is attained by Ireland, a con-

---

[7] This revealed undue suspicion of the Executive and of foreigners, but it was not of fundamental importance. It seems evident that full participation would not have been possible without the approval of Congress anyhow, and that such approval would have been speedily forthcoming if we had joined the League. Even without League membership, Congress voted to join the International Labor Organization in 1934.

summation it is hoped is at hand, it should promptly be admitted as a member of the League of Nations.

Democratic Reservations

Secret Wilson Reservations [1]
(September, 1919)

[1] Inasmuch as Article ONE of the Covenant of the League of Nations provides no tribunal to pass judgment upon the right of a member State to withdraw from the League, the Government of the U.S.understands the provision of Article ONE with regard to withdrawal as putting no limitation upon the right of a member State to withdraw except such as may lie in the conscience of the Power proposing to withdraw with regard to its having fulfilled "all its international obligations and all its obligations under the Covenant" in the sense intended by the instrument.

[2] It understands that the advice of the Council of the League with regard to the employment of armed force contemplated in Article TEN of the Covenant of the League is to be regarded only as advice and leaves each member State free to exercise its own judgment as to whether it is wise or practicable to act upon that advice or not.

Hitchcock Reservations [2]
(November, 1919)

[1] That any member nation proposing to withdraw from the league on two years' notice is the sole judge as to whether its obligations referred to in article 1 of the league of nations have been performed as required in said article.

[2] That the advice mentioned in article 10 of the covenant of the league which the council may give to the member nations as to the employment of their naval and military forces is merely advice which each member nation is free to accept or reject according to the conscience and judgment of its then existing Government, and in the United States this advice can only be accepted by action of the

1 Text in D. F. Fleming, *The United States and the League of Nations*, p. 493; also *Canadian Historical Review*, X (1929), 197–198; both from copies provided by Senator Hitchcock; original now in Wilson Papers.

2 *Cong. Record*, 66 Cong., 1 sess., p. 8800. The order has been changed to parallel the Wilson reservations.

Congress at the time in being, Congress alone under the Constitution of the United States having the power to declare war.

[3] It understands that under Article FIFTEEN of the Covenant of the League no question can be raised either in the Assembly or in the Council of the League which will give that body the right to report or to make any recommendations upon the policy of any member state with regard to such matters as immigration, naturalization, or tariffs.

[3] That no member nation is required to submit to the league, its council, or its assembly, for decision, report, or recommendation, any matter which it considers to be in international law a domestic question such as immigation, labor, tariff, or other matter relating to its internal or coastwise affairs.

[4] It understands, also, that the reference to the Monroe Doctrine in Article TWENTY-ONE of the Covenant of the League means that nothing contained in the Covenant shall be interpreted as in any way impairing or interfering with the application of the Monroe Doctrine in the American Hemisphere.

[4] That the national policy of the United States known as the Monroe doctrine, as announced and interpreted by the United States, is not in any way impaired or affected by the covenant of the league of nations and is not subject to any decision, report, or inquiry by the council or assembly.

[5] That in case of a dispute between members of the league if one of them have self-governing colonies, dominions, or parts which have representation in the assembly, each and all are to be considered parties to the dispute, and the same shall be the rule if one of the parties to the dispute is a self-governing colony, dominion, or part, in which case all other self-governing colonies, dominions, or parts, as well as the nation as a whole, shall be considered parties to the dispute, and each and all shall be disqualified from having their votes counted in case of any inquiry on said dispute made by the assembly.

CHAPTER ELEVEN

THE STRATEGY
OF DEADLOCK

THE CHIEF sources for this chapter are the Wilson Papers, the Hitchcock Papers, the *Congressional Record*, and the New York *Times*. The Wilson letter to Hitchcock of Nov. 18, 1919, is published in the *Cong. Record*, 66 Cong., 1 sess., p. 8768. The Hitchcock-Wilson colloquy on compromise is related in Hitchcock's speech of Jan. 13, 1925 (Nebraska Historical Society). The Borah-Swanson negotiations are discussed in J. M. Roots, "The Treaty of Versailles," pp. 82–83. Roots got the story direct from Borah, who thought that his pressure had some effect. The Lodge-Bonsal incident is set forth in Stephen Bonsal, *Unfinished Business*, pp. 272–280. Bonsal quotes House as suggesting (*ibid.*, p. 279) that Wilson's letter to Hitchcock of Nov. 18 was drawn up in September when the outlook was more favorable, but the context proves that it was written a day or so before sent. Also useful are Edith B. Wilson, *My Memoir*; H. C. Lodge, *The Senate and the League*; J. P. Tumulty, *Woodrow Wilson As I Know Him*; and the more general works previously cited.

WILSON AND RESERVATIONS. Wilson's antipathy to asking Germany to accept our reservations was set forth in his speeches, and also in a letter to John C. Shaffer, Aug. 27, 1919 (Wilson Papers, II–C). On Sept. 18, Vance C. McCormick wired Wilson (then on his tour) that three of the "mild reservationists" had prepared a reservation to Article X which Lodge was said to favor but which Taft opposed; Wilson replied the next day that he would regard such a reservation as a practical rejection of the Covenant (Hitchcock Papers). On Nov. 13 Hitchcock wrote Mrs. Wilson outlining his proposed strategy and saying that the Democrats would like Wilson's guidance; on Nov. 15 he added that it was their plan to vote down the Lodge reservations unless the President advised otherwise. On the back of this letter (which had been brought by a special messenger) appears a notation in the handwriting of Mrs. Wilson to the effect that the program outlined by Hitchcock had Wilson's approval, for the President could not in any case accept ratification with the Lodge reservations. (Wilson Papers, File VIII, vol. 6.) On Dec. 17, after the treaty rejection, Hitchcock told Tumulty that Wilson's instructions (presumably obtained during one of the November interviews) had been to go ahead and do the best he could, which apparently meant that Hitchcock was to secure such mildly interpretive reservations as were possible. (Tumulty to Mrs. Wilson, Dec. 18, 1919 [reporting a conversation with Hitchcock], Wilson Papers, File VIII, vol. 7.) See also New York *Times,* Nov. 8, 1919. When Hitchcock was unable to block the Lodge reservations with his own, the President sent the letter of Nov. 18, 1919.

CHAPTER TWELVE

BREAKING THE HEART OF THE WORLD

THE BEST source for the Senate voting is the *Congressional Record,* which may be supplemented by the New York *Times.* A long and moving letter from Taft to Hitchcock (Nov. 15, 1919), urging compromise and setting forth the reasons therefor, may be found in the Hitchcock Papers. Analyses of the final votes appear in the works by Learned, Holt, Roots, Lodge, and Fleming previously cited. Allan Nevins, *Henry White,* has useful material on French reactions. For the attitude of the League to Enforce Peace, see R. J. Bartlett, *The League to Enforce Peace* (especially pp. 154–155). See also Alice R. Longworth, *Crowded Hours;* A. D. H. Smith, *Mr. House of Texas* (especially p. 343); and J. E. Watson, *As I Knew Them* (especially p. 200).

WILSON'S PRESSURE TO DEFEAT THE TREATY. As late as Jan. 4, 1930, the New York *World* wired Hitchcock, seeking confirmation of certain charges that had recently been made in a public address by Henry Morgenthau. A draft reply appears in Hitchcock's handwriting among his papers. The ex-senator said that both he and the President were convinced that, if they relaxed their opposition, the treaty with the Lodge reservations would be adopted; also, that until the last moment Lodge labored under the delusion that Wilson would give in.

WOULD WILSON HAVE POCKETED THE TREATY? On June 23, 1919, Wilson cabled Tumulty from Paris that since reservations infringed on the President's power of negotiation, ". . . I would be at liberty to withdraw the Treaty if I did not approve of the ratifications." Wilson authorized the publication of the entire telegram, with this sentence omitted. (J. P. Tumulty, *Woodrow Wilson As I Know Him*, pp. 531–532.) In the speech at Pueblo, Wilson virtually declared that he would decline to go through with ratification if objectionable reservations were attached (Woodrow Wilson, *War and Peace*, II, 412). As the treaty approached a vote, it was believed in Washington that Wilson would pocket it (New York *Times*, Nov. 15, 1919); and on Nov. 17 he told Hitchcock that he would do so (*ibid.*, Nov. 18, 1919). The letter of Wilson to Hitchcock of Nov. 18 is so uncompromising as to support the belief that the treaty would be pocketed (*Cong. Record*, 66 Cong., 1 sess., p. 8768). See the President's correspondence with Glass on this subject, in R. Smith and N. Beasley, *Carter Glass* (New York, 1939), pp. 201–204. Wilson's subsequent vetoing of the Knox separate peace resolution (May 27, 1920) lends further support to the belief that he would have dropped the entire treaty had it been approved with the Lodge reservations.

PUBLIC OPINION AND THE TREATY REJECTION. Useful symposia appear in *Current Opinion* and in the *Literary Digest*, especially Nov. 29 (pp. 11–13) and Dec. 6, 1919 (pp. 14–15). Views unfriendly to the treaty are expressed in the New York *Nation* (see Nov. 22, p. 652; Dec. 6, pp. 711–712) and in the *New Republic. Harvey's Weekly* was an "irreconcilable" mouthpiece (see particularly issue of Nov. 22, p. 1). Fairer and more conservative in judgment were the *Review of Reviews* and the *Outlook*, especially *ibid.*, Dec. 3, 1919, pp. 407–408. For this period the New York *Times*, the *Christian Science Monitor*, and the Springfield *Republican* have been rather closely followed. The New York *Times* is gratifyingly full on Hitchcock's relations with Wilson.

A partial list of newspaper editorials which proved useful fol-

lows: Hearst's Boston *American,* Nov. 21 (quoted herein); the
Boston *Transcript,* Nov. 19, 20 (quoted herein); the New York
World, Nov. 20; the Boston *Herald,* Nov. 18, 20, 21; the Phila-
delphia *Public Ledger,* Nov. 22 (the quoted advertisement is
from the issue of Nov. 20); the Cleveland *Plain Dealer,* Nov.
21; the Boston *Post,* Nov. 20; the Boston *Traveler,* Nov. 21; the St.
Louis *Post-Dispatch,* Nov. 20; the Philadelphia *North American,*
Nov. 21; the Boston *Globe,* Nov. 21; the New York *Tribune,* Nov.
18; the San Francisco *Bulletin,* Nov. 21; the San Francisco
Chronicle, Nov. 20. The quotations from the St. Louis *Star* and the
Atlanta *Constitution* appear in *Current Opinion* (Dec., 1919, p.
274) and in the *Literary Digest* (Dec. 20, p. 15). The conclusions
expressed in this study regarding public opinion square generally
with those in W. S. Holt, *Treaties Defeated by the Senate,* p. 288.

CHAPTER THIRTEEN

THE BIRTH OF A SOLEMN REFERENDUM

MOST OF the unpublished materials used for this chapter appear in the Wilson and Hitchcock papers, which were supplemented by the press. The texts of the annual message and the
Jackson Day letter may be found in Woodrow Wilson, *War and
Peace,* II, 428–442, 453–456. See also Edith B. Wilson, *My Memoir;*
David Lawrence, *Woodrow Wilson;* D. F. Houston, *Eight Years
with Wilson's Cabinet,* vol. II; G. S. Viereck, *The Strangest Friendship in History.* Symposia of press reactions to the Jackson Day
letter are published in the *Literary Digest,* Jan. 17 and 24, 1920,
pp. 11–13 and 15–16. The typescript House letters to Wilson of
Nov. 24 and 27 (published in Charles Seymour, *House Papers,* IV,
509–511) were accompanied by brief, longhand notes to Mrs. Wilson, in which the Colonel spoke of his solicitude for Wilson's place
in history, of the necessity of having the great work at Paris live,

and of the possibility of later securing modification of objectionable reservations (Wilson Papers, File VIII, vol. 6).

WILSON'S UNISSUED APPEAL. On Dec. 22, 1919, Attorney General Palmer wrote to Wilson setting forth the laws of the various states regarding vacancies created by the resignation of United States senators. A draft of the note requesting this information for the President appears in the handwriting of Mrs. Wilson (Wilson Papers, File VIII, vol. 8). The senators who were called upon to resign (it is not indicated who made up the list) were all the Republicans, except McCumber, Nelson and Norris, plus nine Democrats: Bankhead, Gore, Kendrick, Kirby, Reed, Smith of Georgia, Thomas, Trammell, and Walsh of Massachusetts. Postmaster General Burleson was asked to criticize this list, which he did in collaboration with Senator Hitchcock. The two men believed that it was not fair to include the Democrats Kirby, Trammell, and Thomas; and that the "irreconcilable" Norris and the "mild reservationists" Nelson, McNary, Kellogg, and McCumber should be added. Some of the "Lodge reservationists" favored the treaty but, said Burleson, were more anxious to promote the welfare of the party than to secure ratification. The "mild reservationists," by voting for the Lodge resolution, had done as much to hinder the treaty as the other Republicans. This group was listed as consisting of Colt, Hale, Jones of Washington, Kellogg, Kenyon, Keyes, McCumber, McNary, Nelson, Spencer, Sterling, and Townsend—a different list from that conventionally accepted. (Burleson to Mrs. Wilson, Jan. 28, 1920, *ibid.*) In writing to Wilson on Nov. 24, 1919, Hitchcock had included, among others, Lenroot, Edge, and Cummins (*ibid.*, vol. 6). The copy of the unissued appeal (tentatively dated Jan. 26 by a custodian of the papers) appears in *ibid.*, vol. 8. Wilson had earlier considered resignation, particularly during the Canal Tolls repeal fight and the campaign of 1916.

WILSON AND HITCHCOCK. In response to rumors that Wilson was dissatisfied with Hitchcock's handling of the fight, Tumulty issued a statement to the press, on Nov. 22, denying all reports of a breach, and declaring that the President was very appreciative of the senator's efforts, he added that Wilson was not taking sides in the fight for minority leadership between Hitchcock and Underwood (New York *Times*, Nov. 23, 1919). On Jan. 13, 1920, Hitchcock wrote to Mrs. Wilson, suggesting that something be done to influence the vote of Senator Harris in the close contest for minority leadership between himself and Underwood. Hitchcock pointed out that he had alienated the support of the Democratic "irreconcilables" by his stand during the treaty fight. A note in Mrs. Wilson's handwriting, attached to this letter, states that the President could not accede to this request, because he did not want to give grounds for the accusation that he had exceeded the proper bounds of executive authority. Nevertheless, he was profoundly grateful for Hitchcock's leadership in the struggle for the treaty. (Wilson Papers, File VIII, vol. 7.) This rough draft was put into final form and appears in the Hitchcock Papers under date of Jan. 13, 1920. Wilson was probably wise, in view of the troubled situation, in keeping out of the fight, though it may be observed that he did not scruple to interfere in Democratic primaries to bring about the defeat of candidates whom he did not like. The note is interesting also as proving that at this late date Mrs. Wilson was still scribbling down the thoughts of her invalid husband.

WILSON AND POSSIBLE COMPROMISE. The letter to Hitchcock, dated Dec. 19, and referred to on p. 213, appears in the Wilson Papers, File VIII, vol. 7. It was drafted in Mrs. Wilson's hand, with Wilson's shorthand notes attached. The finished letter is in the Hitchcock Papers under the same date. The response to Senator Glass's suggestion for a compromise on Article X is drafted in Mrs. Wilson's blue pencil on an undated chit (Wilson Papers, File VIII, vol. 7); the similarity in wording suggests that it was prepared about the time of the Hitchcock letter referred to above. (See also R. Smith and N. Beasley, *Carter Glass*, pp. 201–204.) Another undated chit in Mrs. Wilson's hand, presumably written about Dec. 22, 1919, shows that Wilson was disposed to stress the fact that the attitude of the Senate was encouraging Germany to make a scrap of paper of the treaty (Wilson Papers, II–C).

CHAPTER FOURTEEN

COMPROMISE WITHOUT CONCESSION

FOR DATA relating to the general subject matter of this chapter, see the works by Roots, Fleming, and Bartlett previously cited. Much material on public opinion appears in the daily and periodical press, and in the memorials and petitions listed in the *Congressional Record*.

POLLS ON THE LEAGUE. Newspapers ranging from the (Portland) *Oregon Journal* to the Omaha *Bee* and the Baltimore *Sun* took polls of reader sentiment, which uniformly favored speedy ratification in some form. The most significant poll was conducted by the Intercollegiate Treaty Referendum, which addressed a questionnaire to colleges in every section of the country. The totals from 48 institutions as given by Hitchcock on Jan. 19, 1920 (*Cong. Record*, 66 Cong., 2 sess., p. 1695), follow:

Unreserved ratification	48,232
Complete rejection	13,933
Ratification with Lodge reservations	27,970
Compromise between Lodge and Democratic reservations	61,494

This poll is significant, for it seems to have been the closest thing to a "solemn referendum" on the issue that the country had. Even though the colleges were strongly pro-League, there was much sentiment for the Lodge reservations and for compromise. It seems probable that such sentiment was even stronger among the masses. See also the New York *Times*, Jan. 17, 1920; and particularly the letter of Hamilton Holt to the New York *World* (Jan. 19), published in the *World* on Jan. 20, 1920. It is an impressive recapitulation of various League polls and other expressions of public opinion.

LODGE AND THE BIPARTISAN CONFERENCES. Lodge apparently did not originate the conference, as he suggests (H. C. Lodge, *The Senate and the League*, p. 193), but it was brought about through the initiative of Senator Owen (Hitchcock to Tumulty, Jan. 16, 1920, Wilson Papers, File VIII, vol. 7). The Lodge account contains other errors. The dramatic session described by Borah is taken from notes of a personal interview which the present writer had with the senator on Apr. 21, 1937. A less lurid account appears in C. O. Johnson, *Borah,* pp. 246–247. The press and Lodge both put the meeting in Johnson's office, and Lodge's account says that Senator New was with him. Naturally, Lodge gives no inkling that he was bulldozed by Borah (Lodge, *op. cit.,* p. 194). Lodge also published the tentative changes that were proposed in the bipartisan conferences (*ibid.,* pp. 195–203). His secretary, Charles F. Redmond, later testified that the senator never thought agreement could be reached: he merely went through motions in response to public pressure (J. M. Roots, "The Treaty of Versailles," p. 100). See Hitchcock's speech of Jan. 13, 1925 (Nebraska Historical Society), in which he says that the "irreconcilables" "kidnapped" Lodge; also Senator Johnson's version in the *Cong. Record,* 69 Cong., 1 sess., p. 2351 (Jan. 19, 1926). H. Maurice Darling, "Who Kept the United States Out of the League of Nations?" *Canadian Historical Review,* X (1929), 196–211, throws some light on this whole episode. He reveals that Senators Colt and Kenyon, both "mild reservationists" active in the bipartisan preliminaries, were left off the final committee by Lodge, apparently because they were inclined to be conciliatory (p. 200). The Democrats were willing to accept a Taft reservation to Article X, but Lodge declined to do so. Darling blames Lodge for the final result, unaware of the fact that Wilson (in an undated chit among his papers) also rejected the Taft version. (See also R. Smith and N. Beasley, *Carter Glass,* p. 202.) Senator McKellar, who was one of Darling's informants, testified that Lodge was called to the telephone by Viscount Grey at a crucial moment in the negotiations (p. 209). As a matter of fact, Grey was then in England, or en route to England.

THE GREY MISSION. For general backgrounds see Charles Seymour, *House Papers,* IV, 494–496, 499–500, 508; and A. D. H. Smith, *Mr. House of Texas,* pp. 340–341, 350–354. Smith had a close connection with the British Embassy. See also D. F. Houston, *Eight Years with Wilson's Cabinet,* II, 49; Allan Nevins, *Henry White,* pp. 485–486; and E. S. Corwin, *The President,* pp. 215–216. There is also some material in W. E. Dodd, *Woodrow Wilson*. The undated and unissued White House statement reprimanding Grey appears in the Wilson Papers, File VIII, vol. 7. It is interesting to note that at this late date, about Feb. 2, 1920, Mrs. Wilson was still serving as her husband's private secretary. Lloyd George's views were relayed from London by Ambassador Davis to Lansing, Feb. 6, 1920 (Lansing Papers, vol. 51). For senatorial recollections of the Lloyd George cablegram to Grey, see New York *Times*, Feb. 3, 1920. The Democrats found comfort in a statement by a distinguished British statesman, Arthur J. Balfour, to the effect that American reservations would weaken the efficiency of the League (*Christian Science Monitor*, Feb. 16, 1920).

CHAPTER FIFTEEN

THE NEW
WOODROW WILSON

THE LETTER from Wilson to Hitchcock of Jan. 26, 1920, is published in Woodrow Wilson, *War and Peace*, II, 460–461; the Adriatic notes appear in *ibid.*, pp. 462–479. The Wilson-Lansing interchanges may be found in the *Cong. Record*, 66 Cong., 2 sess., pp. 2882–2883. Further material on the Lansing resignation appears in Robert Lansing, *Peace Negotiations;* D. F. Houston, *Eight Years with Wilson's Cabinet*, vol. II; Edith B. Wilson, *My Memoir;* J. P. Tumulty, *Woodrow Wilson As I Know Him;* David Lawrence, *Woodrow Wilson;* Samuel F. Bemis, ed., *The American Secretaries of State and Their Diplomacy* (New York, 1929), vol. X. On Colby see *ibid.;* also Houston, *op. cit.*, II, 68–69. There exists an interesting memorandum of an interview which R. S. Baker had with Colby on June 19, 1930 (Baker Collection).

HITCHCOCK'S RELATIONS WITH WILSON AND TUMULTY. Hitchcock seems not to have seen Wilson at all during the period between the November and March votes, except when he came with the Fall "smelling committee" (Dec. 5, 1919). He saw Tumulty at least once, and addressed letters to him, and to Mrs. Wilson, and finally to Wilson. Tumulty acted as a go-between, and urged Wilson in two notes to send Hitchcock a statement encouraging compromise (Tumulty to Mrs. Wilson, Jan. 15, 17, 1920, Wilson Papers, File VIII, vol. 7). On Jan. 16 and 17 Hitchcock sent two letters to Tumulty advising him of progress in the bipartisan conferences (*ibid.*). On Jan. 22 Hitchcock addressed a letter to Wilson directly, enclosing a draft of the Article X reservation then being considered (*ibid.;* also printed in New York *Times,* Feb. 8, 1920). On Jan. 26 Wilson, probably responding to Tumulty's prompting, sent his memorable letter to Hitchcock, which was in part a boiling down of a draft submitted by Tumulty with his letter of Jan. 15. Mrs. Wilson added a chit in her own hand saying that in Wilson's judgment the letter should not be published then, but permitting Hitchcock to make what use of it he saw fit (Hitchcock Papers). What is presumably an earlier draft of this letter, in Mrs. Wilson's hand, suggests that she was urging her husband to throw responsibility on the Senate for making the peace (undated memorandum, Wilson Papers, File VIII, vol. 8).

THE WILSON-LANSING BREAK. Wilson had appointed Lansing with misgivings, and had regarded him as an administrative assistant (Houston, *op. cit.,* II, 67). At Paris their views had been sharply divergent on the League (Lansing, *op. cit.*). Lansing's testimony before the Senate committee, though perhaps unavoidable, had displeased Wilson (Tumulty, *op. cit.,* p. 445). The Bullitt affair had also put Lansing in a bad light. Wilson was irritated by the first meeting of the Cabinet (Houston, *op. cit.,* II, 39, 69). His explosion in February may have been touched off by first learning of Lansing's inquiries as to whether Marshall should take over, following the stroke. (See Tumulty, *op. cit.,* p. 444.) It was further rumored that Wilson was angry because Lansing had allegedly influenced the published views of Viscount Grey. The President seems also to have been displeased with Lansing's handling of the Mexican crisis. (*Ibid.;* W. E. Dodd, *Woodrow Wilson,* pp. 406–407.) Dr. Grayson later remembered that Wilson wanted an offensive member of the British Embassy dismissed, and that Lansing had failed to secure satisfactory action (memorandum of Baker interview with Grayson, Feb., 1926, Baker Collection). David

Lawrence, who was rather close to the White House, suggests that Wilson had thought that the Cabinet meetings were purely informal, and that he blew up when he learned otherwise (Lawrence, *op. cit.*, p. 287). Pent-up exasperation, illness, and a new access of energy, combined with some or all of the other factors mentioned above, probably provide the explanation of the President's summary action.

CHAPTER SIXTEEN

THE LAST CHANCE

THE CONTEMPORARY press and the *Congressional Record* are the best general sources. Analyses of the votes on the reservations appear in the works by Fleming, Finch, and Holt previously cited. The tables in Holt are especially useful. For the reservations and the final vote, see H. C. Lodge, *The Senate and the League;* and J. M. Roots, "The Treaty of Versailles." Incidental items appear in Alice R. Longworth, *Crowded Hours,* pp. 299–304; Allan Nevins, *Henry White,* p. 482; J. E. Watson, *As I Knew Them,* pp. 195–196; and N. M. Butler, *Across the Busy Years,* II, 201. The Wilson letter to Hitchcock of Mar. 8 is printed in the New York *Times* of Mar. 9, 1920. Hitchcock gives some personal glimpses in his speech of Jan. 13, 1925 (Nebraska Historical Society).

THE FINAL TREATY VOTE. All Republicans voted affirmatively on Mar. 19, 1920, except the following fifteen "irreconcilables," who voted negatively or were paired against the treaty: Borah, Brandegee, Fall, Fernald, France, Gronna, Johnson, Knox, La Follette, McCormick, Moses, Norris, Penrose, Poindexter, and Sherman. In the previous November all these, except Penrose, had voted against or had been paired against the Lodge resolution of ratification. The following twenty-one Democrats bolted and voted for the treaty: Ashurst, Beckham, Chamberlain, Fletcher, Gore, Henderson, Kendrick, King, Myers, Nugent, Owen, Phelan, Pittman, Pomerene, Ransdell, Smith of Georgia, Smith of Maryland,

Trammell, Walsh of Massachusetts, Walsh of Montana, and Wolcott. The seven who had bolted on the second vote on the Lodge resolution in November were: Gore, Myers, Owen, Pomerene, Shields, Smith of Georgia, and Walsh of Massachusetts. See *Cong. Record,* 66 Cong., 1 sess., p. 8802; 66 Cong., 2 sess., p. 4599.

CHAPTER SEVENTEEN

THE SUPREME
INFANTICIDE

ON THE general subject matter of this chapter see the previously cited works of Holt, Fleming, Roots, and Lodge. The incident of Wilson's telephonic negotiations with Lodge is taken from D. F. Houston, *Eight Years with Wilson's Cabinet,* II, 56–57. R. J. Bartlett, in *The League to Enforce Peace,* holds that the Allied powers would have rejected the Lodge reservations (pp. 164–166). This does not follow from the evidence herein presented, and particularly from the testimony of Grey, Lloyd George, and the French press given in a previous chapter. For further evidence see N. M. Butler, *Across the Busy Years,* II, 200–201.

PUBLIC OPINION AND THE SENATE VOTE. Material was taken from the editorial comments of all the journals listed on pp. 397–398; in addition, the Washington *Post,* the Chicago *Tribune,* and the Portland *Oregonian.*

WAS LODGE SINCERE IN SUPPORTING HIS RESERVATIONS? Much of the evidence about Lodge is contradictory. His daughter believed that his heart was with the "irreconcilables"; his grandson (later senator) denied this. (Fleming, *op. cit.,* p. 476.) A sister of Theodore Roosevelt, who was Lodge's house guest at the time, thought Lodge sincere (*ibid.,* p. 475); Roosevelt's daughter regarded the senator as basically an "irreconcilable" (Alice R. Longworth, *Crowded Hours,* p. 295). Lodge stirred up so much bitterness by his course that we must view with suspicion the numerous reports about him based on hearsay, supposition, and wishful thinking. The often quoted story of ("my dear James") Senator Watson (*As I Knew Them,* pp. 190–191), to the effect that Lodge diabolically sought to defeat the treaty by indirect means, does not have the ring of verisimilitude, as is true of other Watsonian tales. The present writer has preferred to judge Lodge more by his actions than by the guesses of others as to his motives. For what it is worth, it may be noted that Senator Borah told the present writer in 1937 that Lodge at heart was a "League man." (Further favorable evidence appears in P. C. Jessup, *Elihu Root,* II, 402–403.) Charles F. Redmond, then Lodge's private secretary, stated later in an interview that the senator had no strong convictions about the League one way or another, but as the fight developed he put party unity foremost in his thinking (J. M. Roots, "The Treaty of Versailles," p. 88). There is an excellent summary statement in Fleming, *op. cit.,* chap. XIX. Lodge's refusal to respond to White's invitation to submit amendments to the League when he might have done so may be plausibly explained on political grounds (Allan Nevins, *Henry White,* pp. 397–401). Positive judgments regarding Lodge's motives should be tempered pending an opening of his private papers.

JAPAN AND THE TREATY REJECTION. The Japanese press was much concerned about the proposed Shantung amendment, and rejoiced when it was defeated. But the purely negative Shantung reservation aroused no such opposition, largely because it was regarded as having no international weight. (See symposia of editorial opinion in the *Japan Times and Mail* [Weekly Edition], Nov. 22, 1919, p. 1477; Nov. 29, 1919, p. 1505.) This was also the conclusion of Viscount Ishii, former ambassador to the United States (*ibid.,* Nov. 22, 1919, p. 1483). The Japanese newspapers somewhat resented the violent senatorial attacks on Japan, but it was recognized that much of this was pure partisanship (see *ibid.,* Sept. 6, 1919, p. 1171). Of the six prominent Japanese newspapers referred to, none expressed satisfaction over the treaty rejection, either in November or March, and most of them regretted the action of the United States as bolstering Chinese obduracy and further unsettling world peace. The conclusion seems warranted that Japanese opinion preferred treaty ratification (even with the Shantung reservation) to treaty rejection. (*Ibid.,* Nov. 29, 1919, p. 1505; March 27, 1920, p. 405.) For a summation of Senate arguments on the

Shantung question, see Robert E. Hosack, "The Shantung Question and the Senate," *South Atlantic Quarterly*, XLIII (1944), 181–193.

CHAPTER EIGHTEEN

ADVANTAGES
WITHOUT OBLIGATIONS

ON THE separate-peace movement, see the *Congressional Record* and the New York *Times*. For public opinion on this issue and the others herein treated see the journals previously mentioned. The text of the Knox Resolution appears in the *Cong. Record*, 66 Cong., 2 sess., p. 7102, as does the final vote. Nelson was the only Republican voting against it; Reed, Shields, and Walsh of Massachusetts were the Democrats who voted for it. The account of the Cabinet meeting of Apr. 13 appears in D. F. Houston, *Eight Years with Wilson's Cabinet*, II, 69–70. For the Hamaker Oregon letter, the message to Congress on Armenia, and the veto message regarding the Knox Resolution, see Woodrow Wilson, *War and Peace*, II, pp. 483 ff. Some of the same ideas which appear in the Oregon letter also appear in a letter which Wilson wrote to Jouett Shouse, to be read to the Kansas Democratic State Convention. (See New York *Times*, Apr. 23, 1920.)

CHAPTER NINETEEN

A TALE OF TWO
CONVENTIONS

THE TWO most helpful accounts of the nomination of Harding are in Samuel H. Adams, *Incredible Era* (Boston, 1939), and Mark Sullivan, *Our Times*, vol. VI. Useful material appears in Hermann

Hagedorn, *Leonard Wood,* vol. II; Claude M. Fuess, *Calvin Coolidge* (Boston, 1940); William A. White, *A Puritan in Babylon: The Story of Calvin Coolidge* (New York, 1938); Harry M. Daugherty, *The Inside Story of the Harding Tragedy* (New York, 1932); W. F. Johnson, *George Harvey;* N. M. Butler, *Across the Busy Years,* vol. I; C. G. Bowers, *Beveridge;* P. C. Jessup, *Elihu Root,* vol. II; C. O. Johnson, *Borah.* More general accounts may be found in D. F. Fleming, *The United States and the League of Nations,* and in Charles P. Howland, ed., *Survey of American Foreign Relations, 1928* (New Haven, 1928). The smoke-filled room has become something of a legend, for the meeting was more informal, more protracted, and less definitive than is commonly supposed. See Henry L. Stoddard, *It Costs to Be President* (New York, 1938), pp. 73–75.

The materials on the backgrounds and course of the Democratic convention are less full. Consult the previously cited works by Dodd and Tumulty; and James Kerney, *The Political Education of Woodrow Wilson.* The pre-convention photograph of Wilson which was published in the newspapers appears in Gerald W. Johnson, *Woodrow Wilson* (New York, 1944), p. 108, but is four years out of context.

WILSON AND THE THIRD-TERM ISSUE. Wilson had earlier put himself on record as against a third term, and on Feb. 28, 1919, he rather definitely announced his retirement to a private gathering of Democrats (Tumulty, *op. cit.,* p. 378). On Aug. 27, 1919, shortly before leaving on his Western tour, Wilson wrote Cyrus T. Brady that when his *term came to an end* he hoped he would have enough vigor to propose some much-needed university reforms (Wilson Papers, II–C). While on the trip he laughed aside a suggestion of a third term (New York *Times,* Sept. 20, 1919). Mrs. Wilson told Henry White (prior to July 2, 1919) that under no circumstances would Wilson run again (Allan Nevins, *Henry White,* p. 456).

The editorial in the Springfield *Republican* urging Wilson to declare himself out of the running, was published on May 17, 1919. Wilson cabled Tumulty, on June 2, 1919, asking his opinion of it and that of Secretary Glass, Secretary Baker, Secretary Wilson, and Homer S. Cummings. Nothing, Wilson said, should be allowed to stand in the way of the League. On June 3 Tumulty advised against both a third nomination and a public renunciation at that time (Wilson Papers, IX–A). No further action seems to have been taken on this matter. See also pp. 44, 374 of the present book.

The last figures of the *Literary Digest* poll *(ibid.,* June 12, 1920, p. 20) showed the five leading Democratic contenders to have the following votes: McAdoo, 102,719; Wilson, 67,588; Edwards, 61,393; Bryan, 46,448; Cox, 32,343.

In an undated rough draft of some kind of proclamation or statement, tentatively dated by the custodians of the Wilson Papers Oct. 3, 1920, Wilson asked the rhetorical question whether the people wanted to make use of his services as President for another four years. There was no point in raising such a question after the nomination of Cox, and the internal evidence suggests that the statement may have been drafted before the Democratic convention with the thought of promoting a third-term candidacy. (Wilson Papers, File VIII, vol. 7.)

First-hand evidence from Dr. Grayson regarding Wilson's desires was recorded by Glass in his diary (R. Smith and N. Beasley, *Carter Glass,* pp. 205–209).

On June 30, 1920, Cummings wired Wilson that the platform committee was in the hands of friends, and that everything thus far had moved beautifully according to plan (Wilson Papers, II–C). See Colby's press interview (New York *Times,* July 1, 1920). For Colby's statement that he went to the convention as a result of Wilson's personal desire that he should go and also serve as permanent chairman, see Colby to Wilson, June 18, 1920, Wilson Papers, II–C. Stoddard thinks that Colby was sent out to put his chief's name in nomination, but that the "right moment" never came (Henry L. Stoddard, *As I Knew Them* [New York, 1927], pp. 515–518). Colby told R. S. Baker in 1930 that he had been on the point of nominating Wilson, and possibly of stampeding the convention. He promised to develop the story more completely, but evidently failed to do so. (Interview of June 19, 1930, Baker Collection.) A memorandum of Homer S. Cummings, dated Jan., 1929 (in *ibid.*), reveals that Mrs. Wilson told Colby (according to Colby) that the President was receptive to a third nomination, though the Democratic leaders at San Francisco (except Colby) thought such a nomination impossible. This memorandum is paraphrased in Charles W. Stein, *The Third-Term Tradition* (New York, 1943), pp. 248–249.

The code telegram from Colby at San Francisco to Wilson (July 2, 1920) is in the Wilson Papers, File VIII, vol. 7; his follow-up telegram to Wilson (July 4) is in the Baker Collection, A, Box 3 (Cummings).

For Wilson's alleged anger with the Cabinet members after the convention, see I. H. Hoover, *Forty-two Years in the White House*, p. 107, and G. S. Viereck, *The Strangest Friendship in History*, p. 336. Neither is particularly reliable. James Kerney, who is more trustworthy, states in his *Political Education of Woodrow Wilson*, p. 456, that Wilson summarily asked Burleson to resign because he had supported McAdoo. All this does not prove that Wilson had expected a third nomination; he doubtless was displeased over the whittling down of the League plank and the nomination of Cox. For the White House policy of hands-off, see Tumulty, *op. cit.*, pp. 493–496, 498.

Wilson's relation to the third-term issue is most fully developed in Stein, *The Third-Term Tradition,* chap. IX. Although this account is gratifyingly full, the author comes to the incredible conclusion (which he himself admits is flimsy) that, beginning with mid-1918, Wilson decided to exploit the League issue in such a way as to make necessary a third term. Here, says Stein, is the explanation of a long series of deliberate attempts to antagonize the Senate (pp. 263–264). The author not only misreads Wilson's character, but overlooks the fact that there were other and more plausible reasons for each of his acts.

CHAPTER TWENTY

THE GREAT AND SOLEMN MUDDLEMENT

GENERAL ACCOUNTS of the campaign of 1920 appear in the works by Fleming, Howland, Sullivan, Adams, and Berdahl, all previously cited. P. C. Jessup, *Elihu Root*, II, 413–414, throws some new light on the appeal of the Illustrious Thirty-one. On the essential dishonesty of this statement, see R. J. Bartlett, *The League to Enforce Peace*, and the commentary of ex-President Charles W. Eliot of Harvard University in the New York *Times*, Oct. 21, 1920. Samuel Colcord, in *The Great Deception* (New York, 1921), develops fully the thesis that the effort of the "irreconcilables" to misrepresent the result of the election as a clear-cut mandate against the League was "the great deception." A detailed analysis of the 1920 vote appears in Edgar E. Robinson, *The Presidential Vote, 1896–1932* (Stanford University, 1934).

COULD THE ELECTION HAVE BEEN A REFERENDUM? Following the Jackson Day appeal it was widely felt that there could be no clear-cut referendum. See the statements of Taft, Bryan, and Lowell, the comments of Democratic newspapers, and the observations of political experts in the New York *Times*, Jan. 10, 19, 1920. After the March rejection of the treaty such doubts multiplied. The New York *Nation* (Mar. 13, p. 322) recommended a true referendum in the Swiss style, as did the San Francisco *Bulletin* (Mar. 22). The Baltimore *Sun* (Mar. 20) said it was foolish to hope for a mandate; the New York *Evening Post* (Mar. 20) declared the result would be a "solemn muddle"; the Boston *Globe* (Mar. 20) observed that the issues, already muddy, would be further muddied by months of mud-slinging; and the Brooklyn *Eagle* (Mar. 20) remarked that the people would know no more after the election than before about public sentiment on the League. For similar expressions by other journals, domestic and foreign, see *Literary Digest*, Apr. 3, pp. 17–19, July 24, pp. 9–10; *Current Opinion*, Aug., 1920, p. 156. Curiously enough, foreigners, especially the French, seem to have been more realistic about the problem than some Americans. Among the many individuals who declared that domestic preoccupations would preclude a mandate were Senator McCumber (*Cong. Record*, 66 Cong., 2 sess., p. 6853), and Senator Walsh of Montana (*ibid.*, p. 4582).

WAS THE ELECTION A MANDATE? A majority of the newspapers sampled regarded the result as a repudiation of Wilsonism. See Philadelphia *North American*, Nov. 4; New York *Evening Post*, Nov. 3; New York *Sun*, Nov. 4; New York *Call*, Nov. 3; Brooklyn

Eagle, Nov. 3; New York *Herald,* Nov. 3; Springfield *Republican,* Nov. 3; Boston *Herald,* Nov. 3; Detroit *Free Press,* Nov. 4; Kansas City *Star,* Nov. 3; San Francisco *Chronicle,* Nov. 3; San Francisco *Examiner,* Nov. 3. There is a useful symposium in the *Literary Digest,* Nov. 13, 1920, pp. 11–14. Other papers stressed the desire for a change ("normalcy"), among them *Current Opinion* (Dec., 1920, p. 759), which said that the result was a victory for "General Grouch." See also the New York *Times,* Nov. 4; the Portland *Oregonian,* Nov. 3; the Boston *Post,* Nov. 3; the New York *World,* Nov. 4; the Columbus *Dispatch,* Nov. 3; the Boston *Globe,* Nov. 3; the Louisville *Courier-Journal,* Nov. 4; the Chicago *Tribune,* Nov. 3. Those which declared that there could be no mandate, or that the results were confused, were the New York *Times,* Nov. 3, 4; the Boston *Globe,* Nov. 3; the St. Louis *Post-Dispatch,* Nov. 3; the New York *Tribune,* Nov. 2; the Cleveland *Plain Dealer,* Nov. 3; the Philadelphia *Public Ledger,* Nov. 3 (it was "dishonest" to say that a "downright or unmistakable mandate had been written"); the Atlanta *Constitution,* Nov. 4; the Sacramento (Calif.) *Union,* Nov. 3; the San Francisco *Bulletin,* Nov. 1 (the difference on the League issue was that between "Tweedledum and Tweedledee"). See also *Literary Digest,* July 24, pp. 9–11, Aug. 21, p. 14; *Current Opinion,* Dec., 1920, pp. 778–779. Those which stressed the re-action against idealism were the Kansas City *Star,* Nov. 3; *Current Opinion,* Dec., 1920, p. 778. Those which pointed out that it was not a partisan victory but a national upheaval were the Washington *Evening Star,* Nov. 3, and *Current Opinion,* Dec., 1920, p. 761.

Only a few newspapers came out flatfootedly and said that the result was clearly and unmistakably a mandate against the League; among them, the Hearst chain. (See Boston *American,* Nov. 3.) Other isolationist journals, like the Boston *Transcript* (Nov. 2) and the Washington *Post* (Nov. 3), coupled the League with something else, as did the San Francisco *Chronicle* (Nov. 3). Some newspapers accepted the proposition that the election doomed the League, among them the New Yorker *Staats-Zeitung* (Nov. 3); the *Wall Street Journal,* Nov. 4 (the country needed "an audit" rather than a referendum); and the San Jose (Calif.) *Mercury-Herald,* Nov. 3 (the same general result would have been obtained if the League had never been heard of).

Borah and Johnson and other foes of the League of course hailed the result as a clear-cut mandate (New York *Times,* Nov. 4). Lodge later said essentially the same thing (*The Senate and the League,* p. 210). Others, then and later, were of a contrary view. See Samuel Gompers, *Seventy Years of Life and Labor* (New York, 1925), II, 502; D. F. Houston, *Eight Years with Wilson's Cabinet,* II, 58; Walter Lippmann, *Public Opinion* (New York, 1922), pp. 195–196. Calvin Coolidge remarked that the outcome was not a verdict on the League (New York *Times,* Nov. 24). On Nov. 23, Senator Pittman wrote to Wilson that the result was not a mandate but a remarkably successful campaign of "deception" (Wilson Papers, II–C). See also David Lawrence, *Woodrow Wilson,* p. 300; and Colcord, *op. cit.,* who estimates that more than one hundred and fifty pro-League Republican newspapers supported Harding. Consult also *Official Report of the Proceedings of the Democratic National Convention* (Indianapolis, 1924), pp. 250–276, for the debate in 1924 on the plank for a national referendum on the League.

CAMPAIGN ISSUES. In the field of foreign affairs the Republicans talked mostly about the League, which also embraced the Association of Nations, Article X, the Monroe Doctrine, six votes to one, and Shantung. Wilsonism was clearly the most discussed domestic issue. It embraced such items as "one-mannism" and personal rule; autocracy; dictatorship; overcentralization; interference with business; attempting to make over the government; catering to labor; inefficiency; maladministration; extravagance, incompetence, and waste; "socialism"; impractical idealism; and government by deadlock. Reaction to the war government was tied up with Wilsonism, and involved such items as heavy taxation, restrictions on freedom of speech and other civil liberties (Debs), postal censorship and inefficiency (Postmaster General Burleson), Red-baiting (Attorney General Palmer), the railroad muddle (Secretary McAdoo), the price ceiling on wheat, profiteering, and the absence of curbs on the high cost of living.

The Republicans also stressed peace, prosperity (with a high tariff),.and "normalcy," which no doubt was the winning slogan. Other themes were the Armenian mandate; farm relief; soldiers' bonus; justice for the Indians, Jews, and Irish; immigration bars;

Japanese in California; relief for labor; prohibition; a ship subsidy; partisan credit for woman suffrage; Panama Canal tolls repeal; the World Court; Democratic unpreparedness in 1917; the Mexican muddle; failure of the League in Poland; the who-won-the-war issue (the Republicans?); Democratic patriotism, 1917–1918; and the injustices of the treaty.

The Democrats stressed the League, so the Republicans charged, to obscure their failures at home. The Democrats also emphasized progressivism; the straddles of the Republicans; their keeping the nation out of peace; their isolationism; their Senate cabal; their class rule; their appeal to the hyphenates. On other issues the Democrats generally took opposite sides from the Republicans, or promised to do the same thing better.

THE WOMAN VOTE. It is difficult to make sound observations as to how the women responded. Many mothers no doubt voted for Cox because they hoped the League would keep their boys at home. Other mothers no doubt voted for Harding because they feared that Article X would take their boys abroad; the Association of Nations looked somewhat safer. The Woman's Christian Temperance Union was unfriendly to the "wet" Cox. It was generally believed that the women, who had felt the pinch of high prices and wartime restrictions more keenly than the men, joined disproportionately in the anti-Wilson protest vote.

CHAPTER TWENTY-ONE

THE FINAL CURTAIN

FOR WILSON'S final days, Mrs. Wilson's *My Memoir* is the most revealing of the published works. The private Wilson Papers contain much material, and the present writer is deeply indebted to Miss Katharine E. Brand for her invaluable *précis* of the S Street files. The works previously cited, by James Kerney, Tumulty, Josephus Daniels, Houston, and Bonsal all contain some material. Bainbridge Colby, *The Close of Woodrow Wilson's Administration and the Final Years* (New York, 1930), p. 12, indicates that Wilson at times despaired of ultimate success, for he feared that the ene-mies of the League had poisoned the .wells of public thinking for at least thirty years. See also J. P. Tumulty, *Woodrow Wilson As I Know Him,* p. 455. For Wilson's post-presidential third-term aspi-rations, see C. W. Stein, *The Third-Term Tradition,* pp. 252–253.

On the Harding administration in general, consult the works by Adams, Sullivan, and Daugherty previously cited. See also M. R. Werner, *Privileged Characters* (New York, 1935). Bartlett, *op. cit.,* has some important new material on the plight of the Illustri-ous Thirty-one. On the relations of Harding with the League, con-sult the works by Berdahl and Howland previously cited, and D. F. Fleming, *The United States and World Organization, 1920–1933* (New York, 1938).

CHAPTER TWENTY-TWO

THE GREAT BETRAYAL

THIS CHAPTER consists of general conclusions drawn from the materials that were used in preparing this volume and the pre-ceding one on Wilson. A sketchy bibliography would not do justice to the subject or to those who have written about it; a full bibliography would be unmanageably voluminous and not in con-sonance with the author's purposes.

INDEX

Adriatic notes, 252–253. *See* Fiume
Alien Property Custodian, 391
alliances, 7, 48
Allies: and treaty publication, 3; duplicity of, 128; delay ratification, 149; must accept reservations, 155–156, 198–199, 240, 264–265, 281–284; severe with Germany, 206, 207; ratify treaty, 224; U.S. betrays, 358. *See* Adriatic notes; public opinion; *and countries by name*
amendments to treaty: proposed, 150; McCumber on, 152; debated, 153–154; Wilson against, 173. *See* reservations
America. *See* United States
American Bar Association, 124
Anglophobia, 25, 28–29, 236. *See* Great Britain; Ireland; Irish
Armenian mandate, 76, 150, 295–296, 313, 339, 359. *See* mandates
Article X: early attacked, 13–14; Irish hate, 27; Wilson explains, 85–86, 116, 119, 259; misrepresented, 115; Johnson attacks, 128; reservation to passed, 157–160; necessity of, 159–160; and Shantung, 163–164; Wilson opposes reservation on, 171, 177, 244, 395–396; reservations on, 182–183, 226, 254–255; final compromise attempts on, 230–232, 258, 260, 402, 404; aimed at France, 261–262; final reservation on, adopted, 262–263; importance of, exaggerated, 267; Rhode Island Democrats oppose, 308; in 1920 campaign, 323; text of, 385; text of reservations on, 388–389, 393. *See* Bipartisan conferences; League of Nations
Article XI, 116, 118, 385. *See* League of Nations
Article XII, 183, 386
Article XV, 160–161, 386
Article XVI, 158, 183, 386–387
Article XX, 327
Article XXI, 161, 387

Ashurst, Senator H. F., 187, 264, 271, 272, 380, 405
Assembly (of League) : voting in, 164–165. *See* League of Nations
Association of Nations: in Republican platform, 302; Harding on, 326–327; in campaign, 328; dies, 352
Australia: distrusts U.S., 165–166
Austria: peace with, 352
Austria-Hungary: and separate peace, 290–294. *See* Austria; Hungary

Baker, R. S., 225
Balfour, A. J., 403
Baruch, B. M., 81, 183
"Battalion of Death," 59. *See* "irreconcilables"
Belgium: rulers of, in U.S., 136, 142, 176
Beveridge, ex-Senator A. J., 22, 32, 137
bipartisan conferences, 229–232, 244, 254, 258, 401–402. *See* compromise
"bitter-enders," 59. *See* "irreconcilables"
Bliss, Gen. T. H., 377, 384
Bolsheviks, 19, 20
Bonsal, Col. Stephen, 166, 175–176
Borah, Senator W. E.: publishes treaty, 4; a Progressive, 22; irresponsibility of, 31, 33; characteristics of, 61, 63–65; on Foreign Relations Committee, 73; at White House, 85; misrepresents constituency, 96; "trails" Wilson, 127–128; objects to an amendment, 154; fights Article X, 159; on Shantung, 162–163; pressures Wilson, 183; condemns treaty, 187–188; rejoices, 193; urges referendum, 208, 220; wrecks compromise, 230–232, 402; and Grey letter, 238; on reservations, 254; on compromise, 255, 380; threatens bolt, 237; baits Democrats, 257; defends self, 263; against World Court, 282–283; at 1920 convention, 299–300; in campaign, 327–328; presidential aspirant, 374; and

QUADRANGLE PAPERBACKS

American History

Frederick Lewis Allen. *The Lords of Creation*. (QP35)
Lewis Atherton. *Main Street on the Middle Border*. (QP36)
Thomas A. Bailey. *Woodrow Wilson and the Lost Peace*. (QP1)
Thomas A. Bailey. *Woodrow Wilson and the Great Betrayal*. (QP2)
Charles A. Beard. *The Idea of National Interest*. (QP27)
Carl L. Becker. *Everyman His Own Historian*. (QP33)
Barton J. Bernstein. *Politics and Policies of the Truman Administration*. (QP72)
Ray A. Billington. *The Protestant Crusade*. (QP12)
Allan G. Bogue. *From Prairie to Corn Belt*. (QP50)
Kenneth E. Boulding. *The Organizational Revolution*. (QP43)
Robert V. Bruce. *1877: Year of Violence*. (QP73)
Roger Burlingame. *Henry Ford*. (QP76)
Gerald M. Capers. *John C. Calhoun, Opportunist*. (QP70)
David M. Chalmers. *Hooded Americanism*. (QP51)
John Chamberlain. *Farewell to Reform*. (QP19)
Alice Hamilton Cromie. *A Tour Guide to the Civil War*.
Robert D. Cross. *The Emergence of Liberal Catholicism in America*. (QP44)
Richard M. Dalfiume. *American Politics Since 1945*. (NYTimes Book, QP57)
Carl N. Degler. *The New Deal*. (NYTimes Book, QP74)
Chester McArthur Destler. *American Radicalism, 1865-1901*. (QP30)
Robert A. Divine. *American Foreign Policy Since 1945*. (NYTimes Book, QP58)
Robert A. Divine. *Causes and Consequences of World War II*. (QP63)
Robert A. Divine. *The Illusion of Neutrality*. (QP45)
Elisha P. Douglass. *Rebels and Democrats*. (QP26)
Felix Frankfurter. *The Commerce Clause*. (QP16)
Lloyd C. Gardner. *A Different Frontier*. (QP32)
Edwin Scott Gaustad. *The Great Awakening in New England*. (QP46)
Ray Ginger. *Altgeld's America*. (QP21)
Ray Ginger. *Modern American Cities*. (NYTimes Book, QP67)
Ray Ginger. *Six Days or Forever?* (QP68)
Gerald N. Grob. *Workers and Utopia*. (QP61)
Louis Hartz. *Economic Policy and Democratic Thought*. (QP52)
William B. Hesseltine. *Lincoln's Plan of Reconstruction*. (QP41)
Granville Hicks. *The Great Tradition*. (QP62)
Dwight W. Hoover. *Understanding Negro History*. (QP49)
Stanley P. Hirshson. *Farewell to the Bloody Shirt*. (QP53)
Frederic C. Howe. *The Confessions of a Reformer*. (QP39)
Harold L. Ickes. *The Autobiography of a Curmudgeon*. (QP69)
William Loren Katz. *Teachers' Guide to American Negro History*. (QP210)
Burton Ira Kaufman. *Washington's Farewell Address*. (QP64)
Edward Chase Kirkland. *Dream and Thought in the Business Community, 1860-1900*. (QP11)
Edward Chase Kirkland. *Industry Comes of Age*. (QP42)
Adrienne Koch. *The Philosophy of Thomas Jefferson*. (QP17)
Gabriel Kolko. *The Triumph of Conservatism*. (QP40)
Aileen S. Kraditor. *Up from the Pedestal*. (QP77)
Walter LaFeber. *John Quincy Adams and American Continental Empire*. (QP23)
Lawrence H. Leder. *The Meaning of the American Revolution*. (NYTimes Book, QP66)
David E. Lilienthal. *TVA: Democracy on the March*. (QP28)
Arthur S. Link. *Wilson the Diplomatist*. (QP18)
Huey P. Long. *Every Man a King*. (QP8)
Gene M. Lyons. *America: Purpose and Power*. (QP24)
Jackson Turner Main. *The Antifederalists*. (QP14)
Ernest R. May. *The World War and American Isolation, 1914-1917*. (QP29)
Henry F. May. *The End of American Innocence*. (QP9)
Thomas J. McCormick. *China Market*. (QP75)
August Meier and Elliott Rudwick. *Black Protest in the Sixties*. (NYTimes Book, QP78)
George E. Mowry. *The California Progressives*. (QP6)
William L. O'Neill. *American Society Since 1945*. (NYTimes Book, QP59)
Frank L. Owsley. *Plain Folk of the Old South*. (QP22)
David Graham Phillips. *The Treason of the Senate*. (QP20)
Julius W. Pratt. *Expansionists of 1898*. (QP15)
C. Herman Pritchett. *The Roosevelt Court*. (QP71)
Moses Rischin. *The American Gospel of Success*. (QP54)
John P. Roche. *The Quest for the Dream*. (QP47)
David A. Shannon. *The Socialist Party of America*. (QP38)
Andrew Sinclair. *The Available Man*. (QP60)

American History (continued)

John Spargo. *The Bitter Cry of the Children.* (QP55)
Bernard Sternsher. *Hitting Home.* (QP79)
Bernard Sternsher. *The Negro in Depression and War.* (QP65)
Richard W. Van Alstyne. *The Rising American Empire.* (QP25)
Willard M. Wallace. *Appeal to Arms.* (QP10)
Norman Ware. *The Industrial Worker, 1840-1860.* (QP13)
Albert K. Weinberg. *Manifest Destiny.* (QP3)
Bernard A. Weisberger. *They Gathered at the River.* (QP37)
Robert H. Wiebe. *Businessmen and Reform.* (QP56)
William Appleman Williams. *The Contours of American History.* (QP34)
William Appleman Williams. *The Great Evasion.* (QP48)
Esmond Wright. *Causes and Consequences of the American Revolution.* (QP31)

European History

William Sheridan Allen. *The Nazi Seizure of Power.* (QP302)
W. O. Henderson. *The Industrial Revolution in Europe.* (QP303)
Raul Hilberg. *The Destruction of the European Jews.* (QP301)
Richard N. Hunt. *German Social Democracy.* (QP306)
Telford Taylor. *Sword and Swastika.* (QP304)
John Weiss. *Nazis and Fascists in Europe, 1918-1945.* (NYTimes Book, QP305)

Philosophy

F. H. Bradley. *The Presuppositions of Critical History.* (QP108)
E. M. Cioran. *The Temptation to Exist.* (QP119)
William Earle. *Objectivity.* (QP109)
James M. Edie, James P. Scanlan, Mary-Barbara Zeldin, George L. Kline. *Russian Philosophy.* (3 vols, QP111, 112, 113)
James M. Edie. *An Invitation to Phenomenology.* (QP103)
James M. Edie. *New Essays in Phenomenology.* (QP114)
James M. Edie. *Phenomenology in America.* (QP105)
R. O. Elveton. *The Phenomenology of Husserl.* (QP116)
Manfred S. Frings. *Heidegger and the Quest for Truth.* (QP107)
Moltke S. Gram. *Kant: Disputed Questions.* (QP104)
James F. Harris, Jr., and Richard Severens. *Analyticity.* (QP117)
E. D. Klemke. *Studies in the Philosophy of G. E. Moore.* (QP115)
Lionel Rubinoff. *Faith and Reason.* (QP106)
Stuart F. Spicker. *The Philosophy of the Body.* (QP118)
Paul Tibbetts. *Perception.* (QP110)
Pierre Thévenaz. *What Is Phenomenology?* (QP101)
Robert E. Wood. *The Future of Metaphysics.* (QP120)

Social Science

Abraham S. Blumberg. *Criminal Justice.* (QP227)
Shalom Endleman. *Violence in the Streets.* (QP215)
Nathan Glazer. *Cities in Trouble.* (NYTimes Book, QP212)
William J. Goode. *The Contemporary American Family.* (NYTimes Book, QP223)
George and Eunice Grier. *Equality and Beyond.* (QP204)
Morris Janowitz. *Political Conflict.* (QP226)
Kurt Lang and Gladys Engel Lang. *Politics and Television.* (QP216)
Charles O. Lerche, Jr. *Last Chance in Europe.* (QP207)
Raymond W. Mack. *Prejudice and Race Relations.* (NYTimes Book, QP217)
David Mitrany. *A Working Peace System.* (QP205)
Earl Finbar Murphy. *Governing Nature.* (QP228)
H. L. Nieburg. *In the Name of Science.* (QP218)
Martin Oppenheimer. *The Urban Guerrilla.* (QP219)
Martin Oppenheimer and George Lakey. *A Manual for Direct Action.* (QP202)
James Parkes. *Antisemitism.* (QP213)
Fred Powledge. *To Change a Child.* (QP209)
Lee Rainwater. *And the Poor Get Children.* (QP208)
The Rockefeller Report on the Americas. (QP214)
Ben B. Seligman. *Molders of Modern Thought.* (NYTimes Book, QP224)
Ben B. Seligman. *Permanent Poverty.* (QP229)
Clarence Senior. *The Puerto Ricans.* (QP201)
Harold L. Sheppard. *Poverty and Wealth in America.* (NYTimes Book, QP220)
Arthur L. Stinchcombe. *Rebellion in a High School.* (QP211)
Edward G. Stockwell. *Population and People.* (QP230)
Harry M. Trebing. *The Corporation in the American Economy.* (NYTimes Book, QP221)
David Manning White. *Pop Culture in America.* (NYTimes Book, QP222)
Harold Wolozin. *American Fiscal and Monetary Policy.* (NYTimes Book, QP225)